Church of England Record Society
Volume 27

THE RESTORATION OF THE CHURCH OF ENGLAND

CANTERBURY DIOCESE
AND THE ARCHBISHOP'S PECULIARS

THE RESTORATION OF THE CHURCH OF ENGLAND

CANTERBURY DIOCESE AND THE ARCHBISHOP'S PECULIARS

EDITED BY
Tom Reid

THE BOYDELL PRESS
CHURCH OF ENGLAND RECORD SOCIETY

© Tom Reid 2022

All Rights Reserved. Except as permitted under current legislation no part of this work may be photocopied, stored in a retrieval system, published, performed in public, adapted, broadcast, transmitted, recorded or reproduced in any form or by any means, without the prior permission of the copyright owner

First published 2022

A Church of England Record Society publication
Published by The Boydell Press
an imprint of Boydell & Brewer Ltd
PO Box 9, Woodbridge, Suffolk IP12 3DF, UK
and of Boydell & Brewer Inc.
668 Mt Hope Avenue, Rochester, NY 14620–2731, USA
website: www.boydellandbrewer.com

ISBN 9781-78327-688-2

ISSN 1351-3087

Series information is printed at the back of this volume

A CIP catalogue record for this book is available
from the British Library

The publisher has no responsibility for the continued existence or accuracy of URLs for external or third-party internet websites referred to in this book, and does not guarantee that any content on such websites is, or will remain, accurate or appropriate

This publication is printed on acid-free paper

Printed and bound in Great Britain by
TJ Books Limited, Padstow, Cornwall

For my grandchildren:
Iona   Amelie
Henry   Oliver   Noah

Contents

Acknowledgments	viii
Parish lists in 1663	ix
Number of parishes	xxiv
Exempt parishes	xxvi
List of abbreviations	xxviii
Introduction	xxxvii
General description and editorial conventions	lxxii
Transcription	1
Bibliography	72
Biographical index	86
General index	171

Acknowledgments

The research for this edition would not have been complete without utilizing the work of antiquaries and historians of the past who transcribed and annotated manuscripts, many of which have now been lost. They are represented by Edward Hasted in the eighteenth century and crucially for this edition the Rev. Eveleigh Woodruff in the nineteenth century, while the twentieth century brought the Clergy of the Church of England database and the work of its directors and legion of volunteers to stand alongside modern historians.

My early research was done in Canterbury Cathedral Archives and more recently in Lambeth Palace Library and I wish to thank all the staff in these institutions for their help and courteous attention over many years. David Wykes and the staff at Dr Williams's Library were also very helpful, as were the staff at the British Library, the Bodleian Library and the Kent History and Library Centre, Maidstone. My thanks to them all.

Convenors, colleagues and friends at the Institute for Historical Research Religious History of Britain, 1500–1800 seminar have had to endure more than one of my efforts to analyse the events in Canterbury diocese in the seventeenth century. Thanks to them and in particular to Rebecca Warren and Andrew Thomson, who listened often and gave practical advice and assistance.

More than fifteen years ago, Ken Fincham agreed to supervise my Ph.D. thesis and as mentor and friend, he has been of inestimable assistance. He suggested this project to me, read the first and second drafts and offered many critical comments and suggestions for improvements. I am very grateful.

Grant Tapsell has been very helpful and Linda Randall has been a meticulous copy-editor patiently highlighting errors and assisting with inconsistences.

I am most grateful to my wife, Janette who has tolerated my absences and the continual presence of a host of clergymen for many years. Once again, her support was essential.

Parish lists in 1663

The parishes of Canterbury Diocese listed in the Catalogue in 1663

Parish and chapel names are taken from the Clergy of the Church of England database. The parishes in Canterbury, Dover, Sandwich and Thanet have been listed under those locations..

Maps showing the locations of diocesan deaneries, parishes and peculiars can be accessed at https://dhjhkxawhe8q4.cloudfront.net/boydell-and-brewer-wp/wp-content/uploads/2022/02/09141445/Restoration-of-the-Church-of-England-Maps.pdf.

Parish	Status	Deanery	Catalogue Folio No.	Map Ref.
Acrise	Rectory	Elham	23	E3
Adisham with Staple	Rectory	Bridge	8	E3
Aldington with Smeeth	Rectory	Lympne	27	D4
Alkham with Capel-le-Ferne	Vicarage	Dover	20	E4
Appledore with Ebony	Vicarage	Lympne	27	C4
Ash	Curacy	Bridge	9	F2
Ashford	Vicarage	Charing	35	C3
Badlesmere	Rectory	Ospringe	50	D3
Bapchild	Vicarage	Sittingbourne	45	C2
Barfreystone	Rectory	Sandwich	15	F3
Barham chapel annexed to Bishopsbourne	Annexed chapel	Bridge	9	E3
Bearstead	Vicarage	Sutton	39	B3
Bekesbourne	Vicarage	Bridge	9	E3
Benenden	Vicarage	Charing	35	B4
Bethersden	Vicarage	Charing	35	C4
Betteshanger	Rectory	Sandwich	15	F3
Bicknor	Rectory	Sittingbourne	45	B2
Biddenden	Rectory	Charing	35	B4
Bilsington	Curacy	Lympne	27	D4
Birchington chapel annexed to Monkton	Annexed chapel	Westbere	5	F1

Parish	Status	Deanery	Catalogue Folio No.	Map Ref.
Bircholt	Ruined church	Elham	24	–
Bishopsbourne with Barham	Rectory	Bridge	9	E3
Blackmanstone	Ruined church	Lymne	27	D5
Blean	Vicarage	Canterbury	1	D2
Bobbing	Vicarage	Sittingbourne	45	C2
Bonnington	Rectory	Lympne	27	D4
Borden	Vicarage	Sittingbourne	45	C2
Boughton Aluph	Vicarage	Bridge	10	D3
Boughton Malherbe	Rectory	Charing	35	B3
Boughton Monchelsea	Vicarage	Sutton	39	B3
Boughton under Blean	Vicarage	Ospringe	50	D2
Boxley	Vicarage	Sutton	40	B2
Brabourne	Vicarage	Elham	24	D4
Bredgar	Vicarage	Sittingbourne	45	C2
Bredhurst	Curacy	Sutton	40	B2
Brenzett	Vicarage	Lympne	28	C5
Bridge chapel to Patrixbourne	Annexed chapel	Bridge	9	E3
Brook	Rectory	Bridge	9	D3
Brookland	Vicarage	Lympne	28	C5
Broomfield chapel to Leeds	Annexed chapel	Sutton	40	B3
Broomhill	Ruined church	Lymne	32	C5
Buckland	Rectory	Ospringe	50	C2
Buckland near Dover	Curacy	Dover	20	F3
Burmarsh	Rectory	Lympne	28	D4
Canterbury All Saints	Rectory	Canterbury	1	E2
Canterbury Holy Cross Westgate	Vicarage	Canterbury	5	E2
Canterbury St Alphege	Rectory	Canterbury	1	E2
Canterbury St Andrew	Rectory	Canterbury	1	E2
Canterbury St Dunstan	Vicarage	Canterbury	1	D2
Canterbury St George the Martyr	Rectory	Canterbury	2	E2

Parish	Status	Deanery	Catalogue Folio No.	Map Ref.
Canterbury St Margaret	Rectory	Canterbury	2	E2
Canterbury St Martin	Rectory	Canterbury	3	E2
Canterbury St Mary Bredin	Curacy	Canterbury	3	E2
Canterbury St Mary Bredman	Rectory	Canterbury	3	E2
Canterbury St Mary de Castro	Ruined church	Canterbury	5	E2
Canterbury St Mary Magdalen	Rectory	Canterbury	3	E2
Canterbury St Mary Northgate	Vicarage	Canterbury	3	E2
Canterbury St Mildred	Rectory	Canterbury	2	E2
Canterbury St Paul	Vicarage	Canterbury	4	E2
Canterbury St Peter	Rectory	Canterbury	4	E2
Capel-le-Ferne chapel to Alkham	Annexed chapel	Dover	21	E4
Challock chapel to Godmersham	Annexed chapel	Bridge	10	C3
Charing with Egerton	Vicarage	Charing	36	C3
Charlton by Dover	Rectory	Dover	20	F4
Chart Sutton	Vicarage	Sutton	40	B3
Chartham	Rectory	Bridge	10	D3
Cheriton	Rectory	Dover	20	E4
Chilham with Molash	Vicarage	Bridge	10	D3
Chillenden	Rectory	Bridge	10	E3
Chislet	Vicarage	Westbere	6	E2
Coldred	United benefice (to Sibertswold)	Sandwich	15	F3
Cranbrook	Vicarage	Charing	36	B4
Crundale	Rectory	Bridge	10	D3
Davington	Curacy	Ospringe	50	C2
Deal	Rectory	Sandwich	16	F3
Denton	Rectory	Elham	24	E3
Detling	Vicarage	Sutton	40	B2
Doddington	Vicarage	Ospringe	50	C2

Parish	Status	Deanery	Catalogue Folio No.	Map Ref.
Dover St James the Apostle	Rectory	Dover	22	F4
Dover St Mary the Virgin	Curacy	Dover	22	F4
Dover St Peter	Ruined church	Dover	23	F4
Dymchurch	Rectory	Lympne	28	D4
East Langdon	Rectory	Sandwich	15	F3
East Sutton annexed to Sutton Valence	Annexed chapel	Sutton	40	B3
Eastbridge	Ruined church	Lymne	28	D4
Eastchurch	Rectory	Sittingbourne	46	C1
Eastling	Rectory	Ospringe	51	C2
Eastry with Worth	Vicarage	Sandwich	16	F3
Eastwell	Rectory	Charing	36	D3
Ebony chapel to Appledore	Annexed chapel	Lymne	28	C5
Egerton	Curacy	Charing	36	C3
Elham	Vicarage	Elham	24	E3
Elmley	Ruined church	Sittingbourne	46	C2
Elmsted	Vicarage	Elham	24	D3
Elmstone	Rectory	Bridge	11	E2
Eythorne	Rectory	Sandwich	16	F3
Fairfield	Curacy	Lympne	29	C5
Faversham	Vicarage	Ospringe	51	D2
Folkestone	Curacy	Dover	21	E4
Fordwich	Rectory	Canterbury	2	E2
Frinsted	Rectory	Sutton	41	C2
Frittenden	Rectory	Charing	37	B4
Godmersham with Challock	Vicarage	Bridge	11	D3
Goodnestone by Dover	Curacy	Bridge	11	E3
Goodnestone by Faversham	Rectory	Ospringe	51	D2
Goudhurst	Vicarage	Sutton	41	A4
Graveney	Vicarage	Ospringe	51	D2
Great Chart	Rectory	Charing	36	C4

PARISH LISTS IN 1663   xiii

Parish	Status	Deanery	Catalogue Folio No.	Map Ref.
Great Mongeham	Rectory	Sandwich	16	F3
Guston	Curacy	Dover	21	F3
Hackington	Vicarage	Canterbury	4	E2
Halstow	Entered twice (see Lower Halstow)	Sittingbourne	41	–
Ham	Rectory	Sandwich	16	F3
Harbledown	Rectory	Canterbury	2	D2
Harrietsham	Rectory	Sutton	41	B3
Hartlip	Vicarage	Sittingbourne	47	B2
Harty	Curacy	Ospringe	51	D2
Hastingleigh	Rectory	Elham	25	D3
Hawkhurst	Curacy	Charing	37	B4
Hawkinge	Rectory	Dover	21	E4
Headcorn	Vicarage	Charing	37	B3
Herne	Vicarage	Westbere	6	E2
Hernhill	Vicarage	Ospringe	51	D2
High Halden	Rectory	Charing	37	C4
Hinxhill	Rectory	Lympne	29	D3
Hoath chapel to Reculver	Annexed chapel	Westbere	6	E2
Hollingbourne	Sinecure rectory	Sutton	41	B3
Hollingbourne Vicarage with Hucking	Vicarage	Sutton	41	B3
Hope	Ruined church	Lymne	29	D5
Hothfield	Rectory	Charing	37	C3
Hougham	Vicarage	Dover	21	F4
Hucking chapel to Hollingbourne	Annexed chapel	Sutton	42	B3
Hurst	Ruined church	Lymne	29	D4
Hythe chapel to Saltwood	Annexed chapel	Elham	25	E4
Ickham with Wells	Rectory	Bridge	11	E2
Ivychurch	Rectory	Lympne	29	C5
Iwade	Curacy	Sittingbourne	46	C1
Kenardington	Rectory	Lympne	29	C4
Kennington	Vicarage	Charing	37	D3

Parish	Status	Deanery	Catalogue Folio No.	Map Ref.
Kingsdown	Rectory	Sittingbourne	46	C2
Kingsnorth	Rectory	Lympne	30	C4
Kingston	Rectory	Bridge	11	E3
Knowlton	Rectory	Sandwich	16	F3
Langley	Rectory	Sutton	42	B3
Leaveland	Rectory	Ospringe	52	C3
Leeds with Broomfield	Curacy	Sutton	42	B3
Lenham	Vicarage	Sutton	42	C3
Leysdown	Vicarage	Sittingbourne	46	D1
Linton	Vicarage	Sutton	42	B3
Little Chart	Rectory	Charing	36	C3
Little Mongeham	Ruined church	Sandwich	18	F3
Littlebourne	Vicarage	Bridge	12	E2
Loose	Curacy	Sutton	43	B3
Lower Halstow	Vicarage	Sittingbourne	47	B2
Lower Hardres	Rectory	Canterbury	2	E3
Luddenham	Rectory	Ospringe	52	C2
Lydd	Vicarage	Lympne	30	D5
Lydden	Vicarage	Dover	22	E3
Lyminge	Sinecure rectory	Elham	25	E4
Lyminge	Vicarage	Elham	25	E4
Lympne	Vicarage	Lympne	30	D4
Lynstead	Vicarage	Ospringe	52	C2
Maidstone	Curacy	Sutton	43	B3
Marden	Vicarage	Sutton	43	B3
Mersham	Rectory	Lympne	30	D4
Midley	Ruined church	Lymne	30	C5
Milstead	Rectory	Sittingbourne	47	C2
Milton	Vicarage	Canterbury	3	D4
Milton Regis	Vicarage	Sittingbourne	46	C2
Minster	Vicarage	Westbere	7	F2
Minster in Sheppey with Queenborough	Curacy	Sittingbourne	47	C1

Parish	Status	Deanery	Catalogue Folio No.	Map Ref.
Molash chapel to Chilham	Chapel	Bridge	12	D3
Monks Horton	Rectory	Elham	24	D4
Monkton with Birchington	Vicarage	Westbere	6	F2
Murston	Rectory	Sittingbourne	47	C2
Nackington	Curacy	Canterbury	4	E3
New Romney	Vicarage	Lympne	33	D5
Newchurch	Sinecure rectory	Lymne	31	D4
Newchurch	Vicarage	Lympne	31	D4
Newenden	Rectory	Charing	38	B4
Newington next Hythe	Vicarage	Dover	22	E4
Newington next Sittingbourne	Vicarage	Sittingbourne	47	B2
Newnham	Vicarage	Ospringe	52	C2
Nonington with Wymynswold	Curacy	Bridge	12	E3
Northbourne with Shoulden	Vicarage	Sandwich	17	F3
Norton	Rectory	Ospringe	52	C2
Oare	Curacy	Ospringe	53	C2
Old Romney	Rectory	Lympne	33	D5
Orgarswick	Ruined church	Lymne	31	D4
Orlestone	Rectory	Lympne	31	C4
Ospringe	Vicarage	Ospringe	52	C2
Otham	Vicarage	Sutton	43	B3
Otterden	Rectory	Ospringe	53	C3
Paddlesworth chapel to Lyminge	Annexed chapel	Elham	25	E4
Patrixbourne with Bridge	Vicarage	Bridge	12	E3
Petham	Vicarage	Bridge	12	D3
Pluckley	Rectory	Charing	38	C3
Postling	Vicarage	Elham	25	E4
Preston	Vicarage	Bridge	12	E2
Preston next Faversham	Vicarage	Ospringe	53	D2

Parish	Status	Deanery	Catalogue Folio No.	Map Ref.
Queenborough chapel to Minster	Annexed chapel	Sittingbourne	48	C1
Rainham	Vicarage	Sittingbourne	48	B2
Reculver with Hoath	Vicarage	Westbere	7	E2
Ringwould	Rectory	Sandwich	17	F3
Ripple	Rectory	Sandwich	17	F3
River	Vicarage	Dover	22	F3
Rodmersham	Vicarage	Sittingbourne	48	C2
Rolvenden	Vicarage	Charing	38	B4
Royton chapel to Lenham	Ruined church	Sutton	43	–
Ruckinge	Rectory	Lympne	31	D4
St Margaret at Cliffe	Vicarage	Dover	22	F3
St Mary in the Marsh	Rectory	Lympne	30	D5
St Nicholas at Wade	Vicarage	Westbere	7	E2
Saltwood	Rectory	Elham	26	E4
Sandhurst	Rectory	Charing	38	B4
Sandwich St Clement	Vicarage	Sandwich	15	F2
Sandwich St Mary	Vicarage	Sandwich	17	F2
Sandwich St Peter	Rectory	Sandwich	17	F2
Seasalter	Vicarage	Westbere	7	D2
Sellindge	Vicarage	Lympne	32	D4
Selling	Vicarage	Ospringe	53	D2
Sevington	Rectory	Lympne	32	D4
Shadoxhurst	Rectory	Lympne	32	C4
Sheldwich	Vicarage	Ospringe	53	D2
Sheperheath	Not in Canterbury diocese	Dover	23	–
Shoulden chapel to Northbourne	Annexed chapel	Sandwich	18	F3
Sibertswold with Coldred	Vicarage	Sandwich	17	E3
Sittingbourne	Vicarage	Sittingbourne	48	C2
Smarden	Rectory	Charing	38	C3
Smeeth chapel to Aldington	Annexed chapel	Lymne	32	D4

PARISH LISTS IN 1663

Parish	Status	Deanery	Catalogue Folio No.	Map Ref.
Snargate	Rectory	Lympne	33	C5
Snave	Rectory	Lympne	32	D4
Stalisfield	Vicarage	Ospringe	53	C3
Stanford chapel to Lyminge	Annexed chapel	Elham	26	D4
Staple chapel to Adisham	Annexed chapel	Bridge	13	E2
Staplehurst	Rectory	Sutton	44	B3
Stelling chapel to Upper Hardres	Annexed chapel	Bridge	13	E3
Stockbury	Vicarage	Sittingbourne	48	B2
Stodmarsh	Curacy	Bridge	13	E2
Stonar	Ruined church	Sandwich	18	F2
Stone	Ruined church	Ospringe	54	C2
Stone-in-Oxney	Vicarage	Lympne	33	C5
Stourmouth	Rectory	Bridge	13	E2
Stowting	Rectory	Elham	26	D3
Sturry	Vicarage	Canterbury	4	E2
Sutton by Dover	Curacy	Sandwich	18	F3
Sutton Valence with East Sutton	Vicarage	Sutton	43	B3
Swalecliffe	Rectory	Westbere	7	E2
Swingfield	Curacy	Dover	23	E3
Temple Ewell	Vicarage	Dover	21	F3
Tenterden	Vicarage	Charing	38	C4
Teynham	Vicarage	Ospringe	54	C2
Thanet St John [Margate]	Vicarage	Westbere	6	F1
Thanet St Laurence	Vicarage	Westbere	6	F2
Thanet St Peter [Ramsgate]	Vicarage	Westbere	7	F2
Thannington	Curacy	Canterbury	4	D2
Throwley	Vicarage	Ospringe	54	C3
Thurnham with Allington	Vicarage	Sutton	44	B2
Tilmanstone	Vicarage	Sandwich	18	F3
Tonge	Vicarage	Sittingbourne	48	C2
Tunstall	Rectory	Sittingbourne	49	C2

xvii

Parish	Status	Deanery	Catalogue Folio No.	Map Ref.
Ulcombe	Rectory	Sutton	44	B3
Upchurch	Vicarage	Sittingbourne	49	B2
Upper Hardres with Stelling	Rectory	Bridge	11	E3
Waldershare	Vicarage	Sandwich	18	F3
Walmer	Curacy	Sandwich	19	F3
Waltham	Vicarage	Bridge	14	D3
Warden	Rectory	Sittingbourne	49	C1
Warehorne	Rectory	Lympne	33	C4
West Cliffe	Vicarage	Dover	23	F3
West Hythe	Vicarage	Lympne	33	D4
West Langdon	Ruined church	Sandwich	19	F3
Westbere	Rectory	Westbere	8	E2
Westenhanger	Ruined church	Lymne	31	–
Westwell	Vicarage	Charing	39	C3
Whitfield	Curacy	Dover	20	F3
Whitstable	Curacy	Westbere	8	D2
Wickhambreaux	Rectory	Bridge	13	E2
Willesborough	Vicarage	Lympne	34	D4
Wingham	Curacy	Bridge	14	E2
Wittersham	Rectory	Lympne	34	C5
Woodchurch	Rectory	Lympne	34	C4
Woodnesborough	Vicarage	Sandwich	19	F2
Wootton	Rectory	Elham	26	E3
Wormshill	Rectory	Sutton	44	C2
Worth chapel to Eastry	Annexed chapel	Sandwich	19	F2
Wychling	Rectory	Sittingbourne	49	C3
Wye	Curacy	Bridge	13	D3
Wymynswold chapel to Nonington	Annexed chapel	Bridge	14	E3

The peculiars of the archbishop of Canterbury listed in the Catalogue

Parish and chapel names are taken from the Clergy of the Church of England database. The alleged peculiars listed on folio 65 in the Catalogue are not listed below.

The parishes of the deanery of Shoreham in the county of Kent and located geographically within the diocese of Rochester (Map 2)

Parish	Status	Catalogue Folio No.	Map Ref.
Bexley	Vicarage	55	A1
Brasted	Rectory	55	A3
Chevening	Rectory	55	B3
Chiddingstone	Rectory	55	B3
Cliffe at Hoo	Rectory	55	C1
Crayford	Rectory	55	B1
Darenth	Vicarage	55	B1
Downe	Chapel to Orpington	57	A2
East Farleigh	Vicarage	55	C3
East Malling	Vicarage	56a	C2
East Peckham	Vicarage	56a	C3
Eynsford	Sinecure rectory	56a	
Eynsford	Vicarage	56a	B2
Farningham	Vicarage	56a	B2
Gillingham	Vicarage	56a	D2
Grain	Vicarage	56a	E1
Halstead	Rectory	56a	B2
Hayes	Rectory	56a	A2
Hever	Rectory	56a	A3
Hunton	Rectory	56b	C3
Ifield	Rectory	56b	C1
Ightham	Rectory	56b	B2
Keston	Rectory	56b	A2
Knockholt	Chapel to Orpington	57	A2
Lidsing * within the parish of Gillingham	Chapel to Gillingham	57	*
Meopham	Vicarage	56b	C2
Northfleet	Vicarage	56b	C1
Orpington	Sinecure rectory	56b	

Parish	Status	Catalogue Folio No.	Map Ref.
Orpington	Vicarage	56b	A2
Peckham	Not a peculiar	56b	
Penshurst	Rectory	56b	B4
Sevenoaks	Sinecure rectory	57	
Sevenoaks	Vicarage	57	B3
Shoreham rectory	Merged with vicarage	57	
Shoreham	Vicarage	57	B2
Sundridge	Rectory	57	B3
Woodland * united to Wrotham	Ruined church	57	*
Wrotham	Sinecure rectory	57	
Wrotham	Vicarage	57	C2

The parishes of the deanery of the Arches within the diocese of London (Map 3)

Parish	Status	Catalogue Folio No.	Map Ref.
All Hallows ad Fenne [All Hallows the Great]	Not a peculiar	58	
All Hallows Bread Street	Rectory	58	1
All Hallows Lombard Street	Rectory	58	2
St Dionis Backchurch	Rectory	58	3
St Dunstan in the East	Rectory	58	4
St Edmund Lombard Street [St Edmund the King and Martyr]	Not a peculiar	59a	
St John the Evangelist Watling Street [Friday Street]	Rectory	58	5
St Leonard Eastcheap	Rectory	58	6
St Mary Aldermary	Rectory	58	7
St Mary Bothaw	Rectory	58	8
St Mary le Bow	Rectory	59a	9
St Michael Crooked Lane	Rectory	59a	10
St Michael Paternoster Royal	Rectory	59a	11
St Pancras Soper Lane	Rectory	59a	12
St Vedast Foster Lane	Rectory	59a	13

The parishes of the deanery of Croydon in the county of Middlesex and located geographically within the diocese of London (Map 4)

Parish	Status	Catalogue Folio No.
Harrow on the Hill	Sinecure rectory	59a
Harrow on the Hill	Vicarage	59a
Hayes	Sinecure rectory	59a
Hayes	Vicarage	59a
Pinner	Chapel to Harrow	59a
Throckington	Chapel to Harrow	59a

The parishes of the deanery of Croydon in the county of Surrey and located geographically within the diocese of Winchester (Map 5)

Parish	Status	Catalogue Folio No.
Barnes	Rectory	59b
Burstow	Rectory	59b
Charlwood	Rectory	59b
Cheam	Rectory	59b
Croydon	Vicarage	59b
East Horsley	Rectory	59b
Merstham	Rectory	59b
Mortlake	Perpetual curacy	60
Newington	Rectory	59b
Norwood	Chapel to Hayes	59b
Putney	Perpetual curacy	60
Wimbledon	Sinecure rectory	60
Wimbledon	Perpetual curacy	60

The parishes of the deanery of Pagham in the county of Sussex (West) and located geographically within the diocese of Chichester (Map 6)

Parish	Status	Catalogue Folio No.
Chichester All Saints	Rectory	62
East Lavant	Rectory	62
Pagham	Vicarage	62
Slindon	Rectory	63

South Bersted	Vicarage	62
Tangmere	Rectory	63

The parishes of the deanery of Tarring in the county of Sussex (West) and located geographically within the diocese of Chichester (Map 6)

Parish	Status	Catalogue Folio No.
West Tarring	Sinecure rectory	63
West Tarring	Vicarage	63
Patching	Rectory	63

The parishes of the deanery of South Malling in the county of Sussex (East) and located geographically within the diocese of Chichester (Map 7)

Parish	Status	Catalogue Folio No.
Buxted with the dependent chapel of Uckfield	Rectory	63
Lewes St Thomas at Cliffe	Rectory	63
Edburton	Rectory	63
Framfield	Vicarage	64
Glynde	Vicarage	64
Isfield	Rectory	64
Mayfield	Vicarage	64
Ringmer	Vicarage	64
Stanmer	Rectory	64
Wadhurst	Vicarage	64
Linfield	Vicarage	64
South Malling	Sinecure rectory	64

The parishes of the deanery of Bocking in the county of Essex and located geographically within the diocese of London

Parish	Status	Catalogue Folio No.
Bocking	Rectory	60
Borley	Rectory	60
Latchingdon	Rectory	61
Little Coggeshall	Not a peculiar	60

Southchurch	Rectory	61
Stisted	Rectory	60

The parishes of the deanery of Bocking in the county of Suffolk and located geographically within the diocese of Norwich

Parish	Status	Catalogue Folio No.
Ash	Not a peculiar	61
Hadleigh	Rectory	60
Monks Eleigh	Rectory	61
Moulton	Sinecure rectory	61
Moulton	Vicarage	61

The parishes of the deanery of Risborough in the county of Buckinghamshire and located geographically within the diocese of Lincoln

Parish	Status	Catalogue Folio No.
Monks Risborough	Rectory	62
Halton	Rectory	62

The parishes of the deanery of Risborough in the county of Oxfordshire and located geographically within the diocese of Oxford

Parish	Status	Catalogue Folio No.
Newington	Rectory	62
Milton	Not a peculiar	

Number of parishes

Catalogue total of diocesan parishes

		290
Deduct		
Parishes entered twice[1]	2	
Sinecure rectories[2]	3	
Ruined churches[3] (11 of which were sinecure rectories)	17	
Annexed chapels with no incumbents[4]	16	
Annexed chapels with the same incumbent as mother church[5]	4	
United benefice[6]	1	
Parish not in the diocese[7]	1	44
Total 'operational' parishes		246
Deduct vacant parishes[8]		12
Total 'active' parishes		234

---

[1] Halstow and Hartlip.
[2] Hollingbourne, Lyminge, Newchurch.
[3] Bircholt, Blackmanstone, Broomhill, Canterbury St Mary de Castro, Dover St. Peter, Eastbridge, Elmley, Hope, Hurst, Little Mongeham, Midley, Orgarswick, Royton, Stonar, Stone near Faversham, West Langdon, Westenhanger.
[4] Barham chapel to Bishopsbourne, Birchington chapel to Monkton, Bridge chapel to Patrixbourne, Capel-le-Ferne chapel to Alkham, East Sutton chapel to Sutton Valence, Ebony chapel to Appledore, Hoath chapel to Reculver, Hythe chapel to Saltwood, Paddlesworth chapel to Lyminge, Queenborough chapel to Minster-in-Sheppey, Shoulden chapel to Northbourne, Smeeth chapel to Aldington, Stanford chapel to Lyminge, Staple chapel to Adisham, Worth chapel to Eastry, Wymynswold chapel to Nonington.
[5] Broomfield chapel to Leeds, Challock chapel to Godmersham, Hucking chapel to Hollingbourne, Stelling chapel to Upper Hardres.
[6] Coldred with Sibertswold.
[7] Sheperheath.
[8] Canterbury St Mary Bredman, Canterbury St Peter, Chart Sutton, Davington, Egerton, Harty, Kennington, Lenham, Petham, Sheldwich, Waldershare, Warden.

Catalogue total of archbishop's peculiars		117
Deduct		
Sinecure rectories[9]	10	
Ruined church[10]	1	
Parishes/prebends which were not peculiars[11]	14	
Annexed chapels with the same incumbent as mother church[12]	1	
Annexed chapels with no incumbent[13]	2	28
Total 'operational' parishes		89

---

[9] Eynsford, Harrow, Hayes Middlesex, Moulton, Orpington, Sevenoaks, Shoreham, Tarring, Wimbledon, Wrotham.
[10] Woodland.
[11] All Hallows the Great, Ash by Campsey, Castle Rising, Coggeshall, prebend of Cropredy & Tame, Little Milton, Myntling, North Wooton, Peckham, Roydon, St Edmund the King and Martyr, South Wooton, prebend of Sutton & Buckingham Thursford.
[12] Lidsing
[13] Pinner and Throckington.

Exempt parishes

Certain parishes in the diocese were exempt from the jurisdiction of the archdeacon. Churchill attributes the exemptions, in the twelfth century or before, to the collation of their incumbents by the archbishop, archiepiscopal residences in their parishes or incumbents' occupation of 'posts in the Archbishop's administrative economy too important for their subjection to be suitable'.[1] The number of exempt parishes varies according to the source. The table below compares the number of exempt parishes shown in the Catalogue with those enumerated by Nicolas Battely and with those described by William Somner for Archdeacon Sancroft in 1668. The Lambeth Palace Library website in 2022 gives a different, probably later, list. The privilege of exemption was abolished in the nineteenth century.

LPL, MS 1126		Battely[2]	Somner[3]
Folio			folio
1	Canterbury St Alphege	*	202v
3	Canterbury St Martin	*	202v
6	Herne	*	202v
6	Monkton with Birchington	*	202v
7	St Nicholas at Wade	*	202v
8	Adisham with Staple	*	202v
9	Ash		202r
10	Challock which was a chapel to Godmersham		
11	Godmersham with Challock	*	202r
11	Ickham	*	202v
12	Nonington with Wymynswold		202r
13	Staple which was a chapel to Adisham	*	
14	Wingham	*	202r
14	Wymynswold which was a chapel to Nonnington		
16	Deal	*	202v
20	Buckland near Dover		202r
21	Guston		202r
22	St Margaret at Cliffe	*	202r

[1] Churchill, I, 83–111.
[2] Somner, pp. 57–8.
[3] CCA, DCc/LitMS/C/5.

22	Dover St Mary	*	202r
22	Dover St James		202r
25	Lyminge rectory with the chapels of Paddlesworth and Stanford	*	202r
25	Hythe which was a chapel to Saltwood	*	
25	Lyminge vicarage [see rectory above]		
27	Aldington with Smeeth	*	203v
29	Fairfield	*	203v
29	Ivychurch	*	203v
30	Lydd	*	203v
31	Newchurch vicarage	*	203v
31	Newchurch rectory [see vicarage above]		
32	Smeeth which was a chapel to Aldington	*	
33	New Romney		203v
36	Charing	*	202r
39	Westwell	*	203v
40	Detling	*	203v
40	Bredhurst[4]		
41	Hollingbourne vicarage with Hucking	*	203v
43	Loose	*	203v
43	Maidstone	*	203v
50	Boughton under Blean	*	203r
51	Hernhill	*	203r
	Eastry with Worth	*	202v
	Egerton	*	203v
	Reculver with Hoath	*	202v
	Saltwood	*	202r
	Wittersham	*	203v
	Woodchurch[5]	*	203v
	Hoath[6]	*	
	Hucking[7]	*	
	St Nicholas, Harbledown[8]	*	
	Brockhull chapel[9]	*	

---

[4] Bredhurst, a perpetual curacy, was later referred to as being exempt. Hasted, V, 589.
[5] Chapel to Monkton.
[6] Chapel to Reculver.
[7] Chapel to Hollingbourne vicarage.
[8] Chapel to the hospital.
[9] Chapel to Brockhull Manor in Saltwood parish.

Abbreviations

Used in the footnotes, the Biographical index and the Introduction. The place of publication is London unless otherwise stated.

46th report	HMC, *The forty-sixth annual report of the deputy keeper of the public records*. 11 August 1885 Appendix I Nos. 1 and 2 Presentations to Offices, on the Patent Rolls; Charles II, vol. XXXVII, Readex Microprint Edition
AC	*Archaeologia Cantiana*, Transactions of the Kent Archaeological Society, vols. 1–124 (1858–2009)
Armytage	G. J. Armytage, ed., *A visitation of the county of Kent, begun A.D. 1663 and finished A.D. 1668* (Harleian Society, 54, 1906)
Barratt	D. M. Barratt, 'The condition of the parish clergy between the Reformation and 1660, with special reference to the dioceses of Oxford, Worcester and Gloucester', D.Phil. thesis, University of Oxford, 1949
Bate	F. Bate, *The Declaration of Indulgence 1672* (1908)
Beaumont	G. F. Beaumont, *A history of Coggeshall, in Essex* (1890)
Beaven	A. B. Beaven, *The aldermen of the city of London* (1908)
Bennett	N. Bennett, *Lincolnshire parish clergy c. 1214–1968: a biographical register*, Part II: *The deaneries of Beltisloe and Bolingbroke* (Lincoln Record Society, 105, Lincoln, 2016)
Berry	W. Berry, *Pedigrees of the families in the county of Kent* (1830)
Besse	J. Besse, *A collection of the sufferings of the people called quakers* (2 vols., 1753), I.
BL	British Library
Bloomfield	P. Bloomfield, 'The Cromwellian Commission in Kent, 1655–57', in *Studies in modern Kentish history*, ed. A. Detsicas and N. Yates (Maidstone, 1983)
Boodle	J. A. Boodle, ed., *The registers of Boughton-under-Blean* (Parish Register Society, 49, 1903)
Bosher	R. S. Bosher, *The making of the Restoration settlement, 1649-1662* (1951)
Bodl.	Bodleian Library, Oxford

Boys	W. Boys, *Collections for an history of Sandwich* (Canterbury, 1791)
Bradfer-Lawrence	H. L. Bradfer-Lawrence, *A short history of the castle honor and borough of Castle Rising* (King's Lynn, 1932)
Bramston	W. Bramston, *A history of the abbey church of Minster* (1896)
Bray	G. Bray, ed., *The Anglican canons 1529–1947* (Church of England Record Society, 6, Woodbridge, 1998)
Broadway, Cust and Roberts	J. Broadway, R. Cust and S. K. Roberts, eds., *A calendar of the docquets of Lord Keeper Coventry 1625–1640* (4 vols., List and Index Society, Special Series, 34–7, Kew, 2004)
Brydges	E. Brydges, *Peerage of England* (9 vols., 1812)
Bucholz	R. O. Bucholz, ed., 'The chapel royal: chaplains, 1660–1837', in *Office-holders in modern Britain*, XI (revised): *Court officers, 1660–1837* (2006)
Burke	J. and J. B. Burke, *A genealogical and heraldic history of the extinct and dormant baronetcies of England* (1841)
Cardwell	E. Cardwell, *Documentary annals of the reformed Church of England: being a collection of injunctions, declarations, orders, articles of inquiry, from the year 1546 to the year 1716* (2 vols., Oxford, 1839)
Cass	F. C. Cass, *Monken Hadley* (1880)
Cave-Browne (1889)	J. Cave-Browne, *The history of the parish church of All Saints Maidstone* (Maidstone, 1889)
Cave-Browne (1890)	J. Cave-Browne, *The story of Hollingbourne* (Maidstone, 1890)
Cave-Browne (1892)	J. Cave-Browne, *The history of Boxley parish* (Maidstone, 1892)
Cavell and Kennett	J. Cavell and B. Kennett, *A history of Sir Roger Manwood's School Sandwich 1563–1963* (1963)
CCA	Canterbury Cathedral Archives
CCEd	The Clergy of the Church of England database 1540–1835, www.theclergydatabase.org.uk
Chalkin	C. W. Chalkin, *Seventeenth-century Kent* (1965)
Churchill	I. J. Churchill, *Canterbury administration ...* (2 vols., 1933)
Cliffe	J. T. Cliffe, ed., 'The Cromwellian Decimation Tax of 1655: the assessment lists', in *Seventeenth-century political letters and papers. Miscellany, Vol. XXXIII* (Royal Historical Society, Camden 5th series, 7, Cambridge, 1996)

Cobbett	W. Cobbett, *Parliamentary history of England: 1642–1660* (1808)
Cockburn (1989)	J. S. Cockburn, ed., *Calendar of assize records Kent indictments 1649–1659* (1989)
Cockburn (1995)	J. S. Cockburn, *Calendar of assize records Kent indictments Charles II 1660–1675* (1995)
Cockburn (1997)	J. S. Cockburn, *Calendar of Assize Records Kent indictments Charles II 1676–1688* (1997)
Cokayne	G. E. Cokayne, ed., *Complete baronetage* (5 vols., Exeter, 1900–6)
Compounding	HMC, *Calendar of the proceedings of the Committee for Compounding, etc., 1643–1660, preserved in the State Paper Department of Her Majesty's Public Record Office* (3 vols., 1889–92)
Cowper (1887)	J. M. Cowper, ed., *The register booke of christeninges, marriages and burialls in Saint Dunstan's, Canterbury, 1559–1800* (Canterbury, 1887)
Cowper (1888)	J. M. Cowper, ed., *The booke of regester of the parish of St. Peter in Canterbury: for christninges, weddinges and buryalls, 1560–1800* (Canterbury, 1888)
CSPC	*Calendar of state papers colonial, America and West Indies*, V: 1661–8 (1880)
CSPD	*Calendar of state papers domestic: Charles II* (28 vols., 1860–1969)
Daeley	J. I. Daeley, 'The episcopal administration of Matthew Parker, archbishop of Canterbury, 1559–1575', Ph.D. thesis, London University, 1967
Dallaway	J. Dallaway, *A history of the western division of the county of Sussex. Including the rapes of Chichester, Arundel, and Bramber, with the city and diocese of Chichester*, II, pt 2: *The parochial topography of the rape of Bramber, in the western division of the county of Sussex* (1815)
DUL	Durham University Library
Dunkin	E. H. W. Dunkin, C. Jenkins and E. A. Fry, *Index to the Act Books of the archbishops of Canterbury 1663–1859* (2 vols., 1929–38)
Ecton	J. Ecton, *Liber valorum & decimarum: being an account of such ecclesiastical benefices …* (2nd edn, 1723)
EHR	*English Historical Review*
ELJ	*Ecclesiastical Law Journal*

Everitt (1960)	A. Everitt, ed., 'An account book of the committee of Kent, 1646–7', in *A seventeenth century miscellany* (Canterbury, 1960)
Everitt (1966)	A. Everitt, *The community of Kent and the Great Rebellion, 1640–60* (Leicester, 1966)
Fielding	C. H. Fielding, *The records of Rochester* (Dartford, 1910)
Fincham (1984)	K. C. Fincham, 'Pastoral roles of the Jacobean episcopate in Canterbury province', Ph.D. thesis, London University, 1984
Fincham	K. Fincham, *Prelate as pastor. The episcopate of James I* (Oxford, 1990)
Fincham and Lake	K. Fincham and P. Lake, eds. *Religious politics in post-Reformation England* (Woodbridge, 2006)
Fincham and Tyacke	K. Fincham and N. Tyacke, *Altars restored: the changing face of English Religious worship, 1547–c. 1700* (Oxford, 2010)
Fishwick	H. Fishwick, *The history of the parish of Rochdale in the county of Lancaster* (Rochdale, 1889)
Foster	J. Foster, ed. *Alumni Oxonienses* (4 vols., Oxford, 1891–2)
Foster (1889)	J. Foster, ed. *The register of admissions to Gray's Inn, 1521–1889* (1889)
Fox	J. Fox, *The king's smuggler: Jane Whorwood ...* (Stroud, 2010)
Freeman	J. Freeman, 'The parish ministry in the diocese of Durham, c. 1570–1640', Ph.D. thesis, Durham University, 1980
Greaves	R. L. Greaves, *Deliver us from evil: the radical underground in Britain, 1660–1663* (Oxford, 1986)
Green (1973)	I. M. Green, 'The process of re-establishment of the Church of England, 1660–1663', D.Phil. thesis, University of Oxford, 1973
Green (1978)	I. M. Green, *The re-establishment of the Church of England, 1660–1663* (Oxford, 1978)
Gregory	J. Gregory, ed., *The Speculum of Archbishop Thomas Secker* (Church of England Record Society, 2, Woodbridge, 1995)
Gregory (2000)	J. Gregory, *Restoration, reformation and reform, 1660–1828* (Oxford, 2000)
Gregory (2017)	J. Gregory, ed., *The Oxford history of Anglicanism*, II: *Establishment and empire, 1662–1829* (Oxford, 2017)

Haggard	J. Haggard, *Reports of cases argued and determined in the ecclesiastical courts* ... , I (1829)
Hardman Moore	S. Hardman Moore, *Pilgrims: new world settlers and the call of home* (New Haven and London, 2007)
Harrington	D. Harrington, ed., *Kent Hearth Tax assessment Lady Day 1664* (2000)
Harris	T. Harris, *London crowds in the reign of Charles II* (Cambridge, 1990)
Haslewood (1886)	F. Haslewood, *Memorials of Smarden, Kent* (Ipswich, 1886)
Haslewood (1889)	F. Haslewood, *The parish of Benenden, Kent* (Ipswich, 1889)
Hasted	E. Hasted, *The history and topographical survey of the county of Kent* (2nd edn, 12 vols., 1797–1801)
Hegarty	A. Hegarty, ed., *A biographical register of St. John's College, Oxford 1555–1666* (Oxford Historical Society, n.s., 43, Woodbridge, 2011)
Hennessy	G. L. Hennessy, *Novum repertorium ecclesiasticum parochiale londinense* (1898)
Heygate Lambert	F. A. Heygate Lambert, *The registers of Banstead, Surrey* (1896)
HMC	Historical Manuscripts Commission
HoP	www.historyofparliamentonline.org
Horn	J. Le Neve, *Fasti ecclesiae anglicanae 1541–1857*, ed. J. M. Horn *et al.* (13 vols., 1969–2013)
Houston	J. Houston, *Catalogue of ecclesiastical records of the Commonwealth 1643–1660 in the Lambeth Palace Library* (1968)
Ingram Hill	D. Ingram Hill, *The Six Preachers of Canterbury cathedral 1541–1982* (Ramsgate, 1982)
Ivimey	J. Ivimey, *A history of the English baptists* (4 vols., 1811–30)
JEH	*Journal of Ecclesiastical History*
Jones	S. A. Jones, 'The Church of England in the Forest of Arden, 1660–1740', Ph.D. thesis, University of Birmingham, 2009
KFHS	Kent Family History Society, transcriptions of parish registers of baptisms, marriages and burials on CD-ROMs
KHLC	Kent History and Library Centre
Kilburne	Richard Kilburne, *A topographie or survey of the county of Kent* (1659)

Larking	L. B. Larking, ed., *Proceedings principally in the county of Kent ... in 1640* (Camden Society, o.s, 80, 1862)
Lipscomb	G. Lipscomb, *The history and antiquities of the county of Buckingham* (4 vols., 1847)
Littledale	W. A. Littledale, ed., *The registers of St Vedast, Foster Lane and of St Michael le Quern, London* (2 vols., 1902–3)
LJ	*House of Lords Journal*
LMA	London Metropolitan Archives
Lodge	E. C. Lodge, ed., *The account book of a Kentish estate 1616–1704* (1927)
LPL	Lambeth Palace Library
Lutton	R. Lutton, 'Heresy and heterodoxy in late medieval Kent', in *Later medieval Kent, 1220–1540*, ed. S. Sweetinburgh (Woodbridge, 2010)
Lyon Turner	G. Lyon Turner, ed., *Original records of early nonconformity under persecution and indulgence* (2 vols., 1911)
MA	Medway Archives Centre
McCartney	M. W. McCartney, *Virginia immigrants and adventurers, 1607–1635: a biographical dictionary* (Baltimore, 2007)
Mackenzie and Ross	E. Mackenzie and M. Ross, *An historical, topographical, and descriptive view of the county palatine of Durham*, I (Newcastle upon Tyne, 1834)
Marshall	W. M. Marshall, 'The administration of the dioceses of Hereford and Oxford, 1660–1760', Ph.D. thesis, University of Bristol, 1978
Mastin	J. Mastin, *The history and antiquities of Naseby* (Cambridge, 1792)
Matthews, *Calamy*	A. G. Matthews, *Calamy revised* (Oxford, 1988)
Matthews, *Walker*	A. G. Matthews, *Walker revised* (Oxford, 1948)
Newcourt	R. Newcourt, *Repertorium ecclesiasticum parochiale londinense* (2 vols., 1708–10)
ODNB	*Oxford dictionary of national biography* (60 vols., Oxford, 2004–14)
Oechsli	W. Oechsli, *History of Switzerland 1499–1914* (Cambridge, 1922)
Orridge	B. B. Orridge, *Some account of the citizens of London ...* (1867)
Overton	J. H. Overton, *The nonjurors* (1902)

Packer	B. Packer, 'Nonconformity in Tenterden: 1640–1750', *Transactions of the Unitarian Historical Society*, 20 (1992)
Page	W. Page, ed. *The Victoria history of the county of Buckingham* (2 vols., 1905–8)
Parkin	C. Parkin, *An essay towards a topographical history of the county of Norfolk*, IX (1808)
Pearce	E. H. Pearce, *Sion College and Library* (Cambridge, 1913)
Pearman	A. J. Pearman, *Ashford: its church, vicars, college, and grammar school* (Ashford, 1886)
Peile	J. Peile, *Biographical register of Christ's College 1505–1905* (2 vols., 1910–13)
Pepys	R. Latham and W. Matthews, eds., *The diary of Samuel Pepys* (11 vols., 1970–83)
Plantagenet	M. H. Massue, *The Plantagenet Roll of the Blood Royal… (the Mortimer-Percy Volume, Part 1)* (1911)
Plomer	H. R. Plomer, *A dictionary of the printers and booksellers who were at work in England, Scotland and Ireland from 1668 to 1725* (Oxford, 1922)
Potter	J. M. Potter, 'The ecclesiastical courts in the diocese of Canterbury, 1603–1665', M.Phil. thesis, University of London, 1973
Pruett	J. H. Pruett, *The parish clergy under the later Stuarts: the Leicestershire experience* (Urbana, 1978)
Reeves and Eve	A. Reeves and D. Eve, 'Sheep-keeping and lookers' huts on Romney Marsh', in *Romney Marsh environmental change and human occupation in a coastal lowland*, ed. J. Eddison, M. Gardiner and A. Long (Oxford, 1998)
Reid	Thomas Reid, 'The clergy of the diocese of Canterbury in the seventeenth century', Ph.D. thesis, University of Kent, 2011
Richardson	D. Richardson, *Magna Carta ancestry: a study in colonial and medieval families*, I (Baltimore, 2011)
Robinson	C. J. Robinson, *A register of the scholars admitted into Merchant Taylors' School 1562–1874* (Lewes, 1882)
Rushworth	J. Rushworth, *Historical collections of private passages of state …* (8 vols., 1721)
SA	Shropshire Archives
SAC	*Sussex Archaeological Collections*
Salter	J. L. Salter, 'Warwickshire clergy, 1660–1714', Ph.D. thesis, Birmingham University, 1975

Scott	J. R. Scott, *Memorials of the family of Scott, of Scot's-hall* ... (1883)
Shaw (1870)	W. F. Shaw, *Memorials of the royal ville and parish of Eastry* (1870)
Shaw (1900)	W. A. Shaw, *A history of the English church during the civil wars and under the Commonwealth, 1640–1660* (2 vols., 1900)
Shaw (1906)	W. A. Shaw, *The knights of England* (2 vols., 1906)
Smith	G. Smith, *Royalist agents, conspirators and spies* (Oxford, 2016)
Snow and Young	V. F. Snow and A. S. Young, eds., *The private journals of the Long Parliament*, II (New Haven, 1987)
Somner	W. Somner, *The antiquities of Canterbury* ... , rev. N. Battely (2nd edn, 1703)
SP	State Papers
Spaeth	D. A. Spaeth, *The church in an age of danger: parsons and parishioners, 1660–1740* (Cambridge, 2000)
Spurr	J. Spurr, *The Restoration Church of England, 1646–1689* (1991)
Squibb	G. D. Squibb, *Doctors' Commons: a history of the College of Advocates and Doctors of Law* (Oxford, 1977)
SRS	Surrey Record Society
Sterry	W. Sterry, *The Eton College register 1441–1698* (Eton, 1943)
Stevens	R. Stevens, *Protestant pluralism: the reception of the Toleration Act, 1689–1720* (Woodbridge, 2018)
Stifford	F. A. Crisp, *The parish registers of Stifford, Essex* (privately printed, 1885)
Surrey AC	*Surrey Archaeological Collections*
Sussex RS	*Sussex Record Society*
Tarbutt	W. Tarbutt, *The annals of Cranbrook church* (Cranbrook, 1870)
Thomas and Ryan	H. R. Thomas and J. Ryan, eds., *Wolverhampton Grammar School register* (Kendal, 1926)
Thomson	A. B. de L. Thomson, 'The diocese of Winchester before and after the English civil wars: a study of the character and performance of its clergy', Ph.D. thesis, University of London, 2004
Thoroton	J. Throsby, ed., *Thoroton's history of Nottinghamshire* (3 vols., 1790–7)
TNA	The National Archives

Tomlinson	E. M. Tomlinson, *A history of the minories London* (1907)
Topographer	*The Topographer*, 1, no. IV, July 1789
Venn	J. and J. A. Venn, eds., *Alumni Cantabrigienses*, Part 1: *From the earliest times to 1751* (4 vols., Cambridge, 1922–7)
West Tarring	T. P. Hudson, ed., *A history of the county of Sussex*, Victoria County History of Sussex, VI, Part 1: *Bramber Rape (Southern Part)* (1980)
Whiteman	A. Whiteman, ed., with M. Clapinson, *The Compton Census of 1676: a critical edition* (1986)
Whiteman (1955)	A. Whiteman, 'The re-establishment of the Church of England, 1660–1663', *Transactions of the Royal Historical Society*, 5th series, 5 (1955)
Wilkie (1891)	C. H. Wilkie, ed., *The parish registers of Elmstone, Kent, 1552–1812* (Kingston, 1891)
Wilkie (1893)	C. H. Wilkie, ed., *The parish registers of St. Giles, Kingston* (Brighton, 1893)
Wilkie (1896)	C. H. Wilkie, ed., *The parish registers of St. Peter's, Beakesbourne, Kent, 1558–1812* (Canterbury, 1896)
Wilkins	D. Wilkins, ed., *Concilia magnae Britanniae et Hiberniae* (4 vols., 1737)
Willis (1733)	B. Willis, *Parochiale anglicanum: or the names of all the churches and chapels within the dioceses of Canterbury, Rochester, London, Winchester ...* (1733)
Willis (1972)	A. J. Willis, comp., *Canterbury licences (general) 1568–1646* (Chichester, 1972)
Willis (1975)	A. J. Willis, ed., 'Canterbury licences (general) 1660–1714' (unpublished typescript, Canterbury, 1975) (see also KHLC, DCb/L/R/17–27)
Wilson	H. B. Wilson, *The history of Merchant-Taylors' School, from its foundation to the present time* (1814)
Woodruff and Cape	C. E. Woodruff and H. J. Cape, *Schola Regia Cantuariensis: a history of Canterbury School* (1908)

Introduction

The story of the Church of England over the course of the seventeenth century is complicated and multifaceted, and the most complex period, both at the national and local level, is from 1660 to 1700. The latter period has had the sometimes doubtful privilege of being endowed with a heavy burden of historical opinion.[1] Charles II was restored to his kingdom in 1660 and the Church of England was re-established by law in 1662, but it was a fractious kingdom and the church was not universally accepted. The period from 1660 to 1663 was characterized by small rebellions, many executions for treason, large-scale movements of parish incumbents and the persistence of dissent. This Introduction is intended to assist in the understanding of a single document which is itself devoted to a comparatively small number of parishes located, in the main, within the confines of a small area of England. Attention is therefore directed at what the document says and whether any revelations of shortcomings should or could have been remedied in the years immediately following the Restoration, rather than attempting to discuss national issues. Many historians have explicated the national political and religious problems and a few have examined local communities, but this document reveals the problems facing the re-established local church hierarchy, at the parish level.

The Church of England had been officially banned for nearly twenty years and while some of the Canterbury diocesan parishes clung on to their ministers or individuals continued to use the old rites clandestinely, the majority of the parishes, if they had a pastor at all, were subjected to an ever changing mélange of presbyterians, congregationalists, baptists, quakers and itinerant preachers. By 1663, it was apparent that church attendance was alarmingly low and nonconformists survived in numbers and influence, despite the national laws enacted between 1660 and 1663 designed to control matters. The machinery of the church courts was not yet fully operational, making local control more difficult, and support from county leaders was not always guaranteed. Adding to these challenges were the structural problems caused by pluralism, non-residence, low clerical incomes, ruined churches, dilapidated clerical residences and vacant livings.

The document popularly referred to as the 'Sheldon survey' presents a blurred and flawed view but assists our understanding of the state of the church, by the end of 1663, in the diocese of Canterbury and the archbishop's peculiars.[2] The information it gives is restricted to a comparatively small number of parishes in the south-east of England, but it may suggest that similar problems existed elsewhere.

Gilbert Sheldon was consecrated bishop of London in October 1660 and, following the death of William Juxon, installed as archbishop of Canterbury on the last day of August 1663.[3] There is no documentary evidence, but it appears likely

---

[1] Bosher; Green (1978); Spurr; J. Gregory and J. S. Chamberlain, eds., *The national church in local perspective. The Church of England and the regions 1660–1800* (Woodbridge, 2005); Gregory (2017); Stevens.
[2] See 'Parish lists in 1663' for lists of diocesan parishes and peculiars.
[3] John Spurr, 'Sheldon, Gilbert', *ODNB*.

that, soon after his elevation, he gave instructions for a survey of his new diocese to be prepared. As we will see, multiple informants needed to contribute, but the final document was compiled under the supervision of Sheldon's secretary, Miles Smyth. Given the title 'A catalogue of all the benefices and promocions within the diocese and jurisdiction of Canterbury. With the state of every particular parish as it stood at October 1663',[4] it includes a table of benefices in the gift of the archbishop of Canterbury, with their values, and a table of advowsons granted to Sheldon by various bishops at their consecrations and translations.[5] As the Catalogue[6] is dated very shortly after Sheldon's installation as archbishop, it was probably the result of an early occurrence of his demands for information during his archiepiscopate, but what distinguished it was the inclusion of views of the religious temperature of some parishes, and the naming of men, lay and clerical, and women, who were known to be hostile to the church and therefore (in the eyes of Sheldon and others) the state.

Historians, principally Professors Green and Gregory in their early work,[7] have quoted from the comments in the Catalogue about the conformity or otherwise of incumbents and parish congregations but it has not previously been subjected to detailed critical analysis. The compilers of the Catalogue provided Sheldon with evidence of continuing disaffection with the religious settlement of 1662, coupled with intelligence as to those of the gentry who could be relied upon to support the wing of the church that would not allow for any compromise with dissenters. This was vital, given the uncertainty of the times, but its usefulness was diminished by error and the extent of missing information. Nevertheless, as we shall see, the Catalogue indicates that religion was far from settled, the Church of England being far from secure by 1663: in other words, the practical work of the re-establishment had only just begun.[8] The Catalogue is the forerunner of a series of surveys conducted during the 1660s but it is unique in its inclusion of opinions about individual clerics, laymen and parish congregations, and on the state of the church fabric and furnishings. In Canterbury, this practice is usually only found in the notebooks compiled by men commencing their archdeaconries.[9] The later archiepiscopal surveys, undertaken by Sheldon, extended beyond the diocese but were confined to factual matters.[10]

Miles Smyth arranged the format of the Catalogue and presumably determined the detailed questions to be asked of informants but, as we will see, the answers he received vary in quantity, quality and subject matter.[11] The Catalogue evolved over time, accumulating alterations and additions made over a period of nearly twenty years. Its compilation may have begun in September 1663, with major additions in

---

[4] LPL, MS 1126.
[5] The table of benefices in the gift of the archbishop may be contemporaneous with the date of the parish entries as it was copied from Archbishop Grindal's register. For the table of advowsons see the Catalogue, p. 69 n. 191.
[6] This abbreviation will be used in the text and notes below.
[7] Green (1973), (1978); Gregory.
[8] Expanded on in Grant Tapsell 'The Church of England, 1662–1714', in Gregory (2017).
[9] Examples are William Sancroft and Thomas Green. Bodl., MS Sancroft 99 (1668); KHLC, DCb/J/Z/3/34 (1711).
[10] The later survey results are contained in LPL, MSS 639, 923, 943, 951, and Whiteman.
[11] The shortcomings of the answers to the Catalogue enquiries can probably be attributed to missing or incomplete returns whereas the returns for the Compton census of 1676 were affected by poor framing of the questions. Whiteman, pp. xxix–xlvii.

late October giving rise to its title, followed by editing by Miles Smyth. The original would only have shown the information relevant to the parishes and incumbents in late 1663 or early 1664 and, for the diocesan portion, there are indications that it was completed after 16 December 1663 but before 9 January 1664. The entry for John Campleshon, who subscribed as vicar of Upchurch on 16 December 1663, notes that he was 'lately put in' and the vicarage of Lenham is said to be vacant, before the incumbency of John Lord, who was collated and subscribed as vicar on 9 January 1664.[12] The latest dated entry for the diocese can be found on folio 11 'Mr. James Christmas – 10 July 82'. Unless otherwise indicated the analysis on the following pages refers to the first named incumbents in each parish who are documented as being there by the end of 1663. Most of the entries for the archbishop's peculiars could have been made before the end of 1663 but there are exceptions. The deanery of Shoreham has two initial entries in September and December 1664, one in 1666, one in 1670 and one in 1672.[13] The deanery of Croydon has entries in 1665, 1667 and 1672;[14] Monks Risborough, one in 1675;[15] Pagham, one in 1674 and two in 1676[16] and South Malling has entries in 1664, 1666 and 1667.[17] In addition, there are many blank spaces throughout the peculiars.

This introduction is in two parts: the first, by far the largest, concerns the diocese, and the second, although very small, attempts to pierce the veil obscuring the archbishop's peculiars. The diocesan part is further divided into four sections: first, an outline of geographical location and ecclesiastical administration; secondly, an explanation of how the Catalogue was compiled and its provenance; thirdly, a discussion of the problems facing the church in the diocese in 1663, including inequality of incomes, pluralism and nonconformity exacerbated by the chaos of the previous twenty years and finally, an explanation of two extant instances of the Catalogue format being used again.

THE DIOCESE OF CANTERBURY

The county of Kent consists of two dioceses, Rochester and Canterbury and, in the seventeenth century, the diocese of Canterbury comprised all of the parishes in Kent east of the River Medway.[18] The Isle of Sheppey, located off the north coast, was part of the diocese, and two other areas were islands in the seventeenth century: Thanet, in the north-east, and Oxney, in the south-west. The rivers and channels forming these two islands gradually changed direction, silted up or were drained to join them to the land in the eighteenth and later centuries. There were large areas of marshland in the north-west and north-east and particularly in the south, with the Romney Marsh. Drainage and land reclamation was still incomplete in the seventeenth century, so while the northern part was called Romney Marsh, the southern

---

[12] The CCEd entry for John Campleshon includes his collation on 23 Apr. 1664, but this must have been a tidying up exercise. Catalogue, fos. 42, 49; CCEd Person ID: 1390, 139924; LPL, VG 1/4 fos. 2v, 2r.
[13] Blackstone, Richard Marsh, Stacey, William Pawley and Philip Jones.
[14] Millington, Fly and Thompson.
[15] Wooley.
[16] Betton in 1674 and 1676 and Holder in 1676.
[17] Peck, Thomas Clarke and Ireland.
[18] See Parish lists in 1663.

area had Guldeford Marsh, Denge Marsh and Walland Marsh. The Kentish Weald lay to the south-west of the diocese with 'scattered and fragmented settlement in large parishes'.[19] These geographical features served to protect some parishes from external influence. There were two main roads through the diocese: the old Roman Watling Street, from London through Dartford, Rochester and Canterbury to Dover with a branch to Deal, described in the seventeenth century as 'the most frequented road in England',[20] and another linking Maidstone to Ashford and Hythe, which was of lesser quality. All other routes were narrow, winding lanes, almost impassable in winter with horses sinking to their girths and wagons to their axles, and in summer, travellers still encountered mud or had to endure clouds of chalk or clay dust.

Canterbury had only one archdeaconry, coterminous with the diocese, but thirty-nine parishes were exempt from the jurisdiction of the archdeacon[21] and answerable only to the archbishop, thus giving them some measure of independence. The Catalogue lists 290 'parishes' but, as we will see later, this number is misleading. Between the archbishop, archdeacon, dean and chapter of Canterbury and of Rochester and St Paul's and some parish incumbents, the church held the patronage of over 60 per cent of the livings in 1663,[22] a high percentage compared to other dioceses. In Bath and Wells, in 1643, private individuals held over 67 per cent and in Oxford and Worcester they held over 46 per cent.[23] Canterbury cathedral is not included in the Catalogue, as it was exempt from archiepiscopal oversight except at visitations, although it notes where several parish incumbents are also cathedral canons or Six Preachers.[24] The latter, unique to Canterbury, were a college of six preachers set up under the royal charter for the new foundation of the cathedral in 1541. Every Preacher was expected to preach at least twenty sermons a year, in the city churches, their own living, if they held one, or in one of the other churches in the gift of the dean and chapter and they also preached in the cathedral on holy days or as substitutes for the canons.[25]

Canterbury was therefore a diocese with a relatively small number of parishes, located reasonably near the archbishop's residence at Lambeth Palace, under the eye of the archdeacon and senior clergy in the cathedral and with one of the best roads in England into its heart. These factors were advantageous to governance but other factors gave rise to problems. The rivers and their tributaries meant that many parishes or groups of parishes were remote and isolated. Well-qualified clergymen were reluctant to serve in these areas and in the large areas of marshland; there were frequent dispensations for non-residence granted because of the 'unhealthy air'. The malarial mosquitoes that bred in the marshes were to the detriment of the

---

[19] Lutton, p. 179.
[20] Chalkin, p. 164.
[21] See 'Exempt parishes'.
[22] Reid, p. 30; Gregory (2000).
[23] M. Stieg, *Laud's laboratory. The diocese of Bath and Wells in the early seventeenth century* (1982), pp. 96–7; Barratt, pp. 42–55. For a detailed table for the situation in *c*.1835, see G. F. A. Best, *Temporal pillars: Queen Anne's Bounty, the ecclesiastical commissioners, and the Church of England* (Cambridge, 1964), Appendix vi.
[24] Dean Thomas Turner and Canons William Barker, Peter Gunning and Thomas Pierce are omitted from the Catalogue as they did not have livings in the diocese and there is no reference to Robert Wilkinson, Miles Barnes and Elias Juxon being Six Preachers.
[25] P. Collinson, 'The protestant cathedral, 1541–1660', in *A History of Canterbury Cathedral*, ed. P. Collinson, N. Ramsay and M. Sparks (Oxford, 1995), p. 159; Ingram Hill, *passim*.

health of the inhabitants.[26] The state of the minor roads were another impediment; in the summer of 1675, John Bargrave, canon and receiver general of the revenues of Canterbury cathedral, accompanied by the dean and another canon, ventured forth by coach to survey the cathedral's estates. The roads were so bad that the party had often to resort to leaving their coach and walking across the fields to inspect manors and churches.[27]

PROVENANCE AND SOURCES OF INFORMATION

We can determine from the contents of the Catalogue that Sheldon asked for a list of all the benefices, their values, patrons and incumbents and, crucially, 'the state of every particular parish'. We may have expected that the archdeacon of Canterbury would provide the required information, but, by 1663, he was elsewhere. During the chaotic period from 1660 to 1663, Archbishop Juxon, who was in his late seventies, instituted 120 rectors and vicars to the parishes but there are no surviving records of visitations in 1660 or 1661. The archidiaconal visitation of 1662 was carried out by James Master,[28] while the vicar-general Sir Richard Chaworth, together with the bishop of Hereford, Herbert Croft, conducted the metropolitan visitation of 1663. Juxon can perhaps be excused because of his age and infirmity but similar sympathy cannot be extended to George Hall, his archdeacon. The son of a former bishop, Hall had been a vicar, prebendary and archdeacon in Cornwall but was sequestered from all his preferments during the civil wars. In 1660, he became a canon of Windsor and archdeacon of Canterbury and by 1661 he was a chaplain to Charles II. In May 1662, Hall was consecrated bishop of Chester. John Ramsbottom says that, during his bishopric, Hall 'resided at the comfortable rectory of Wigan … while failing to supervise the routine business of his see, where in his time presentations to livings or subscriptions by clergy were recorded only "by chance"'.[29] Even more unfortunate for the diocese of Canterbury, therefore, that in addition to the rectory of Wigan, Hall was dispensed to hold in commendam the archdeaconry of Canterbury from October 1662 until his death in 1668.[30] At a critical time for the recovery of the Church of England, in its mother diocese, its archbishop was incapacitated and its sole archdeacon was hundreds of miles away.

Some surviving manuscripts provide insight into how Miles Smyth, Sheldon's secretary, managed the production of the Catalogue. The whereabouts of the administrative documents of the province of Canterbury (usually held at Lambeth) are unknown for the 1640s to 1650s but, by the end of 1663, Smyth would have had ready access to the registers of Archbishops Juxon and Sheldon, and the clergy subscription books. He then devised the format for the Catalogue, which he adapted in a later request for information in 1665. In a letter to Bishop Cosin of Durham, he says: 'I have now withall sent a Patterne to show them [Cosin's Register and Receivers of Tenths] the Manner of it.'[31] His 'Patterne' was a set of papers ruled to

---

[26] Dobson, M. J., 'Death and disease in the Romney Marsh area in the 17th to 19th centuries', in *Romney Marsh environmental change and human occupation in a coastal lowland* (University of Oxford Committee for Archaeology, Monograph No. 46, 1998), pp. 165, 175.
[27] *AC*, 38, pp. 29–44.
[28] KHLC, DCb/V/V/56.
[29] John D. Ramsbottom, 'Hall, George', *ODNB*.
[30] LPL, F I/C fo. 95.
[31] DUL, Cosin Letter Book 1B, 122.

give four columns, lined in red, to each page. Across two facing pages, six columns were headed 'Benefices', 'Common Reputed Value', 'Value in the King's Books', 'Subsidy at 4s per £', 'Incumbents' and 'Patrons'. This pattern is very similar to that of the Catalogue which has column headings written by Smyth. Parish names would then have been arranged in alphabetical order within deaneries and written into the Catalogue. In the meantime, instructions would have been sent to the diocesan officials to provide information. The initial answer may have been 'A note taken of the Clergie within the Archdeaconry of Cant.' dated 15 October 1663[32] but this was only a list of parishes and incumbents' names and omitted the parishes which were exempt from the jurisdiction of all except the archbishop.[33] We can see from the wording of the Catalogue comments that what would now be called a questionnaire was probably sent by Smyth to the church authorities in Canterbury. As examples, the phrases 'Church in good repayre' and 'all things decent' are frequently used and it is unlikely that the same informant wrote them as the comments are about parishes in different deaneries and spread far apart in the diocese. The questions and answers will be discussed below.

The crucial components of the Catalogue are the comments made about the incumbents and parishioners, and the names of dissenters. Ian Green and Jeremy Gregory both suggest that this information may have come from the metropolitical visitation in April 1663, but the surviving documentation belies that notion.[34] In addition, there were changes in incumbents between the visitation in April 1663 and the preparation of the Catalogue. These changes can be found by comparing the April/May 1663 visitation call book with the 'note taken of the Clergie'[35] referred to above. The changes include eight parishes which had no incumbents in April but where the vacancies had been filled by October 1663,[36] allowed for the death of Edward Fellow, in May 1663, and included the ejections of Clement Barling and John Dodd. The visitation record also omits the exempt parishes. There are further, minor, differences between the 'note' and the Catalogue, but the major difference is that the Catalogue lists the incumbents in the exempt parishes. The clue to the source for the comments can be found in transcriptions published in 1895 by Rev. Eveleigh Woodruff.[37] He had found manuscripts among the Sancroft correspondence, within the Tanner collection in the Bodleian Library, Oxford, which gave comments about some of the incumbents and parishes in Canterbury diocese, and speculated that they might have been drawn up for Sancroft's use 'when entering upon his duties as Archdeacon' (in 1668). He partially transcribed the comments for twenty-seven parishes, but there are 111 extant, in entries for six out of eleven deaneries.[38] These are now divided between MSS Tanner 124 and 125 and are the remnants of what the title-page calls 'A note of all the benefices within the jurisdiction of the archdeacon of Canterbury.'[39] There is no date on the manuscript. If we refer to these as the Archdeaconry Notes and compare them

---

[32] CCA, DCc-ChAnt/C/255D.
[33] The exempt parishes are discussed and listed in 'Exempt parishes'.
[34] Gregory, p. 276; Green (1978), p. 170; see the 'Archdeaconry Notes' discussed below.
[35] KHLC, DCb/J/Z/7/4; CCA, DCc-ChAnt/C/255D.
[36] Fordwich, Waltham, Westbere, Sandwich St Peter, Stone-in-Oxney, Leysdown, Newnham and Teynham.
[37] AC, 21, pp. 176–8.
[38] Canterbury, Westbere, Sandwich, Bridge, Dover and Lympne.
[39] Bodl., MSS Tanner 124, fos. 207–21; 125, fos. 145–55.

to the Catalogue, it becomes clear that they have been used as the basis for the remarks in the Catalogue. A further connection between the Archdeaconry Notes and the Catalogue is that a working sheet for the Catalogue's Index of Persons and Places is archived in the Bodleian Library along with the Notes.[40] Not all of the parishes are listed, the major exception being those exempt from the jurisdiction of the archdeacon, and many others only give values and patrons with no mention of the incumbent. The Notes and the Catalogue are not included in either of the two catalogues of the manuscripts in Lambeth Palace Library written between 1666 and 1691.[41] Presumably, these documents were regarded as purely administrative and therefore not of historical interest, forming part of a class of documents which included the Archbishops' Registers. The Catalogue remained at Lambeth, perhaps because it was a bound volume, but the Archdeaconry Notes, which were unbound papers, were probably included among other manuscripts retained by Sancroft, when he was deprived of his archbishopric in 1690. His nephew sold his papers to a London bookseller, purchased by Bishop Tanner and bequeathed to the Bodleian Library, Oxford, in his will of 1733.[42]

The Archdeaconry Notes were used, verbatim or paraphrased, to prepare the first draft of the Catalogue, which was then altered, in minor and major ways; by scoring through text to eliminate scribal errors, by inserting text to correct, expand or elucidate and by deliberately making text illegible, presumably where Miles Smyth considered it inappropriate.[43] There were also alterations and additions made to monetary values. One example illustrates a major amendment. The Catalogue entry for Canterbury St Mildred, where the rector, 1664–6, was James Arderne, reads: 'A yong man of good Schollerlike parts' and is followed with four lines of text which have been made illegible but the entry in the Notes reads: 'A yong man of good Schollerlike parts, but vaine & unlike a Clergyman in his hayre & habit & garbe, proud of his popularity followed by Presbyterians & Schismatiques & proud of his Popularity.'[44] At Alkham, the Notes name one of the inhabitants as 'Mr. Evering of Evering a deray[ng]ed person' but the Catalogue has the name scored out and the accusation of insanity expunged.[45] Smyth's micro-management continued with his instruction to consult his 'Large Booke of Entries' on folio 49. This is the Act Book commenced in August 1663, in which he wrote and signed every entry until 26 June 1665.[46] He also pointed to information contained in the registers of Archbishops Warham, Parker and Bancroft,[47] and was responsible for the thirty-nine annotations of 'Q', for query or question, in the Catalogue. Fourteen of these concerned augmentations to parishes and twelve suggested the right of patronage of the archbishop.

There are two remaining puzzles: the source of information about the exempt parishes and the identity of the writer of the Archdeaconry Notes. The former was probably William Somner, known in his own lifetime as an antiquary and Anglo-Saxon scholar but he was also intimately connected, through family, friends and

---

[40] Bodl., MS Tanner 124, fo. 206.
[41] LPL, MS 1047; Bodl., MS Tanner 270; LPL, MS Facsimile 6.
[42] Plomer, pp. 24–5; R. A. P. J. Beddard, 'Sancroft, William', *ODNB*.
[43] See St Georges and St Mildred both in Canterbury for examples. Catalogue, fo. 2.
[44] LPL, MS 1126, fo. 2; Bodl., MS Tanner 124, fo. 208.
[45] Bodl., MS Tanner 125, fo. 151; LPL, MS 1126, fo. 20.
[46] Catalogue, fo. 49; LPL, VB 1/1.
[47] Catalogue, fos. 38, 29, 44.

offices, with the affairs of Canterbury diocese.[48] He was a proctor of the consistory court at Canterbury from 1638 and acted as deputy registrar from 1639 to 1643.[49] In 1660, as a notary public, he was appointed as registrar of the commissary and consistory court for the city and diocese of Canterbury and auditor and deputy receiver general of the cathedral. He collected tenths from the clergy in the diocese of Canterbury for one year ending Christmas 1660, and in 1662, he was the effective deputy to the principal registrar to the archbishop.[50] In 1668, Somner provided Sancroft with information about the exempt parishes.[51]

The author of the Archdeaconry Notes has remained elusive. Green points to the presence of William Stede, official of the archdeacon from 1628 to 1672,[52] but he must be eliminated along with Somner, as their handwriting does not match the 'Notes'. Another possible candidate is Martin Hirst, as he had been the registrar of the archdeacon's court since 1661, but we do not have a sample of his handwriting.[53] It is also important to be aware that four surrogates were appointed to preside over both the consistory and the archdeacon's courts[54] and apparitors were engaged to carry citations to the parishes who, as Potter says, had 'many opportunities to hear gossip, or "common fame", which might then be passed on'.[55] There is also evidence of views being sought from incumbents. The comments for eleven parishes include their answers. Nicholas Dingley, at Kingston, 'complaynes of one Quaker & one Anabaptist, but sayes nothing of Presbyterians' and Great Chart was 'by the Definition of the Incumbent made generally good'. The other nine reported comments about the commonly accepted value of the livings, with John Cooper, at Cranbrook, saying 'he makes not much more now than £60 tithes, & that very ill payed'. This in a parish thought to have a value of '£80 or neere it'.[56] Somner, Stede, the surrogates, apparitors and incumbents could have contributed to what was known but Hirst may have written the Archdeaconry Notes.

In sum, then, the Catalogue was commenced in 1663, altered and added to until 1682 and remained in the archives of Lambeth Palace. Its major source (Archdeaconry Notes), of uncertain authorship, was removed from the Palace in 1690, left, amongst many other manuscripts, to Sancroft's nephew in 1693, sold to a bookseller, purchased by Bishop Tanner and bequeathed to the Bodleian Library in 1733.[57] In 1895, an antiquarian found some of the manuscripts but thought them to be written in 1668.[58] Nearly four hundred years after the Catalogue was written the link has been made to its antecedent.

Whoever wrote the Archdeaconry Notes, the likely informants were the apparitors, using the questions sent from Lambeth. Judging by the consistency of the Catalogue comments, the questionnaire probably included the following questions:

---

[48] Peter Sherlock, 'Somner, William', *ODNB*.
[49] Fincham, 'Somner and Laud', unpublished paper, 2019.
[50] CCA, DCc-ChAnt/S/406, BB/W/12, VP/6, 9; LPL, CM 28/4.
[51] CCA, DCc/LitMS/C/5.
[52] Green (1978), p. 122.
[53] CCA, DCc-BB/W/13; Wilkins, IV, 583–4; Hegarty, p. 326.
[54] Edward Aldey, William Jordan, James Lambe and William Lovelace.
[55] Potter, pp. 166, 182–3.
[56] Catalogue, fos. 11, 36.
[57] Plomer, pp. 24–5; Richard Sharp, 'Tanner, Thomas', *ODNB*.
[58] *AC*, 21, pp. 176–8.

- Is the incumbent 'right' for the church?
- How many families or communicants are in the parish and how many took communion last Easter?
- Are there any nonconformists or sectaries in the parish, of what type and who are their leaders?
- Are there men of quality friendly to the church and any justices of the peace living in or near the parish and what are their names?
- Are the church, chancel and rectory or vicarage houses in good repair?
- Is the church decently furnished with bible, Book of Common Prayer, font and surplice?

If all or most of these questions had been answered for all of the parishes, we would be in an excellent position to judge the state of the diocese in 1663 but unfortunately, this was not the case, as we will see in the sections below, but here we should be aware that the comments column is completely blank for 25 per cent of the parishes.

THE STATE OF THE CHURCH IN THE DIOCESE IN 1663

Consideration of the state of the diocese should be prefaced by an examination of how the church served its parishioners by the provision of places of worship. In his 1970s analysis of the Catalogue, Ian Green states that 'In the diocese of Canterbury there were about 400 churches and chapels' and footnotes that this figure is based on a count of cures in Lambeth MS 1126.[59] Unfortunately, this analysis is based on two misconceptions: that the peculiars were part of the diocese and that the 'places' listed in the Catalogue could properly be considered, in the later seventeenth century, as working parishes. His subsequent characterization of the clergy is therefore skewed by the error in the original number. The Catalogue lists 290 parishes in the diocese but, although the ancient parishes still existed as legal entities, the numbers of churches and chapels given inflate the availability of places of worship. This availability was also reduced by sinecure rectories and ruined churches. The realistic number of active parishes in the diocese is 234 and details are given in 'Number of parishes'.

There were several issues facing the restored church in 1660, some of them interrelated structural problems. The low incomes of many clergy encouraged pluralism and those with higher incomes sought even more wealth, again by pluralism, but canonical strictures meant that curates had to be employed, thus reducing income. This could often lead to parishes being bereft of ministers for extended periods. More recently, the turmoil in the parishes in the 1640s to 1650s contributed to the disaffection of parishioners, and exacerbated the problems of vacant livings, ruined churches and dilapidated clergy houses. Few, if any, of these problems appear to have been addressed by 1663; some low incomes were augmented but pluralism may have seemed intractable. The overriding problem for the church authorities was the extent of dissent and its putative connexion to civil unrest. The following sections provide a brief overview of these issues, and linked with information from the Catalogue they will assist the understanding of its content.

---

[59] Green (1978), p. 168, (1973), p. 360.

Incomes

Clerical incomes can only be estimated but, using the higher of the common values shown in the Catalogue[60] as the basis, we can add the approximate additional amounts received by those who were canons and Six Preachers of Canterbury cathedral, to arrive at an income for the year 1663. After allowing for pluralism, this exercise reveals that 68 per cent of the men had incomes of less than £100 and the remaining 32 per cent had incomes ranging from £100 to nearly £500. The median incomes for the low earners is £50 and for the greater earners £140, this latter figure being skewed mainly by the incomes of the canons, who held many of the wealthy livings, sometimes in plurality, and who received dividends from entry fines for the leases of cathedral lands. Three examples of high earners will give some insight into what was going on.

First, John Lee was rector of Bishopsbourne with the chapel of Barham annexed to it,[61] the richest living in the diocese, but he would have rarely honoured it with his presence. William Lunne, 'A yong very ordinary man, but seems right enough' held the rectory of Denton,[62] two miles from Barham and a further two miles from Bishopsbourne, and he acted as Lee's curate at Bishopsbourne. Lunne had £80 a year from Denton and although his stipend from Lee is unknown, it may have been generous. Lee could well afford it as his income from Bishopsbourne was £350 and he had further income from the rectory of Southfleet, in Rochester diocese, and the archdeaconry of Rochester. He was also a canon of Rochester cathedral.[63] Secondly, following his sequestration from the perpetual curacy of Dover St Mary the Virgin in 1643, John Reading was instituted rector of Cheriton in 1644, where he survived the Interregnum. This earned him a reputation in the Catalogue as 'A Swerving man'.[64] In 1660, he was appointed a canon of Canterbury cathedral and instituted to the rectory of Chartham, which was worth at least £200 a year.[65] His two rectories, canonry and share of entry fines would have given him an income of approaching £500 a year. Significantly more than his colleague, William Belke who was rector of Wickhambreaux and canon of Canterbury, from 1660 until his death in 1676. He had to be content with a total annual income of, at least, £350.[66] At the other end of the scale, James Penny, vicar of Canterbury St Dunstan from 1615 until his sequestration, in 1646, was restored by 1662 and received the princely sum of £25 a year until his death, in 1664. The Catalogue describes him as 'A good honest, but poore man, hath been in it many yeares, Aged neer 80, or full so much.'[67]

Pluralism

Pluralism had been controversial since Elizabethan times. Archbishop Whitgift defended pluralities in 1584: 'as they are now used pluralities are not against anie

---

[60] Two estimations of value are frequently given – see All Saints Canterbury '20.00.00 or 30.00.00 at most'. Catalogue, fo. 1.
[61] Catalogue, fo. 9.
[62] Ibid., fo. 24.
[63] CCEd Person ID: 1366; Horn, III, 52, 58, 70.
[64] Catalogue, fo. 10.
[65] CCEd Person ID: 14929; Matthews, *Walker*, p. 224; *AC*, 5, p. 120; Foster, III, 1242.
[66] CCEd Person ID: 67593; Dunkin, I, 57; LPL, COMM I/21, II/717; Matthews, *Walker*, p. 211; Venn, I, 127.
[67] CCEd Person ID: 39038; Matthews, *Walker*, p. 223; Cowper (1887), pp. 126, 128; Catalogue, fo. 1.

parte of the holie scriptures'.[68] The proponents of a Bill against Pluralities of Benefices in 1601 argued that 'This Statute takes away no Benefices from the Clergy; but only better orders the Distribution of Benefices amongst the Clergy.'[69] Professor Fincham has outlined the further legislative attempts to curb pluralism in the early part of the reign of James I.[70] At the beginning of the reign of Charles I, a petition concerning religion was presented to the king, one of the pleas being that 'Nonresidency Pluralities and Commendams be moderated'. His remarkable reply was that

> For Pluralities and Nonresidences, they are now so moderated, that the Archbishops affirm, there be now no Dispensations for pluralities granted; nor no Man now is allowed above two Benefices, and those not above thirty miles distant: And for avoiding Non-Residence, the Canon in that case provided shall be duly put in execution.[71]

Historical research has proved the error of the above. Canon 41 of 1604 strictly defined pluralism as 'the keeping of more Benefices with Cure than one'.[72] Using this definition, the percentage of parochial pluralists in the dioceses of Oxford, Worcester and Gloucester 'on the eve of the civil war' was 10 per cent; in Winchester diocese in 1631, 25 per cent; in Leicestershire it rose from 13 per cent in 1603 to 23 per cent in 1642 and in the diocese of Durham, pluralism increased from 18 per cent of benefices, in 1603, to over 33 per cent in 1634.[73] In the diocese of Canterbury, only 9 per cent of the parish clergy held more than one benefice in the years 1600–40 but during the same period, 35 per cent of those who held cathedral offices were pluralists. The limited definition of Canon 41 meant in practice that men could hold any number of cathedral offices simultaneously with impunity, only constrained by residency requirements, they could combine these offices with a benefice, one or more sinecures, one or more perpetual curacies and one or more sequestrations, as the last three were not accounted as benefices. By obtaining a dispensation, additional benefices could be held along with all of the other positions. If the canonical definition is then widened to include all offices held (and remunerated) the percentage of actual pluralism in Canterbury diocese was 35 per cent in 1603, declining to 29 per cent in 1637 following the vigorous recruitment of clergy by Archbishop Laud. By 1700, the figure was in excess of 50 per cent.[74]

---

[68] LPL, MS 2004, fos. 14–15v; There is a detailed discussion of the Tudor legislation intended to control pluralism in D. Crankshaw, 'The Elizabethan Faculty Office and the aristocratic patronage of chaplains', in *Patronage and recruitment in the Tudor and early Stuart church*, ed. C. Cross (Borthwick Studies in History, 2, York, 1996); see also C. Hill, *Economic problems of the church* (Oxford, 1968), pp. 225, 232–4.
[69] Heywood Townshend, 'Proceedings in the Commons, 1601: November 16th – 20th', *Historical collections: or, an exact account of the proceedings of the four last parliaments of Q. Elizabeth* (1680), pp. 216–36, www.british-history.ac.uk/report.aspx?compid=43555. A full exposition of the reasons advanced against the abolition of pluralities proposed in the parliamentary bills of 1589 and 1601 can be found in R. M. Haines, 'Some arguments in favour of plurality in the Elizabethan church', *Studies in Church History*, 5 (1969), 166–92.
[70] Fincham, pp. 62–3.
[71] J. Rushworth, *Historical collections: 1625 (Charles I), historical collections of private passages of state*, I: 1618–29 (1721), pp. 165–219, www.british- history.ac.uk report.aspx?compid =70142.
[72] Bray, p. 327.
[73] Barratt, p. 137; Thomson, p. 104; Pruett, p. 52, Freeman, p. 87.
[74] Reid, pp. 51–93.

Pluralism was again debated in the House of Commons, in 1663, and the 'arch-royalist, and quasi-official spokesman for king and court',[75] Sir John Birkenhead, was of the opinion that

> There are not Loyal Ministers enough to Supply the Cures of the Land without Pluralities, The Bawling against Pluralities was the first Engine of bringing the Loyal Clergy (in whose hands the most were) into Contempt, and the bringing them into Contempt the first Engine of the late Rebellion.[76]

But in the same year, a pamphlet raged against pluralism: 'It's but latelie that you were thought uncapable of one Living; and now three, four, five, cannot suffice you. It's not long since you wanted necessaries, and do you now heap up superfluities?'[77] In 1665, Archbishop Sheldon sent detailed questions to his bishops, one of which concerned pluralists, but no subsequent action can be traced and only five diocesan returns of pluralists are extant, all, except Norwich, from Wales and the West Country. It is unrealistic to assume that the missing diocesan returns reflect the absence of pluralism.[78]

In 1663, only 187 men served the 234 'active' diocesan parishes[79] because fifty-one of them were pluralists. Thirty-seven held two livings in the diocese; five held three livings[80] and six held a living in the diocese and another in a different diocese (five in Rochester and one in Norwich).[81] Five men were canons of Canterbury cathedral and also held a living in the diocese.[82] Three men formed the only links between the diocese and the archbishop's peculiars: John Castilion, Thomas Browne and Richard Marsh. Castilion, a canon of Canterbury cathedral, held the rectory of Minster along with St Dionis Backchurch, in the deanery of the Arches and Colsterworth, Lincolnshire. Browne held the rectory of Newenden until December 1664, along with the vicarage of Farningham in the deanery of Shoreham. Marsh was restored to his rectory of Ruckinge in 1660, and is noted in the Catalogue as the vicar of East Peckham, in Shoreham.

Non-residency

Non-residency could be a concomitant of pluralism. It would have been very difficult, if not impossible, for any pluralist minister to provide proper pastoral care and exercise moral discipline in two or more parishes at once. The distance between two parishes held in plurality was limited by canon law to thirty miles, although this was often ignored, but the real difficulty was the time it took to ride from one parish to another.[83] The legal solution was to employ a curate.

---

[75] Charles Clay Doyle, 'Birkenhead, Sir John', *ODNB*.
[76] BL, Lansdowne MS 958, fos. 21–4.
[77] *Ichabod: or, Five groans of the church:* .... (Cambridge, 1663), Early English Books Online http://eebo.chadwyck.com, no longer attributed to Bishop Thomas Ken; William Marshall, 'Ken, Thomas (1637–1711)', *ODNB*.
[78] Cardwell, II, 271–5; LPL, MS 639.
[79] See 'Number of parishes'.
[80] Arderne, Cole, Eve, Pulford and Thomas Russell.
[81] Codd, Crompe, Dixon, Ellis, Lee and Sherman.
[82] Aldey, Belke, Casaubon, Du Moulin and Hardres.
[83] Bray, p. 329.

In 1664, the mayor and jurats of New Romney wrote to their vicar, Robert Bostocke:

> we wonder that (keeping still in your hands this Vicarridge of New Romney) you provide not that the cure therof be duly officiated; you cann be content to receive tithes, but you will neither reside on your benefice your selfe nor provide a curate ... These things if complayned of will neither sound to your commendation nor proffitt, for sure wee are that if you cann obtain a dispensation for your non residence (whereof we much doubt), yett must it be conditionally, and noe longer in force then you provide that the cure bee well and sufficiently supplyd.[84]

Bostocke was vicar of New Romney from 1662 until 1680, but in 1664, he was given dispensation to hold it along with the vicarage of Hougham and also granted the sequestration of Dover St James the Apostle. In 1668, the churchwardens of New Romney were granted sequestration 'for stipend of curate' and this must have stung Bostocke into action as he gave consent, as vicar, to the licensing of Thomas Theaker as curate in 1672. He was the first of three curates appointed in the succeeding six years.[85]

Curates

Curates and their importance to the functioning of the Church of England in the sixteenth to the eighteenth centuries have largely been overlooked in historical writing. Five postgraduate theses have been found[86] which address some of the aspects but only two secondary sources attempt to grapple with the subject.[87] The Clergy of the Church of England database provides definitions of perpetual curates and donatives but does not indicate in its records where certain parishes were curacies or donatives. This reticence is primarily due to the absence of primary documents which clearly set out the status of ministers or parishes. This is hardly surprising as it would appear that, at least in seventeenth-century Canterbury diocese, the church authorities were themselves often ignorant of the detail or tended to ignore most curates.

The Canons of 1604 regulating pluralism required that a man given dispensation must hold the MA degree, be a licensed preacher and reside in each of his benefices for at least two months a year, the benefices not being more than thirty miles apart. He also had to provide a graduate curate, licensed to preach, in each of the livings where he was not resident, where 'the worth of the benefice will bear it', the latter phrase providing scope for avoidance. In addition, the dispensation was 'for the keeping of more Benefices with Cure than one', thus providing room for opportunism. In theory, an incumbent who employed a curate to serve his rectory or vicarage could accept pecuniary office in a cathedral, obtain a sinecure, become the temporary sequestrator of a vacant benefice and act as a perpetual curate, although the lay donor of the perpetual curacy may well have protested by ceasing payment.[88] Curates did not have the security of tenure of their beneficed betters but they could only be removed for misconduct, by revocation of their

---

[84] *AC*, 13, p. 213.
[85] Willis (1975), pp. 45, 49, 48.
[86] Daeley; Fincham (1984); Jones; Marshall; Salter.
[87] Gregory (2000), and Spaeth.
[88] Bray, pp. 327, 329, 335.

licences. Although all were referred to simply as curates, there were actually two types: those who served in perpetual curacies and donatives, and those who were employed by rectors or vicars to serve their cure. The latter can often be absent from church records. They were all paid a stipend and in what follows, men who served the cure of a vicar or rector will be referred to as curates and the others as perpetual curates.

The incumbents of the thirty-one perpetual curacies in the diocese were licensed by the archbishop but were not instituted or inducted. Perpetual curacies first appeared after the dissolution of the monasteries, when impropriators of parishes were required to nominate a clerk to provide for the cure of souls. The curate was paid a stipend by the impropriator and, most importantly, was perpetual in the sense that he could only be removed, by the church authorities, for misconduct.[89] The term perpetual curate only began to be used in the early eighteenth century when, under the regulations of Queen Anne's Bounty, augmented parishes were made perpetual curacies 'to protect the augmentation against depredations'.[90] The perpetual curacies included a special class, called donatives. The men serving these parishes were licensed as curates and put in place by a deed of donation of the patron, without presentation, institution or induction. Their office is very similar to that of the other curates but with the important exception that 'the patron alone was empowered to deprive the incumbent'.[91] In 1663, there were five donatives in the diocese,[92] but only Bredhurst was named as such in the Catalogue. Eight perpetual curates also held a benefice in the diocese without having to apply for dispensation and three more each held two additional benefices.[93]

The only curate identified in the diocesan part of the Catalogue as serving in 1663 is Robert Master: 'Curate, a person lately come, and not much knowne yet'. He was licensed to the cure of Molash chapel in 1662 and would have been paid by Robert Cumberland, the vicar of Chilham. Henry Hurt is mentioned under St Mary in the Marsh, but this was not until, at least, 1668 and Thomas Finney is called 'Curat' of Warehorne, but that was in 1681.[94] Four curates are named among the archbishop's peculiars: Edward Oliver at Shoreham, Ralph Twisse at Lidsing, a chapel of Gillingham, William Fly at Norwood, a chapel of Hayes and William Pawley at Knockholt. The first three were in place in 1663 but Pawley was not appointed until 1670. The foregoing underlines the difficulty in identifying curates in the diocese and the peculiars in the latter part of the seventeenth century, notwithstanding the existence of what appears to be a robust system of licensing.[95] However, there is evidence of the presence of unlicensed curates. The possibility is illustrated by the Catalogue entry for the vicarage of Lydd.[96] Edward Wilford was born the third son of Sir Thomas Wilford, around 1611, and graduated BA from Peterhouse, Cambridge, proceeded MA in 1636 and was a Fellow of

---

[89] CCEd/reference/glossary.
[90] *ELJ*, 5 (1998), pp. 90–1.
[91] *ELJ*, 5 (2000), p. 326.
[92] Goodnestone by Dover, Hawkhurst, Bredhurst, Minster-in-Sheppey with Queenborough, and Davington. Stodmarsh became a donative in the eighteenth century. Hasted, IX, 146.
[93] Alderne, Thomas Brett, John Davis of Otham and Maidstone, Dicas, Nairne, William Osborne senior, Perne, Pulford, Scarlett and Mathew Smith.
[94] Catalogue, fos. 30, 32.
[95] See Willis (1975).
[96] Catalogue, fo. 30.

Peterhouse from 1638 to 1644. He made two good marriages: first to a daughter of the earl of Castlehaven and second to Elizabeth, a daughter of Isaac Bargrave, the dean of Canterbury, briefly vicar of Lydd in 1627. Reputed to be a staunch royalist who had been present at the battle of Worcester in 1651, Wilford gathered the gentry and nobility to meet Charles II at Dover in 1660. His degree of DD, awarded by royal mandate in 1660, was not his only reward as, in June 1660, he petitioned for presentation to the vicarage of Lydd and in August, he asked for the next vacant prebend in Canterbury. This latter petition pleaded that he had raised a troop of horse at his own charge for the late king, and suffered much in estate and by imprisonments.[97] He never received preferment to the cathedral, although he resided in a seven hearth house in the precincts of the archbishop's palace in Canterbury, but he was presented to the vicarage of Lydd by the king on 4 July 1660.[98] It was worth £250 a year and Wilford remained as vicar until his death in 1669 but, in 1661 he was granted a dispensation for three years' non-residence, renewed for a further three years, by Archbishop Sheldon, in 1664.[99] After an extensive search in all the relevant sources,[100] the only curate at Lydd traced during this period is John Tudor, who was licensed in 1668.[101] The parish of Lydd is situated at the extreme southern tip of Kent, over thirty miles from Canterbury. Wilford would have attended the church for his induction but that may have been the last time he was seen there. A curate or succession of them must have served at Lydd from 1660 to 1668 but no substantiating records have been found. There is further evidence of unlicensed curates in the diocese in the years following 1663. In 1668 William, Somner recorded their presence in Goodnestone by Dover, Charing, Egerton, Ivychurch and New Romney.[102]

Vacant livings, ruined churches and dilapidated residences

Fifteen livings are noted in the Catalogue as vacant but, as with so many of the entries in the Catalogue, caution is required. Three of the livings marked vacant did have incumbents. William Russell held River along with Lydden; John Malbon held Lympne and Peter Pury served Goodnestone by Dover. The remaining twelve took longer to fill. Lenham in January 1664, Kennington in April and Warden (by sequestration) in May 1664. The vacancy at Chart Sutton affords a glimpse of difficult times. The presentations of Richard Whitlock in June 1662, Daniel Alderne in October 1662 and Richard Morris in June 1663 did not result in an appointment;[103] that had to await the presentation of Peter Browne, in December 1663 and his subsequent institution, in May 1664. It would appear that the eight remaining parishes were without ministers for much longer periods but this may be due to incomplete records.[104]

---

[97] *CSPD*, 1660–1, pp. 32, 92.
[98] CCEd Person ID: 38049; Catalogue, fo. 30; *46th report*, p. 123; Mathews, *Walker*, p. 228; Horn, III, 9; Dunkin, II, 482; Harrington, p. 380; Venn, IV, 271. The living was part of the patrimony of the archbishop of Canterbury but Juxon was not named until 2 Sept. 1660.
[99] LPL, F II/1/205a, 205b, VB 1/1/64.
[100] Willis (1972), (1975); CCEd *passim*; Hasted, VIII, 420–39; LPL.
[101] KHLC, DCb/L/R 17–27, p. 44.
[102] CCA, DCc/LitMS/C/5, fos. 202v–203v.
[103] The entries in the Biographical index for these men suggest that Chart Sutton was not their first choice.
[104] Canterbury St Mary Bredman, Canterbury St Peter, Davington, Egerton, Harty, Petham, Sheldwich and Waldershare.

Seventeen ruined churches are noted as *desolata* in the Catalogue but in addition there were four not described as such, but which were in ruins or demolished by 1663: Canterbury St Mary de Castro, West Langdon, Bircholt and Hope. St Mary de Castro was demolished in the sixteenth century and united with St Mildred.[105] In 1778, Hasted comments about West Langdon

> The church, which was dedicated to St Mary, has been long in a ruinated state. In 1660, Sir Thomas Peyton, bart. of Knolton, had a design to repair it, for which purpose he provided a quantity of timber, but in the night the country people stole the whole of it away, and besides took away the pulpit, pews, &c. which had been left standing, out of the church; in which dilapidated situation it still continues.[106]

At the visitation for 1578, it was declared that there was no church standing in the parish of Bircholt,[107] and Hope had been in decay since 1578 and would have been a ruin in 1663. Further evidence of the church's desuetude is provided by the appointment of John Bale as rector. He was a doctor of medicine and there is no record of him being ordained.[108] The age-old system of freehold tenure of vicarages and rectories was not ideal in encouraging maintenance of the properties, notwithstanding that dilapidations could be a charge on a deceased minister's estate. The consequent deterioration of the houses caused, or at least provided the excuse for, non-residence. The Catalogue reports that Upchurch had 'A poore Vicaridge house (if any, for it is disputed)' and at Lyminge the vicarage house was 'halfe fallen downe'.[109] Five other parishes had semi-ruined clergy houses.[110] Those clergy who persevered in dilapidated houses had many problems to surmount and they sometimes failed. Giles Hinton was the pluralist minister of Westbere and Faversham from 1666 to 1681 and following his collation to Biddenden, in 1682, he received dispensation for the rectory of Wormshill, in 1683. He was appointed rural dean of Charing, in the same year and reported that:

> The parsonage house [of Biddenden] was once doubtless a large fair building, but noe Rector having dwelt in it for neer fourscore years I found it a most ruinous and dreadful spectacle, and my immediate predecessor without lands, goods, or chattells. The roof only was tolerably covered, but the floors, windows, doors, stairs, and walls within broke and spoyld beyond the possibility of reparation, and without doors, all fences lost, one great barne and malt house soe demolished and carried away that the foundations are hardly now discerned. Into this condition this house came the more speedily, for that it was tenemented out to vile and vicious people who made it soe ragged and unclean that I never saw any building stand more in need of a lustration. However I brought my family into it, and since I have had a title to it I have laid out neer two hundred pounds only to make it capable of a bed, and a table, a stoole, and a candlesticke. I was not borne in a pigstie though I may die in a worse place, soe thicke have been upon me my charges in removing, in first fruits (£35) and necessary reparations.[111]

---

[105] Catalogue, fo. 5; LPL, VG 1/2 fo. 33, 1/4 fo. 5v; Hasted, XI, 271.
[106] Catalogue, fo. 19; Hasted, IX, 404.
[107] Catalogue, fo. 24; Hasted, VIII, 12.
[108] Catalogue, fo. 29; Hasted, VIII, 419; *AC*, 37, p. 191.
[109] Catalogue, fos. 49, 25.
[110] Boughton Aluph, Cranbrook, Eastry, Ickham and St Margaret at Cliffe.
[111] *AC*, 21, p. 185.

In a 1685 letter to Archbishop Sancroft, he pleaded that he may retain his two livings, although he was about to be committed to Maidstone jail, as he could not satisfy his creditors. He said that he had been forced to pay 'faculties, first fruits, and reparation of dilapidated houses (amounting to above £300)'. It is not known how long he spent in prison but he kept his two rectories until his death, in 1702.[112]

Dilapidated residences obviously caused problems for incumbents but what of the parish churches and the furnishings required by the canons? There are only forty-eight comments addressing the physical state of the churches and their ancillary buildings, such as barns. Of these, thirty churches were said to be in good repair, eight were reasonable and ten were bad. The latter category including, among the many 'out of repayre', Sandwich St Peter 'Church fallen downe, but now rebuilding' and the necessity for the incumbent at Great Mongeham to preach in the chancel. There are only forty-three comments referring to the essential church furnishings, ranging from the ubiquitous 'all things decent in it' to 'Communion table, Font, Surplice, and all things decent' at Saltwood. The Catalogue entries for the parishes in the deanery of Canterbury do not include references to the fabric of churches or church furnishings. Church fabric goes unreported in the deanery of Westbere and the deanery of Bridge does not report on church furnishings. Among the reports made, the biggest problem was the twenty-four churches with 'noe surplice' although five were being made. At Alkham, the churchwardens were 'unwilling to provide it'. Finally, five churches had no font. The deaneries of Canterbury and Westbere have a common boundary in the north-east of Kent and it is plausible that the same informant reported on both, but possibly without visiting, or being informed about, the churches. It may be that the temper of the incumbent or his parishioners was such that access could not be gained to some churches. The reports for the deanery of Charing, which had the greatest number of parishes not 'well affected' to the church, only include four remarks about church fabric or furnishings. At Charing and Eastwell, two of the few parishes without dissenter problems, the churches were in good repair and all things were decent, perhaps indicating an inspection. However, Cranbrook, with above 1,000 nonconformists, and Smarden, noted as 'very disorderly', perhaps did not welcome an investigator. There was nothing said about church furnishings, only reports that the vicarage house was ruined at Cranbrook and the church was out of repair at Smarden. The Catalogue comments, or the lack of them, may suggest that some at least of the parish congregations were hostile to church enquiries.

In seventeenth-century Kent, in addition to the county town of Maidstone, the cathedral city of Canterbury and the market towns, there were a multitude of small communities, some of them parishes in their own right, and others gathered into parishes, but all of them having their own church or chapel. The parishioners were legally bound to attend their parish church regularly and they therefore needed and expected it to be within walking distance of their homes. Forced to pay tithes for the upkeep of their minister, they looked to him to live among them and literally minister to their needs. In addition to performing the rites of passage of baptism, churching, marriage and burial, he was expected to provide charity to the poor, attendance on the sick and dying and possibly assistance with the wills of the latter. The problem for the church was that many of the places of worship were dilapidated, as were many of the rectory and vicarage houses and continuing emigration from

[112] *Ibid.*, p. 186; Dunkin, I, 412.

rural areas to the towns reduced the size of many of the rural congregations. This made it difficult to attract and pay ambitious clerics. However, the multiplicity of parishes meant that most of them were close to one another and it can be suggested that it would have been sensible to amalgamate some of them,[113] but a contemporary archdeacon or archbishop had to be mindful of parishioners who would not relish a much longer walk to their church and, more pertinently, the owners of the advowsons of the dispossessed churches would have had to be compensated. The latter problem was not insoluble, as a very high proportion of patronage was in the hands of the church by 1663, over 60 per cent of the livings.

Turmoil in the parishes

In a letter to Richard Chaworth, Archbishop Juxon's visitor in the metropolitical visitation of 1663, the churchwardens attribute the ruination of the church of Hope in Romney Marsh to 'the late great stormes, what with the constant neglect of forty years continuance or more, especially in the late times which so much countenanced and connived at such neglects'.[114] Ruined or dilapidated churches and houses and vacant livings contributed to the turmoil in the parishes, but the high turnover of ministers was even more corrosive.

Of the incumbents in the diocese, 119 shown in the Catalogue in 1663, were appointed in the years 1660–3 but, according to Matthews, there were only forty-seven ejections from the diocesan parishes during these years.[115] The discrepancy between these two figures is due to unexplained changes in ministers: the arrival and departure of incumbents caused by death, voluntary or involuntary resignation, desertion of cures or ejections, that were either unrecorded or where the records have not survived. Figure 1 illustrates events.

These findings may suggest that the widely accepted number of ejections, based on the work of Matthews, is too low.[116] In all of these years, the number of changes in ministers exceeds the number of surviving recorded ejections. The sixteen ejections, which occurred on the return of the king in 1660, were more than matched by the eighteen changes in minister; and in 1661, the two ejections were dwarfed by the twenty-eight changes. The provisions of the Act of Uniformity, in 1662, caused the number of ejections to increase to twenty-seven in that year, but in an additional forty-three parishes there was a change of minister, and although there were only two ejections in 1663, there were another forty-one changes. The Act for Confirming and Restoring of Ministers, in December 1660, may have spurred the changes in 1661. The provisions of the Act of Uniformity in 1662 could have prompted many ministers to abandon their cures, rather than repudiate their oath under the Solemn League and Covenant or deny their previous ordination in favour of another one by a bishop.[117]

---

[113] There is evidence of recommendations to unite some parishes during the Commonwealth period, particularly in Norfolk. In Canterbury diocese, Sibbertswold had been united to Coldred since 1584 and Archbishop Sancroft reaffirmed this in 1680. LPL, COMM XIIa/3, 4, 7, 10, COMM XIIb/2–7, 9, 12; Whiteman (1955), p. 127.
[114] KHLC, DCb/J/Z/7/4, fo. 262. Quoted in Potter, pp. 198–9.
[115] Matthews, *Calamy, passim*.
[116] *Ibid.*; Reid, pp. 177–205, and see the findings in K. Skea, 'The ecclesiastical identities of puritan and nonconformist clergy, 1640–1672', Ph.D. thesis, Leicester University, 2015.
[117] Matthews, *Calamy*, p. xi; Green (1978), pp. 144, 150; Reid, pp. 177–205.

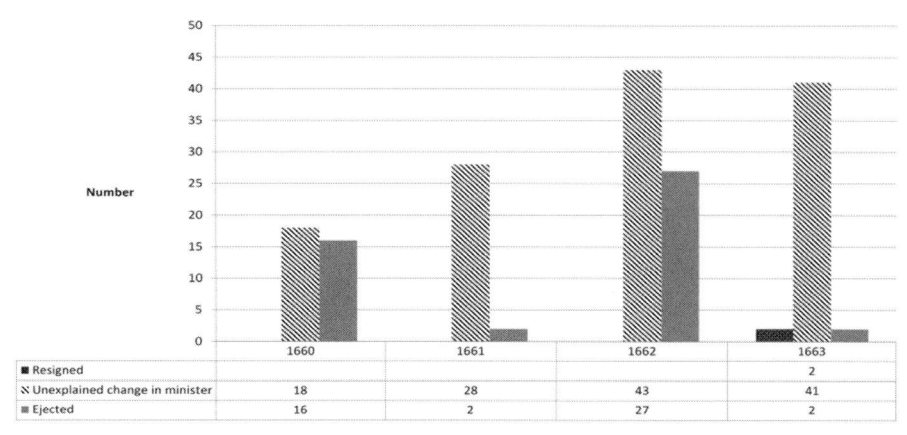

Figure 1 Changes in the diocesan parishes, 1660–3.

	1660	1661	1662	1663
Resigned				2
Unexplained change in minister	18	28	43	41
Ejected	16	2	27	2

In 1663, pluralism enabled 187 men to serve the 234 'active' parishes in the diocese.[118] In twenty of these parishes the incumbents had been appointed in the years between 1612 and 1642 and no evidence has been found to suggest that they were ever supplanted by others in the years leading up to and beyond 1663. In a further thirty-three parishes, the incumbents had been appointed between 1643 and 1656 and they also retained their positions beyond 1663. These fifty-three parishes were the only ones with no change in minister from 1660 until 1663 compared to the remaining 181 parishes where the incumbent was changed in the space of these four years.

A short parochial case study will illustrate the chaotic movement of clergy in the diocese, particularly in the years immediately following the Restoration. The parish of Boughton under Blean suffered from more turmoil than most. Samuel Smith was collated to the vicarage in 1637 but was sequestrated in 1641. There was then a procession of ministers. Richard Harding resigned in 1646 and was succeeded by John Baker, who died in 1648. Hercules Hill took over and probably stayed until the appointment of Thomas Seyliard in 1653. John Dalton became vicar in 1657 but resigned in 1658. Samuel Smith was restored in 1660 but he resigned in the same year. Philip Holland was collated in 1660 and in April 1662 he consented to the licensing of Ralph Roundtree as curate but, in the same year, Paul Griffith subscribed as vicar, only to be succeeded by Percival Radcliffe in 1663.[119] The reasons for the frequent changes at Boughton under Blean cannot be determined now. Some fifty miles from London, the parish was not particularly valuable or large, for it was worth £60 in 1640 with around four hundred inhabitants, but its situation, between Faversham and Canterbury, may have meant that nonconformists from these towns had influenced events.

This evidence challenges the work of Green and Spurr in two important ways. First, in his work on the re-establishment of the church after the Restoration, Green

---

[118] See 'Number of parishes'.
[119] CCEd Person ID: 47108; Matthews, *Walker*, p. 225; Ingram Hill, p. 66; KHLC, DCb/L/R 17–27, pp. 70, 87; Houston, p. 148; *46th report*; LPL, VG/1/2.

addressed what had happened in the diocese of Canterbury and concludes that his evidence

> enables us to throw new light on certain aspects of the Restoration church settlement ... it allows us to put the ejections of 1662 in a better perspective: far more Commonwealth clergy conformed to the Restoration settlement, at least outwardly, than were ejected for nonconformity. Against the forty ejected in Canterbury diocese, we should place the hundred Commonwealth conformists who decided to continue serving in the church.[120]

This statement implies that in the great majority of the parishes, there was no upheaval, but the scale of the changes occasioned by the Restoration and its aftermath was far greater than that portrayed by Green. Spurr accepts the total number of national ejections given by Matthews and does not therefore consider the consequences of missing data.[121] The second major difference is the lack of attention paid to the year 1663. Green acknowledges that 'nearly half of the [Canterbury] livings were still vacant after three months, and even in the new year a quarter had not been filled', but he does not explore the events in the parishes in 1663.[122] In her examination of the re-establishment of the church, using records from Exeter, Salisbury, Lincoln and Oxford, Whiteman found evidence of parish vacancies still being filled in 1663 and she concludes that '1663 is a more significant date,[123] for not till then was episcopal administration in full working order and the re-establishment of the church a reality in most parishes throughout the land'.[124]

The Catalogue gives us the opinions of its informants about the incumbents in place in 1663. There are 187 of these incumbents, and we are able to divide them into three periods according to the date they were appointed or restored to their parish. Thirty-six were appointed before the civil wars, of which eighteen had been sequestrated but restored between 1660 and 1662. There are no comments on four of them and the others are given general approval. Thirty-two men were appointed between 1643 and 1656; two with no comment, twenty approved of but Thomas Nightingale was 'an empty impertinent man'. The remaining nine were more contentious; four were thought to be 'Presbyterian' and the other five were either suspected, conforming intruders or converts. During the final period from 1658 to 1663, 119 men took up their livings. There are no comments for nineteen and eighty-four received approval. Five were not liked, with comments ranging from 'a yong vapouring blade' (John Fidge) to 'vaine, bragging, & somewhat Dissolute' (Richard Burney). A further eight were accused of being 'Presbyterian', converts from it, or favouring presbyterianism.

The comments in the Catalogue show that the investigators and compilers were suspicious of incumbent intruders and of the motives of converts and conformists, but their main concern appears to be about those who were suspected to hold presbyterian views. The term is used to describe incumbents and parishioners thirty-six times but it was probably not meant in the classical sense, merely being used as a pejorative term to describe undefined nonconformist views. As the term 'Sectaries'

---

[120] Green (1978), p. 177.
[121] Spurr, p. 43; Matthews, *Calamy*, p. xiii.
[122] Green (1978), p. 160.
[123] Rather than 1661, which had been suggested by Bosher, p. 216.
[124] Whiteman (1955), pp. 111, 113, 115, 124.

is employed forty times in the Catalogue, it may be that the two descriptors were interchangeable. Independents are only mentioned four times.

The nonconformist incumbents were in the minority of the incumbents in place in 1663. Although 18 per cent of the comments give no information about the orthodoxy of incumbents, 76 per cent of the incumbents are said to be orthodox or probably so. These are the men of 'Right Principles' who are 'right for the Church' and they are spread fairly evenly throughout the diocese. Most of the uncertainties about the orthodoxy of incumbents occur only in the deaneries of Dover and Lymne and some of these may be accounted for by difficulty in interpreting comments such as 'An indifferent good person'. Only 6 per cent are suspected to hold nonconformist opinions.

After the Restoration, there is evidence that some of the parish intruders conformed, but the many changes of ministers dwarf the 'official' ejections and cast doubts on any claim that there were large numbers of conformers. The misconception may have arisen because the scale and timing of the ejections has previously been based on the assumption that the 'Bartholomew' ejections of 1662, as listed by Matthews,[125] marked the endpoint of the re-establishment of the church, albeit that, for some, physical removal did not take place until 1663. The evidence introduced here indicates that there were many more changes of minister, thus reducing the probability of large numbers of conforming intruders and extending the longevity of instability in the parishes. The data given above can be summarized and analysed as follows:

Appointments between 1612 and 1642 36
Appointments between 1643 and 1656 <u>32</u>
                                      68 Representing 36 per cent of the incumbents in place in 1663
Appointments between 1658 and 1663 <u>119</u>
                                     187 **Total number of incumbents in 1663**

the researched data for parishes with incumbents is slightly different because of pluralism, sinecures, annexed chapels and ruined churches:

Appointments between 1612 and 1642 20
Appointments between 1643 and 1656 <u>33</u>
                                      53 Representing 23 per cent of the active parishes in 1663
Appointments between 1658 and 1663 <u>181</u>
                                     234 **Total number of active parishes in 1663**

These figures show that 64 per cent of the incumbents in 1663 were recent appointments and 77 per cent of the active parishes had recent changes of incumbents. These figures mean that claims that 70 or 75 per cent of all parish ministers were left in possession of their benefices until their death or the Restoration certainly do not apply to those in Canterbury diocese. Fincham and Taylor have highlighted the large number of episcopal ordinations during the Interregnum thus adding to the

---

[125] Matthews, *Calamy, passim*.

pool of men, presumably loyal to the Church of England, available for appointment to parishes, but we do not know if any of these men were appointed but subsequently ejected and if so, when.[126]

The problem of dissent

Since the restoration of the monarchy and the re-establishment of the church, religious and political dissent had been of great concern to the church and state authorities nationally and in Kent. The civil authorities relied on the assizes and the reports of informants, many of which remain in the state papers, and the church courts disciplined clerks and laymen. However, the latter relied on visitation and presentments and although the consistory court and the archdeacon's court started work again in the autumn of 1661, full ecclesiastical jurisdiction was not achieved until the end of 1663.[127] The Catalogue can be considered as an additional strand of information around the same time.

At the national level, there were civil disturbances, small in military terms, but their regular recurrence was taken very seriously by the authorities, particularly as they appeared to be motivated by continued resistance to the re-establishment of episcopalian church government. The Restoration regime was concerned from the beginning that radical sectarians would plot with ex-Cromwellian soldiers to revolt against the new order.[128] Venner's Fifth Monarchist uprising in London in 1661, the Tong Plot to seize Windsor castle in 1662, an attempt led by Colonel Blood to seize Dublin castle in 1663 and a series of risings in northern counties in the autumn of that year (variously referred to as the Derwentdale, Kaber Rigg, Yorkshire or Northern plot) were all countered by the savage execution of perpetrators and repressive legislation embodied in the Corporation Act of 1661, the Act of Uniformity and the Quaker Act of 1662 and the Conventicle Act of 1664.

In Kent, Thomas Palmer, a Fifth Monarchist preacher and conspirator, and ejected rector of a Derbyshire living, was arrested at Egerton in 1662 and threatened with summary execution, for his radicalism, but he was spared and imprisoned in Canterbury jail for some time. He was imprisoned again for his part in the Farnley Wood plot, in 1663, and travelled to Ireland with Thomas Blood, in 1666, to organize Fifth Monarchist activities, but left no further trace in the records.[129] Colonel William Kenrick was suspected of involvement with the 1662 Tong Plot along with Edward Riggs, the ejected vicar of St John in Thanet.[130] Riggs was imprisoned in the Tower of London, confessed and after giving a bond, he was allowed to cross to Rotterdam, where he became a government informer. In the autumn of 1663, there were reports of large groups of armed horse and foot meeting at Egerton and Canterbury and that nonconformists at Waltham and Reculver were armed and organized. Kenrick and others were reported to be behaving suspiciously.[131] The Catalogue does not report dissenting parishioners at Egerton, Waltham or Reculver.

---

[126] Spurr, pp. 6–7; K. Fincham and S. Taylor, 'Episcopalian conformity and nonconformity, 1646–1660', in *Royalists and royalism during the Interregnum*, ed. J. McElligott and D. Smith (Manchester, 2010), pp. 18–43.
[127] Potter, pp. 184–8.
[128] Harris, p. 88.
[129] Alan Marshall, 'Blood, Thomas', *ODNB*; Matthews, *Calamy*, p. 380.
[130] Margate St John the Baptist. CCEd.
[131] Greaves, pp. 122–3, 171–2; Matthews, *Calamy*, p. 412.

At the Maidstone Assizes, in July 1661, the rectors of Monkton and of Hawkhurst were indicted for refusing to administer the sacraments according to the Book of Common Prayer and three laymen were indicted for attending unlawful conventicles.[132] Thirty-four laymen were indicted for the same offence in July 1662 and a further twenty-three in March 1663, while at the Canterbury Assizes, in July 1663, John Cooper, vicar of Cranbrook, swore that 'when he and his parishioners were assembled to celebrate communion on 19 Apr. 1663 Thomas Morreland and several others approached the communion table with their hats on, laughing and deriding the vicar, and when asked to behave themselves reverently, obstinately refused and persisted in disturbing the service'.[133] At the end of 1663, it was reported that, at Dover, 'On Christmas evening 200 Presbyterians met at a brewer's in the town; the preacher was Matthew Barry, former minister of St Mary's parish, a dangerous fanatic, who preached rebellion 20 years ago, and is maintained by a factious party.'[134]

Another source in the state papers refers to dissenters in the hundreds of the lathe of St Augustine in Kent.[135] Since before the Norman conquest in 1066, Kent had been divided, for administrative purposes, into lathes subdivided by hundreds. These divisions were still being utilized in the seventeenth century, as witnessed by the Hearth Tax returns for Kent in 1664.[136] Notwithstanding its title, it names only a very few dissenters; but it does provide the number of independents, anabaptists and quakers in each parish in the lathe, along with those of their number who were women. When it is used as a comparison, it reveals, in thirty-five parishes, the presence of dissenters who are not mentioned in the Catalogue. The dissenters named in the lathe return were referred to as the 'teachers' (preachers), with seven of them being called anabaptists and three independents. Four can be traced; John Mockett and Richard Mills in Ash or nearby, Isaac Slaughter lived in Northbourne and Charles Nichols, who is not named in the Catalogue. The ten dissenters were located in four parishes, Harbledown (1), Eyethorne (2), Northbourne (Slaughter and another two) and Ash (Nichols and another three). Only Slaughter is named in the Catalogue although the presence of 'factious persons, 'Anabaptists & Quakers' and 'fanaticks' is noted in three of the parishes. Charles Nichols is a surprising omission from the Catalogue as he was notorious and his family background links a nonconformist association of Elizabethan times to incumbents of the Interregnum who were ejected, excommunicated or imprisoned after the Restoration, but who survived and continued to preach. In the 1660s, he was part of a large network of nonconformists, which included John Durant and Samuel Taverner, both mentioned in the Catalogue, and Nathaniel Barry.[137] A possible explanation for the exclusion of Nichols from the Catalogue is that he was never ordained in the Church of England

---

[132] Cockburn (1995), pp. 25–7.
[133] *Ibid.*, pp. 61–95.
[134] This was Nathaniel Barry. *CSPD*, 19–31 Dec. 1663.
[135] BL, SP 29/93, Register of the names of 116 Independents, 156 Anabaptists, and 96 Quakers, in the several parishes and hundreds of the lathe of St Augustine's, Kent, with the names of their teachers, fos. 123–4.
[136] Harrington, pp. xxiii–xxv; Hasted, I, 250–6. The lathe of St Augustine covered eighty-three parishes in the deaneries of Bridge, Canterbury, Dover, Elham, Sandwich and Westbere. The source includes three parishes not in the lathe and omits eleven parishes in the lathe.
[137] See footnote 134, above; Reid, pp. 148–73.

and therefore was considered a layman, but he could have been mentioned as a lay dissenter under Adisham or Ash.

There are two types of information about dissent in the Catalogue: parish congregations and named individuals. The Catalogue informants used a multiplicity of terms to describe the religious inclinations of parishioners. What follows is an attempt at placing subjective remarks into a few categories but, as will be seen, the absence of comment far outweighs the rest. Of the 234 active parishes in the diocese, 14 per cent are said to be 'much infested' with nonconformists. Amongst the 'infested' congregations, the much-written-about parish of Cranbrook is said to be 'Pestered with all sorts of Non-Conformists above 1000' and far to the east, the three parishes in the town of Sandwich are all condemned; St Clement's is 'Full of Sectaries and grossly ignorant persons', St Peter's is infested with 'Presbyterians & Sectaries' and St Mary's has 'Many Sectaries & Enemies to the late King, & some Petitioners for his death.' The deaneries of Canterbury (23 per cent) and Sandwich (25 per cent) are well behind Charing, where 48 per cent of the parishes are said to be full of sectaries. These figures perhaps consolidate the impression that dissent was strongest in the coastal areas, the Weald[138] and the major towns[139] (Maidstone was 'much infected with presbyt. & Fanaticks'), but we must suspend judgment until we reflect on the proportion of parishes without comments.

Seventy-three dissenters, laymen and excommunicated ministers are named in the Catalogue, of which thirty-three are located in the deanery of Charing, ten in Bridge, nine in Sutton, eight in Sandwich and the remainder in the deaneries of Canterbury, Dover, Elham, Lympne, Sittingbourne and Westbere. The greatest number were in the parish of Smarden, with nine, and George Hammond is named as a bad influence in seven parishes in the deanery of Charing. The only names found in both the Catalogue and the civil sources are Barry, Durant, Slaughter and Taverner.

The most glaring deficiency in the Catalogue is the number of parishes which lack information on the behaviour of the parishioners. Of the parish entries, 55 per cent do not comment on their religious behaviour. It would be tempting to assume that lack of comment meant conformity, but only 31 per cent of the comments confirm that the parishes are 'well affected' or 'indifferently well affected' to the church and therefore we must assume that lack of comment means lack of information. One of the surest indicators of conformity, occasional or regular, is attendance at church, particularly at Easter, and judging by the comments, one of the questions asked was: how many families or communicants are in the parish and how many took communion last Easter? Unfortunately, the question is only answered for 25 per cent of the parishes. The church relied on 'the quality' to be a bulwark against dissent: namely the aristocrats, knights, gentry, landowners and justices of the peace, very many of whom leased land and properties from the church and were therefore expected to give it their support and who, in return, may have been given favourable terms for the renewal of their leases. Here, the Catalogue disappoints once more, as for 79 per cent of the parishes there are no comments about friends of the church. They are only identified in 16 per cent of the parishes and in the

---

[138] See P. Collinson, 'Cranbrook and the Fletchers: popular and unpopular religion in the Kentish Weald', in *Reformation principle and practice*, ed. P. N. Brooks (1980), pp. 171–202.

[139] The dissenting councillors dominating the municipal governments in Dover and Sandwich were dismissed in 1662. C. Lee, '"Fanatic magistrates": religious and political conflict in three Kent boroughs, 1680–1684', *Historical Journal*, 35 (1992), pp. 43–61.

remaining 5 per cent there are no gentlemen or friends. This lack of comment may suggest that in some parishes the chief men were not in favour of ruthless persecution of dissenters providing that they did not threaten political disorder. The Hearth Tax returns for 1664 list many men in the parishes whose residencies were the equal of those occupied by aristocrats or justices of the peace, inferring a prominent position in their parishes.[140]

These results highlight two difficulties: obtaining information in a relatively short period of time (probably less than three months) in a season of the year where communications would have been hampered by bad roads, and the problem of standardizing the format of information gathering and reporting. However, we can assume that those who had access to the reports of the civil authorities referred to above would have considered the Catalogue a useful adjunct. Our conclusion must be that the Catalogue gives valuable information about dissent in some of the parishes but it is flawed by the omission of information in more than half of the parishes.

Later inquiries about dissent

In attempts to quantify and locate dissenters, a series of demands for information were sent to the bishops in the following years. In February 1665, Sheldon demanded the compilation and return to him of a survey of benefices and Miles Smyth set out how the survey results were to be formatted. Judging by the returns, it was intended to include all of the parishes in the provinces of York and Canterbury. Many returns were either not submitted or were lost[141] before they were bound together in the eventual *Notitia Episcopatuum*.[142] The return for London is on smaller paper, has no column headings and does not give incumbents' names. The Rochester return includes the archbishop's peculiars in the deanery of Shoreham and the return for Canterbury does not relate to 1665; it is a return to the governors of Queen Anne's Bounty of livings under the annual value of £80 in October 1705. In July 1665, Sheldon issued instructions for returns of a wider and more detailed nature. Names were to be submitted of pluralists and their curates, lecturers, schoolmasters, doctors and nonconformist ministers.[143] Only five are extant, all from Wales and the West Country except Norwich, and none gives complete answers.[144] We know that a return was demanded of Canterbury because of the survival of a letter from Smyth to Sir Edmund Peirce, commissary of Canterbury, enclosing the orders from Sheldon.[145] In June 1669, Sheldon required 'what and how many conventicles or unlawful assemblies, or church meetings are held in every town and parish, what are the numbers that meet at them,

---

[140] A. Fletcher, 'The enforcement of the Conventicle Acts 1664–1679', *Studies in Church History*, 21 (1984), pp. 235–46; G. Tapsell, 'Pastors, preachers and politicians: the clergy of the later Stuart church', in G. Tapsell, *The personal rule of Charles II, 1681–85* (Woodbridge, 2007), pp. 74–8; Harrington, *passim*; see also David Wykes who suggests that the impact of the Acts 'was greater than has been appreciated because of the enforcement of other statutes and the harassment of ejected ministers and their supporters', in D. L. Wykes, 'Protestant dissent and the law: enforcement and persecution, 1662–72', *Studies in Church History*, 56 (2020), pp. 306–19.

[141] Sodor and Man, Bristol, Chichester, Coventry and Lichfield, Ely, Hereford, Lincoln, Oxford, Salisbury and Winchester.

[142] LPL, MS 923.

[143] Cardwell, II, pp. 321–6.

[144] Norwich, Bristol, Exeter, St Asaph, St David's. LPL, MS 639, fos. 300r–309v, 310r–316v, 346r–354v, 390r–395v, MS 943, pp. 380a–g, MS 951/1, fos. 54r–61v, 62r–68v.

[145] CCA, DCc/BB/P/154.

and of what condition or sort of people they consist'.[146] This elicited detailed replies but eight are not extant.[147]

Sheldon was not the author of the census of catholic recusants and protestant dissenters of 1676. Lord Treasurer Danby was the instigator and Henry Compton, bishop of London, performed the administrative function only, but historians have given his name to the survey.[148] A comparison of the Catalogue to the 1669 returns and the 1676 census should give an indication of success in quelling the dissenting tide, or failure to stem it, but detailed examination reveals shortcomings. Twenty-five parishes are missing from the 1669 returns and eight are missing from 1676. The proximity of the Romney Marsh perhaps inhibited investigators from searching the deanery of Lympne too closely; ten of its parishes are missing from 1669 and three from 1676. Comparisons from a selection of parishes give concern about the accuracy of reporting. We have seen previously that there was great concern expressed in the Catalogue about the dissenters in the deanery of Charing. Rolvenden, Sandhurst and Smarden are listed as free from dissenters in 1669, although in the Catalogue they are classified as being pestered and infested with violent fanatics and, in 1676, they have 40, 75 and 100 nonconformists respectively. Tenterden is 'a parish much corrupted' in the Catalogue, but in 1669 has only 'anabaptists chiefly women', and in 1676, 300 nonconformists. Finally, Hawkhurst is 'Pestered with all manner of Sectaries' in the Catalogue, but is listed as free from them in 1669, and reported to have 150 nonconformists in 1676.

Gilbert Sheldon died in 1677, having tried and failed to extirpate dissent from his own diocese and the country at large.[149] It is perhaps significant that, of his frequent demands for information, only two of the returns include his diocese and, in a third, that of 1669, a large number of parishes are missing.

THE CATALOGUE FORMAT USED AGAIN

The format Miles Smyth devised for the Catalogue gives ample space for comments, amendments and further entries but only two other uses of the format have been found covering the diocese and the peculiars. The Survey of Canterbury Diocese[150] commences as a poor copy of the Catalogue. A scribe was obviously told to start copying the Catalogue by lining a volume and copying the headings and parish names. This was done exactly, and Canterbury St Alphege is entered in the first page and then repeated overleaf; the same error made in the Catalogue. Page numbers are used instead of folio numbers. The copying of the incumbents' names has been badly done. A good example can be found in Ospringe deanery, where the name has first been written in the parish above his own and then scored out and the correct name added below. This happens in four consecutive parishes. Incumbents' names were omitted if they had died or moved and this gives an indication that it was compiled in 1668 or early 1669. Two examples illustrate this. In the parish of Brook, Nairne

---

[146] Wilkins, IV, 588.
[147] Bristol, Gloucester, Hereford, Peterborough, Oxford, Rochester, Sodor and Man and St David's. LPL, MS 639; Lyon Turner, I, 3–20, 27–127, 136–47, 148–76.
[148] Whiteman, p. xxiv; Andrew M. Coleby, 'Compton, Henry', *ODNB*.
[149] Spurr, pp. 47–52, 55–8, 63–4; Gregory (2000), pp. 182–3, 191–2.
[150] LPL, MS 1137.

and Johnson are omitted; Nairne died in 1667 and Johnson resigned in 1669. John Stokes, who was appointed in 1669, is included. At Sandwich St Peter, Wilkinson is omitted; he resigned in 1665 and died the following year. Thomas White was appointed in 1668. Entries continued to be made in the Survey but on an irregular basis; William Balderston is noted as vicar of Northbourne in 1678[151] and the final entry is John Maximilian De L'angle's appointment as rector of Chartham in 1695.[152] William Sancroft, proven to be an accomplished administrator in previous positions as master of Emmanuel College, Cambridge, dean of York and then of St Paul's was appointed archdeacon of Canterbury in 1668, around the time when this Survey was commenced, and he may have suggested the compilation of the Survey, but he wrote his own small notebook in 1668. This is in alphabetical order of parishes, one per page, and he has written the parish name, deanery, patron and value at the top of the page, with the incumbent's name at the foot of the page along with brief comments and, occasionally, a remark taken from the Catalogue. Thus, for the parish of Eyethorne, he has written: '[16]68. Rect. Mr Tho. Walton, reg.[ular] & res.[ident] – [16]63. pr[e]sb.[yterian]'.[153] He has obviously studied the Catalogue but has only taken comments from forty-three parishes. The notebook is incomplete, as it does not include thirty-eight parishes that were exempt from the jurisdiction of the archdeacon. Sancroft asked William Somner to give him information on these parishes and the latter produced a short document, giving the details of incumbents, which is now in Canterbury Cathedral Archives.[154]

After he became archbishop of Canterbury, Sancroft ordered the preparation of another list of incumbents. This one was given the title 'A catalogue of all the benefices and spirituall promotions within the diocesse & jurisdiction of Canterbury with the patrons and values'.[155] The Catalogue was copied again in a very fine hand, but with the same Canterbury St Alphege error on the opening folios. The date can be derived from the appointment dates, which are no earlier than 1677. From the many annotations he made over the next few years, it appears that Sancroft kept it as his personal copy.

DIOCESAN CONCLUSION

The diocese of Canterbury has a comparatively small number of parishes and so may be thought easy to monitor, but its difficult terrain and historical structure meant that archbishops could struggle to assert their authority and correct canonical error, abuses of incumbents and dissent among the populace. Sheldon and his predecessors were also limited in the time they could devote to the diocese because of their national religious and secular responsibilities. Sheldon was particularly hampered by the absence of his archdeacon until 1668. Nevertheless, analysis of the Catalogue shows that the diocese was in a poor state in 1663. Three years after the restoration of the church, the administration could not produce a complete and accurate summary of parishes and incumbents and the extent of dissent was either unknown or

[151] LPL, MS 1137, pp. 35–6; VG 1/5, p. 70.
[152] CCEd Person ID: 24486.
[153] Bodl., MS Sancroft 99, p. 74.
[154] CCA, DCc/LitMS/C/5. I owe this reference to Professor Ken Fincham.
[155] Bodl., MS Tanner 122, pp. 1–89.

concealed. Sheldon was only appointed in 1663 but the information provided by the Catalogue and succeeding surveys did not provoke radical changes in the structure of the church. In 1663, there were derelict churches in parishes where the residents were still paying tithes; dilapidated churches and incumbents' houses; a high amount of pluralism and non-residence, and large inequalities in income between incumbents, all of which engendered contempt for the clergy and served to further the cause of dissent. These problems persisted until at least the end of the century.

THE ARCHBISHOP'S PECULIARS

It is clear that the archbishop's peculiars were not considered to be a part of the diocese. The Catalogue includes information about them but separates them from the diocesan parishes. The title begins: 'A catalogue of all the benefices and promocions within the diocese and jurisdiction of Canterbury' and we should understand that, in this context, 'Canterbury' was the archbishop. Paul Barber explains that an 'Archiepiscopal Peculiar ... forms no part of any diocese although it may be completely surrounded by one ... it is like a mini-diocese in its own right ... it forms part of the province, and is therefore visitable by the metropolitan'.[156] They were situated in locations where the archbishop, or his predecessors, held manors and land and they had been in existence for many centuries. The grouping of the peculiars into deaneries was complete by the end of the thirteenth century, with the archbishop appointing deans, by collation and commission, and giving them powers of archidiaconal jurisdiction.[157]

The Catalogue lists 117 parishes as peculiars in 1663, grouped into eight deaneries,[158] within seven geographical dioceses,[159] in ten counties[160] and the city of London.[161] This administrative and geographical structure prohibits any assumption of homogeneity and underlines their differentiation from the diocese. It also means that any attempt to analyse what the Catalogue tells us must be done by individual deanery. As with the diocese, the Catalogue listing of peculiars is distorted by error and omission. These will be indicated below. Compared to the diocesan parishes, the reporting on the peculiars is far less detailed and there are very few comments.

At the time of the compilation, Giles Sweit, president of Doctors Commons, was dean of the Arches, having been appointed in September 1660; by September 1663, he was also official principal of the court of Canterbury and dean of Shoreham, Croydon, and Risborough.[162] Stephen Roborough was dean of South Malling and Richard Colebrand was dean of Bocking.[163] The identity of the dean of Pagham and Tarring, assuming that there was one, is unknown for 1660–3 but Thomas Briggs became dean of South Malling, Pagham and Tarring from 1678.[164] One of the Shoreham parishes illustrates the possible complexities of the peculiars: Cliffe

---

[156] *ELJ*, 3 (1995), p. 301.
[157] Churchill, pp. 62–83.
[158] Arches, Bocking, Croydon, Monks Risborough, Pagham, Shoreham, South Malling and Tarring.
[159] Chichester, Lincoln, London, Norwich, Oxford, Rochester and Winchester.
[160] Buckinghamshire, Essex, Kent, Lincolnshire, Middlesex, Norfolk, Oxfordshire, Suffolk, Surrey and Sussex.
[161] Locations of the deaneries can be found in the 'Parish lists in 1663' section.
[162] Squibb, pp. 46, 117; LPL, VH 98/3/84.
[163] Venn, I, 368.
[164] LPL, VB 1/4/36.

at Hoo was a peculiar exempt from the jurisdiction of the dean of the peculiars. The rector was ordinary in his own parish and was visited only by the archbishop. He held his own visitations without special commission, and had his own court and seal.[165] The church held the patronage of over 60 per cent of the peculiars in 1663. Their 'peculiar' status was abolished in the nineteenth century, when the parishes were absorbed into their geographical diocese.

The compilers of the Catalogue entries for the peculiars could not rely on 'A note of all the benefices within the jurisdiction of the archdeacon of Canterbury'[166] as they did for the diocesan parishes. The only extant reference in that document to the peculiars is a simple list of the parishes in the deanery of Shoreham.[167] No evidence has been found to suggest who provided the information about the peculiars. The Catalogue compilers would have had sufficient information available to them to enable the entry of parish names, incumbents, values in the King's Books and patrons, but contemporary values and any comments must have come from local sources. Obtaining information about the peculiars in the same detail as achieved in some of the diocesan parishes proved impossible within a limited timescale. The distances involved and the state of the roads in winter were probably the main reason although the semi-independence enjoyed by many of the peculiars may have led to reticence. In the entries for the fifty-eight parishes, excluding those in the deanery of Shoreham, 83 per cent are without any comment and the remaining ten parishes have no comments that address matters of importance.

The **deanery of Shoreham** embraced the largest number of parishes and it was the nearest to the diocese, situated within the diocese of Rochester, Kent. This proximity suggests that one of the diocesan informants may have been able to provide information about some of the Shoreham parishes. The Catalogue lists thirty-six livings and three chapels in Shoreham but this figure includes Peckham, which probably refers to the sinecure rectory of East Peckham, which was not a peculiar by the seventeenth century.[168] There were four sinecure rectories in the deanery and Shoreham rectory was merged with the vicarage.[169] Allowing for the annexed chapel of Lidsing and the ruined church of Woodland, the total number of operational parishes was therefore thirty-one and this number of men are shown in the Catalogue as their incumbents. However, three of these men were not admitted to their vicarages until November and December 1664,[170] one was appointed to a rectory in 1666,[171] and two to chapels, in 1670 and 1672.[172]

There were eleven pluralists in the deanery. Thomas Browne and Richard Marsh held Farningham and East Peckham, respectively, along with parishes in the diocese, as detailed above.[173] Six men held one of the Shoreham peculiars along with parishes in other dioceses[174] and Edward Layfield held the sinecure rectory of Wrotham along

---

[165] Catalogue, fo. 55; LPL, VH 70; Hasted, III, 513–14. See also Gregory, p. 271.
[166] Bodl., MSS Tanner 124, fos. 207–21; 125, fos. 145–55.
[167] Bodl., MS Tanner 125, fo. 155.
[168] Catalogue, fo. 56b; Hasted, V, 105.
[169] Eynsford, Orpington, Wrotham and Sevenoaks. Sevenoaks was held by the writer Edward Chamberlain.
[170] Blackstone, Bosse and Marsh.
[171] Stacey.
[172] William Pawley and Philip Jones.
[173] See above p. xlviii.
[174] Edward Clarke, William Gibson, William Pindar, Thomas Potter, John Williams, George Stradling.

with the peculiar of Barnes, in the deanery of Croydon. Francis Porter and Robert Say each held sinecure rectories along with a living in the dioceses of York and Lincoln. Of the incumbents, 65 per cent had incomes of less than £100, with a median of £60, and the higher earners received incomes of £100 to over £300, with a median of £150.

In contrast to the diocesan parishes, there are very few comments made about parish incumbents (four), behaviour of the parishioners (twelve, generally approved) or the condition of the church fabric and furnishing (eight); the last said to be in good condition and 'all things decent'. There were no comments about incumbents, parishioners or churches for fifteen parishes. Robert Whittle was instituted to East Malling in 1628 and possibly served it until his death, fifty-one years later. Eight were appointed between 1644 and 1654 and served throughout the Interregnum and into the Restoration era,[175] and the remaining fifteen gained their livings between 1658 and 1663.[176] Matthews lists four ejections from the Shoreham peculiars but John Petter probably resigned from the rectory of Hever as he was replaced by his nephew, George Boraston, previously his curate. There were three ejections: Thomas Seyliard from Chiddingstone, George Latham from Hunton and John Mauduit from Penshurst.[177] It follows that in eleven parishes there were unexplained changes in incumbents due to deaths, resignations or ejections, which were either unrecorded or for which the documents have been lost. However, this result indicates a much greater degree of stability in the deanery (over 60 per cent of the parishes remained undisturbed) than in the diocese (25 per cent of the parishes undisturbed). This stability is exemplified by the life of Thomas Browne. He has been referred to above: as one of the only three men linking the diocese and the archbishop's peculiars, as one of the eleven pluralists in the deanery of Shoreham and as one of the eight incumbents of peculiars who served throughout the Interregnum and into the Restoration era. A curate and teacher in Shoreham deanery in 1636, he began his ministry in Farningham in 1646 and was the resident vicar there until his death in 1678.[178] The presence of a communion table is commented on at Saltwood and Stowting in the diocese but Farningham is the only parish in the Catalogue having a comment which refers to rails: 'Commun. Table rayled in'.[179] They could have been in place before the civil wars but it is more likely that they were installed after the Restoration and paid for by Sir John Cotton, who lived in the parish.

The Catalogue lists fifteen rectories in the **deanery of the Arches**, within the diocese of London, but the remarks by Miles Smyth against All Hallows ad Fenne and St Edmund's Lombard Street make it clear that they were not peculiars.[180] Of the thirteen incumbents, four were pluralists, including John Castilion.[181] Charles Adams and Christopher Shute each held another living along with their rectories[182] and Elkanah Downes held the peculiar of St Leonard Eastcheap, Holy Trinity Mino-

---

[175] Browne, Clarke, Cottingham, Gibson, Hickford, Sharpe, Twisse, Wood.
[176] Allen, Boraston, Davis, Greene, Thomas Lee, Oliver, Palmer, Pindar, Potter, Smith, Smoult, Stradling, Williams, Yardley, Yates.
[177] Matthews, *Calamy*, pp. 315, 345, 387, 433.
[178] See the Biographical index for details and references. Professor Fincham alerted me to the misidentification of Browne in Fincham and Tyacke, p. 327.
[179] Catalogue, fos. 26, 56a.
[180] Catalogue, fos. 58, 59a.
[181] See p. xlviii above.
[182] Adams the vicarage of Great Baddow, Essex, and Shute the rectory of Watton, Herts.

ries and Ashstead in Surrey. There are no remarks about the incumbents, parishioners or the condition of the churches, eleven of which were destroyed in the Great Fire of London in 1666 and St Dunstan in the East and St Vedast Foster Lane were badly damaged. Four were not rebuilt but united to other parishes, in 1670: St John the Evangelist Friday Street to All Hallows Bread Street; St Leonard Eastcheap to St Benet Gracechurch; St Mary Bothaw to St Swithin London Stone and St Pancras Soper Lane to the parishes of All Hallows Honey Lane and St Mary le Bow.[183]

The **deanery of Croydon** is listed as having six parishes within the geographical diocese of London and thirteen within the bounds of Winchester diocese but the rectories of Hayes, Harrow and Wimbledon were sinecures, and Pinner and Throckington were chapels to Harrow. This left only fourteen working parishes but the Catalogue only gives incumbents for eleven of them in 1663, as the curates listed at Putney, Wimbledon and Mortlake were appointed in 1664, 1665 and 1672 respectively. Ralph Cooke ministered to the parish of Burstow from 1637 until his death in 1685, but there were many changes in the other parishes. The vicar of Hayes was appointed in 1662 and Henry Hesketh was instituted to Charlewood in 1663, both following the deaths of their predecessors. The vicars of Harrow and Croydon and the rector of East Horsley were admitted following the ejection of the previous incumbents and James Megges, sequestered rector of Newington, in 1643, was restored in 1661. The rectors of Barnes, Cheam and Merstham were appointed in 1662 and 1663 after ejections but we have no evidence of the previous incumbents. The rectories of Burstow, East Horsley, Charlwood and Newington were all held by pluralists. Dissenters or suspect incumbents in the deanery are not mentioned.

Eleven parishes in the **deanery of Bocking**, in Essex and Suffolk, are shown in the Catalogue but Little Coggeshall and Ash by Campsey were not peculiars,[184] and Moulton rectory was a sinecure held by Francis Seyliard. Only four other incumbents are named. Martin Alderson had been appointed to Latchingdon by Lord Protector Cromwell in 1656, but conformed and remained until his death in 1680. Daniel Nicolls held Hadleigh and Stisted, having been appointed to the former following the resignation or ejection of his predecessor. There are no surviving records of the incumbents at Bocking, Southchurch and Stisted before 1660 and there were no comments about dissent.

Of the four parishes listed as being in the **deanery of Risborough**, Milton was not a peculiar of the archbishop. The first incumbent named at Monks Risborough, John Wooley, was not appointed until 1675 and died in the same year. The incumbent at Newington held it along with the vicarage of Northolt, Middlesex. There are no comments about dissent.

The same pattern of lack of information is repeated in the **deaneries of Pagham** (six parishes) and **Tarring** (three parishes), both in Sussex. At Pagham, the rector of Slindon was not James Hering, as he was at Slinfold, also in Sussex. There were no incumbents named in the other five parishes, as the pluralist John Betton and John Holder were not appointed until the 1670s. West Tarring rectory was a sinecure and the vicarage was held along with Albourne, Sussex, by Thomas Negus. The incumbent of the remaining parish of Patching is not named. There are no comments.

Finally to the **deanery of South Malling**, Sussex. There are twelve parishes named, of which South Malling was a sinecure rectory. Buxted had the dependent

[183] LMA, P69/JNE, LEN1, MRY6, PAN.
[184] CCEd; Beaumont, *passim*; Gregory, p. 262, fo. 338.

chapel of Uckfield which did not become a parish until 1846.[185] Framfield, Glynde and Lindfield were vacant and the incumbents of Mayfield, Lewes St Thomas at Cliffe and Ringmer were not appointed until later in the 1660s. The Edburton and Stanmer incumbents had been in place since 1656 but had conformed at the Restoration. John Smith became vicar of Wadhurst after the death of his predecessor but Robert Middleton, at Buxted, replaced an ejected minister, and Thomas Mell at Isfield had probably done the same. The vicarages of Framfield and Glynde were vacant following the presentations of candidates deemed to be insufficient and there is a revelation of dissent at Mayfield.

Catalogue folio 65 lists six parishes in Norfolk and two prebends in Lincoln cathedral and refers to them as peculiars, but this was an error. Castle Rising was, as of itself, a peculiar, exempted from all episcopal and archidiaconal jurisdiction except induction by the archdeacon of Norwich, and the lord of the manor, the duke of Norfolk, was patron. The rector of Rising had his own court for the probate of wills. He was known as the commissary and corrector general within the parishes of Castle Rising, Roydon and North and South Wooton, and had a seal of office. There was, however, confusion. In 1574, Castle Rising is described as in the diocese of Canterbury, rather than the diocese of Norwich, and, in 1640, the same parish is referred to as a peculiar of the archbishop of Canterbury. It is significant that in the Survey of the diocese of Norwich, 1603–14, the names of incumbents and patrons are not given, in contrast to the other benefices in the Survey, including Thursford. Mintlyn is not listed. In the updated version of the Catalogue, prepared for Archbishop Sancroft, the six parishes are shown, but without comment.[186] The parishes are listed by Archbishop Secker, in his *Speculum*, but the tenor of his remarks suggest he accepted that they were not peculiars.[187] Mintlyn was originally the property of the Benedictine priory of Lynn in Norfolk and became part of the possessions of the dean and chapter of Norwich cathedral, after the dissolution.[188] It was in the deanery of Lynn, and curates were licensed to it in the sixteenth and seventeenth centuries. Thursford was a rectory in the deanery of Walsingham, in the diocese of Norwich.[189] The prebends were not archbishops' peculiars. The prebends of Cropredy and Sutton-cum-Buckingham were in the presentation of the crown. There may have been confusion with the parish of Cropredy (one of the Banbury peculiars) and the peculiar of Thame, but both were in the jurisdiction of the dean and chapter of Lincoln.[190]

There is very little information in the Catalogue about dissent in the peculiars. In the deanery of Shoreham, the parishes of Crayford, Gillingham and Hunton are each noted as having a named nonconformist and Sundridge is said to be recovering from the attentions of unnamed Quakers. The only other named dissenter is the ejected minister of Mayfield, in South Malling, where John Maynard has 'much poysoned the people'. The remaining six deaneries are devoid of comment. The absence of

---

[185] *SAC*, 26, p. 10.
[186] Bodl., MS Tanner 122, fos. 74–5.
[187] CCEd Person ID: 77233, 80469; Bodl., MS Tanner 122, fos. 74–5; Bradfer-Lawrence, *passim*; Parkin, pp. 57–8; Gregory, pp. 261–2; Whiteman, p. 230.
[188] *Monasticon anglicanum: or, the history of the ancient abbies, and other monasteries, hospitals, cathedral and collegiate churches in England and Wales* ... , collected in Latin by Sir William Dugdale, ed. J. Caley, H. Ellis and B. Bandinel (8 vols., 1823), IV, p. 462.
[189] CCEd; Whiteman, p. 229.
[190] Horn, IX, 60, 118; Whiteman, p. 373.

comment can be taken as a sign of stability but it is probably only because of a lack of information.

The answers to the enquiry of February 1665 included all of the Shoreham peculiars, except for the chapelries of Knockholt, Lidsing and Downe and the listing for the diocese of London includes All Hallows Lombard Street and St Edmund's Lombard Street.[191] The remaining peculiars were not included in any of the other diocesan returns. There are no surviving returns for the peculiars in answer to the enquiry of July 1665,[192] and we only have a record of ten peculiars in the 1669 returns. Listed within the return for the diocese of Chichester, six of them are reported to have no dissenters[193] and four contain many: Lindfield 'many factious persons'; Cliffe 60 sectarians; Pagham 20 or 30 sectarians; South Malling 500 presbyterians.[194] This last figure must be an estimate of those attending conventicles in the deanery; the parish of South Malling had a population of under 100. Finally, for the returns to the Compton census of 1676, we must resort to deanery totals, for reasons of space. Shoreham declared a total of 188 nonconformists; Arches 175 with St Michael Crooked Lane missing; Croydon 161 but Croydon and Newington missing; Pagham 73; Tarring 4; South Malling 93 but Glynde missing. There are no returns for Risborough and Bocking.[195] In a similar way to the returns for the diocesan parishes, the figures for the peculiars suggest that the extent of dissent was unknown.

Having examined the peculiars within their separate deaneries, it may be instructive to take a view of them in aggregate. The Catalogue lists 117 parishes but fourteen of them were not peculiars, one church was in ruins and there were ten sinecure rectories and three annexed chapels. This left eighty-nine churches available for worship but nineteen of these did not have an incumbent in late 1663. Only twenty-six of the 117 peculiars listed comment on the orthodoxy or otherwise of parish priests or dissent among parishioners. It is perhaps not surprising that the Catalogue compilers found it very difficult to obtain details about the incumbents and parishioners in the peculiars, but it is noteworthy that this extended to the entries for the deanery of the Arches, where there is a complete absence of comment about orthodoxy or dissent. The bishop of London, Humphrey Henchman, and his archdeacon, John Dolben, both allies of Sheldon, the former bishop, and Giles Sweit, dean of the Arches, must all have had knowledge of the situation in the thirteen parishes. The lack of comments on them was perhaps because they were thought to be unnecessary as the facts were already known.

CONCLUSION

We can judge the usefulness of the Catalogue by asking two questions. Did it assist Sheldon's efforts to find and root out the dissenters and did it provide enough information to assess the state of his diocese? The Catalogue should be viewed as only a part of the efforts being made by the religious and secular authorities to subdue

---

[191] LPL, MS 923, pp. 305–6, 201.
[192] LPL, MS 639.
[193] East Lavant, Tangmere, West Tarring, Patching, Isfield and Ringmer.
[194] Lyon Turner, I, 32–3.
[195] Whiteman, pp. 66–7, 103, 409–11.

dissent. Serving and ejected ministers and laymen were indicted at the Maidstone Assizes, clergy and laymen were brought before the archdeaconry and consistory courts and informants sent regular reports to London about the activities of suspects. The information provided in the Catalogue was, perhaps, less than would have been expected from the diocesan hierarchy and the deans of the peculiars but the errors and omissions revealed by modern analysis may not have been apparent to Smyth. Modern judgment must be that the Catalogue contributed to the battle against dissent but could have been improved upon. If Sheldon read it (he did not annotate it), it may only have reinforced what he probably already knew, that there were problems with dissenters in the Kentish Weald, the main towns and the ports. However, he may have been heartened to know that most of the incumbents in the diocese were thought to be orthodox, and perhaps considered that they would have the same success as that in the peculiar of Hunton, where 'Latham the late intruder hath much infected the Parish, but begins to be reduced.'

The Catalogue subtitle is 'With the state of every particular parish as it stood at October 1663'. A reader in the seventeenth century could have gained a general impression of the state of the parishes but what did they think of the frequent blank spaces intended to be filled with information about church premises, incumbents and parishioners? They may have been told, or assumed, that all was well in these parishes, but why then are there many other approving comments when they could have been left blank? The likeliest explanation is that the blanks signified lack of information. The Catalogue does reveal ruined churches, vacant livings, unsuitable incumbents, pluralism, inequality of incomes and poor church attendance but these may all have been considered as part of the normal way of things. The information providers for the Catalogue were men who patronized ordinary parishioners describing them variously as 'good dull earthworms' and 'playne, conformable country fellowes' and at the same time deferring to 'friends of the church' and 'persons of best quality'. The latter being aristocracy, lords of the manor and JPs who supported the church and protected their tenure of church lands and property. The modern reader may begin to feel that the Catalogue, devoid of pastoral care, is more of a political than a religious document.

Can the state of the church in the diocese, as shown by the Catalogue, assist an attempt to judge the state of the wider church in 1663? The topographical features of Kent, with its towns, scattered parishes, bad roads and malarial marshes were repeated in many other areas of England. The archbishop was preoccupied by national affairs, but the other bishops were often absent from their dioceses through regular attendance at parliaments. For some twenty years of chaos, the Canterbury parishes had been heavily influenced by nonconformist ministers and preachers or, perhaps worse, had received no pastoral care while they lay vacant. This probably also happened in other dioceses but while local studies are available, the proof can only be obtained by detailed examination of the succession of incumbents in each parish in an attempt to reveal hidden deaths, desertions or ejections.[196] Skea's research suggests that Calamy's numbers for ejected ministers are much too low and considers that 'contemporary research is essential in the quest to provide a more accurate rendering of the numbers of ejected ministers'.[197]

---

[196] Pruett; J. S. Chamberlain, *Accommodating high churchmen: the clergy of Sussex, 1700–1745* (Illinois, 1997); Spaeth; Salter; Marshall; Freeman; Thomson; Jones.

[197] Skea, 'The ecclesiastical identities of puritan and nonconformist clergy, p. 176.

The Catalogue reveals that, although the Church of England was re-established by the Act of Uniformity in 1662, acceptance and support by parishioners fell far short of being enthusiastic and wholehearted. It also reveals that, under the leadership of Sheldon, the church authorities displayed an attitude of mind that would not admit of tolerance and an unwillingness to attempt to change practices inimical to an age which was becoming more enlightened. The dissenters survived the years of persecution and the legislation against them and, as Sheldon's influence diminished and the court's interest waned, they grew stronger. Less than thirty years after the compilation of the Catalogue, changes were to come, which would strip the Church of England of its legal exclusivity to forms of worship. Nevertheless, it was not until after the 'Glorious Revolution' of 1688–9 that the so-called 'Toleration Act' of 1689 was passed. This Act did not repeal the penal laws against the dissenters enacted since 1660 but only gave exemptions from some of them and did not apply to catholics, any protestants who contradicted Trinitarian theology or any who refused to swear allegiance to William and Mary. This less than wholehearted granting of tolerance was further diminished by those who remained loyal to the Church of England who considered religious deviance a 'self-evident cause of political disunity and social upheaval'. Prejudice, legal harassment, verbal abuse and the threat of violence continued. Additional laws were passed against the dissenters late in the reign of Queen Anne but they were completely repealed in 1718 excepting for the disablement from office of magistrates who attended dissenting services in their robes of office.[198] Stevens sets out the continued problems for dissenters with regard to public offices, education of children, baptism and the uses of chapels, but he concludes that 'the long campaign to coerce the nation to be of one religion had failed'.[199]

Sheldon, the progenitor of the Catalogue, his Canterbury officials and investigators and Miles Smyth and the other compilers did not live to see the blossoming of religious toleration and the founding of new denominations but their achievement was the production of the forerunner of a series of similar documents intended to assist with the control and administration of the parish clergy by the archbishops and bishops. Perhaps wisely, successive variants of the Catalogue did not include pejorative comments about incumbents or parishioners.

---

[198] 'An Act for strengthening the protestant interest in these kingdoms', 1718, D. Pickering, *The statutes at large*, XIV (Cambridge, 1765), p. 15.
[199] Stevens, *passim*.

General description and editorial conventions

GENERAL DESCRIPTION

The Catalogue is in the form of a book measuring 304 x 206 mm, vellum bound, rebacked, with paper leaves. The front cover bears the main title 'A Catalogue of all the Benefices & Promocions Within the Diocese and Jurisdicion of Canterbury' and 'With the State of every Particular Parish as it stood at October 1663' is added below. The main title is repeated over the first two pages but the left-hand page has been cut off 50 mm from the spine. Each pair of facing pages has been treated as a folio by the compiler, and has been given a single folio number which is used in the transcription from folio 1 to folio 65 without reference to rectos and versos. The folios have been vertically lined to provide columns of varying widths with headings at the top, and these column headings vary slightly between the entries for the diocese and those for the peculiars. The left-hand side of each folio has six columns: 'Folio number'; 'Benefices', containing the name of the parish and whether it is a rectory, vicarage or chapel; a column without a heading, which was used to indicate which parishes were exempt from the jurisdiction of the archdeacon, designated as 'Ex'; 'K^s Bookes' ('King's Books' the value in the *Valor Ecclesiasticus* of 1535); 'Com. Value' (the contemporary assessment of the value of the living); 'Patron'. In the entries for the peculiars, the first column is used for the folio number and also for the type of living and the third column is used only to indicate an alternative value for the *Valor Ecclesiasticus* figure for four parishes in the deanery of the Arches, London. The right-hand side of the folio has a column to list incumbents and a much broader, unheaded column to accommodate notes. Folios 1–54 have been ruled horizontally so that six parishes or headings can be entered. This gives sufficient space so that when an incumbent's name is scored out two or three more can be entered. On folios 55 to 65 the spaces are increased to accommodate ten parishes. The first folio has no number and has only one entry under the headings:

St. Alphege in Cant.   R   Ex   08.13.04   Arch-Bp   Mr John Stockar

The next folio makes it obvious that the writer has started again, with the addition of 'Canterbury Deanery' under the folio headings. The entry for St Alphege is then repeated, followed by the other parishes of the deanery of Canterbury. The folio numbers are contemporary with the text but on the right-hand top corner of folio 65 the number 66 has been added by another hand. This marks a change to using each folio to accommodate two pages, and in this latter hand, the folios are numbered on the right side only. This necessitates referring to rectos and versos for folios 70 to 73 to clarify the location of text. Folios 68 to 69 are blank with no rulings. Text begins again on folio 70 and continues to folio 73. Folios 74 to 78 inclusive are blank. The final folio is unnumbered and gives a list of deaneries with their starting folio numbers, all in the original hand. There are two places in the text where the folio numbers have been repeated. In this edition, these are distinguished by the addition of a suffix thus: '56a' and '56b', '59a' and '59b'. There are 82 double pages with text.

The original has an index. Folio 79 gives the title 'An Alphabeticall Table of Persons and Places' and the index commences on folio 80 extending to folio 87. Each folio is divided into six columns, two for each letter with the first listing incumbents and the second giving place names. The incumbents and places are not listed alpabetically but in the order the compiler found them in the document. Many personal names have been scored through, probably as incumbents died or moved, but there is no indication of dates and the process is incomplete. The index has not been included in this edition but folio 80 has been reproduced as an example.

EDITORIAL CONVENTIONS

The arrangement of the original complicates the presentation of a modern edition, so the following format has been adopted. The first line of text gives the parish name in bold. The second line gives information about the benefice but it is not always complete. The first entry is either R[ectory], V[icarage, Cur[acy] or Cap (chapel) and the next is Ex[empt] where that applies. The following two entries are monetary values prefixed by K[ing's Book's Values] or C[ommon Value] and the last entries give patronage detail. Note that two or more monetary values often occur as do different patrons. The third line starts with the name of an incumbent in bold and then the associated comment and further incumbent names appear, in bold, below. The comments usually refer to the first-listed incumbent, whether or not his name is crossed out. All exceptions are given in a footnote or, on two occasions where the manuscript has an arrow indicating the correct incumbent, the arrow is reproduced (folio 27 Aldington Allan Eales; folio 46 Kingsdown Thomas Allen). The archbishop's peculiars commencing on folio 55 are entered slightly differently. The type of benefice (R, V, Cur or Cap) is entered on the first line before the name of the parish. All other entries are in the same format as the diocesan parishes.

The original spelling and punctuation has been retained except where additional silent punctuation clarifies the text. Contractions and some abbreviations have been expanded, again for clarification. Entries that have been scored through, mainly indicating a change in incumbent, have been reproduced as written and scored through. Erased, completely obscured or illegible entries are indicated by {…}. Places where the original does not provide expected information are marked with brackets ( ) and editorial additions are marked with square brackets [ ]. Interlineations are marked thus ^ ^. Text underlined in the manuscript is underlined in the transcription. Where text has been made partially or completely illegible, but is available from the Archdeaconry Notes, the recovered text is shown in a footnote. Many variations of the notation of parish values occur in the manuscript but in this edition, they are uniformly written, thus: 13.04.04, 13:04:04 and 13.4.4 are all given as 13.04.04, meaning thirteen pounds, four shillings and four pence. There were twelve pence to the shilling and twenty shillings in a pound. The £ sign has been used where values are rounded in the original.

The folio numbers are given in their original location, at the upper left-hand side of the folio. The cross-references within the text and the footnotes, and the folio numbers given in the Index, refer to these folio numbers and not to the pagination of the modern edition.

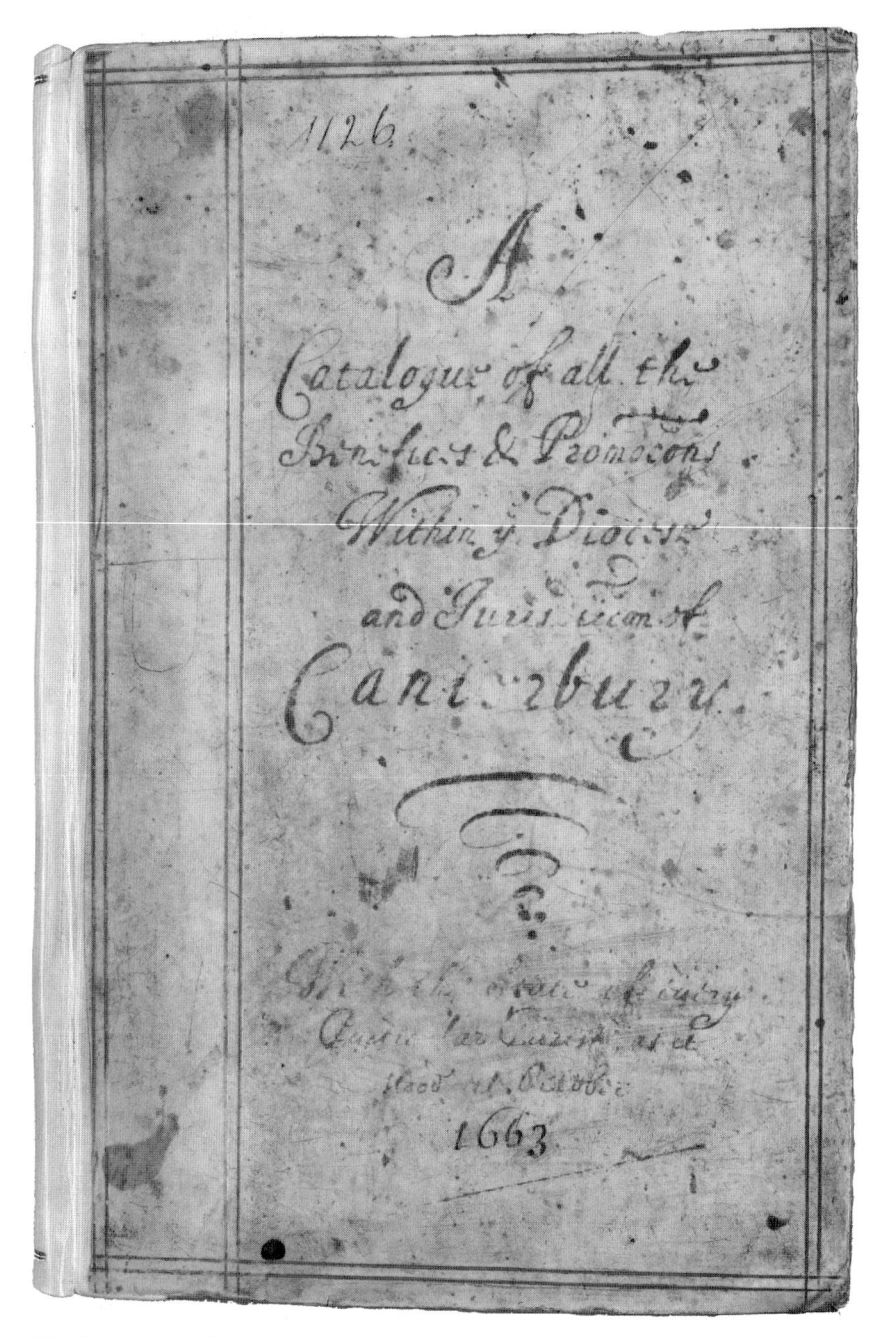

A
Catalogue of all the
Benefices & Promocons
Within ye Diocess
and Jurisdiccon of
Canterbury

1663

The front cover of MS 1126. Image courtesy of Lambeth Palace Library.

A
CATALOGUE OF ALL THE
BENEFICES AND PROMOCIONS
WITHIN THE DIOCESE
AND JURISDICTION OF
CANTERBURY.
WITH THE STATE OF EVERY
PARTICULAR PARISH AS IT
STOOD AT OCTOBER
1663

Folio 0[1]

St. Alphege Cant.
R; Ex; 08.13.04; C 30.00.00; ArchBp.

Folio 1

Canterbury Deanery

St. Alphege Cant.[2]
R; Ex; K 08.13.04; C 30.00.00; ArchBp.
Mr. John Stockar   A ~~Frenchman~~ ^Switzer^ by Birth; Recommended by Mr. Durell: ~~A scholler of good parts. The Parish full of Walloons,~~[3] ~~of the Presbyterian stampe, & some Anabaptist~~ to your Grace. Preaches a little the Presbyterian modell, & gives measure enough, but sound in his judgment for & conformable to the government & Ceremonies of the Church. The Parish full of Walloons of the Presbyterian stampe, & some Anabaptists.

St. Andrews Cant
R; K 13.06.08; C 60.00.00; ArchBp.
~~Mr. Edw. Aldey~~   Preb. Of Cant: A soft man, of weake resolutions, & heretofore a little inclining to Presbyterianism. The living was heretofore accounted well worth £100 a yeare, & is so still, if an Active man had the managing. The tithes here as in all the Churches in Cant: arise by so much a household. About a 100 in this Parish, whereof many let now by Lease at low Rent & fines, which causes the abatement. Parish full of Sectaries and Schismatiques. The Incumbent professes he makes not much more than £40 of it.
Arthur Kay

All Saints Cant
R; K 07.00.00; C 20.00.00 or 30.00.00 at most; The King
Mr. Rich. Burney   A person of parts sufficient, if a good man had them in keeping. A smooth tongued man, but vaine, bragging, & somewhat Dissolute; He is much in debt, & for his Protection sworn Chap: to his majesty in Extraordinary. Does things many times irregularly, as marry without License or Bannes to which end a little money goes far with him. Yet in all companies talks of nothing so much as his Loyalty, Conformity & sufferings upon those Accts.

---

[1] A false start.
[2] United to St Mary's Northgate in 1681. Hasted, XI, 210.
[3] French-speaking refugees, from what is now Belgium, engaged in weaving. They had been allowed to use their own form of worship in the undercroft of the cathedral, but Archbishop Laud had forced them to conform and attend their parish church. Hasted, XI, 93.

Parishes	Kg Books	Com. Value	Patron	Incumbents	
2 Gorinich — R.	05.15.02½ 40.00.00.	E. Finch	Mr Wm Osborn:	Old person favouring Presbytery; The Sumer — a pretty lyge place, chiefly Freeholders and mingled w a last — principall part: most part.	
St George's Cant: — R.	07.17.11. 30.02.40	Cb. of Cant.	Mr Solo: Potier Bury Canon of Cathedrall.	For Cath: Lingdon fol. 15. [Insufficient for Scholarship, [crossed out text] ... fol. about 80. or 90. Comfirm. the Cach: Rate left by 2d of Cold Hugh Park.	
				Mr Elias Robinson	
Herbaldown — R.	09.02.06. 100.00.00.	Arch. Bp.	Dr Jo: Bargrave Canon of Cant:	Inc Thomas fol.18. Will Known to ye Grace. Has neg[lec]ted his Living now, not about 70. Sim. Fanatical in ye Parish but not contentible, about 40. Families, ye Easter about 30. Communicants, not was thought a great Reformation.	
Had 2 for 9 parva — R.	07.19.09½ 60.0. Bar.	Tho: King.	Mr Greg: Gulford.	A good man, L. of good parts. A gentleman in ch. Leach, Vic. Clausum of com: in difficulty will to Ch. att. but his misfor. [illegible] cheap. off. 40. Families in ye Parish, ch. 10. Chief of gone to Ceylon.	
St Michells Cant — R.	07.19.02. 50.00.00.	Tho: King.	Mr Sam: Andrew. [illegible] Curate Mr John Augusten.	A young man of good Schollarlike parts. Endeavours [illegible] ... [illegible] ...	
St Margarets Cant — C.	00.00.00.30.02.40.	Arch D. Cant.	Mr Wm Hawkins, City Canon of Cath. Pauls. A man of good Parts, Regular in his Judgment and in Church, to well Read by Several men.		

Cosmus Bleane
V; K 10.00.00; C £40 or £50; Eastbridge Hospital[4]
Mr. Stephen Sackett   ~~An Ancient man Mr of the said Hospitall, of wary Principles, But shows himselfe conformable enough to the Church.~~   See Westhith in Limpne.

St. Dunstans Cant
V; K 05.00.00; C £20 or £25; ArchBp. Imp
~~**Mr. James Penny**~~ Dead   ~~A good honest, but poore man, hath been in it many yeares, Aged neer 80, or full so much.~~
~~**Mr. Robert Boys**~~ Dead   Vacant[5]

Folio 2

Fordwich
R; K 05.15.02½; C 40.00.00; Lord Finch
Mr. Wm. Osborne[6]   A person favouring Presbytery; The Towne a pretty bigge place, And the Inhabitants and minister alike principled for the most part.   See East Langdon fol. 15

St. Georges Cant
R; K 07.17.11; C £30 or £40; Ch. of Cant.
~~**Mr. Blasé White**~~   Petty Canon of the Cathedrall, {…}[7] of ~~good~~ ^sufficient^ parts for Schollership, {…}[8] About 80 or 90 houses in the Parish. Tithe rises by 2d per £ House Rent.   See Stonar fol. 18
Mr. Elisha Robinson

Harbledown
R; K 09.02.06; C 100.00.00; ArchBp.
Dr. Jo. Bargrave   Prebend of Cant: well known to your Grace. He says he makes of his living now, not above £70. Some Fanaticks in the Parish but not considerable, About 40 Families. Last Easter above 30 Communicants, which was thought a great Reformation.

Hardres parva
R; K 07.19.9½; C £60 or better; The King
Mr. Gregory Pulford   A good man, & of good parts. No gentleman in the Parish; The Parishioners come indifferently well to Church, all but two inconsiderable Anabaptists. 40 Families in the Parish, And 10 Acres of glebe to the Parson

---

[4] Founded in the twelfth century for lodging poor pilgrims, it was, by the seventeenth century, an almshouse for some ten poor, elderly, residents of Canterbury, but it also had a school for poor children. A Master governed it. Hasted, XII, 115.
[5] Probably vacant from 1666 until Henry Hughes became vicar in 1676. John Sargenson, James Fowler and Henry Hughes were curates in 1671, 1674 and 1675 respectively. KHLC, DCb/L/R/17–27, pp. 45-7.
[6] This is William Osborne junior. The reference to 'East Langdon fol. 15' is an error.
[7] '& best singer there', Bodl., MS Tanner 124, fo. 208.
[8] 'and every way to be liked; if he be not a little too much a good fellow. About 100 houses.' *Ibid.*

St. Mildred Cant
R; K 07.19.02; C 50.00.00; The King
~~Mr. Jam. Arderne~~   A yong man of good Schollerlike parts. {…}⁹
~~Mr. Simon Louth~~
Mr. John Sargenson

St. Margaret Cant
C;¹⁰ K 00.00.00; C £30 or £40; ArchDeac. Cant.
Mr. Wm. Hawkins   Petty Canon of Cathedrall; A man of good playne parts. Right in his judgement for the Church, & well liked by discreet men.

Folio 3

St. Mary Bredman Cant
R; K 09.00.00; C £20 at most;
Long time vacant¹¹ This is a very poor living, now hardly worth £15 a year. There have been heretofore endeavours to have it united to St. Andrews aforesaid. The Church standing within 60 paces of it, and a very small parish.

St. Mary Bredin Cant
V; K 04.00.7½; C 20.00.00; Heirs of Mr. James Hales Imp.
Mr. Wm. Lovelace   A man of good parts & Principles, & very well liked.

St. Mary Magd. Cant
R; K 04.10.0; C £20 or £25; Ch. of Cant.
Id. **Mr. Lovelace**

St. Mary Northgate Cant
V; K 11.19.04½; C £25 or £26; ArchBp.
Mr. John Stockar aforesd   See St. Alphage aforsd

St. Martins Cant¹²
R; Ex; K 06.05.02½; C 30.00.00; ArchBp.
Mr. Wm. Osborne ~~aforsd~~¹³   See Walmer fol. 19.   See Guston fol. 21.   ~~See Fordwich Page 2~~

---

[9] Richard Burney was the rector, 1662–4, followed by James Arderne, who was 'A yong man of good Schollerlike parts but vaine & unlike a Clergyman in his hayre & habit & garbe, followed by Presbyterians & Schismatiques & proud of his Popularity.' *Ibid.*

[10] Hasted says that St Margaret's was a rectory and institutions of rectors are recorded. Hasted, XI, 233; CCA, AddMs-79.

[11] Francis Taylor was rector from 1648 to 1662. The parish was vacant in April 1664 but Edmund Burges was licensed to the cure in December of that year and signed the Compton census as curate in 1676. The dean and chapter of Canterbury cathedral was patron, and the church was united to that of St Andrew's in 1681. Matthews, *Calamy*, p. 477; Hasted, XI, 210; Whiteman, p. 19.

[12] United with Canterbury St Paul in 1682. LPL, CM I/52.

[13] This is, again, William Osborne junior. The 'aforsd' and 'See Fordwich' should not have been deleted and the references to Walmer and Guston are errors.

Milton by Cant
V; K 04.14.04½; C 30.00.00;
Mr. Greg. Pulford aforsd   See Hardres Parv Page 2

Folio 4

St. Peters Cant
R; K 03.10.10; C £20 or £25; Chu. of Cant.
Vacant[14]
~~Pead Duel~~[15]

Nackington
Cur; K 00.00.00; C £10 ~~Stipend~~ ^Church Dues^ £40 Augment: lately, out of St. Gregories Lease.[16] In all £50; ArchBp.
Mr. Greg. Pulford aforsd   A small Parish, & of meane persons.   See Hardres Parv

St. Pauls Cant
V; K 09.18.09; C £20 or £22; Chu. of Cant:
Mr. Wm. Jordan   Petty Canon of the Cathedrall: A good, sober, Civill person, and of good ordinary parts. Tithe 2d per £ House Rent. Communicants in the Parish (if they would come) about 400. Durant a Washball maker, & Minister there in Cromwells Dayes now a great keeper of Conventicles in the Parish, & elsewhere in Cant.

St. Stephens als Hackington
V; K 05.02.07½; C 80.00.00; ArchDeac. Cant
Mr. Wm. King   A person of good parts, & discretion, well esteemed, betweene 30 & 40 yeares old.   See Hothfield fol. 37.

Sturry
V; K 13.01.08; C £36 or £40 at most; ~~Lord Strangford Imp~~.; {…} ArchBp. Patron
Mr. Tho. Jones   Lord Strangford Impropriator. The Incumbent a good old poore man, of parts sufficient for so meane a living, & so small a Parish.

Thannington
C; K 00.00.00; C £40 Augment. Out of St. Gregories. Surplice dues £10 in all £50; ArchBp. Imp.
~~Mr. Jam. Arderne~~ aforsd   See St. Mildreds Page
~~Mr. Paul Boston~~
~~Mr. Simon Bayley~~   v. St Mary in the Marsh fo. 30
Mr. Robert Garret

---

[14] The living was probably vacant until Elisha Robinson was noted at the 1670 visitation. The parish register transcript of 1671 is signed, as rector, by Richard Burney, and by Duel Pead in 1672, but in 1673, the churchwardens report that 'Our Minister, Mr Duel Peade, is gone away wee know not whether.' Burney resumed signing from 1675 until 1692. United to Canterbury Holy Cross Westgate in 1681. Cowper (1888), p. x; Hasted, XI, 210.

[15] Duel Pead.

[16] The estate of the ancient priory of St Gregory, Canterbury, became part of the revenues of the see of Canterbury in the sixteenth century and augmentations were made to several parishes. Hasted XII, 144.

Folio 5

Westgate Holy Cross ^Cant^
V; K 13.00.02½; C £30 or better; ArchBp. Imp.
~~Mr. Arderne aforsd~~   See St. Mildreds Page
Mr. Simon Louth

St. Maries by the Castle Cant.[17]
R; K 02.18.01½

Westbere Deanery

Birchington Chapel annexed to Monkton vide;   See Monkton Parva[18]

Folio 6

Chislett
V; K 29.19.11; C 40.00.00; ArchBp. Imp. Pat
~~Alex. Cooke~~   Mr. Rose Tennant, who as is sayd alliaged the Vicaridge to be worth about £80 and so no further examination being made, he has his lease sealed, with no Augmentacon to the Vicar, which now the Vicar & Parish peticon for; The Vicar a crazy man, but ~~of~~ a good man, & of parts sufficient for a better living.
Rchd. Howard

Hoath Cap. annexed Vic: de Reculver   vid. 7
C 40.00.00; ArchBp. Imp. Pat

St. Johns Thannet
V; K 08.00.00; C 50.00.00 No Augmentation; ArchBp. Imp. Pat
~~John Overing~~   The Incumbent a ~~yong~~ sober man of good ~~ordinary~~ abilities. Makes not above £43 of the living. Viz Stipend of the ArchBp. £8 Small tithes 14.10.0 Brookland 30 Acres 1.10.0. Glebe & Barne 18.0 Wheat from the Parsonage 2 Bush. 10s Vic: house £3. Parishioners about 1000 Men women & children, of which Capt. Newman & Capt. Petitt the chiefe both friends of the Church. Not 100 Commun: last Easter. Easter booke ought to be 3d a person. Parishioners come all to the Church, but not very conformable in it, rather out of a rude clownishnesse, than any factious or peevish opposition.   See St. Nicholas at Wade 7
Nicholas Chowney

Hearne
V; Ex; K 20.16.03; C 80.00.00 rather more; ArchBp. Imp. Pat
John Webb   A conforming Intruder.

---

[17] Demolished, probably in the sixteenth century, and united with Canterbury St Mildred. Richard Burney and Simon Louth were among those instituted as rectors of St Mildred with St Mary de Castro. LPL, VG 1/2 fo. 33, 1/4 fo. 5v; Hasted, XI, 271.

[18] 'Parva' is an error.

St. Laurence in Thannet
V; K 07.00.00; C 50.00.00 viz Patron £46 Stipend out of Newland Grange Glebe £3 Besides the Easter booke which if duly payd worth £12; ArchBp. Imp. Pat
Mr. John Young
A person of abilities sufficient, but his Discretion questioned. In the parish 2 parsonages viz. Newland Grange Mr. Barker tennant to the ArchBp. at £300 Ozington Grange, La: Finch tennant to the Dean & Chap. at £200. All the small tithes goe in the Lease of Salmeston Grange which belongs to the ArchBp. which Grange is accounted worth £300. The Parish full of Presbyterians of whom the leader is Johnson the late Minister put out for Non-Conformity.

Monckton cum Capella de Birchington predicta
V; Ex; K 13.08.04; C 80.00.00 if the most made; ArchBp. Patron Dec. Cap. Cant. Imp
Mr. John Ayling A yong man of good parts. Bp. of Rochester Warner Tennant to the Impropriacon. Families in the parish viz in Monckton 20. in Birchington 100 or more. Out of most houses there were Communicants last Easter. Parish in pretty good order. In the parish the chiefe are Capt Rooke, Capt of the County troupe, & Capt. Crips of Quexe, honest gent & Justices of Peace.

Folio 7

St. Nicholas At Wade
V; Ex; K 15.19.07; C £50 or £60; ArchBp.
Nicholas Chowney A person of Right Principles. See St. Johns 6

Minster
V; K 33.03.04; C £200 or £250; ArchBp.
Dr. Castilian Prebend of Canterbury. The Impropriacon belongs to the Church of Canterbury. The Parishioners indifferent good.

St. Peters in Thanet
V; K 09.00.00; C 80.00.00 so made up by Augmentation from the Church of Canterbury; ArchBp.
~~**Mr. James Shipton**~~ A good man, Mr. Adey Church tennant; worth £80 a yeare about Rent. Families in the Parish about 60. Heretofore about 500 Communicants. No gentleman in it, But Culmers sonne ^whose father was^ an Independent Preacher Anabaptist, Quaker, anything now dead; This Culmer comes to Church. Parish full of Seamen: The most all dull ~~wordly~~ worldly men. The place a Member of Dover.[19]
Mr. Luke Proctor

Reculver cum Cap de Hoath predicta
V; K 09.12.03½; C 50.00.00 £20 Augment; ArchBp.
~~**Mr. Rob. Godden**~~ A person right for the Church.
Mr. Hen: Hughes

---

[19] The parish was within the jurisdiction of the Cinque Port of Dover. Hasted, X, 236.

Seasalter
V; K 11.00.00; C £30 or £40; Chu: Cant. Imp. & Pat:
Mr. Math. Smith A man of right principles & parts good enough for his Living but poore.

Swalcliffe
R; K 11.09.04½; C 80.00.00; Mr. Ayres, or Mr. Barnham of London
Mr. Dan. Cuckow An honest man & right for the Church.

Folio 8

Westbere
R; K 07.00.00; C £40 or therabouts; The King
Mr. Giles Hinton A person ~~not~~ ^yong &^ well ~~knowne~~ ^esteemed^ ~~because lately put in~~. See Faversham Fol: 51

Whitstable
C; C £10 Stipend; ArchBp. Imp. Pat
Mr. Math Smith aforesaid   Sir Wm. Willoughby that married Sir Morrice Abbot's daughter tennant
Bps present £30 Improvement £100 Parish well affected, All farmers & but meane. About 400 soules. The lease for 3 lives, and in being only. Memorandum to move for Augmentation to the Curate, when{…} renewed.   See Seasalter fol. 7.

Bridge Deanery

Adisham cum Capella de Staple
R; Ex; K 28.03.01½; C 200.00.00; ArchBp.
Dr. Du Moulin Prebend of Canterbury. Speaks well of his Parish.

Folio 9

Ash
C; Ex; K 00.00.00; C Old Stipend 16.13.04, £50 Aug. out of Ash, £10 St. Gregories, £10 out of Marshland,
[Total] 86.13.04; ArchBp.
Mr. Benchskyn An Ancient grave man Bachelor in Divinity, of Right Principles, & scholler sufficient, A quiet man, but not much relished by his parish which is large, about 700 Communicants, pestered with Presbytery, & some factious persons, but the greatest part good dull Earthworms.

Bridge Chapel annexed to Patrixbourne   See Patricksbourne fol. 12.

Bishopsbourne cum Cap de Barham
R; K 39.19.02; C 350.00.00; ArchBp.
Dr. John Lee Arch-deacon of Rochester. A good charitable man. The Parishioners for the most part well affected to the Church.

Barham Chapel annexed to Bishopsbourne   See Bishopsbourne aforesaid

Beakesbourne

V; K 06.00.00; C 40.00.00 10 Augment. out of St. Gregorys; ArchBp. Imp.

~~Mr. John Edmonds~~   mort   A good man. Sir Rob. Honywood tenant to the parsonage worth about £60. Persons of quality in the parish Sir Rob. Hales & Dr. Sabin an Aldermans sonne of Cant. of a great estate. About 20 houses in the parish 5 of which Farmers the rest most labourers. Independents about a 3rd part and come not to Church. The heads of them Capt. Monings, Mr. Jo. Francis under tenant to Honywood Geo. Simpson once keeper of Cant. jayle. Wm Lorrington Carpenter with their whole families. Chancell bad, Church worse, Steeple falling. No Clarke, No font, No Surplice, No Kings Arms.   See Fol. 29 Ivychurch   Mr. Aldworth accused to be hinderer of the Augmentacon, that it was no incr.

~~Mr. Edw. Ladbroke~~
Mr. Obadiah Brokesby

Brooke

R; K 07.07.01; C 30.00.00; Chu. of Cant.

~~Mr. David Nairne~~ lately resigned   ~~A Scott, but a good man.~~
~~Mr. Wm. Johnson~~[20] resigned   ~~A good Scholler, But a meacke man.~~[21]
~~Mr. John Stokes~~
Mr. John Ansell

Folio 10

Bocton Aluph

V; K 06.05.00; C 60.00.00 of which a Gleabe worth £12; La. Moyle married Th. Godfry Esqr at Mayhoe

Mr. Henry Nicolls   A pittifull man, of parts scarse sufficient for a minister, Once an Apothecary, after a Petty Cannon of the Cathedr. at Cant. The Church finding him weake, gave him £10 to quitt his place there. In the Parish, there were last Easter Communicants about 60. The Church & Chancell in pretty good repayre, The Vicaridge house much in decay. The Incumbent says the living is not worth about £40 a yeare in all. Mr. Godfry the Patroness husband & Impropriator holds the Parsonage in his own hands. Anabaptists Ralph Frembley & Daniel Savery ordinary fellowes. The Church is provided of Surplice & Com. Prayer booke.

Chilham cum Capella de Mold:Ash

V; K 13.06.08 vid. Id. fo. 12; C £80 in good times £60 at most now; Heirs of Sir Thom Kempe

Mr. Rob. Cumberland ~~Bach of Arts~~   A Presbyterian. In the Parish about 50 or 60 houses, in all about 120 Communicants, Last Easter about 40 recd. Parishioners for the most part well enough affected all but 5 persons, whereof 2 Anabaptists, 3 Quakers all meane persons. Chu. & Chancell in indifferent repayre; No Font; No Surplice. Persons of quality in the parish Mr. Diggs a melancholy crackd man. Mr. Fagge sonne (as I take it) of Col. Fagge in Sussex and one Mr. Spraling.

---

[20] Johnson was preceded by Henry Cuffen, who was instituted in April 1667, but died within three months.

[21] Comment refers to Johnson.

Chartham
R; K 41.05.10; C 200.00.00 £250 of old; ArchBp.
~~Mr. Jo. Reding~~ mort   ~~Prebend of Canterbury, well enough known to be no extraordinary man.~~_ A Swerving man. The Chancell is sayd to be in good repayre. The Church not soe, or but indifferently well. Noe Surplice. Families about 60 in the parish. Parishioners for the most part come to church. Parish troubled with three or foure Quakers, whereof one Perry the Chiefe, the rest inconsiderable.   See Cheriton fol. 20.
Dr. Sam. Parker

Chillenden
R; K 05.00.00; C £40 at most; The King
Mr. Joh. Cullen   Usher of the Ks Schoole at Canterb. About 20 Houses in the Parish No Gentleman in it All are Farmers & husbandmen; And come all to Church except one Silvester Neame a farmer who is Independent. Church & Chancell newly repayred. They have Com. Prayer Booke, but no Surplice.

Crondale
R; K 11.10.10; C £70 or £80; Heirs of Mr. Reynold Kempe
Mr. Rich. Allen   An honest good man.

Challock Chap to Godmersham
Chap; Ex; C £10 Augmentacon vid. Godmersham fo. 11.
~~Mr. Nath. Collington~~[22]   A person of right principles. There is £10 Augmentation pd ~~by~~ to the Minister by the Earle of Winchilsey Tennant to the ArchBp.   See Godmersham fol. 11.
~~Mr. Dan. Butler~~
Mr. Richard Munn

Folio 11

Elmstone
R; K 06.07.08½; C £40 or thereabouts; Heirs of Mr. ^Wm.^ Gibbs
Alex. Bradley   A good ingenious yong man.

Godmersham with Chap of Challock
V; Ex; K 09.03.09; C 50.00 of old and by Augment from the ArchBp. £10 The Church - £10 in all £70 The Church pays but £10; ArchBp. or Chu. of Cant Imp
~~Mr. Nath. Collington~~[23] aforesaid Resigned ~~A good man~~. Major Brodnax the chiefe of the parish. No persons in it very refactory, But some Disputers.   See Tenterden fol. 38
Now ~~Mr. Dan. Butler~~
Mr. Richard Munne
^~~Mr Q~~^[24]   **Mr. James Christmas** - 10 July 82

---

[22] Nathaniel Collington senior.
[23] Nathaniel Collington senior.
[24] A query whether James Christmas had an MA. It was noted when he was ordained in June 1682. His institution to Godmersham is stated to be in July 1682 but this may be an error. CCEd Person ID: 138305; Foster, I, 275.

Goodnestone by Dover
C; ArchBp.
Vacant[25]

Hardres mag with the Chap. of Stelling
R; K 19.13.01½; C 160.00.00; Sir Edw. Hardres
Dr. Hardres   Prebend of Canterbury. The Parishioners well affected all but one woman an Anabaptist. Church in good repayre. The Tithes farmed out by the Dr. now at £120.

Ickham cum Cap. de Wells
R; Ex; K 29.13.04; C 180.00.00; ArchBp.
~~Dr. Meyrick Casaubon~~   Prebend of Canterbury. A little Parish, but tainted with Presbytery. No person of fashion in it but one Mrs. Southland. Their lives in it 2 Brothers Goddards, a Carpenter & a Mason both Anabaptists. The Church in good repayre, but no Font nor Surplice; both in making. The Parsonage house much decayed.
Dr. Parker

Kingston
R; K 16.00.00; C 100.00.00; Sir Anths Aucher now Dr. Primrose Sr Ant Aucher
~~Mr. Nich. Dingley~~   A pure Presbyterian, came in first upon the Sequestration of Dr. Blechinden He acknowledges the living £80 in tith, £10 glebe. Houses about 46. in the parish Sir James Wilford & Mr. ~~Marsh~~ John Marsh chief Inhabitants. The rest ordinary persons & many poore. Incumbent complaynes of one Quaker & one Anabaptist, but sayes nothing of Presbyterians. Church & Chancell sayd to be in good repayre.
Mr. Robt Aucher

Folio 12

Littlebourne
V; K 08.02.06; C £30 in Tithes £50 Augment.; Chu. of Cant. Imp.
~~Mr. Rich. Langham~~   Petty Cannon of Cant. a good sober man, Mr. Norton tennant to the Church payes the Augmentacon. Families in the Parish about 60 amongst which some but inconsiderable persons, Anabaptists. Church in good repayre & Surplice providing.
Mr. John Gostling

Molash Chap. to Chilham   vid fo. 10;
Mr. Rob. Master   Curate, a person lately come, and not much knowne yet.

Nonnington with the Chap. of Wymingswold
 C; Ex; C 13.06.08 Stipend 20.00.00 Aug.; ArchBp. Imp.
Mr. Sam. Wells   Of right Principles.

---

[25]   Peter Pury senior signed the parish register in 1661 and probably remained in this perpetual curacy until his son took over in 1682. CCA, U3/232/1/1.

Petham
V; K 08.00.02½; C 30.00.00; Mr. Haddes his heirs Improp.
~~Vacant~~[26]
Mr. David Terry   Jul 9th ^1669^

Preston by Wingham
V; K 09.15.00; C £30 or £40 at most; Chu. of Cant. Imp. ArchBp. Q
Mr. Alex Bradley aforesaid   See Elmstone fo 11.

Patricksbourne with the Chap. of Bridge
V; K 05.07.03½; C 40.00.00; Sir Edw. Partherich
~~Mr. John Fidge~~   ~~A yong vapouring Blade~~
Mr. Jo. Mackallir   A Scott, of ordinary parts.[27]

Folio 13

Stelling, Chap. to Hardres mag.
K 00.00.00; Sir Edw. Hardres
Dr. Hardres   See Hardres mag. fol. 11.

Stodmarsh
Cur; K 00.00.00; C 40.00.00; ArchDeac. Imp
Mr. Tho. Russell   See Brensett fol.

Sturmouth
R; K 19.00.00; C 120.00.00; Bp. of Rochester
Dr. Hen. Parkhurst   A right man for the Church. The Parish small, not above 14 houses. The best person a Farmer; All orderly enough.

Staple Chap. annex. to Adisham
Ex; K 00.00.00   See Adisham fol. 8.

Wickhambreux
R; K 29.12.06; C 250.00.00; Mr. Brown of Bucks
~~Dr. Belke~~[28]   ~~Prebend~~ of Canterbury. In the Parish houses about 40 But not a quarter of them come to the Communion, though most goe to the Church.
Dr. Tho. Belke

Wye
Cur; K 00.00.00; C £40 old stipend; ArchBp. Imp.
Mr. Jeremy Dodson   A person right for the Church.

---

[26] No incumbents or curates have been found, so it may have been vacant until the appointment of David Terry in 1669.
[27] Comments refer to Mackallar.
[28] William Belke.

Folio 14

Waltham
V; K 07.15.05; C £30 of old, £20 Augment. out of St. Greg. in all £50; ArchBp. Imp.
Mr. David Terry   A good honest playne man lately put in by your Grace; at the recommendation of Dr. Casaubon.   See Petham fol. 12.

Wingham
Cur; Ex; C 23.13.04; Sir Tho. Palmer
Mr. Samuel Stephens   Right for the Church.

Wymingswold Chap. to Nonnington
Cur; Ex   See Nonnington fol. 12.

Folio 15

Sandwich Deanery

Barfrayston als Barston
R; K 07.14.02; C £50 almost £60; Sir Tho. Boise heirs now Mr Ewell of Herne
Richard Edwards   A person but little known. Parishioners all commers to Church. Church in good repayre, but noe Surplice.

Bettishanger
R; K 06.04.04½; C 40.00.00; ~~The King~~
Mr. Tho. Brett   A St. Johns man, not long since putt in, conceived to be right.

Coldred
V; K 06.02.06; C £30 at most £20 Augm.; ArchBp. Imp
Mr. Jonas Owen   Bachr. in Divinity. A grave good man.   See Sibertswold fol.

East Langdon
R; K 07.00.00; C 40.00.00; Rich. Master Esqr
~~**Mr. Wm. Osborne senr**~~   A Presbyterian. Parishioners of meane quality, a Carpenter & a Cobler the most refractory in the parish.   See Fordwich fol. 2.[29]
Mr. John Dawling

St. Clements in Sandwich
V; K 13.16.10½; C 100.00.00; ArchBp. Imp. Pat. Q if not Arch. Deac. Arch. Deacon Q de Jure Archi. Epi
~~**Mr. Benj. Harrison**~~ cession   A good man. Parish consists of about 200 houses, which pay tithes at 2d. 3d. 6d. & some 12d per £ Rent. Full of Sectaries and grossly ignorant persons.
~~**Mr. Wm Coleman**~~

St. Clements in Sandwch.
Mark Parker[30]

---

[29] An error. William Osborne junior was rector of Fordwich.
[30] An addition made in 1677.

Folio 16

Deale
R; Ex; K 19.10.0; C 120.00.00; ArchBp.
Mr. Edm. Ibbott   a yong man of good parts. A Convert from Presbytery or Independency. 1500 Commun. whereof 200 or thereabouts received last Easter. They all generally come to Church. Not above 20 Sectaries, whereof Capt. Taverner the Chiefe. Church & Parsonage house in good repayre. But they have no Font nor Surplice. a member of Sandwich.
Mr. Henry Gerrard

Eythorne
R; K 15.12.06; C £100 or 120; Sir Ed. Boys & Sir Wm. Monings
Tho. Walton   A Presbyterian. A very good Parsonage house.

Eastry with Chap. of Worth
V; K 19.12.01; C £60 or £70; ArchBp. Pat.
Mr. John Whiston   a ~~right~~ good man. ^& a good Scholer, but weake in his discretion ^ Chu. of Cant. Imp. Sir Geo. Sonds tennt for the Corne tithes worth £55 per annum. No Augmentation here although he hath 2 Churches to serve. Sir Geo. that he should be forced to make an augmentacon holds off from renewing. Mr. John Boys of Betshanger holds 300 Acres of marsh in the parish of the ArchBp. for which no tithes to the Vicar worth £300 per annum at least. 300 or 400 Commun. in the parish. Not above 120 recd. last Easter. Eastry free from both Presbyterians & Sectaries but Worth pestered with Sectaries. Church in pretty good repayer. Vicaridge house very ill.

Hamme
R; K 05.06.01½; C 60.00.00; The King
~~Mr. Jam. Burville~~   One of the 6 Preachers at Cant. A right man. The Tithes are lett now to Mr. Rich. Sands for £50 per annum. Church in good repayre. Families but two in the parish.
Mr. John Plymley   inst. May 78;

Knowlton
R; K 06.05.02; C 40.00.00; Sir. Tho. Payton
Mr. Petr. Pury   A man much commended for his parts & life.

Mongham mag
R; K 18.05.00; C 120.00.00; ArchBp.
~~Mr. Jo. Sackett~~   {...}[31] The Church is much out of Repayre. preaches in the Chancell. Parish much infested with Sectaries, poore persons. One third of the parish at least absenters from Church. Noe Surplice. Sir Rich. Sandys, Sir Tho. Payton Sir Edw. Monins the nearest Justices.
Mr. Henry Ullock

---

[31] 'kept in all these late tymes Presb. heretofore but now Conformable, speaks much of his being well known & beloved by Sir Thomas Moore. Noe Gleabe.' Bodl., MS Tanner 124, fo. 217.

Folio 17

Northbourne with the Chap. of Shoulden
V; K 12.11.08; C 50.0.0 or £60 at most for both.; ArchBp. Imp.
Mr. Jam. Burville aforesaid   ArchBp. Imp. Mr. Aldworth tennant. No Augmentation, though two Churches to be served. Sir Rich. Sandys Justice of Peace inhabitant. About 40 families. Full of Anabaptists & Quakers, whereof Wildbore, Slaughter and Verier are the Chiefe, poor fellowes. Church in good repayre; Font and Surplice in making.   See Hamme fol. 16.

St. Peters Sandwich
R; K 08.00.00; C £40 or £50; King and the Towne by turns.
~~Dr. ^Rob.^ Wilkinson~~   ~~Entered into the parish upon the Sequestracon of Dr. Oliver living at Adisham.~~ [32] Mayor & Jurats live most in this Parish and are so so *sic* affected. Presbyterians & Sectaries much infest this parish & whole towne. Capt. Wilson once Dep. Governor of Dover and one Peake heade the Factions. Noe Surplice, nor any will be indured. The Church fallen downe, but now rebuilding. Incumbt. hopes well (as to his part) of the Parish, because he comes in at their desire.   See East-Church in Shephey. fol. ( )
~~Mr. Tho. White~~[33]
~~Mr. John du Bray~~
Mr. Gervas How

St. Mary Sandwich
V; K 08.01.00½; C £50 at most £60; Arch.Deac. Cant.
John Lodowick   A Fleming, lately put in; Of parts very sufficient. A sober man, & right for the Church, though he seemes to affect preaching after the Presbyterian modell & measure. 200 Houses in the parish. Many Dutch & Flemings. Many Sectaries & Enemies to the late King, & some Petitioners for his death.

Riple
R; K 05.19.04½; C 60.00.00; Sir Wm. Crayford ~~Inc. hath the next advowson~~
Mr. Wm Stanley   Thought to be a very good man.

Ringwould
R; K 13.12.06; C £100 or little less; Sir Ch. Sedley. Incumbt hath the next Advowson.
Mr. Rich. Dawling   Conceived to be a very right man. Houses about 30 in the Parish. Parishioners for the most part frequenters of the Church. Church in good repayre. Village a Member of Dover port.

---

[32] Dr John Oliver was sequestrated from Adisham in 1655 and replaced by Francis Quinton. In 1656, Robert Wilkinson was appointed to Staple, chapel to Adisham. Robert Lovell was rector of Sandwich St Peter from 1639 until, at least, 1642, but there is then a gap in the records until the appointment of Robert Webber in 1654, ejected in 1662. Oliver may therefore have been at St Peter's. Matthews, *Calamy*, pp. 223, 516; LPL, COMM III/4, fo. 114, III/5, fo. 656; CCEd Person ID: 46220.

[33] As rector, John Lodowick approved the appointment of the parish clerk in 1666, but by 1668 he had been sequestered. White would have been the sequestrator. Willis (1975), p. 34; Bodl., MS Sancroft 99, p. 162.

Sibbertswold, als Shepheardswell united to Coldred
V; K 06.00.00; C 20.00.00 £20 Augment. in all £40; ArchBp. Imp. Pat.
Mr. Jonas Owen aforesaid   See Coldred; fol. 15.

Folio 18

Sutton next Dover
Cur; C £10 Old Stipend; ArchBp.
Mr. Tho. Brett   see Bettishanger   See Bettishanger fol. 15.

Mongeham parv Ecctia Desolata
R; K 05.15.00; C 30.00.00; ArchBp.
Mr. Clemt. Corutier   a Frenchman.

Shoulden Chap.
see Northbourne   See fo. 17.   See Northbourne fol. 17.

Stonar Ecctia Desolata
R; K 03.06.08; C 10.00.0; Sir Hen. Crips
~~Mr. Blasé White~~ aforesaid   See St. Georges Cant. fol. 2.

Tilmanston
V; K 07.12.06; C 40.00.00 £40 Augment.; ArchBp. Imp. Pat.
~~Mr. Hump. Dicas~~   A man of good parts & principles, but in some things indiscreet; He is tennant to the ArchBp. at £6 rent, Improved worth £50. 20 houses in the Parish, but not above 20 ~~that~~ persons that comes to the Commun. Sir Tho. Payton Ld. of the Mannor. Mr. Fogg the Chiefe man in the parish. Wm Neale Taylor, John Ayres Carpenter notorious Anabaptists. Church much out of repayre, Chancell well. No Surplice.   See Beauxfeild fol. 20.
Mr. James Burvil junr.

Waldershare
V; K 05.06.01½; C £20 at most £20 Augment. when the tenant enjoyes the Lease.; ArchBp. Imp. Pat.
Vacant

Folio 19

West-Langdon
Cur; C £12 old Stipend Q What Augment.; ArchBp. Imp. Pat.
Mr. Wm. Stanley[34]   see Riple   See Riple fol. 17.

---

[34] Should be William Osborne senior, for this and the Walmer entry have been transposed.

Walmer
Cur; C £8 old Stipend £20 Augment.; ArchBp. Imp. Pat.
Mr. Wm. Osborne senr[35]   see East Langdon   See St. Mart. Cant. fol. 3.[36]   See Guston. fol. 21.   See East Langdon fol. 15.

Woodnesborough
V; K 10.00.07½; C 40.00.00 Q What Augment.; Dec. Cap. Rochr.
Mr. Joseph ~~Jackson~~   A good grave able man, & well esteemed.   ~~See Eastry fol. 16.~~
~~Mr. John Beck~~
Mr. Isaac Lovell

Worth Chap. to Eastrye   See Eastry fol. 16.

Folio 20

Dover Deanery

Alkham cum Cap. de Capleferne
V; K 11.00.00; C 30.00.00 no Augment.; ArchBp. Imp. Pat.
Mr. Sam. Pownall   an old man formerly sequestered; An indifferent good person. Wm. ~~Thornham~~ ^Sherman^ Tennt. to the ArchBp. The Vicars sonne his undertennt. at £245 a yeare. ~~Mr. Evering of Evering.~~ Communicants 200 at least but not above half receivers now. Many Anabaptists Independents & Quakers followers of Mr Davis of Dover. ~~No~~ Church out of repayre. No Surplice. The Churchwardens unwilling to provide it: The Living once worth £50 a year.

Beauxfeild, als Whitfield
Cur; K 07.08.09; C £20 at most £20 Augment.; ArchBp. Imp. Pat.
~~Mr. Humph. Dicas~~ ~~aforesaid~~   Wm. Baker tenant to the ArchBp. Tho. Cullen undertenant at £70. About 30 families in the parish. Communicants about 60 but not above 10 last Easter. Church & Chancell in good repayre. A Surplice in making. Sir Edw. Monins & Mr. Masters next Justices.   See Tilmanstone fol. 18.
Mr. James Burvile[37]

Buckland by Dover
V;[38] Ex; C 20.00.00 £12 Augment.; ArchBp.
~~Mr. Tho. Perne~~ ^ mort^   A person whose principles are doubted.
~~Mr. Jo. Harman~~[39] ~~A German~~
~~Barney Wm~~
Mr. Wm. Burney[40]

---

[35] Should be William Stanley.
[36] William Osborne junior was rector of Canterbury St Martin.
[37] James Burville junior.
[38] Buckland was a perpetual curacy. Hasted, IX, 468-9.
[39] This is John Herman Romswinckell and the comment refers to him.
[40] The scored-through William Barney is correct.

Charleton
R; C 30.00.00; Tho. Monings olim
~~Mr. Tho. Perne aforesaid~~ ~~mort~~ See Buckland fol. 20.

Cheriton
R; K 16.12.06; C £100 or £120; Jam Brockman Esq. of Bichborough
~~Dr. John Reading~~[41] ~~aforesaid mort~~ The Parishioners generally well affected & come to Church. Chancell in good repayre. Church pretty well. No Surplice. The Incumbent sayes he makes little above £80 of it. See Chartham fol. 10.
~~vacant~~
Mr. Jonathan Dryden

Folio 21

Capleferne chap. to Alkham
See Alkham fol. 20.

Ewell
V; K 06.13.04; C £20 at most; Ed. Ducy and Andr. Asthare
Mr. Wm. Russell   A Peevish man, otherwise indifferent good.

Folkstone
Cur; K 10.00.02½; C £10 old Stpd. £70 Augment.; ArchBp. Imp. Pat.
~~Mr. Nich. Brett~~ ~~resigned~~   The Rectory & Vicaridge leased to Sr Arnold Brames at £300 R. Parish very full of Fanaticks.
~~Mr. Tho. Tomkyns~~
Mr. Miles Barnes   A grave good old man.[42]

Guston
Cur; Ex; C 13.06.08 old stipend; ArchBp. Imp. Pat.
Mr. Wm. Osborne sen   Right in his judgmt & practise for the Church.

Hougham St Lawrence
V; K 06.13.04; C 50.00.00 £25 Augment.; ArchBp. Imp. Pat.
~~Dr. Swadlin~~   A {…} person well known. Mr. Percivall tenant to the ArchBp. Parsonage worth about £160. The Vicaridge accounted heretofore £50 a yeare before the Augmentation.
~~Mr. Bostock~~
Mr. Wm. Brewer

Hawking
R; K 07.08.01½; C £40 or £50; ArchBp.
~~Mr. Alex. Udney~~   ~~A Scotsman~~ Recommended by Sir Arnold Brames.
~~Mr. Peter Bonny~~
Mr. John Barham

---

[41] Called 'Dr. Reading' here but 'Mr.' on fo. 10. DD not found but Foster, III, 1242, says BD.
[42] The comment refers to Barnes.

Folio 22

St James Dover
R; Ex; K 04.17.08½; C 50.00.00; ArchBp.
~~Dr. Swadlin aforsd~~   A Parish full of Sectaries. The Incumbent sayes he makes not £30 of it. The tith arises on land tith is £20. The rest on the pound Rent by houses. Mr Davis formerly an ordayned minister a cheife countenancer of Sectaries & Conventiclity. Luke Howard a Shoemaker chiefe of the Quakers. Church and Chancell in good Repayre, and a Surplice providing.   held as heretofore by Sequestr.   See Hougham fol. 21.
~~Mr Bostock aforsd~~
Mr. Brewer aforsd

Liddon
V; K 06.06.00½; C 10.00.00; ArchBp. Imp. Pat.
~~Mr. Wm. Russell~~ aforsd   See Ewell fol. 21
~~Mr. Pearne Andrew~~[43]
Mr. Tho. Griffin[44]

St Mary Dover
Cur; Ex; C £05 stipend Q What allowance from the towne.; King
~~Dr. Hind~~   a Person travelled much, and well knowne
~~Dr. Swadling~~
~~Hind~~
Dr. Hind sed Q[45]

St Margarett le Cliffe
V; Ex; K 06.10.00; C 40.00.00 £26 Augment.; ArchBp. Imp. Pat.
Mr. Wm Barney   A Person very right. Sayes he makes of the tithes but £15 a yeare & £26 Augmentation. Dr. Wilford tenant to the ArchBp. Lease worth about £140. Mr. Tuck & Mr. Gibbons very good persons, dwellers in the parish. John Finnis a Carpenter, his wife & daughter Anabaptists, & so one Oliver a Schoolmaster. Noe other irregular persons in the parish. 80 Communicants last Easter; Surplice providing. Church in good repayre. Vicaridge house decayed and not habitable.

Newington by Hythe
V; K 07.12.06; C 40.00.00; Sir Wm. Brockman
Mr. Cha. Harfleete   Conceived to be right, as he ought.

River
V; K 07.01.00; C £10 or little more; ArchBp.
~~Vacant~~[46]
Mr. Jo. Harman[47]

---

[43] John Herman Romswinkell held the sequestration of Lydden from 1666 and was vicar from 1670 until his death in 1673.
[44] Thomas Griffin junior.
[45] Hind resigned in 1663, but returned after a short incumbency by Swadling.
[46] Probably held by William Russell.
[47] John Herman Romswinckell.

Folio 23

Swinkfeild[48]
Cur; C £16 stipend; Sir Tho. Palmer Lo. Strangford ArchBp.
Mr. David Nairne   See Brook fol. 9.

Sheperheath[49]
V
Mr. John White

WestCliffe
Vic. or Cur;[50] K under value; C £09 old Stipend £24 Augment.; Chu. of Cant.
Mr. Wm. Barney   But 2 Families in the parish: Church much out of repayre.   See St. Margarets at Cliffe fol. 22.

St. Peters in Dover[51]
R; K 04.00.00
Ecctia desolata

Elham Deanery

Acryse
R; K 07.00.00; C 80.00.00 £100 if the best made of it; King
Mr. John Floate   A person indifferently well qualified. About 20 houses in the Parish. last Easter, and so ordinarily at other times about 20 Communicants. No Papists nor Sectaries in the parish. Church in good repayre. No Surplice: Mr. Lewknor a well affected person lives in the parish. Mr. Brockman, & Sir Norton Knatchbull next Justices.

Folio 24

Brabourne
V; K 11.12.06; C 40.00.00 £16 Augment.; Mr. John Cadman Q now ArchBp. Imp. & Pat.
~~Mr. John Rosse~~   ~~An ancient weake timorous man~~ Dead
Mr. Wm. ~~Brabo~~[52] **Johnson**   Mr. of Arts of parts sufficient; Married & a good playn man.[53]   See Brook fol. 9.

---

[48] Swingfield.
[49] Sheperheath is not one of the parishes of Canterbury diocese or one of the archbishop's peculiars. It is the parish of Shepreth, in the diocese of Ely, in Cambridgeshire. John White was instituted as vicar on 5 September 1672 but not inducted.
[50] Barney subscribed as vicar in 1662. CCEd Person ID: 67490.
[51] Last recorded as in use in 1611. Hasted, X, 542.
[52] The scribe about to write Brabourne.
[53] The comment refers to William Johnson.

Bircholt

R; K 02.10.10; C 10.00.00; Mr. Hawke Ob Q
~~Mr. John Rosse~~ aforsd[54]   See Brabourne before fol. eodem
Mr. Christopher Harris

Denton

R; K 05.19.04½; C £100 at least of old. Now as the Incumbt sayes not more than £80; Mr. Andrewes of Denton
Mr. Wm. Lunne   A yong very ordinary man, but seems right enough. Parish very well affected, About 30 Families. Usually about 40 Communicants at the great times. Church & Chancell in good repayre: & Com. prayer booke & Surplice.

Elham

V; K 20.00.00; C 50.00.00; Coll. Merton Ox: Imp. & Pat. ArchBp. noiacun Q
Mr. Hen. Hannington   {…}

Elmstead

V; K 06.13.04; C 30.0.0 £20 Augment out of St. Greg. in all £50; ArchBp. Imp. Pat.
~~Mr Spencer~~[55]   A person suspected to favour Presbyterianism
~~Mr. Charles Kay~~[56]   A Scott
~~Mr. Richards Samuel~~
Mr. Samuel Ricards

Horton monachorum

R; K 07.10.10; C 50.00.00 reall value by old composition for tithes. House & glebe worth £10 [Total] 60.00.00; ArchBp.
~~Mr. Sam. Smith~~ ^resigned^   A good man. ~~A long time sequestered & restored.~~ Capt. Rooke Ld of the manor. The Church in good repayre & all things decent & fitt in it   See Braborne fol. 24 ante hac fol   ~~See Eastbridge fol. 28~~
~~Mr. Wm. Johnson~~
Mr. John Richards

Folio 25

Hithe ~~with the~~ Chapell to ~~of~~ Saltwood annexed

Ex
See Saltwood fol. 26.

Hastingleigh

R; K 10.05.00; C 80.00.00; ArchBp.
Mr. Henry Pibus   A good honest playne man. He says he makes but £60 at most. The Hosp. of St. Thomas in Southampton Lds of the Mannor. Families about 20. The best, Farmers & tenants to the Hospital. They come indifferently well to Church. No Sectaries or Schismatiquies, but some few a little leaning. Chancell in good repayre, Church in repayring. No Surplice. Sir Norton Knatchbull next Justice.

---

[54] Rosse was instituted to Bircholt in September 1662, but must have died sometime before the institution of Simon Howe in January 1664. The latter should have been listed after Rosse.
[55] John Spencer.
[56] Arthur Kay succeeded John Spencer and was succeeded by Charles Kay, the Kays were both Scottish.

Liminge with the Chappels of Paddlesworth and Stanford
R; Ex; K 21.10.00; Sir Anthony Aucher ArchBp. Q
I do not find that any of late have been presented or Collated to the Parsonage. The Cure with the Chappells belongs to the Vicars charge. Sid Quare.

Liminge V
V; Ex; K 10.18.09; C 40.00.00; ArchBp. Q. Mr. Roberts of Lyminge, presented the last time & claymed the Patr.
Mr. Miles Barnes   An ancient good man. Sequestered all the times of trouble. Deserves a better place. Mr. Roberts holds the Parsonage. Parish indifferently well affected About 300 Commun. of which Last Easter 150 or more. Mr. Scott brothers sonne to Sir Ed. Scott of Scotshall a Refuser to come to Church. No Papists, Some Quakers, of which Rich. Holman the Chiefe. The Church in good repayre. The Chancell mending. Vicaridge house halfe fallen downe.

Postlinge
V; K 06.08.01½; C £30 or £40; ArchBp. Imp. Pat.
~~Mr. James Kay~~   vid. Dymchurch.
Mr. Basil Kennet

Paddlesworth Chap. annexed to Lyminge R.
See Lyminge V fol. eodem

Folio 26

Saltwood
R; K 34.00.00; C £120 of old. The incumbt sayes but £80 at most now.; ArchBp.
~~Mr. Thomas Carter~~   Hath beene in a long time. An Intruder but now a Convert & conformable. Families in the parish about 16. No Sectaries. Church in good repayre. Communion table, Font, Surplice, and all things decent.   Lady Honywood   v. East Bridge 28   See Hith fol. 25.
Mr. Francis Peck

Stowting
R; K 07.17.11; C 100.00.00 old; Sir Tho. Kempe The Incumbt hath bought the perpetual patronage with 6 acres of land to which the Patr. is appendant.
Mr. Reginald Ansell   Presbyterianly affected as is thought. About 30 Houses in the Parish and 90 Communicants. No Papist, nor notoriously fanatick. Church well repayred. Commun. Table, Font & Surplice. Mr. Brockman & Mr. Norton Knatchbull next Justices.

Stanford Chap. annexed to Lyminge   See Lyming. fol. 25.

Wodeton als Wotton
R; K 08.10.02½; C £80 Coibus an; Jo. Coppin Esqr
~~Mr. Jonas Owen~~ aforsd   A good grave man. Two women only 2 refusers to come to Church. Sir Tho. Peyton, Sir Ed. Monins & Major Boys of Nonnington the next Justices.   See Sibertswold fol. 17.
– Garret[57]

---

[57] Robert Garret.

Folio 27

Limpne Deanery

Aldington cum cap. de Smeth
R; Ex; K 38.06.08; C 150.00.00; ArchBp.
~~Mr. Elias Juxon~~ mort   A person of about 36 or 40 of good parts, & well esteemed. On *sic*
Mr. Allan Eales[58]

Appledore cum Cap. de Eboney
V; K 21.00.00; C £100 or £120 140 as the Curate there for 25 years tells me;[59] ArchBp. Imp. Pat.
Mr. Francis Drayton   A yong man of ~~good~~ parts & esteeme, indifferently good. The parish well affected. Sir Cheyney Culpepers Lady Lessee to the ArchBp. of the Parsonage.

Bonnington
R; K 10.13.01½; C £60 or neere it; Sir Wm. Man
Mr. Joyner Brook   Indifferent good man. The Glebe worth £16. Parish lyes on the Edge of the Marsh. Some tith corn, but the most Marsh. Marsh land pays 12d per Acre and is about 500 Acre. The upland pasture, which is much more payes 6d. Earl of Thannett & Capt. Tuck are the owners of the marsh land and a good deale of the parish. The Parishioners almost all Lookers[60] They have Com. Prayer booke & Surplice.

Blackmanston sine Cura Ecctia desolata
R; K 04.00.00; C £40 or ~~£50~~ really worth as is sayd heretofore.; ArchBp.
~~Mr. Wm. King of Warlingham in Surrey~~   No Church, or Chappell, But one shepheards house, & one Cottage in the parish. I am told, it is now farmed out at less than £20. v. Burmarsh 28   See Sittingbourne p. 48.
Mr. Geo. Jones

Bilsington
Cur.; Sir Mart. Barnham
Mr. Norton Knatchbull

Folio 28

Burmarsh
R; K 20.10.10; C £50 or £60; ~~ArchBp~~.   King
Mr. John Hurt   A person right for the Church. vid. Sittingbourne 48 & Blackmanston 27.   See Milton fol. 46.
Mr. George Jones

---

[58] The arrow is in the manuscript.
[59] From 1646 until 1660, Appledore had been served by three vicars: John Richards, John Vaughan and Thomas Hieron, all of whom had moved on, or died, by 1660.
[60] Looker was the local name for a marshland shepherd. The term is used again in fos. 28, 30, 31, 38, 46 and 48 below (Brenzett, Brookland, Eastbridge, St Mary in the Marsh, Orgarswick, Ruckinge, Newenden, Eastchurch and Tonge) but they were also present in other parishes. Reeves and Eve, pp. 191–207.

Brensett
V; K 07.18.11½; C 60.00.00; Sir Wm. Brockman
~~Mr. Tho. Russell~~   An ancient person & an ~~very~~ ^ordinary^ good man ^long sequestered^. Sir Wm. Brockman Ld of the Manor & Parson. The vicar his tenant to the Parsonage. Parish consists all of Lookers, who all come to Church.
Mr. George Gipps

Brookland
V; K 17.12.08½; C 80.00.00 Q whether so by Augmentation.; Chu. of Cant. Imp. & Pat.
Mr. Tho. Russell aforsd.   A parish all of Lookers, playne, conformable country fellowes. Church in good repayre; ~~but~~ no Surplice.   See Brensett immediately next before.

Dimchurch
R; K 07.02.08½; C £50 or £60; King
~~Mr. Rich. Burton~~   Sir Edw. Deering Lord of the Manor. Parishioners about 200. None of quality Come to Church generally well.
Basil Kennet   w. Postling

East-Bridge   sine cura Ecctia desolata
K 05.06.08; C £30 or little more; ArchBp.
~~Mr. Sam. Smith~~ ~~aforsd~~   A very good man. The tith consists all in pasture at 6d per Acre. Sir Edward Deering hath a good part of the land of which a ~~good~~ ^great^ part tith free. No Church. Not above 3 or 4 houses in the parish. All marsh land. Parishioners only Lookers.   v. Saltwood f. 26   See Horton Monachor fol. 24.
Mr. ~~Francis Peck~~[61]

Eboney   Chap. to Appledore
See Appledore fol. 27.

Folio 29

Fairfield
Cur; Ex; C 13.06.08 Stipend Q Augmentation.; Chu. of Cant.
Mr. Henry Cuffen   A person of right Principles.

Hinkshill
R; K 07.16.08; C 50.00.00; Lady Knollis & Now Sir Geo. Chute
~~James Wilkinson~~ ~~Mr. of Arts~~   mort   Conceived to be a good man. Sir Geo. Chute Lord of the Manor. Parishioners 18 Families. Most frequenters of the Church.
Mr. Jo. Jemmett

Hope All Saints[62]
R; K 10.01.00½; C 50.00.00; King
Joh. Bale Med. Dr.   A very good man.

---

[61] Francis Peck was preceded by John Hurt.
[62] The church would have been a ruin by 1663. Hasted, VIII, 419.

Herst als Falconherst sine cura Ecctia desolata
R; K 04.18.04; C 20.00.00; Parker fo. 390 Rev. Contulit racoe Lapsus
Mr. Reginald Carew   A good man.

Ivechurch
R; Ex; K 44.16.08; C 200.00.00 or not much less; ArchBp.
~~Mr. Robert Boys~~   mort   A person very right.   See fol. 9 Beaksbourne
~~Mr. Edw. Ladbroke~~
Mr. Obadiah Brokesby

Kenardington als Kenarton
R; K 12.01.00½; C 50.00.00; King
~~Mr. Rich. Lightfoot~~ mort[63]   Conceived to be a right man.
Mr. Nath. Collington[64]

Folio 30

Kingsnothe
R; K 11.09.09½; C £50. or better; Sir Nath. Powell ArchBp.
Mr. Nath. Wilson   Not well knowne, but by report conceived right. Sir Tho. Scot Lord of the Mannor. Yong Honywood a Roundhead lives here. Parish generally well affected. One Godden the only Non-conformist & he promises faythly.
Mr. Timothy Wilson

Limpne als Limne
V; K 09.01.03; C £30 or £40; ArchDeac. Cant.
vacant[65]

Lydd
V; Ex; K 55.12.01; C £250 or better; ArchBp.
~~Mr. Edw. Wilford~~[66]   Parish very full of Sectaries & Schismatiques which must trouble the parson & are ill paymasters of the tithes.
Mr. Henry Jeriard

St. Mary in the Marsh
R; K 23.03.09; C £80 by the Incumbt. Acct. but £60 at most.; ArchBp.
^Mr. Henry Hurt Curat & likewise of Burmarsh under Mr. Jones of Sittingbourne^[67]
~~Mr. Wm. Hawkins~~[68]   Recom. Per Ld. Halyfax   A good able man, and one of the Petty Canons of Cant. Parishioners not above 50 persons. All of meane quality, Marsh Lookers. All come well to Church. The way of tithing is 12d per Acre payment by Custom. Corne but little; Sir Charles Sedley, Sir Edw. Hales & Sir Rob. Honeywood

---

[63] Lightfoot was not dead; he had ceded the rectory and moved to Chadwell St Mary, Essex. CCEd Person ID: 46162.
[64] Nathaniel Collington senior.
[65] John Malbon was vicar, 1662–6, and Peter Bonny was curate in 1670.
[66] Wilford was followed by George Screven and then Jeriard (Gerrard).
[67] This comment, in a different hand, could not have been inserted until George Jones was instituted to Burmarsh in 1673. LPL, VB 1/3/193.
[68] Henry Hurt was curate to William Hawkins who was the 'good able man'.

owners of all land in the parish. 1734 acres of Pasture Land which after the rate of 12d per acre amounts £80 14d per annum. House & Glebe Rented at £3 15s per Annum {…} comp. for all the Corn Tith at the Rate of 5s per acre amounts but to £6.7.6 scarse not like to be recovered.   v. Thannington   See St. Margaretts Cant. Fol. 2.
~~Mr. Simon Bayley~~
Mr. Henry Hurt   1 Sept. 79

Mersham
R; K 26.16.10½¼; C £180 of old £120 now; ArchBp.
~~Mr. Geo. May jun   A person of good very good parts, modest & discreet. Very well esteemed and one of the 6 Preachers at Cant.~~ There is 40 or 50 acres of glebe worth £20 or £25 at least. Parishioners in all points very conformable by the discretion of the Incumbt. & the Helpe of Sir Norton Knatchbull who lives in the Parish.
~~Dr. Castilion Preb. of Cant.~~
Mr. John Cooke

Midley Ecctia desolata
R; K 30.00.00; C £80. or better; ArchBp. Onim ex concessione Dni Windsor. Mr. Alan Cliff
~~Mr. Duke~~[69]
Dr. Henry Eve

Folio 31

Newchurch
R; Ex; K 08.04.02; C 10.00.00; ArchBp.
~~Mr. Paul Knell~~   ~~A person right for the Church~~.
Mr. May senior   A worthy grave man.[70]

Newchurch
V; Ex; K 19.16.0½; C 100.00.00; The Parson
~~Mr. Paul Knell~~   ~~aforesaid~~ who was presented by the late Parson Mr. Yates.
~~Mr. May senior~~
Mr. Ed. Sleighton   A person of good parts and life.[71]

Orlaston
R; K 04.10.10; C £45 or £50; Sir Tho. Scott of Scott Hall
~~Mr. Mark Sherman~~ mort   ~~A man of Right principles.~~ Glebe 140 Acres worth £10 Sir Tho. Scott Lord of the Manor. None of Quality in the parish. No Sectaries. Church in repayre. No Surplice yet.
Mr. Robert ~~Richards~~[72]
            Powel

---

[69] Duke was followed by Henry Bankes, noted in visitations until 1680. KHLC, DCb/V/V/64, 69, 74.
[70] The comment refers to May.
[71] The comment refers to Sleighton.
[72] Richards was succeeded by William Stringer, followed by Roger Powel.

Orgarswick sine cura Ecctia desolata
R; K 03.00.00; C 15.00.00; Chu. of Cant.
Mr. Wm. Jorden　　But one Lookers house in the Parish & no Church. Lett to farmer by the Incumbt. at 13.10.00
See St. Pauls Cant. fol. 4.

Ostenhanger Ecctia desolata
R; K 07.12.06
Church fallen down. Lord Strangford lives in the parish.

Rucking
R; K 14.13.04; C 120.00.00 by the Incumbents Acct.; ArchBp.
Mr. Rich. Marsh　　Prebend of Tottenham[73] in St. Pauls London. A good scholler But some question his discretion. Parish on the Edge of the marsh. Tith 12d per Acre. Pasture Parishioners all Lookers. The Parson hath a pretty deale of tithe wood & Corne Compoundable at pleasure.

Folio 32

Promehill Ecctia desolata

Seavington
R; K 08.13.11½; C £30 or £40; Sir {...}Boys[74]
~~Mr. Simon Howe~~ afsd.[75]
Mr. Edw. Sleighton M.A.　　See V. Newchurch fol. 31.[76]

Sellinge
V; K 06.19.02; C £40 at most; King ArchBp. Q
Mr. Rich Burton　　Sir Peter Heyman Lord of the Manor Parishioners indifferently well affected. Church out of repayre. No Surplice. 24 Apr. 76.[77]　　See Dimchurch Fol. 28.
Abdias Morris

Shaddoxherst
R; K 07.12.11; C £40 at best; King
~~Mr. Robt. Cole~~ ~~of Bethersden~~　　A small parish of inconsiderable persons for quality. Some pretty good Families, most husbandmen. Quiet & pretty free from Sectaries.　　See Bethersden fol. 35.
vacant
Timothy Wilson

Smeth Chap. annex. to Aldington
Ex
See Aldington fol. 27.

---

[73] Totenhall.
[74] Sir John Boys.
[75] See under Bircholt fo. 24 and fo. 24 n. 54.
[76] This refers to Sleighton.
[77] Institution date of Abdias Morris.

Snave
R; K 19.07.11; C 50.00.00 or thereabouts; ArchBp.
Mr. Tho. Snelling   A person right for the Church.

Folio 33

Snargate
R; K 17.06.08; C £50 or thereabouts; ArchBp.
~~Mr. Wm. Lawder~~
Mr. Tho. Snelling

Stone in Oxney
V; K 08.12.08½; C £60 at most. No Augmentation.; Chu. of Cant.
Mr. Wm. Bryan   A yong man, right for the Church. Parishioners about 100 meane quality. Indifferently well affected. Church much out of repayre. No surplice yet.

Romney nova
V; Ex; K 06.16.03; C 60.00.00; All Souls Coll. Oxon.
Mr. Rob. Bostock S.T.B.   ~~A very good man & well accounted~~ Sid Qu

Romney Ventris
R; K 15.19.02; C 100.00.00; ArchBp.
Mr. Wm. Carre   A good man, Beneficed in Essex. Q where & if dispensed.[78]

Warehorne
R; K 19.00.00; C 80.00.00 100.00.00; King
~~Mr. John Asherst~~[79]
Mr. John Coventry
James Perkins
Mr. Thomas Finney Curat

Westhith
V; K 08.14.04½; C £20. not much more; ArchDeac. Cant.
Mr. Steph. Sackett   Well enough for conformity.

Folio 34

Willesborough
V; K 08.16.08; C £30 scarse so much; Chu. of Cant.
~~Mr. Geo. May sen~~   A grave worthy man. One of the 6 Preachers of Canterbury. Mr. Masters Impropriator. Mr. Anth. Aucher & Mr. John Boys persons of about £200 a yeare, honest gent. live in the Parish. Parishioners indifferently well affected. About 200 Communicants in all.
~~Warley John~~
~~Mr. John Warley~~[80]
Henry Walker

---

[78] This probably refers to his failed presentation to Bexhill, Sussex.
[79] Succeeded by John Bromskell.
[80] Succeeded by Edmund Burges.

Wittersham
R; K 15.08.06½; C 100.00.00 140.00.00; ArchBp.
~~Mr. Sam. Crosswell~~ ~~A Conforming Intruder.~~ Persons of quality in the Parish none. Some Sectaries, one Wm. Tufton & his wife Anabaptists & Henry Beane that went about with a petition against Monarchy. Church in pretty good repayre. They have a Com. Prayer booke, but noe Surplice. See Appledore fol. 27.
Mr. Francis Drayton[81]

Woodchurch
R; K 26.13.04; £130 some say £150; ArchBp.
Mr. Steph. Mund A Converted Presbyterian.

Folio 35

Charing Deanery

Ashford
V; K 18.04.02; C 80.00.00; Chu of Rochr
~~Mr. Rich. Whitlock~~ A person of very sufficient parts, and acknowledged by his Parishioners to be of a good life. But for his asserting & maintaining the Doctrine & Ceremonies of the Church of England hated by his Parish; who are all generally stiffly Presbyterian. Bate & Stringer the worst, And Naylor a Lawyer & one of Oliver's justices a great Patron of them. One Hawtry is the best principled man in the town. Sir Norton Knatchbull a new Justice, a good friend to the Church. The living worth in small tithes £30 Glebe £30 Easter Book & Casualties about £20.
~~Mr. Tho. Risden~~
~~Mr. Tho. Warren~~[82]
Mr. Sam. Warren

Bennenden
V; K 17.12.06; C £40 or £50 at most; Sir Joh. Henden or Mr Watts
Mr. Rich. Monyman[83] Accounted a good honest man. Mr. Watts aforesaid Lord of the Manor of Fanatick principles. The Parish generally Presbyterian. Geo. Hammond James Blackmore, Starre, & Hadley great ringleaders of the Sectaries and poysoners of the People.

Bethersden
V; K 12.00.00; C £40.00.00 and £30.00.00 Augment. Out of St Gregories. In all neer £80.00.00; ArchBp. Imp. Pat.
Mr. ~~Rob. Cole~~ A man of good parts & sound principles. ^but full of vaine bragging intercourse^ Sir Rob. Honywood Impropriator. Sir Geo. Chute, Rich. Hulse Esqr, Andrew Liddell Esqr persons of best quality in the Parish, & Mr. Hulse a good friend to the Church. Those that come to Church are very Conformable; But there are many absentees. Parishioners about 800 of them 120 Communicating persons. The

---

[81] Francis Drayton junior.
[82] An error.
[83] Nicholas Monyman.

Parish much poysoned by Geo. Hammond, Wm. Pollard, Jo. Rich. Steph. Chapman, & Tho. Birchin Violent fanaticks.
{…} **vacant**
Mr. Richd. Rands

Biddenden
R; K 35.00.00; C 200.00.00 formerly, now £160 or thereabouts; ArchBp.
Mr. Moses Lee   A person of ~~god~~ good parts & sound principles, thought by some to be too busily zealous for the Church. The living formerly lett for £200. Hath £20 glebe, but the incumbent sayes he makes not £160. Sir Jo. Henden the only person of quality in the parish; About 120 Families in all of which 80 are Schismatiques & Fanaticks. Geo Hammond a taylor Jam. Blackmore a farmer, Rob Hurst a Thatcher, Tho. Moore a Shewman, all Teachers & great Poysoners of this parish & parts neere.

Bocton Malherbe
R; K 13.15.00; C £60 or £70; La. Wotton
~~Mr. Rob. Ellis~~
Mr. Michael Stanhope

Folio 36

Charing Cum Cap. de Egerton Q.[84]
V; Ex; K 13.00.00; C50.00.00 Q. what Augm.; Chu. of St. Paul Lond.
~~Mr. Hen. Ridgeway~~   A person very Orthodox & of good ordinary parts, & good life Diligent in preaching & Catechising. Dr. Sabin tenant to the Parsonage worth £140. Sir Rob. Honywood & his Sonne in the parish, some speake well of the Sonne. Major Wheeler a Low-Country Soldier very Orthodox exhorts his children to Catechising. Parish of 6 miles Extent in length. Last Easter about 100 Communicants. Church in pretty good repayre & all things decent enough, though in a playne manner.
Mr. John Shephard

Chart mag.
R; K 25.06.00½; C 200.00.00 total worth; ArchBp.
~~Mr. Wm Axon~~ mort   A very worthy man, sober, grave, & well esteemed by Clergy & Laity. Ch. of Cant. Ld. of the Mannor. Capt. Tuck an honest gentleman, & of a great estate lives in the parish, a great friend of the incumbent. The Parish by the Definition of the Incumbent made generally good. Not above 2 Families Presbyt. or Sectaries. The Incumbent put in by ArchBp. Laud, sequestered 17 years, restored at the Ks returne. Letts his living for no more than £140.
~~Mr. Tho. Tomkins~~

Chart par.
R; K 13.10.10; C £80 or better; ArchBp.
Mr. Fran. Drayton senr   A very good grave man. Sir Jo. Darell Lord of the Mannor. lives in the parish. Parishioners indifferently well affected to the Church.

---

[84] Egerton was a perpetual curacy. Hasted, VII, 454; *AC*, 30, p. 184.

Cranbrook
V; K 19.19.04½; C £80 or neere it; ArchBp.
Mr. John Cooper   A man of good parts, & zealous principles for the Church, if he knew how to govern them to his best advantage. The parish very great, at least 3000 Communicants in it, of such not above 200 usually come in a year. Pestered with all sorts of Non-Conformists above 1000. Geo. Hammond aforesaid Nich. Birch, Bennet, Colvill, Remmington etc Ringleaders; Wm. Goodrich the late Intruder a dangerous fellow. 500 anabaptists in the parish. Noe Justices nor gentlemen in the parish. The incumbent sayes he makes not much more now than £60 tithes, & that very ill payed. Vicaridge house much ruined. The Church of Canterbury Impropriators.

East-Well
R; K 09.16.08; C 60.00.00; Earle of Winchilsey
Mr. Nich. Toke   A very good painful and diligent man. The glebe is worth £12 a year being £16 clear No Sectaries in the parish, But some loose persons Drinking Ale the parish Impropriate to the Earle. Church in good repayre & all things decent in it.

Egerton
Cur; Q. whether a Cure of itself or appendant to Charing
Vacant & in private hands

Folio 37

Frittenden
R; K 15.18.09; C 80.00.00 at least; Mr. Web of the same place
~~Rob. Clarke   Somewhat suspected, because he hath kept in for 17 years together during all the troubles & changes~~ Mr. Web aforesaid Lord of the Mannor.
Stephen Worgar

Halden, als High-Halden
R; K 19.04.07; C£100 or £80 at least well worth; ArchBp.
Mr. John Crawford   A good Scott. Says he makes not above £60 a yeare. Sir John Henden Lord of the Manor. Lieutenant Jordan a good man the Chief man in the Parish. Parish ill affected, Much poysoned by Hammond & his complices the great Seducer.

Hawkhurst formerly a Vicaridge; now goes as a Curacy
Cur; K 12.10.00; C £20 Salary no Augment.; Eocscl. x^{ti} Coll. Oxon Eccl. X^{ti}. Oxon. Dec & Canon ibin.
Mr. Jonath. Pleydall   A good ordinary man, of parts much better than his stipend. The Dean & Can. of Xti Church Oxon Improp. Wm. Skinner brother to Augustine, the tenant to the Parsonage, which is worth £160. A large parish of about 1500 Communicants, but not above 20 or 30 receive. Pestered with all manner of Sectaries, Geo. Hammond the great Seducer; Wm. Hosman, Tho. Goldsmith, John Payne, & Tho. Chittenden, great abbetters & Maintayners of conventicles in their houses.

Hedcorn
V; K 15.13.04; C 60.00.00 at most; ~~St. Jo. Coll. Cambr.~~ ArchBp. Q
Mr. Tho. Philips   A poor meane qualified man. The Parsonage appropriate to St. Jo. College
Mr. Samuel Whiston

Hothfeild
R; K 17.05.00; C 100.00.00 Acknowledged by the Incumbent; Earle of Thannett
Mr. Wm. King   A very good man, Diligent, modest, & of good parts. E of Thannett lives in the Parish. Parishioners very conformable, no Sectaries, Nor stiffe Presbyters. Last Easter 160 Communicants; The parish but small.   See St. Stephens[85] fol. 4

Kennington
V; K 12.00.00; C 30.00.00; ArchBp. Imp.
~~vacant~~[86]   A place pestilently infested with all manner of Sectaries, About 50 Families in the Parish. Single one but Schismaticall.
~~Henry Walker~~

Folio 38

Newenden
R; K 07.13.04; C 50.00.00 £80 Reall value; ArchBp.
~~Mr. Hieron~~   {…}
~~Mr. Brown~~   litigious
       ~~The incumbent a poore honest man, in prison at Maidstone for debt upon an Executorship.~~ The Parish full of Fanaticks, & Schismatiques. Lookers and Labourers are most of the Inhabitants. No considerable person. Bothell a Shoemaker & Willsted a Farmer two Insolent & turbulent Quakers live in the Parish.
~~Mr. Brown Thomas~~ prsbyt
~~Mr. Walter Collins~~[87]
Mr. David Maccorne

Pluckley
R; K 20.01.05½; C £100 or £120; ArchBp.
~~Dr. John Bargrave~~   Parish indifferently well affected.   See Harbledowne fol. 2.
Mr. Nathaniel Collington[88]

Rolvenden
V; K 10.00.00; C 40.00.00 Q What Augm. £10 Augm. by the liste; Chu. of Rochester
Mr. Rich. Morris[89]   A friend of Dr. Cooke of Rochester. A Parish much infested with Sectaries. Mr. Hammond a Merchant. Farmer to the Chu. payes to them £29 a yeare Renting Letts it to an Undertenant at £70.

---

[85]   Hackington.
[86]   The surname Sympson is noted as the vicar of Kennington in 1662, and Nicholas Toke was vicar, 1664–70.
[87]   Succeeded by James Kay.
[88]   Nathaniel Collington junior.
[89]   Instituted, but may not have been inducted.

Sandhurst

R; K 20.00.00; C 140.00.00 reall worth; ArchBp.

Mr. Walter Drury A good honest man in an ill parish. Makes (as he says) not £80 of the living £12 the glebe worth £10. About 60 houses in the parish, 300 Communicants, which of not above 20 receive in a yeare. All sorts of Sectaries pester it. Ringleoday Starre a New England Minister lived once at Carlisle; Bennet of Rolvenden great Preachers both. No gentleman of note in the parish. Mr Fowle the only gentleman like man & he not right; No Churchwarden, No Bible No Surplice. The best gentlemen neare hand, Sir Joh. Henden, Mr Sam. Boys. Mr. John Horsmonden of Goodherst & Colpeper of the same.

Smarden

R; K 24.02.06; C 120.00.00 reall worth; ArchBp.

~~Mr. Rob. Cole at Bethersden~~ Makes not £80 of it. A very disorderly parish. 1000 Parishioners, not above 200 come to Church. Att Easter last but 8 Communicants. Ringleaders of Sectaries Adman, Hirst, Arinir, Greene, Cooke, 2 notorious Pells, & Willis all violent fanaticks. Geo. Hammond the great poyson of these parts. Persons friends to the Church Richard Hulse Esqr in the first place, Sir Jo. Henden. No Fence to the Churchyard, Church out of repayre to the value of £200 at least.
Mr. Richd. Rands

Tenterden

V; K 33.12.11; C 100.00.00; Chu. of Cant. Imp. & Pat

Tenterden Free Schoole

Smallhith ^Chappell^ Curacy Both belong to the gift of the vicar, as is said by the Vicar. Vid. The Acts of ArchBp. Warham 1. Hen 8th[90]

Mr. Nath. Collington[91] A very good man. Sir Ed. Hales tenant to the Church of Cant. A parish much corrupted; Geo. Haw late Incumbent Presbyter: a great Seducer. A corporate Town & not one honest Justice in it. Mr. Hulse lives neare, but hath no power there. The towne is a Member of Dover. The Court there can only protect the minister, who is dayly affronted, but Q of Dover Justices.

Folio 39

Westwell

V; Ex; K 13.00.00; C 40.00.00 £30 Augment.; ArchBp.

Mr. Samuel Walsall A person right in his principles & conformity, & of indifferent good parts, well liked, of a good life & Diligent in his duty.

---

[90] This appears to be a claim, by Collington, to the patronage of Smallhythe Chapel and Tenterden School. In 1509, Archbishop Warham ordained that the inhabitants of Smallhythe could present a chaplain to the vicar of Tenterden for his approval. If his approval was not received within six days, then they could present to the ordinary. During the late sixteenth and early seventeenth centuries, the vicar of Tenterden sometimes recommended an appointee. There is no evidence that the vicar appointed the schoolmaster, although the school was built on glebe land. It was frequently the case that the curacy of Smallhythe and the mastership of the school were held by the same man. For details, see A.H. Taylor, 'The chapel of St. John the Baptist, Smallhythe', *AC*, 30, pp. 133–92, and 'The Grammar Free School at Tenterden', *AC*, 44, pp. 129–46, at pp. 133–4.

[91] Nathaniel Collington senior. His son, Nathaniel junior, was curate of Smallhythe in 1668 and 1670.

Sutton Deanery

Bersted
V; K 06.07.06; C 40.00.00; Church of Rochester
~~Mr. Fran. Drayton jun~~   See Appledore fol. 27.
~~Mr. Jo. Collins~~
Mr. Thomas Gregory

Bocton Munchelsey
V; K 07.13.04; C 60.00.00; Church of Rochester
Mr. Math. Rutton[92]   A person of parts sufficient.

Folio 40

Boxley
V; K 12.19.02; C 80.00.00 by Aug. Q how much; Church of Rochester Imp. & Pat.
~~Mr. Tho. Haynes~~ stet   A person of a little too loose a life, & too much a good fellow. ^{…} for the Presbyterian way^ Parsonage lease renewed to Mr. Rob. Parker worth £140. Presbyterian Fanatick or any thing. Debauched to a Proverbe. Little Tho. Haynes as drunke as a Devill.
~~Ben. Huntington~~[93]
Mr. Hum. Lynde

Broomfeild a member of Leeds
Cur; ArchBp.
~~Mr. John Moore~~   See Leeds fol. 42.
Mr. James Wilson

Bredhurst
Cur; Ex; C £26 or £30 per annum; Parson of Hollingbourne
A member of Hollingbourne & is disposed of as a Donative by Dr. Pory to Mr. Haynes Fellow of K's Coll. Cambridge, by Lease for term of Haynes his Life at 4 Nobles rent. All the tithes there being worth about £26 or £30. Dr. Boys possessed it in the same manner.
Mr. Tho. Haynes   Serves this Cure but not licensed. In many things he does too much patrizare. He hath besides this a Fellowship, or Schollership in Cambridge which makes him often neglect his cure. A small parish and but one considerable person in it.   See before Boxley fol. 40.[94]

Chart next Sutton
V; K 08.11.08½; C £30 or £40; Church of Rochester
~~vacant~~[95]
Mr. Peter Browne

---

[92] Matthew Rutton senior.
[93] An error, see under Bexley, fo. 55.
[94] The curate of Bredhurst was the son of the vicar of Boxley.
[95] Richard Whitlock was presented in June 1662, Daniel Alderne in October 1662, Richard Morris in June 1663 and Peter Browne was instituted in 1664. CCEd Person ID: 7215, 18, 64597, 7188.

Detling
V; Ex; K 09.00.00; C 30.00.00 Q what Augm. from the Church. The ArchBp. allowes 07.06.08 Aug. 02.13.04d.; ~~Chu. of Roch~~. ArchBp. Improp.
~~Mr. John Fryday~~   Right in his opinions for the Church & in his practise. But a weake man. Sir Charles Doe tenant to this impropriation, with Maydstone & all in one lease.
Mr. Andrew Reny

East-Sutton chap. annex. to Sutton Valence   See Sutton Valence fol. 43.

Folio 41

Frinsted
R; K 09.11.08; C £60 or £70; Mr. Haddes obt. Now one Thatcher an inveterate Enemy to the Church. Simon Hopper presented last.
~~Mr. Isaac Atkinson~~   A poor good man, but suspected to come in by Symony. att the Presentation of Sibil Nitingale by conveyance from Thatcher but controversial.
Mr. Wm. Payn A.M.

Goodherst
V; K 26.19.02; C 100 or better; Church of Rochester
Mr. Edw. Thurman   A Parish much infected with Sectaries & Presbyterians.
Mr. James Fenne

Harrietsham
R; K 11.10.00; C £100 or £120; All Soules Coll. Oxon
Mr. John Linch   A grave good man.

Hollingbourne with the Chap. of Hucking
R; K 28.16.05; C 120.00.00; ArchBp.
~~Dr. Rob. Pory~~[96]   ~~A person very well known.~~ ^stet^ Parsonage leased to Sir Tho. Culpeper at £039 Rt Reserved & £100 every 6 yeares. Worth upon Improvement £150 per annum.
Mr. Ralph Stanton

Hollingbourne with Hucking Chap.
V; Ex; K 07.06.08; C 060.00.00 by Augment.; ArchBp.
~~Mr. John Shrawley~~   A person of ~~parts sufficient & right judgement.~~ ^stet^ His Endowment is 40 in tithes, £20 Augmentation & from the La. Culpepers will Guarantee benefaction of £20. Parish ~~indifferently well affected~~ No noted ~~factious persons. All generally come to Church. Church in Repayre, Chancel in mending. Vicaridge~~ house well for the dwelling ~~part~~, but the Barne & stable are fallen downe.
~~Mr Ralph Stanton~~[97]

---

[96] Pory was succeeded by Anthony Saunders.
[97] Stanton was never the vicar of Hollingbourne. William Thomas was collated in 1668.

~~Halstow~~
Belongs to Sittingbourne Deanery.
V; K 08.02.00; Chu. of Cant.
Mr. Hen. Deering[98]

Folio 42

~~Hartlippe~~
Belongs to Sittingbourne Deanery
V; K 09.10.00; Church of Rochester
~~Mr. Ben. Crompe~~[99]   mort
Mr. Jo. Edwards

Hucking Chap to Hollingbourne
Mr. John Shrawley   See Hollingbourne fo. 41.

Langley
R; K 07.19.00; C 080.00.00; Sir. Edw. Hales
Mr. Peter Browne   A person sufficient for parts. Hath a glebe of 16 Acres. About 30 Families in the parish. Church & Chancell in good repayre. with Surplice & all things decent. Abell Beeching a Brownist a very troublesome & dangerous fellow & he is the Cheife man of the parish.

Lenham
V; K 13.15.02½; C £50 or £60; Sir Tho. Wilford Lo. Montague of Cowdrey Qu.
Vacant   Parish well affected. A large parish few pepoul of any quality one Mr. Wilkinson a justice ^of the^ peace. Church in good Repayre Font Common Prayer booke and all things decent. One Hammond who lives six or 7 Miles off comes there sometymes preaching & endeavours to drawe aside the weaker people as weomen etc.
Mr. ~~Laud~~ Lord[100]

Leeds with the Chap. of Broomfeild
C 12.06.08 Stipend £30 Augment.; ArchBp.
~~Mr. John Moore~~   See Broomfeild fol. 40
Mr. James Wilson

Linton
V; K 07.13.04; C 40.00.00; Mr. Martin a Minor Dr. Dukeson & Mr. Abberfeild guardian
~~Mr. Phineas Cosby~~   A good man for parts & principles. A parish well affected. Com. Prayer booke & Surplice. Church & Chancell in good repayre. No justice in the parish nor person of great note.
Mr. Andrew Reny

---

[98] See fo. 47.
[99] See fo. 47.
[100] Collated in January 1664.

Folio 43

Loose   Q Vic. or Cur[101]
Ex; ArchBp. Imp. Pat.
~~Mr. Lucius Seymour~~   A person of right Principles. Recommended by Capt. Buffkin
Mr. Walter[102]

Maydston
Cur; Ex; C 100.00.00 by Augment.; ArchBp. Imp. Pat.
~~Mr John Davis~~   A very good man, both for parts & life. The towne & parish much infected with presbyt. & Fanaticks, amongst whom none worse than the Jaylours widdow & her under Varlets. Adm he holds the Curacy by Licence durand beneplito And the stipend anciently but £20 per annum but no augmentation Seftis Grace grants him a Lease of all the small Tithes of the Boroughs or Towns of Brick and Stone within the Parish all the benefits of the Church yard of Maidstone all Surplice dues oblations that are known by the name of Alterayiat with the moyety of the Small Tithes or Vicarage Tithes of Maidstone.
Mr. Humprey Lynde   10 July '77[103]

Marden
V; K 07.14.04; C 60.00.00 20.00.00 Augment.; ArchBp. Imp. Pat.
Mr. Geo. Amherst   Lady Whitmore tenant to the Parsonage worth £120 per annnum.

Otham
V; K 09.17.03½
~~Mr. John Davis aforsd~~   See Maidstone fol. iod.
Matthias Rutton[104]

Royton Chap. annex. to Lenham   now Desolate

Sutton Valence with the Chap. of East Sutton annexed
V; K 07.09.06; C £80 of old not £50 now £24 Augment. to East Sutton by the ArchBp.; Church of Rochester
~~Mr. Tho. Pollington~~   A person of good life & abilities beyond his salary. The parish full of Sectaries above ~~a third part~~ 3 parts of 4. Communicants about 400 but scarce 20 attenders in a yeare. James & Henry Wickings Quakers, Tho Turner, Smith, Tho. Watkins & James Spier, Thomas & John Bp all very factious & pestilent Sectaries. resigned
Mr. James Browne

---

[101] Loose was a curacy.
[102] Henry Walter.
[103] This was the date that Lynde was licensed as the curate of Maidstone.
[104] Matthew Rutton junior.

Folio 44

Staplehurst
R; K 26.05.10; C 240.00.00; Mr. Clayton of London Scrivener
Mr. Steph. Sowton   A yong man ~~newly~~ not long since come in.
See ArchBp. Bancroft Regr. about an award & settlement of the Parsons dues & tithes fol. 125.176.

Thornham Cum Capella de Allington
V; K 08.00.10; C £40 or £50; Church of Rochester Mr. John Goddin of Paternoster Row sid. Qu.
Mr. Wm. Sutton
Henry Deering

Ulcombe
R; K 16.05.10; C 240.00.00; Sir Fran. Clerke
~~Dr. John Codd~~   mort   Prebend of Rochester. The Parish in pretty good order, but troubled with some Presbyterians.
Merick Head

Wormshill
R; K 10.00.00; C £70 or £80; Mr Dingley olim
Mr. Tho. Nightingale   An empty impertinent man. Vox et praetera nihil.

Folio 45

Sittingbourne Deanery

Bapchild
V; K 08.00.00; C 30.00.00 Q what Augm.; Chu. of Chicester
Mr. George Jones   A very good man. The Parish small, all of ordinary people.   See
Blackmanstone   See Sittingbourne fol. 48.

Bicknor
R; K 05.10.00; C 30.00.00; Boys King Qu.
~~Mr. Stephen Newman~~[105]   A parish indifferent orderly.
Mr. William Elward

Bobbing
V; C £20 or £30; Mr. Sandford Sir George More
~~Mr. Wm. Scarlett~~   ~~A right man~~.   See Iwade fol. 46.
~~Mr. George Wren~~ A.B.   Formerly Demie of St. Mag. Coll Oxon & now Petty Cannon of Rochester.[106]
Mr. Titus Otes

---

[105] Newman was succeeded by Isaac Bates. CCEd Person ID: 139865.
[106] The comment refers to Wren.

Borden
V; K 08.10.00; C £30 or £40; Mrs. Anne Colt
~~Mr. Thomas Griffin~~[107]   Colt Esqr Parson. Parsonage worth £100 a yeare. The incumbent says the Vicaridge is not worth £30.
Mr. Thomas Milway

Bredgar
V; K 09.00.00; C £40 at most; Mr. {…} Henry Aldersey Esqr. ArchBp. Q
Mr. Nathan Winsmore   Conceived to be a right man.

Folio 46

East-Church in Shepey
R; K 13.00.00; C 200.00.00; Trustees named by the King
~~Dr. Robert Wilkinson~~   A person well known. Parish consists most of Lookers: is a great Circuit of land & in it 2000 Acres tithe free; Particularly a peice called Shurlands.[108] Not above 50 Communicants in all, if they attend. No Justice on the Island; Templeman a farmer, who is a Quaking Preacher lives in the parish & is the Ringleader of the Sectaries. Keeps a whore the wife of a man beyond sea, with whom he lives (as he calls it) on the Land.
Mr. Thomas White

Elmeley Ecctia desolata
R; K 05.00.00; C 40.00.00; All Souls Coll. Oxon
Mr. John Prestwich   Known well enough.

Iwade
Cur; ArchDeac. Cant.
Mr. Wm. Scarlett aforsd.   See Bobbing fol. 45.

Kingsdown
R; K 05.19.02; C £40 or £50; Thomas Finch of Kingsdowne Esqr.
~~Mr. Rich. Tilden~~ A.B.   Mr. of Arts. ~~from~~ Ordayned Priest by the Bp. of Lond. 1664 formerly beneficed at St. James in Grayne. Ins
~~Mr. Ed. Archbold~~[109]
Mr. Tho. Allen[110]

Leesdowne in Shepey
V; K 10.10.00; Mr. Marshall of Totterlane London.
Ralph Roundtree   But lately come, and not much known yet. Conceived to be a good man. A small parish of meane people, and pretty orderly.

---

[107] Thomas Griffin senior. He was succeeded by Thomas Haymes junior.
[108] Shurland and other estates claimed exemption. There is a full explanation in Hasted, VI, 245–58.
[109] Archbold was rector of Kingsdown with Mappiscombe in the diocese of Rochester.
[110] The arrow is in the manuscript.

Milton by Sittingbourne
V; K 13.02.06; C 80.00.00 By Augment.; Chu. of Cant.
~~Mr. John Hurt~~   A person very right in judgement for the Church. A towne & parish infected with Sectaries, but not much; Rob. Honywood an Anabaptist the worst.   See Burmarsh fol. 28
Mr. Thomas Turner

Folio 47

Halstow
V; K 08.02.00; C 40.00.00 ~~Q what~~ ^£20^ Augm.; Chu. of Cant. Imp. & Pat.
~~Mr. Hen. Deering~~   mort   A person of abilities sufficient & of right principles. James Dorrell Esqr Lessee of the Parsonage at £20 per acre rent £60 improved value. A small parish. None but fishermen & farmers. Not above 16 Houses. Come all to Church. Noe sectaries; Church in good repayre, But no Surplice yet.   See Newington Post hoc folio.
Mr. John White

Hartlip
V; K 09.10.10; C 50.00.00 Q what Augm.; Church of Rochester
~~Mr. Ben. Crompe~~   ~~Prebend of Rochester~~ A good man.
Mr. Jo. Edwards
Mr. John Crew

Milsted
R; K 08.15.00; C 50.00.00 so lett; ~~Mr.~~ Tooke Esqr by Ashford
Mr. Rich. Tilden aforsd.   See Kingsdowne fol. 46.

Minster in Shepey cum Cap. de Queenborough
Cur; **Mr. Hensly**. d.
Mr. Sam. Symonds

Murston
R; K 10.14.02; C 160.00.00; Sir Edw. Hales
~~Mr. Rich. Tray~~   mort   An able, and a {…} good man. ~~Parishioners all but ordinary fellows. Infested with some Sectaries,~~ ^The Sectaries^ ~~who about 4 yeares ago sett fire on the Parsonage barne & burnt it, full of Corne.~~ A very small Parish not above 12 Communicants in all. No person of quality. All orderly & come to Church. Church in good repayre. They have Surplice & Com. prayer booke. Parsonage barne burnt downe by Sectaries 4 yeares ago.
Mr. Sam. Symonds

Newington by Sittingbourne
V; K 14.00.00; C £40 at most 50.00.00 Q what Augm.; Eaton Coll. Imp. and Pat. ArchBp. Q
~~Mr. Hen. Deering~~ ~~aforsd~~   mort   See Halstow above fol. 47.
Mr. Adam Reve

Folio 48
Queenborough Chap. to Minster   See Minster fol. 47.

Rainham
V; K 14.04.07; C 50.00.00 or 60.00.00; ArchBp. Imp. Pat.
~~Mr. Joh. Campleshon~~   A person of sufficient ordinary parts; but a little vaine. A parish of about 40 Families. Last Easter 80 Communicants. Church in good repayre, with a Surplice & all things decent. The parishioners indifferent orderly: But one Whittaker an Excommunicate Anabaptist troubles the parish: he is a Farmer at the £120 Rent. Parsonage worth £200 or £250. Hickford tenant. Mr. Frere & one Mr. Smith gentlemen of Acct. live in the parish.   ~~See Upchurch fol. 49.~~
~~Mr. Wm. Walter~~
Mr. Thomas Cradock

Rodmersham
V; K 08.06.08; C 30.00.00 or litle more; Sir Edw. Hales
~~Id. Mr. Campleshon~~[111]   Bachelr. of Arts. Mr. Pordage a Popish Recusant (yet a gentleman of a fayre carriage) Parson. Parish ~~but small~~ ^about 40 families^ Come well to Church all but the Papists.
Mr. John White

Sittingbourne
V; K 10.00.00; C 60.00.00; ArchBp.
Mr. Geo. Jones aforsd.   A very good man. v. Burmarsh 28.   See Bapchild fol. 45.

Stockbury
V; K 09.11.00½; C 40.00.00 Q What Augm.; Chu. of Rochr.
Mr. Tho. Lorkin   A very honest good able man. A small parish.

Tonge
V; K 08.06.08; C 40.00.00 Aug. 10.00; ArchBp. Mr. Steed
Mr. Wm. Pell   A poor weake man A parish of ordinary farmers and meane people & Lookers.
Mr Tho. Cradock
Mr. John Napleton

Folio 49

Tonstall
R; K 14.08.04; C 100.00.00; ArchBp.
Mr. Rob. Dixon   Prebend of Rochester; sayes he makes not above £80 of the living. Sir Edward Hales lives in the parish. The parish not great most ordinary men; indifferent orderly.

---

[111] Probably not inducted.

Upchurch

V; K 11.00.00; C £30 or £40; All Soules Coll. Oxon
~~vacant~~ ^~~Mr. John Campleshon~~^ lately put in A small parish in an unhealthy place ordinary people, farmers, husbandmen & fishermen. Steph. Alleyn tenant to the College for the Parsonage worth ~~£80 and~~ neere £200 a yeare. A poore Vicaridge house (if any, for it is disputed) Church much out of repayre. ~~See Rainham 48 fol.~~
~~Mr. John Campleshon~~
Mr. Ben Phineas

Warden in Shepey

R; K 04.15.00; C 30.00.00; ArchBp. Q It seems to be in Alderman Meynell of London by title derived from the Duke of York & the King.
vacant[112]   See my Large Booke of Entries fol. 91.[113]
Mr. John Tudor   Sir Leol. Jenkins   Lord Keeper per Lapse

Wicheling

R; K 04.01.08; C 40.00.00; Sir Wm. Stede. olim
Mr. Tho. Conway   A person orthodox, & of parts sufficient.

Folio 50

Ospringe Deanery

Buckland by Faversham

R; K 05.13.04; C 30.00.00; King Q. or Sir Bas. Dixwell
Dr. Henry Eve   A person of good esteem. The parish not above 4 houses small farmers.   See Linsted fol.

Badlesmere

R; K 05.02.01; C 50.00.00; Sr. Geo. Sonds
Mr. Wm. Bagnoll   A person of parts very sufficient.

Bocton Bleane

V; Ex; K 09.14.09½; C 60.00.00; ArchBp.
~~Mr. Percivall Radcliffe~~ mort   A good ~~playne~~ man of good parts. Burnt downe in London. Lives Curate at Bromley to the Bp. of Rochester.[114]
Mr. David Barton

Davington

Cur; Heyres of Jo. Edwards Esqr.
vacant

---

[112] The sequestration was held by Ralph Roundtree, 1664–7, and Obadiah Paul, 1669–1670. Dunkin, II, 157.
[113] An annotation by Miles Smyth. His 'Large Booke of Entries' is the Act Book, commenced when Gilbert Sheldon became archbishop in 1663. Smyth wrote and signed all of the entries until 26 June 1665. The entry in fos. 91–2 concerns the presentation to the rectory of Warden of 'Lunne of Jesus College, Oxon. (as presented) but of no degree … lately … an Apothecary or Chirurgion in Canterbury exhibits a Presentation of himselfe by Alderman Meynell of London … found insufficient upon examination by Dr. Stradling was ejected October 20 1664.' LPL, VB 1/1/91.
[114] These comments refer to David Barton.

Doddington
V; K 06.13.04; C £30 at most; ArchDeac. Cant.
Mr. Wm. Dunbarr   A poore Scott, seems to be a good man & of parts sufficient. A small parish.

Folio 51

Eastling
R; K 16.00.00; C 200.00.00; Earle of Winchilsea
~~Mr. Sam. Jemmatt~~   mort   A Covetous fatt Presbyterian Conformist. Not above 40 houses in the parish; All farmers & husbandmen. And come orderly to Church.
Mr. Wm. Wickens

Faversham
V; K 26.17.06; C £100 heretofore now scarse £40; Chu. of Cant.
~~Mr. Fran. Worrall~~ resigned   A ~~grave~~ ^yong^ good & able man, well esteemed.[115] The towne a member of Sandwich. The Corporation pretty well reformed but yet in the towne a great many Schismatiques & Sectaries. Many Hoygh[116] men and fishermen.   See Westbere Fol. 8
now **Mr. Giles Hinton**

Graveney
V; K 12.00.00; C 60.00.00; ArchBp. Imp. Pat.
~~Mr. Mich. Bisson~~   mort   ~~Right but poor.~~
Mr. Francis Worrall   A very good man.

Goodnestone by Faversham
R; K 05.02.07; Sir Ed. Patheriche's Lady by turns ArchBp. Q. v. Reg. Pool fol. 82 ex Jurispatr Dni Tho Kemp milites.
Mr. Tho. Cater   A small parish   See Ospringe fol 52

Hartye
Cur; Thornhill olim. Sir Ed. Hales now Q.
Vacant

Hearnehill
V; Ex; K 15.00.00; C 50.00.00; ArchBp. Imp. & Pat.
~~Mr. Rob. Skeane~~ ~~a Scott~~   Convert from Presbytery About 50 Families 40 Com. last Easter. No Sectaries nor Schismatiques. No Gentleman in the parish Church in good repayre. And all things fitt & decent in it.
Mr. John Gamlyn

---

[115] Worral was probably the 'grave' man, this being scored out when he resigned with 'yong' interpolated to describe Hinton.

[116] A variant of hoy – 'A small vessel ... employed in carrying passengers and goods ... in short distances on the sea-coast': *OED*.

Folio 52

Leaveland
R; K 04.00.00; C 60.00.00; Sir Geo. Sonds
Wm. Bagnoll aforsd.   A small parish & orderly.   See Badlesmere fol 50.

Linsted
V; K 08.03.11½; C 60.00.00; ArchDeac. Cant.
~~Dr. Hen. Eve aforsd~~.   {…} Parish indifferent orderly. Most farmers and husbandmen. Sir Wm. Hugeson lives in the parish & Lord Roper.
Mr. Wm. Wickins

Luddenham
R; K 12.08.04; C 80.00.00; King
~~Mr. James Cowes~~   Once a Presbyterian, now a Conformist. No person of quality in the parish. None but farmers & husbandmen. Pretty orderly.   v. Owre v. f. 53
Mr. John Sherwin

Norton
R; K 10.18.04; C 120.00.00; Bp. of Rochester
Dr. Henry Parkhurst   A Parish pretty regular.   See Sturmouth fol. 13.

Newnham
V; K 05.12.06; C 15.00.00; Mr. Hulks & Dr. Hood
Mr. Wm. Dunbar aforsd   See Doddington fol. 50.

Ospringe
V; K 10.00.00; C 50.00.00; St. Johns Coll. Cambr.
Mr. Tho. Cater aforsd   A good honest playne man. And a pretty good Parish.   See Goodnestone fol. 51.

Folio 53

Ottrinden
R; K 06.14.02; C 50.00.00; Geo. Curtis Esqr.
Mr. Wm. Sclater   An honest good man. A Pretty regular parish; Lives in it The Lady Bamster; All the rest Farmers & husbandmen.

Owre
Cur; C £8.00 Stipend £15 Augment. out of St. Greg.; ArchBp.
Mr. John Mackaller   A man of right principles. A very small parish of meane people.

Preston by Faversham
V; K 08.12.06; C 60.00.00; ArchBp.
Mr. Fran. Worrall aforsd.   ^ vi 52 Regr Parker^   Chu. of Cant. Impropriator. A small parish of about 14 families. Farmers & husbandmen. Indifferently regular. See Faversham fol. 51.

Selling
V; K 06.13.04; C 30.00.00 or little more; Sir Mart. Sonds olim ~~ArchBp~~. Lewis Watson Esq. in right of his wife The Lady Faversham[117]
~~Mr. W. Davis~~[118]
Edward Fisher   Instituted 10 Aug. living void by deprivation of John Sydway.

Sheldwich
V; K 06.16.08; C 20.00.00; Chu. of Cant.
vacant

Stalisfeild
V; K 05.06.08; C £20 or £30 £25 Augm.; ArchBp.
~~Mr. Rob. Trott~~   mort
Mr. Tho. Conway

Folio 54

Stone Ecctia desolata [119]
ArchBp. Q or Chu. of Cant.

Tenham
V; K 10.00.00; C 60.00.00; ArchDeac. Cant.
Dr. Henry Eve aforsd   See Buckland fol. 50.

Throwleigh
V; K 07.11.08; C £30 or £40; Chu. of St. Paul Lond. or some Prebend there
Mr. Geo. Robertson   A Scott. Presbyter.

Folio 55

Livings within the Peculiar, or Immidiate Jurisdiction, of Canterbury Shorham Deanery. being all of them in the Diocese of Rochester

R; **Brasted**
K 22.06.08; C 160.00.00 Whereof £50 Annual Gleab.; ArchBp.
Dr. Pindar   An old man beneficed in Essex.

V; **Bexley**
K 13.04.04; C 80.0.0 140.0.0 or £200 per annum; ~~Mr. Tho. St. John~~ Mr. Tho. St. George
~~Mr. Tho. Smoult~~   A parish very Conformable tho greater in the past. Church and chancel in good repair & surplice. Common prayer book and a font. Sir Robt. Austen, Sir John Wroth Good conformable men.
Mr. Ben. Huntingdon

---

[117] This entry must have been made after the marriage date in July 1677. *HoP*.
[118] Succeeded by Onesiphorus Paul, 1669–71, James Kay in 1671 and John Sidway, 1677–80. Edward Fisher was instituted as vicar in 1680. LPL, VG 1/3 fo. 38, VB 1/3/48, VB 1/4/111.
[119] This was Stone near Faversham, originally a chapel to Teynham. Hasted, VI, 393–6.

R; **Chevening**
K 21.06.08; C 150.00.00; ArchBp.
Dr. Edw. Clarke

R; **Chiddingstone**
K 28.09.04; C 150.00.00; ArchBp.
~~Dr. Thomas Potter~~
~~Mr. Rich. Nurse~~

R; **Clive als Cliue als Cliffe**
K 50.00.00; C £300.00.00 Olim nunc +200; ArchBp.
Dr. Geo. Stradling

V; **Darenth**
K 09.18.10; C 50.00.00; Church Rochester
Mr. John Davyes £20 a year out of the parsonage from the Church of Rochester the parish very conformable. Church & chancel in good repair and all things in correct order. Noe person of quality lives in the parish.
Mr. John Chadwick

R; **Earde als Crayford**
K 35.13.04; C 120.0.0; Earl Northumberland
John Yates The Lady Say comes not Church but keeps one a person in her house which hath been and still is a great sectary by name of Josua Sprigg. Sir Robt. Austen dwells within half a mile the Church in good repair Common prayer book etc. One Mr Romwinkle[120] a person formerly a preacher but now in orders, and Mr Gould comes not to Ch and hath a Child not baptized

V; **East Farley**
K 06.16.08 06.18.08; C 35.00.00; Lord Chancellor Dno rege
Francis Greene All yeomen: Very Orderly & tidy Church. Font, Surplice & Com Prayer Booke; The Parson reported to be regular.

Folio 56a

V; **East Malling**
K 10.08.04; C 50.00.00
Mr Rob. Whittle

V; **East Peckham**
K 14.00.00; C £50 or £60; ~~Dec. Cap. Cant~~. Dec. & C. Cant.
Mr Rich. Marsh per Ent Prebend Capit Cant. See Rucking fol. 31.

---

[120] John Herman Romswinckell.

R; **Eynsford**
K 12.16.08; C £250.00.00 £100 cleare; ArchBp.
Geo. Gifford Esq Sinecure Rector of Grayne[121] Pays £40 toward Rent to the Parson & £20 Aug. To the Vicar. The improved value over & besides has Rt & Augmnt is by common Acct £190.
Mr Porter Incumb Clerke sine Cura
Mr Porter is a Incumbent Clerke beneficed in Nottinghamshire at (   )[122]

V; **Eynsford**
K 12.00.00; C £45 or £50 besides £20 augm. from the Lessor of the Rect.; Rector Eccliae qts Rector
Mr Samuel Palmer mort cession   v. Cranmer fo. 402.
Mr. Nich. Felton
Mr Edward Tilson

V; **Farningham**
K 09.05.08 09.10.10; C 40.00.00 20.00.00 Aug.; ArchBp.
Mr Tho: Browne   See Newenden, Fol. 38. The Parish very Conformable Commun. Table rayled in. Surplice Font etc. Sir Jo. Cotton in the Parish Sir Rob. Austin Sir Wm. Swan Justices neare.

V; **Gillingham Ch Upbury** Donativa in Gillingham
K 15.13.08 11½ 06.13.04; C 80.00.00; Brazenose Colledg in Oxon Brase:nose Coll. Oxon:
Ralph Twiss   Allington Paynter Esq a pensioner to His Majesty a good Conformable man. All the people very Conformable except one John Prolling a fisherman a Quaker. Church in good repair etc.
Mr Moses Pengry
Mr Wm Yates

V; **Grayne**
K 09.11.08; Sr Ed. Hales
Mr Tho Alleyn   Hath left it and is possessed of the R. of Kingsdowne in Cant. Dioc.
Henry Goodwin

R; **Halstead**
K 05.17.10 11; C £30 or £40; ArchBp.
Mr Cottingham John   A small living in a private place; Not above 14 or 15 householders.
Mr Tho Browne

R; **Heavor Als Hever**
K 15.07.04 03½; C 00 if not £100
George Boraston

---

[121] There had been a sinecure rectory in the Isle of Grain, in lay hands, since the sixteenth century. Hasted, IV, 256-7.
[122] North Wheatley.

R; **Hays**
K 06.18.00; C £50 or £60; Rector of Orpington Dr Say Provost of Oriole
Mr Tho Wood   A Parish indifferently affected. Church & Chancell in tolerable Repayre. La. Scott the only person of Quality.

Folio 56b

R; **Hunton als Huntingdon**
K 16.12.01 16.13.00½; C 200.0.00 Reale Value £120 £100; ArchBp. Of Cant.
Tho Yardley   Mr of Arts of both universities. Latham the late intruder hath much infected the Parish, but begins to be reduced. All things decent in the church.

R; **Ifeild**
K 04.07.00; C 25.00.00; William Child gent
~~Mr Jo Stacey~~[123]
Mr Geo Kelley

R; **Ightham**
K 15.16.08; C 80.00.00
James Hickford

R; **Keston**
K 06.10.00; C £50 or £60; ArchBp.
Mr Edw. Smith   A conformable Parish. No person of greater quality than a farmer.

V; **Meopham**
K 16.03.04; C £50 tithes Pens. £5.06.8d Augm. £30; Dec. & Cap Cant ArchBp. Q. vide Whitgift Rgst 319.326 fs 2a
Mr Wm Gibson   Mr of Arts, putt in since His Majesties Restauration; Seemes to be a discreet man. An orderly Parish, & noe Sectaries in it. The Church of Cant. Impropriate.

V; **Northfleete**
K 21.00.00; C 100.00.00; The King
~~Mr Cunningham~~ mort   ~~An old man.~~ A Scott; ~~Kept in att the Rstn.~~
Mr Wm Scott
Thomas Haymes

R; **Orpington cum Cap. de Cray**[124]
K 13.14.04; ArchBp.
Dr. Say

---

[123] His predecessor, Thomas Burley, did not resign until 1666.
[124] St Mary Cray.

V; **Orpington**
K 11.10.04 10.10.05; C £40 or £50; Dr Say Rector of Orpington ArchBp. Q.
~~Benjamin Blackstone~~[125]
Robert Bourne

R; **Penshurst**
K 30.06.00; C 300.00.00; Earle of Leycester Q of the ArchBp. title
Mr Thomas Lee A grave, sober, pious, & well learned man. A large parish consisting of many Hamletts. At least 500 Communicants, very orderly people in generall, as much, as any in England, at this time. Earl of Leycester lives in the parish, as also Mr John Drury & Mr Seyliard.

R; **Peckham**[126]
K 23.00.00; ArchBp.

Folio 57

R; **Shorham cum Cap de Otford**
K 34.09.08; C To the curate £50 tithes & Pension 19.6.0d paid by the Deane & Chap. Besides £20 p annum Cur. De Otford.; D. & Chapter of Westminster
~~Mr Edward Oliver~~ curate mort
Mr. Wm. Wall
Att the Presentation of the D. & Chapter of Westminster

V; **Shorham**
K 14.06.08; D & Chapter of Westminster
Instituted to the R.[127]

R; **Sevenoke**
K 13.06.08; Edw: Impr. R.
Edward Chamberlain

V; **Sevenoke**
K 15.03.00; C £60 if not £70 per annum; Edward Chamberlain Rector of the same
Richard Bosse

R; **Wrotham cum cap. de Stansted**
K 50.08.00 50.09.09½; C £200 Leased out by the incumbent for 21 years Jan. 1774-5. Rent Received £60 per annum; ArchBp.
~~Dr. Layfield~~
Mr Charles Layfield

---

[125] Blackstone was preceded by Philip Holland, vicar 1663–4. CCEd Person ID: 97367, LPL, VH 2/44/1, 2.

[126] This may refer to the sinecure rectory of East Peckham, which was not a peculiar by 1663. Hasted, V, 103–5.

[127] Edward Oliver died as vicar and William Wall was instituted as vicar.

V; **Wrotham**
K 22.05.10 22.10.10; C £60; Rector de Wrotham
Mr John Wms.

V; **Woodland**[128]
K 03.14.06; C £19.10.00

R; **Sundrich als Sundridge**
K 22.13.04; C £140; ArchBp.
Mr Sam. Sharpe. Presb.   A Parish pretty Conformable. Hath beene troubled with some Quakers, but begining to be in good order.

Nockholt
K nil; C £60 if not £70
Mr Pawley curat[129]

Lidsing als Lidging
K nil; £40.00.00
Ralph Twisse curate

Down Capella
K nil; £20.00.00;
Philip Jones

36[130]

Folio 58

Deanery of the Arches, within the Citie of London.

R; **All-hallowes Lombard Streete**
K 22.06.08; Dec. & Cap. Cant.
Dr. John Aucher

R; **Allhallowes Breadstreete annexed to St. John Evangelist**
K 37.17.09; Sir W.W.[131] 37.13.09; C £140 by Act of Parliament.; ArchBp. & Dean & Chapr. of Canterbury by Turnes
Mr. Tho. Risden   Dr. Blomer presented by the Dean & Chap. next turne is the ArchB. 1681.
Edward Fowler
Collated by Dn & Ch.

---

[128] United to Wrotham in 1573, and in ruins since then. Hasted, II, 488.
[129] Pawley became curate in 1670, following the death of Francis Collins.
[130] This is the total number of the livings listed in Shoreham deanery.
[131] This notation appears to report advice of differing values in this and three other churches below, all in the deanery of the Arches. In every case, Ecton confirms the value first written. 'Sir W.W.' may be Sir William Wilde.

R; **Allhallowes ad Fenne**[132] ~~Q. whether this be a Peculiar~~ It is not Vid. Whitgift Regr. 2 f. 328
K 41.18.01; C £150 or £160 per annum; ArchBps Presentation
~~Dr. Geo. Gifford~~[133]   {…}
~~Mr. Blemell~~
Mr. Thom. ~~White~~
Dr. Cave

R; **St. Dunstans, East**[134]
K 60.07.11; ArchBp.
Dr. **Geo. Gifford**

R; **St. Dionis Backchurch**
K 25.00.00; Dec. & Cap. Cant.
Dr. **Jo. Castilion**
~~Mr. Geo. May jun.~~
Mr. Gatford

R; **St. John Evangelist Watling St.**[135]
K 15.19.07; Dec. & Cap. Cant.
Jo. Stoyning   Annexed to Allhallows Bredstreet

R; **St. Leonard Eastcheape**
K 25.10.00 Sir W.W. 15.10.00
Elkanah Downes Dr.

R; **St. Mary Bothaw**
K 10.10.00; C 35.00.00; Dec. & Cap. Cant.
Mr. John ^~~Dalton~~^ ~~Dawson Mr. of Arts~~
John Mereton M.A.

R; **St. Mary Aldermary**
K 41.00.00; C 140.00.00; Ld. ArchBp. of Cant.
~~Dr. Robert Gell~~   This Rectory hath 6 Houses besides the Parsonage house in Glebe. Fines when they fall. The tithes amount not to more than £030 per annum. Easter Booke small.
~~Mr. Tomkins~~[136]
Mr. Spinedge

Folio 59a

R; **St. Mary le Bow**
K 33.12.03½; ArchBp. is to grant the next turn.
George Smallwood

---

[132] All Hallows the Great, which was not a peculiar.
[133] An error. See under St Dunstans, East.
[134] St Dunstan in the East.
[135] St John the Evangelist Friday Street.
[136] John Rudge became rector, following the resignation of Thomas Tomkins in 1669. LPL, VG 1/5, p. 31.

R; **St. Michael Pater noster Row or St. Michs in Ruola**[137]
K 07.00.00 Sir W.W. 09.07.04½; Bp of Worc
~~Charles Adams~~   It is no Peculiar, Nor *sic*
Salter Nathaniel

R; **St. Michael Crooked Lane**
K 26.08.04; C £100 per Act Parl.; ArchBp.
~~Mr. Joseph Browne~~ mort
~~Mr. John Bradshaw~~
~~Mr. Henry Myles~~
~~John Wooley~~
Mr. Richard Pearson

R; **St Pancras Soper Lane**
K 13.06.03; ArchBp.
Mr. Sam. Dillingham

R; **St. Vedast Foster Lane**
K 33.05.10 Sir W.W. 34.05.10; ArchBp.
~~Dr. Christopher Shute~~
Mr. Masters

R; **St. Edmunds Lumbardstreete**[138]
K 21.14.02; C 100.00.00; ArchBp. presentation
Wm. Bradford[139]   It is no peculiar of Cant only in the ArchBp. gift.
Mr. Swift

14[140]

In Comitat Midds London Diocess Jurisnis Cant. under the Deanery of Croydon

R; de **Hayes**
K 40.00.00
Litigious betweene **Mr. Selby** & **Dr. Caldicott** which last hath recd. Institution from his Grace.

V; **Hayes**
K 20.00.00; Q of the ArchBp. Title. Miles Wolfe & John Knight presented Mr. Selby Nov. 27 1661. Id Wolfe et Knight Jan. 16 1661 presented Timothy Morton A.M.
~~Mr. Timothy Morton~~[141]
~~Mr. Edward Caldwall~~ ~~presented by John Knight Esq. of Bristol~~;
joseph Waldron

---

[137] St Michael Paternoster Royal, which was a peculiar.
[138] St Edmund the King and Martyr, which was not a peculiar.
[139] Should read John Bradford, who followed Swift. CCEd Person ID: 62029.
[140] The number of livings in the deanery of the Arches, excluding All Hallows ad Fenne.
[141] William Fly followed Morton as vicar.

R; **Harrow**
K 88.04.04

V; **Harrow**
K {...} 33.04.04;
Mr. Joseph Wilcox

Cap Pynnor[142]

Folio 59b

Throckington Lib. Cap[143]
K 04.13.04

5[144]

R[145]   **In the Countie of Surrey and same Deanery of
            Croydon** ~~Winton Dioc.~~ **& Jurisd of Cant**

R; **Barnes**
K 09.03.02; C £200 heretofore now £150; Dean & Chapter of St. Paul London
Dr. Edw. Layfeild

R; **Burstow**
K 15.13.04; C £200 olim ArchBp. vid. Catal. in R Cranmer; The King and ArchBp. title v. Reg. Laud 321 ubi Cook fuit admisg ad prntacoe Regit plene Jure
Dr. Ralph Cooke

R; **Charlewood**
K 19.16.08; C £200; Assignes of Lord W. Throckmorton
Henry Heskith

R; **Cheham**
K 17.05.04; C 160.00.00; ~~St. John Coll Oxon~~ King Raone Promocais ArchBp. Q St. Johns Coll
~~**Dr. Doughty**~~[146]   Prebend of Westminster
Mr. Osborne Thomas

V; **Croydon**
K 21.18.10; C 150.00.00; ArchBp.
Mr. Clewer

---

[142] Pinner was a chapel to Harrow.
[143] Throckington or Thokyntone was another chapel to Harrow but possibly derelict by 1663. Gregory, pp. 256, 260.
[144] The number of livings in the deanery of Croydon, in Middlesex, excluding Throckington.
[145] An error.
[146] Doughty was succeeded by Edward Bernard. CCEd Person ID: 7672.

R; **East horsley**
K 12.16.03½; C £60 now £45; ArchBp.
~~John Bonwick~~ ~~BD~~   Collated by ArchBp. Juxon Possessed before of the R. of Newdigate in Surrey dist. 10 miles and dispensed with by the sd. ArchBp.
Wm. Turner

R; **Merstham**
K 22.01.08; C £160 £200 heretofore; ArchBp.
Mr. John Harris   A Clownish Parish But one Gent. Sir Jo. Soutchote Noe sectaries Glebe £40 a yeare.

R; **Newington**
K 16.00.00; C £100; ArchBp.   Bishop of Worcr.
~~Dr. Megges~~   Olim ad prntacoe Archi Epi sed ex concess Thomae Cranmer ad sedem Wigorn devenit 1546
~~Mr. Lloyd Nich~~
Mr. Edward Webster

Cap; **Norwood Cur**
K nil; C 30
Wm. Fly

Folio 60

Cap; **Mortlake**
K nil; C £40.00.00; Preb of Wigorn
Mr. Thompson[147]   cav

Cap; **Putney**
R; ~~St. Thomas als St. Cliff~~
C £40 Stipd. & Chu Duties; D et Cap. Wigorn
~~Mr. Wm. Slaughter~~[148]   A person of good parts & Integrity well known
Mr. John Shore

R; **Wimbaldon als Wimbledon**
K 63.04.02

Cap; **Wimbaldon**
C £300.00.00
~~Mr. Tho. Millington~~
Mr. Tho. Willmot
Dr. Tho. Thomas

11[149]

---

[147] Robert Anderson preceded Thompson.
[148] An error; should be Edward Slaughter or Sclater.
[149] The number of livings in the deanery of Croydon, in Surrey, excluding Norwood, a chapel of Hayes, Middx., and the sinecure rectory of Wimbledon.

In the Counties of Essex, and Suffolk of the Peculiar Jurisd. of Canterb under the title of Bocking Deanery

R; **Bocking**
K 35.10.00; C 300.00.00; ArchBp.
Dr. Colebrand
Mr. Nathaniel Sterry

R; **Stisted** ~~Stistand~~
K 22.00.00; C 260.00.00; ArchBp.
~~**Dr. Nicolls** Chap to the late ArchBp. Juxon~~   ~~mort~~
Mr. Th. Cooke Chap. to his Grace
Mr. Denzill Price[150]

R; **Boreley**[151]   Hedingham Dec
K 09.00.00

V; **Coxhall als Coggeshall^parva^**[152] Dec. Lexden
K 11.03.04

R; **Hadleigh** Dec. Rochford
K 11.14.06 45.02.01; C 00.00.00; Earl Warwick ArchBp. Q. vid Reg, Parker where ever in the ArchBp.
~~**Dr. Nicolls** Chap. to the late ArchBp. Juxon~~   See hac page ante Stisted
Mr. Tho. Cooke aforsd.;

Folio 61

R; **Lachingdon et Lalling** in Dec. Chelmsford
K 37.00.00; C 120.00.00; ArchBp.
Mr. Martin Alderson

R; **Southchurch** in Dec. Chelmsford
K 27.00.08; C 100.00.00; ArchBp.
~~**Mr. Rich. Harris**~~
Mr. Wm. Master

R; **Ely Monachorum** in Suff[153]
ArchBp.

---

[150] Price was rector of Stifford, Essex.
[151] William Plaine had been rector from 1661.
[152] Little Coggeshall was always held with Coggeshall, and may have been derelict by 1663. CCEd; Beaumont, *passim*.
[153] William Baker was rector 1660–1706.

R; **Multon ^als Moulton^** in Suff. Dec. Clare ~~Moulto in suff~~
K 13.06.08; ArchBp. olim but passed away by ArchBp. Cranmer temp
~~Mr. Francis Selyard~~
~~Mr. Wm. Huxley~~
Dudley Bradbury   was collated to the Rectory

V; **Multon** in eod: Com: et Dec[154]
K 04.07.08; Sir Francis North Patron of both

{...}

R; **Ash als Ash by Campsey** in Suff in Dec Looes[155]
K 14.05.00

Hamletts within the said Deanery of Bocking & County of Essex	{	Milton Shore within the Parish of Prittlewell Runsell within the Parish of Danbury Callow green within the Parish of Purleigh

12[156]

Folio 62

Peculiars of Canterbury under the title of } **In the Counties of Bucks & Oxon.**
        Risborough Deanery

R; **Risborough Monachor. cum Cap. St. Petri** infra Villam de Owlswick in eadem poch. de Risborough in Co. Bucks.
K 30.00.00; C 200.00.00; ArchBp.
~~Mr. Johes Wooley~~[157]
~~Dr Tompkyns~~
Mr. Campian Abrah.

R; **Halton**[158] ~~in eod: Com: et Dec~~ ~~Q. is not Halton in Com. Oxon or Halton in Com. Surrey~~ In Comit. Bucks.
K ~~13.06.08~~ 12.19.00½; C £60 or £70; ~~Mr. Fermor olim~~ ArchBp. ~~ArchBp.~~ v. Reg. Bourhier[159] & Courtenay f. 219.

R; **Newington cum Cap. de Brightwell** in Com Oxon. et Decanatu Cuddesdon
K 18.13.04; C 150.00.00; ArchBp.
Dr. Brabourne

---

[154] Frances Seyliard was curate until his institution as rector in 1663.
[155] Not a peculiar. Gregory, p. 262, fo. 338.
[156] The alleged number of livings in the deanery of Bocking, but only eleven are listed.
[157] Preceded by William Harward.
[158] John Latimer was restored in 1660.
[159] Thomas Bourchier.

V; **Milton**[160]
K 15.00.00

4[161]

Peculiars of Canterbury under the title of } Com. Sussex
Pageham Deanery

R; **All-hallows Chichester, als in Palenta**
K 05.17.06; C pauper; ArchBp. Q R Parker Sir Wm. Morley Q
John Holder[162]

R; **East Lavant**
K 20.18.00; C 120.00.00; ArchBp. v R Parker fo 394 where the incumbent had Institution uppon the Presentation of the Earle of Dorsitt.
John Betton[163]   Horsham Vicaria in Comitatu Sussexiae spectat ad presentationem Reverendissimi etc vid. Abbot Fol. 159 b prima parte

V; **Pageham**[164] cum cap de Berghstead
K 10.00.00; ArchBp.

V; **Berghstead**[165]
K 08.00.00

Folio 63

R; **Slindon**[166]
K 14.13.00
Mr. Ja Hering

R; **Tangemere**
K 13.05.00; ArchBp. Q Sir Wm. Morley of Chich. see ArchBp. Lauds Regr 312 plene jure
Betton John[167]
Stephen Robins

6[168]

---

[160] Milton was not a peculiar.
[161] The number of livings in the deanery of Risborough.
[162] Holder was not appointed until 1676 but no rectors can be traced after the death of John Peyto in 1662 until 1676.
[163] Preceded by Thomas Gumble, 1663–76.
[164] George Payne was collated to the vicarage in 1662.
[165] South Bersted. Matthew Speed was vicar from 1650 until 1678.
[166] An error – Herring was at Slinfold, also in Sussex, and the incumbent was John Mellis.
[167] Betton was preceded by Paul Lawrence.
[168] The number of livings in the deanery of Pagham.

Peculiars of Canterbury under the title of Terring Deanery } Com. Sussex

R; **Terring**[169]
K 22.13.04; C £170 or £160; ArchBp.
~~Mr. Tho. Dale~~
Mr. Provost Jo

V; **Terring**
Heene Capella
Durrington Capella
K 08.13.04; C 80.00.00 By tithes Pensions and Augmentation.; ArchBp.
~~Mr. Tho. Negus~~
~~Dr. John Harrison~~
Richard Pauley

R; **Patching**[170]
K 11.13.04; ArchBp.
HeadAcre Hamletta in poa St. Pancrasii Cicestrens.
Playstow Hamletta in poa de Kirdford
Bpridge Hamletta in poa de Horsham

3[171]

Peculiars of Canterbury under the title of South-Malling Deanery } Com. Sussex

The Deanery of South Malling is a Dignity rurall upon payment of £20 a yeare {…} given by (   ) & pd by one Kemp,[172] & by him nominated; & £20 more pd out of the estate of one Mr. Smith. He holds it by no Institution, nor Subscription, against the Covenant. Mr. Roborough[173] now holds it, & is a very conformable man; Surrogate at Living to Sr. Rich Chaworth and Henry Thurman.

R; **Bucksted cum Cap de Uckfield**
K 37.05.02; C 200.00.00; ArchBp. & as some say with him the Earle of Dorsit by turnes. But ~~I am informed~~ the Earle never presented but by leave of the ArchBp. {…}
~~R Beckley~~[174]
~~11.06.00~~
~~Mr. Middleton~~
Mr. Anthony Sanders
~~Mr. Henry Alexander~~[175]

---

[169] West Tarring.
[170] Nicholas Garbrand was rector, 1660–71.
[171] The number of livings in the deanery of Tarring.
[172] William Kempe.
[173] Stephen Roborough.
[174] Entered in error.
[175] Should read Erwin Alexander, who was curate.

R; **Cliffe als St. Thomas Martyris** ad Clivam iuxta Lewes
K 05.13.04; C 40.00.00; ArchBp.
~~Mr. Thomas Clarke~~ AB.[176]   Recommended by the Bp. of Chichester.
Mr. Wm Snatt A.B.   Simile

R; **Eadburton als Adburton**
K 16.00.00; C 100.00.00; ArchBp.
Mr. Shepheard

Folio 64

V; **Framfield**
K 13.06.08; Earl of Thannet ArchBp. Q The King vid ArchBp. Whitgift Rg. VI 2.342 E. Dorsett Vid Banc: 309[177]
vacant ar   An ~~incumbent~~ ^Clerke^ presented & sequestered for insufficiency Oct. 1663[178]

V; **Glynde**
K 05.01.01; C 50.00.00; Coll Morley by leave from the Ch. of Windsor. ArchBp. Q. Dec. & Preb. Windsor Abbot 1 Reg 397.
vacant   A Clerke presented & refused for insufficiency[179] The Parsonage is impropriate to the Ch. of Windsor & they lease that with the Patronage of the Vicaridge to Coll Morley.

R; **Isfeild**
K 09.12.08; C 100.00.00; ArchBp.
Tho. Mell Mr of Arts   Who is also Vicar of Letherhead in Surrey Dioc. Winton Dispensed with for 2 Benefices by ArchBp. Juxon.

V; **Mayfeild**
K 17.13.04; C 120.00.00; John Baker Esqr ArchBp. Q
~~vacant~~[180]
Mr. Rob. Peck   One Maynard[181] a rigid Presbyterian ejected thence at the Ks returne, But since yet may be still lives or lately lived there & much poysoned the people.

V; **Ringmere**
K 13.00.00; C 100.00.00; ArchBp.
~~Mr. Rich. Ireland~~[182]
John Lillie

---

[176] Thomas Clarke was succeeded by John Shore. *SAC*, 26, p. 27.
[177] Patronage passed to John Tufton, 2nd earl of Thanet in 1629 and remained with his successors, until the nineteenth century. *SAC*, 26, p. 41.
[178] Thomas Hammond.
[179] Henry Mountague.
[180] Francis Seyliard was instituted in 1663, ceded in March 1664 and immediately followed by Robert Peck.
[181] Ejected in 1662.
[182] Richard Ireland was succeeded by Luke Garnons.

R; **Stanmer**
K 16.00.00; C £70 a yeare at the utmost value: yet Mr. Thurman sayes £80 in his papers; ArchBp.
Mr. Leversidge   Came in heretofore in the troubles by the Presentatcon of one Michenbourn Esqr of the same place, & continues in by the confirmacon Act The Tithes heretofore were considerably more than now. The ground being much arable, but now converted into sheep feedings.

V; **Wadhurst**
K 15.01.00; C 80.00.00; Private Patron
Mr. ^John^ Smith

Linfeild
Is wholly unendowed & therefore now & for the most part unsupplyed.[183]

South Malling
K 33.00.00
Stephen Roborough[184]   A Conformable man Surrogate to Sir Rich. Chaworth
The tithes are wholly impropriate both Parsonage & Vicaridge. One Mr. Kemp[185] is the Impropriator or possessor of all & tithes glebe & houses: Allowed only to the Vicar but £13 per annum and £20 which one Mr. Smith, commonly called Dog Smith left by Will, both which together make up the £33. See Mr. Thurmans Papers in the Bundle 1666.1667.

Hundreda of Locksfeild
1 Wotton Hamletta in Parish of Dallington
2 Hamletta in parish of Wivelsfeild.
3 Hamletta in parish of Worth
4 Hamletta in parish of Grinsted
5 Hamletta in parish of Wittersham
6 Hamletta in parish of Lamberhurst

12[186]

Folio 65

Peculiars of Canterbury within the Diocese of Norwich, and County of Norfolk.[187]

R; **East Rising** Lyn. Dec Als Castle Rising
K 08.00.00

V; **North Wooton** Eodem Dec
K 10.00.00; The King vid. ArchBp.Banc. 271

---

[183] See Alexander Erwin.
[184] Dean of South Malling. Henry Mountague was curate in 1662.
[185] William Kempe.
[186] The number of livings in South Malling deanery.
[187] These six parishes were not archbishops' peculiars.

R; **Roydon** Eodem Dec
K 05.00.00

R; **South Wooton** Eodem Dec
K 08.06.08; The King vid. ArchBp.Abbot 1. Fol. 396.

Myntling juxta Lynne Regs.

Thursford by Fakenham

6[188]

Peculiars of Canterbury in the ~~Diocese~~ Church of Lincoln.[189]

Prebend of Cropredy & Tame in the County of Oxon
K 46.00.00

Prebend of Sutton, & Buckingham cum Horley et Horton
K 110.03.06

Folio 66/67

Master of the Free schole at Rochdale in Lancashire[190]
Usher of the same Schole
K 00.00.00; 17.00.00 whereof to the Usher 40s; ArchBp. of Cant.

Folios 68 and **69** are blank.

---

[188] The number of livings, in Norfolk, alleged to be peculiars.
[189] These prebends were not archbishops' peculiars.
[190] The endowment deed of 1565 specified that the master of the school was to be appointed by Archbishop Parker or his successors. Fishwick, pp. 270–1.

Folio 70r Benecficea ad Collaconem Presentaesem sive noiaconem Rmi. Pris Dmi Archi-Epi Cantuar ptinen

Comitat
Ex Regro Dni Edmundi Grindall Dni Archi Epi Cantuar Fol. 571.

			Valor Censie Regis		
Viz 1ª 4ᵗᵃ 6ᵗᵃ			£	s	d
		Prebenda 3ˢ in Eccl. Cath. Cant. A Rege Ed: 6ᵗʰ viz. 1ª 4ᵗᵃ 6ᵗᵃ singula ad	040	00	00
		Archionatus Cantuar	163	01	09
	R	St Alphege in Cant	008	13	04
Canty	R	Andrea in Cant	013	06	08
	R	Adisham	028	01	00
	R	Aldington	038	06	08
	V	Appledore	038	06	08
	Cur	Ashe			
London	R	Bta Maria de Arcubus	033	12	03½
	R	Bta Maria Aldermary	041	00	00
Sussex	R	Adburton	016	00	00
	R	Barstead a D Rege per 1ⁱⁿ Excamb			
	R	Bishopsbourne	039	19	02
	R	Biddenden	035	00	00
Canty	R	Beatersden	012	00	00
	R	Blackmanston	004	00	00
	R	Beauxfeild a Johhannes Gage, milite	006	00	00
	R	Barstead	022	06	08
	Cap	Barmingett. Whitgift 1 per 1 468 Pntaco Roff. Dni			
Essex	R	Bocking	035	10	00
	V	Barking prope Turrim Lond. Presentacon	029	13	04
Sussex	R	Burstead Buckstead Q Abbot 2 pt 320	037	05	02
	V	Beaksbourne			
Canty	V	Boughton subtus Bleane			
	V	Bredgar			

Folio 70v

Lancastria	V	Blackbourne			
Bucks	V	Brickhill a Johhannes Gage milite			
	V	Cranbrooke			

	R	Charing a Reg. Ed.[6]			
	R	Chartham	041	05	10
Canty	V	Chislet in 3⁰ Excamb	029	19	02
	R	Chart magna	024	18	06
	R	Chart parva	013	10	10
	R	Cleve^ als Clive als Cliffe Roffam	050	00	00
	R	Chidingstone	028	09	04
	R	Chev^n^ing	021	06	08
	V	Coldrede			
	R	Chayham als Cheyham als Cheame ˘permutat˘	017	05	04
Surriae	V	Croydon	021	18	10
	R	Charlewood permutat	019	16	08
	R	Cullesden Anno 1⁰ Edw 6ᵗʰ R a Rege ad pEntaronem	021	17	01
London	R	St Michael in Crooked Lane	026	08	04
	R	St Dunstane in Orien	060	07	11
Canty	R	Deale	019	10	00
	V	Elham Noiaco to the Coll. of All Soules & they to present	020	00	00
	V	Estry	017	11	09
Canty	R	East Peckham	013	00	00
	R	Eynsford	012	16	08
	R	Eastbridge	005	06	08
Surriae	R	East Horsley	013	09	11
London	R	St Edmonde in Lombardstreete	021	14	02
Sussex	R	Eastlavant per 3ⁿⁿ Excamb			
Canty	V	Far^n^ingham	009	05	08
	V	Folkestone			
	V	Framfeild			
Sussex		Prebend in Colleg.de Southmalling	017	00	07
	V	Framfeild	013	06	08

Folio 71r

	V	Godmersham	009	03	08
Canty	Cur	Goodnestone			
	V	Graveney			
Sussex	V	Glynde Q Dec. et Chap. Windsor	005	01	01

Canty	V	Herne		020	06	01
	R	Horton in 3⁰ Excamb		007	10	08
	R	Harbledowne		009	02	06
	R	Hollingbourne		028	14	10
	V	Hernehill		015	00	00
	R	Huntington ^als Hunton		016	12	01
	R	Halstead		005	17	10
	V	Headcorne		015	13	04
	R	High Halding		019	04	06
Suffolke	R	Hadleigh		045	02	01
Essex	R	Highhonger	a Rege per 1ᵃᵐ Ind.	039	10	04
Sussex	V	Horsham	a Rege per 1ᵃᵐ Ind.	025	00	00
Middx	V	Heyes				
Surriae	R	Hastingley a Rege Edw. 6⁰				
		Haies als Heese A⁰ 1⁰ Rege Edw. 6				
	R	Halton A Rege Edw. 6⁰ in Com Surr.				
Canty	R	Ickham		029	13	04
	R	Ivechurch		044	16	00
Sussex	R	Isfeild		009	12	08
Suffolke	R	Ilight als Monkskilly		013	18	10
Canty	R	Kingnoth		011	09	10
	R	Kaston Keston		006	10	00
	V	Kenington				

Folio 71v

Canty	V	Lydde		055	12	00
	R	Lyming		021	10	00
	V	Lyming		010	18	08
	V	St Lawrenty in Thanett		007	00	00
	V	Lydden		006	02	00
	Cur	Leeds				
Essex	R	Lachingdon et Lalling		037	00	00
Surrey	R	Lambehith	ad {…}	032	15	06½
	R	Laborne				
	V	Minster		033	03	04
	R	St Martin in Civitat Cantuar		006	05	08

	R	Mongham magna	078	00	00
	R	Mongham parva	005	16	00
Canty	R	Mersham	026	16	00
	V	Mopham	016	03	04
	V	Moncton	013	08	09
	V	Marden			
	Cur	Maidstone			
Surrey	R	Merstham	022	01	08
Suffolk	R	Multon x			
	V	Multon x			
Sussex	V	Mayfield x			
	V	Newington	014	00	00
	R	Newington^den^	007	13	04
Canty	R	Newchurch	008	04	00
	V	Norborne	012	11	08
	V	St Nicolai in Thanet	015	19	07
	V	Nonington			
Oxon	R	Newington cum Capella ^Pool fo 72 6^	017	03	08½

Folio 72r

Canty	R	Orpington	030	14	04
	V	Orpington Q if not the Parson	011	10	04
London	R	All Souls in Breadstreete	037	13	04
	R	All Souls maior als ad Fen	041	18	01
	V	Postling Vid. Abb. 2 per fol. 352			
	V	Preston	009	15	00
Canty	R	Pluckley	020	01	05
	V	Preston	008	12	06
	R	Penshurst Q Earle of Leycester	030	06	00
Middx	R	Pancrass	013	06	03
Sussex	R	Patching			
	V	Reculver	009	12	03½
Canty	R	Romney Vet	015	19	02
	R	Rocking ^als Rucking	014	13	05
	V	Raynham			
Sussex		Ringmere Prebend	022	10	00

	V	Ringmere	013	00	00
Bucks	R	Risborough	030	00	00
Lancastria	R	Rochdale Pool fo 74v	011	04	08
Canty	R	Redley			
	Cur	Shulden Capella			
Canty	R	Snave	019	07	09
	V	Sturrey	013	01	08
	V	Sandhurst	019	12	06
	R	Smarden	24	02	06
Canty	R	Saltwood	034	00	00
	R	Snargate	017	06	08
	R	Sandwich	022	13	04

Folio 72v

	V	Selling			
Canty	V	Sittingbourne			
	V	Sibbertswould			
	R	Stistead	022	00	00
Essex	R	Southchurch	027	00	08
		Southmalling ^{…}^	045	12	05½
		Q de Vicaria			
Sussex		Southerham Prebend	019	14	11½
	R	Stanmer	016	00	00
Canty	R	Tonstall	014	08	04
	V	Tilmanstone			
Sussex	R	Terring	022	13	04
	V	Terring	008	13	04
Bangor	R	Towin merioneth	060	13	04
	V	Towin merioneth	006	13	04
Sussex	R	Tangmere	013	04	08
	R	St Thomae Martiris de Cliva iuxta Lewis	005	13	04
Hereford	R	Tringe			

Canty		R	Wyttersham	015	08	08
		R	Woodchurch	026	08	00
		R	Wrotham	050	08	00
		V	Westwell	013	00	00
		Cur	Whitstable			
Lancastria		V	Whalley	006	03	08
London		R	Vedasti	033	05	10

Folio 73r

Prerogative Advowsons Granted to His Grace Gilbert Ld ArchBp. of Canterbury by severall Bps. at their Consecrations & Translations respectively[191]

Person	Bprick	Advowson	
~~Humph. Henchman~~	~~London Transla.~~	~~Chancellor of the church of St. Paul~~	To Mr. Saunders
~~Robt. Skinner~~	~~Worcester Transl.~~	~~Fladbury Rect~~	Vacat mort Epi.
Seth Ward	Sarum Transl	Treasurer of the Ch. of Sarum	
~~Rob. Morgan~~	~~Bangor Conf.~~	~~mediety of Comport; of Landinan~~[192]	Com Montgom. Vicar to Mr Worth
~~Benjamin Laney~~	~~Ely Trans~~	~~Cottenham Rectory~~	Given to Dr. Compton
~~Walter Blandford~~	~~Oxon Cons~~	~~Archdeaconry of Oxon~~	Vacat Transl. Epi.
( ) Davis	Llandaffe Conf	Archdeac. Llandaffe	Vacat morte Epi.
~~Henry Glemham~~	~~St Asaph Conf~~	Llanarmon & Llansanfrayd Rect which first falls upon election death	Voyd by the Bps

---

[191] This table is in at least two hands. It could have been commenced when the Catalogue was first compiled, as Henchman and Skinner were appointed in September and October 1663 respectively, but Saunders only became chancellor of St Paul's in 1672 and Compton was instituted to Cottenham in 1671. It was probably started after the death of Skinner in 1670 and added to or entries deleted thereafter.

[192] Probably Llandinam with Banhaglog.

William Fuller	Lincolne Trans	Preb. Leighton Buzzard	
~~Anth. Sparrow~~	~~Exon Cons.~~	~~Chancellor Ch. of Exon~~ Sped	Mr. Thomkins
~~Petr Gunning~~	~~Cicestrens Ep. Trans~~	~~Vic. de Bexhill Susp~~	Vacat trans Ep
Isaac Barrow	Asaphens Trans	Rect. de Llansanfrayd	
Nath Crew	Oxon Consecr.	Archdeaconry of Oxon	Vacat morte Ep
Walter Blandford	Wigorn Translat.	Fladbury Rect	
Tho Wood	Lich. & Co Ep. Cons	Treasurership of the Church	
John Pritchett	Gloucester Ep. Cons	Standish Rect	
Peter Mews	Bath & Wells	Treasurership of the Church	
Humfrey Lloyd	Bangor Ep. Cons	Llanyrys R; Sine Cur. Sped.	
Henry Compton	Oxon. Ep. Transl	Arch.-Deaconry of Oxon.	
Peter Gunning	Elieni Ep. Trans.	Glemsford	

Folios 74 to 78 are blank.

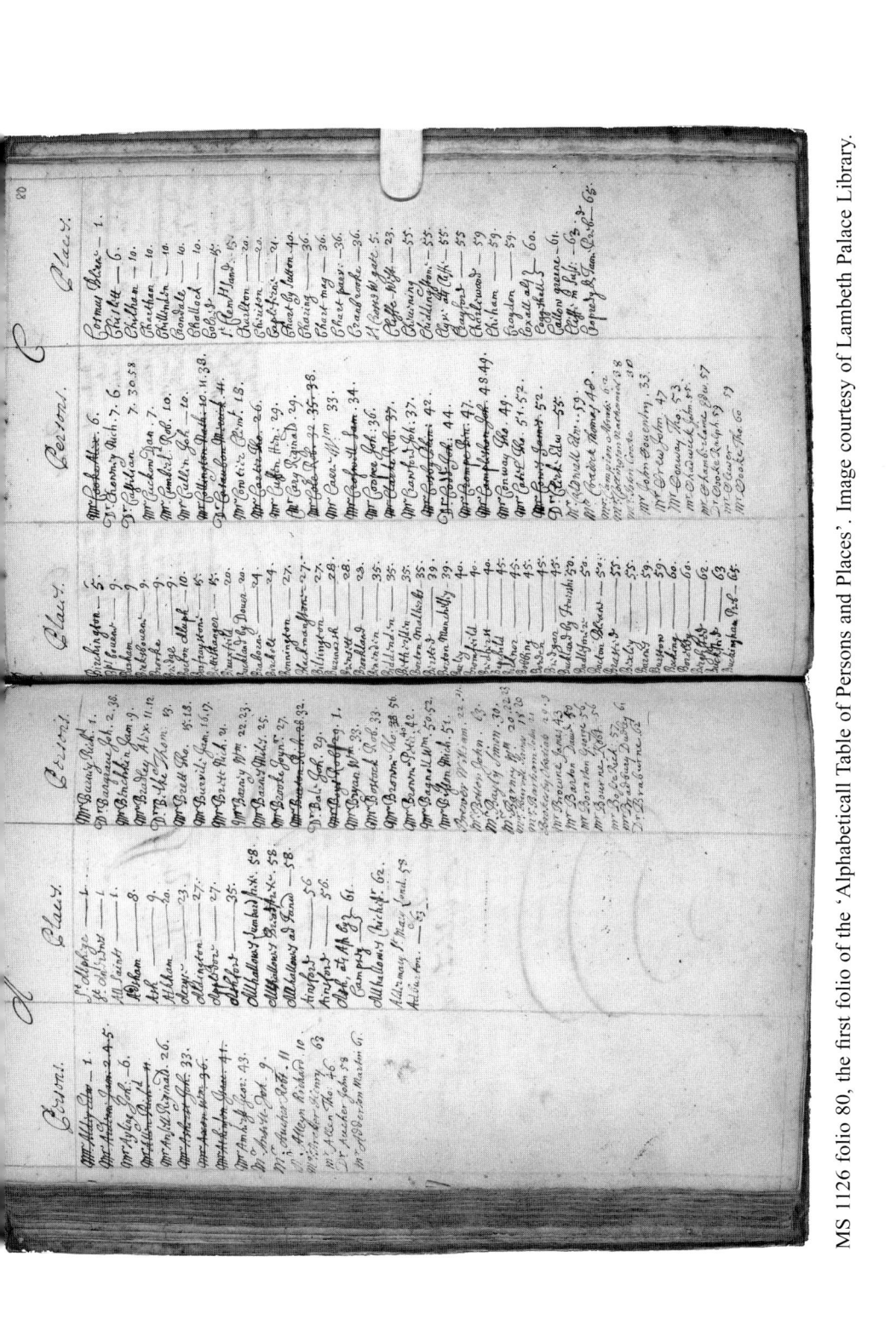

A

Persons	Place
Mr Aldryton — 1.	St Aldrige — 1.
Mr Allen Jam. 2. 4. 5.	St Alban's — 1.
Mr Aylin Joh. — 6.	All Saints — 1.
Mr Ellis Paul. — 7.	Aldham — 8.
Mr Anglet Rayn.D. 26.	Ash — 9.
Mr Ant: ap Feb. 33.	Azay — 20.
Mr Askew Jer. 36.	Atlington — 33.
Mrs Ashton Jam. 41.	Aldpons — 27.
Dr Ashrt. Pet. 9.	Alger-s — 35.
Mr Austin Roff. 11.	Allhallows Lumbard H. St. 58.
Dr Ancher Rich.D. 10	Allhallows Bread St. — 58.
Whiteacre Henry. 63.	Allhallows ad Fænum — 58.
Mr Atkin Tho. 46.	Strafort — 56.
Dr Ancher John 79.	Austin — 56.
Mr Apperton Martin 6.	Abel ch Ap. 62. 61.
	Campsy
	Allhallows Crich.F 62.
	Aldermary St Marie Conh. 58
	Ashburton — 65

Persons	Place
Mr Banny Rich. 1.	Bishington — 5.
Dr Bargrave Joh. 2. 36.	St Bennet — 1
Mr Brichlin Jam 9.	Baham — 3.
Mr Baxley Alex. 11. 12.	Belgrave — 7.
Dr B. ye Thorn. 13.	Burke — 9.
Mr Brett Tho. 6. 13.	Boyge — 10.
Mr Bucrvill Jam. 16. 17.	Burton chapl — 15.
Mr Bratt Rich. 21.	Burlayton — 15.
Mr Bassey Wm. 22. 23.	Ashinge — 10.
Mr Bassey Walt. 25.	Dudley by Down — 20.
Mr Brooke Jun. 27.	Coate — 26.
Mr Barnes Rich. 32.	Bennington — 27.
Dr Bal. Joh. 29.	Rockmasham — 27.
Mr Doyer Geff. 9. 1.	Bilington — 27.
Mr Bagnall Wm. 33.	Braunch — 28.
Mr Botford Rich. 33.	Burlo. 9 — 23.
Mr Barron Ala. 22. 56.	Avinton — 35.
Mr Burton Rich. 42.	Battersdon — 35.
Mr Bagnall Wm. 50. 52.	Bostow Malkah — 35.
Mr Coffm Rich. 51.	Buck — 39.
Brooke Wilham 22. 70.	Burton Manchtby — 39.
Mr Brett John 68.	Burly — 40.
Mr Bayly Simon 20.	Buffold — 47.
Mr Stone Wm 20.12.24	Bull — 43.
Mr Sevins Rob. 18.20	Uppell — 45.
Mr Bartrom Inn —	Betham — 45.
Bondeley David —	Sewing — 45.
Mr Braunt James 43	B. Swan — 43.
Bullr 9 G. Jariste 70.	Bulls 9 G. Jariste. 70.
Mr Berntow Inn 80	Ipson — 50.
Mr Bourne — 53.	Butow — 59.
Mr Baxtad Reb. 56.	Ballsy — 60.
Dr Brahm Dudley 6.	Buck Red. Stly 6.
Dr Brabourne 60	Brauls. 3
	Burgh feed
	Buckingham R.L. — 63

C

Persons	Place
Mr Cook Alex. 6.	Cotmas Plane — 1.
Dr Cherony Rich. 7. 6.	Grillt — 6.
Dr Colgate. 7. 30.58	Chillan — 6.
Mr Cuckow Jam. 7.	Cranham — 10.
Mr Cumbrel. Rod. 10.	Crallyn — 10.
Mr Cullen Col. — 10.	Condale — 10.
Mr Caulson Pick. 10. 11. 38.	Challack — 10.
Mr Cranck Marc. 11.	Col.y. — 15.
Mr Contic. Rebt. 13.	St Ctem Jane — 15.
Mr Curtis Tho. 26.	Cuillon — 20.
Mr Curtis Hin. 29.	Chision — 20.
Mr Car Rayn.D. 29.	Capt.Jack — 21.
Mr Cox R.D. 32. 35.38.	Chiosly Jaden 40.
Mr Casa Wm. 33.	Charing — 36.
Mr Caswell Jam. 34.	Chart my — 36.
Mr Cooper Joh. 36.	Chart prey — 36.
Mr Coll Ro. 37.	Cranbrook — 36.
Mr Cartes Joh. 37.	St Clemn W gate — 23.
Mr Cox Joh. 37.	Criffe Wm — 55.
C: Bull Rich. 42.	Cilaney — 55.
Mr Sigm R. 44.	Chiddligham — 55.
Mr Campron Int. 47.	Cage. ad Clifse — 55.
Mr Camprenborough. 48.49.	Earpes. — 55.
Mr Coaway Ro. 49.	Childwood. — 59.
Mr Chiel Bo. 51. 52.	Chitham — 59.
Mr Grave James 53.	Croydon — 59.
Dr Stoot Elia — 55.	Coxall ad f. — 60.
Mr Oswolt Hor — 59.	Cagshall. 3
Mr Crudot Thomas AP.	Culdon greene — 61
Campton ad Ahrende. 60.	Coff Cliffe. 63. 9.
Mr Cyrington Wardsworth 58	Cooke Right 63 — 19
Mr Corington — 10	Copely Sam Oxb. 62. 65
Mr John Bogentry. 53.	
Mr Crow John 47.	
Mr Danvsy Tho. 53.	
Mr Chadwick John 68.	
Mr Chamberlaine Bro. 57	
Mr Cooke Right 63 — 19	
Mr Cooke Tho. 60 — 17	

Bibliography

(I) MANUSCRIPTS

Canterbury Cathedral Archives

AddMs-79	The rectors of St Margaret's, Canterbury
BB/W/12	Appointment of William Somner as chapter auditor, 1660
DCc/BB/P/154	Letter from Miles Smyth to Edmund Pierce, 1665
DCc/LitMS/C/5	Willam Somner's notes on exempt parishes, *c.* 1668
DCc-BB/W/12	Appointment of William Somner as deputy receiver general, 1660
DCc-BB/W/13	Bond of William Somner and Mart Hirst to pay William Sherman, 1663
DCc-Bond/525	Thomas Turner presentation bond, 1673
DCc-CantLet/121	Letters patent for a commissary for Bocking granted to Dr Colbrand
DCc-ChAnt/C/255C	Rectories and vicarages in Canterbury diocese, *c.* 1610
DCc-ChAnt/C/255D	Incumbents in the archdeaconry 15 Oct. 1663
DCc-ChAnt/C/825E	Elisha Robinson presentation bond, 1666
DCc-ChAnt/S/406	Appointment of William Somner as registrar of the commissary and consistory courts for the city and diocese of Canterbury, 1660
DCc-MAND/SP/1671/1	Mandate to appoint William King as a Six Preacher to replace George May, 1671
DCc-PET/45	Petition from Richard Langham, minor canon, seventeenth century
DCc-PET/211	Petition from William Gibson, vicar of Meopham, *c.* 1661
DCc-SVSB/2/167/2	Presentation of John Sidway to the vicarage of Selling, 1677
DCc-TB/1–35	Treasurers' Books, 1660–1700
U3/232/1/1	Goodnestone by Wingham composite register, 1558–1812
U108/2/25	Augmentation Books, Commonwealth period

U108/16	Frampton Collection
VP/6	Agenda for visitation of cathedral and diocese, William Somner, seventtenth century
VP/9	Appointment of William Somner to act for the principal registrar to the archbishop, 1662

Durham University Library

Cosin Letter Book 1B	Letter from Miles Smyth to Bishop Cosin, 17 Feb. 1665

London, British Library

Add 36792	Register of benefices and ecclesiastical preferments 1649–54
Add 39506	Names of persons compounding for first fruits, 1536–1660, in Kent ...
Lansdowne MS 958	Sir John Birkenhead: notes for a Commons speech in March 1663
SP 29/93	Register of the names of 116 independents, 156 anabaptists, and 96 quakers, in the several parishes and hundreds of the lathe of St Augustine's, Kent, with the names of their teachers

Lambeth Palace Library

Arches A 2	Act Books Nov. 1660–23 Oct. 1663
Arches A 5	Act Books 23 Oct. 1666–22 Oct. 1668
Arches A 14	Act Books 23 Oct, 1678–21 Oct. 1680
Arches Ff 314	Elizabeth Marsh against Jane Smith, wife of Miles Smith, *c.* 1665
CM 28/4	Declared account of William Somner, 22 Nov. 1661
CM 48/3	Presentation of Richard Bosse MA to the vicarage of Sevenoaks, 10 Dec. 1664
CM I/52	Union of St Paul and St Martin, Canterbury 24 Mar. 1681–2
COMM I	Presentation deeds and institution papers, 1643–6
COMM II	Presentation deeds and institution papers, 1650–9
COMM III	Registers of presentations and approvals of ministers, 1654–60
COMM V	Day books, 1652–60
COMM XIIa	Copies of surveys, 1647–57

F I/C	Muniment Book, 1660–9
F I/D	Muniment Book, 1669–81
F I/G	Muniment Book, 1723–33
F II	Fiats, 1660–
F V/1	Registers of noblemen's chaplains
MS 639 fos. 139r–445v	Papers relating to Sheldon surveys, 1665–76
MS 923	Survey of benefices, 1665
MS 943 pp. 380a–g	Return from bishop of St Asaph relating to Sheldon survey, 1665
MS 951/1 fos. 54r–86v, 110r–113v	Papers relating to Sheldon surveys, 1665–76
MS 1047	Catalogue of the manuscripts in Lambeth Palace Library, as arranged 1663–1677
MS 1104	Papers of the trustees for the maintenance of preaching ministers, 1649–57
MS 1126	Survey of Canterbury diocese, 1663–82
MS 1137	Survey of Canterbury diocese, 1668–95
MS 1643	Jenkins papers: index of parochial clergy, c. 1620–63
MS 1753 fos. 1–17	Sermon on Proverbs 8, v. 15, preached by John Sargenson
MS 2004 fos. 14–15v	Paper entitled 'Reasons in defence of pluralities', 1584
MS 2216 fo. 20	List of advocates in Doctors' Commons, 1600–1
MS Facsimile 6	Copy of manuscript in the Bodleian Library relating to Lambeth Palace Library
TA 696/4	Counterpart lease to William Barker, 1662
Vb 1/1–8	Act Books, 1663–1734
VG 1/2–7	Subscription Books, 1660–1736
VH 2	Peculiar jurisdiction: presentation deeds
VH 5	Peculiar jurisdiction: nominations of perpetual curates
VH 70	Peculiar jurisdiction: Cliffe-at-Hoo visitation papers
VH 77	Peculiar jurisdiction: cause papers: clergy and churchwardens
VH 95	Peculiar jurisdiction: wills and inventories: Arches
VH 96	Peculiar jurisdiction: wills and inventories: Croydon and Shoreham
VH 97	Peculiar jurisdiction: registers of wills
VH 98	Peculiar jurisdiction: Probate Act Books

VX IA/10   Licences to practise medicine

London Metropolitan Archives
P69/ALH2   Parish records, All Hallows, Bread Street
P69/ANN   Parish records, St Ann, Blackfriars
P69/JNE   Parish records, St John the Evangelist, Friday Street
P69/LEN1   Parish records, St Leonard, Eastcheap
P69/MRY6   Parish records, St Mary Bothaw
P69/PAN   Parish records, St Pancras, Soper Lane

The National Archives
PROB 11/172/178   Will of Thomas Pordage of Rodmersham, Kent
PROB 11/221/153   Will of Richard Alleyn, rector of Stowting, Kent
PROB 11/337/545   Will of Paul Boston, vicar of St Bride and curate of St Giles in the Fields
PROB 11/346/372   Will of William Pawley, late curate of Knockholt
PROB 11/360/410   Will of John Nayler of Grays Inn, Middlesex
PROB 11/539/376   Will of Thomas Turner, president of Corpus Christi College, Oxford
PROB 11/380/282   Will of Sir John Southcote of Merstham, Surrey
PROB 11/593/387   Will of Thomas Cradock, vicar of Rainham, Kent

Maidstone, Kent History and Library Centre
DCb/J/Z/3/34   Archdeacon Greene's account of parishes, 1711–15
DCb/J/Z/3/44   Oath Book: curates and schoolmasters, 1681
DCb/J/Z/7/4   Libri Cleri, 1663
DCb/L/R/17–27   Registered licences, 1644–65
DCb/PRC/18/30/152   Claim for dilapidations, Nicholls v Collington senior
DCb/V/V/43   Visitation Call Book, 1630
DCb/V/V/56–71   Visitation Call Books, 1662–77
DCb/V/V/74   Visitation Call Book, 1680
DCb/V/V/79   Visitation Call Book, 1685
DCb/V/V/84   Visitation Call Book, 1690
DCb/V/V/89   Visitation Call Book, 1695
DCb/V/V/95   Visitation Call Book, 1700
Q/J/C/8–12   Commissions of the peace 1657–70

| TR/2322/23 | Farningham parish registers |

Medway Archives Centre
DRc/AC3/7	Chapter of Rochester Minute Book III
P153/1/2	Gillingham composite register
P314/1/1	Isle of Grain composite register

Oxford, Bodleian Library
Sancroft 99	Parochial notebook, 1668
Tanner 59	Letter from the committee of Kent to Speaker Lenthall, 21 Apr. 1646
Tanner 122	A catalogue of all the benefices and spiritual promotions within the diocese and jurisdiction of Canterbury, with the patrons and values; corrected by archbishop Sancroft up to the year 1688
Tanner 124, fo. 206	Working sheet from Lambeth Palace Library MS 1126 Index of Persons and Places
Tanner 124, fos. 207–21	A note of all the benefices within the jurisdiction of the archdeacon of Canterbury
Tanner 125, fos. 145–55	A note of all the benefices within the jurisdiction of the archdeacon of Canterbury
Tanner 270	Codex chartaceus, in folio, fr. 22, sec. xvii. Catalogus librorum in bibliotheca Lambethana, auctore Gul. Sancroft

Shropshire Archives
| X7381/225/1246-IMG1653 | Extracts from Stottesdon register, 1565–1687 |

(II) PRIMARY PRINTED SOURCES

Unless otherwise specified the place of publication is London.

Bird, R., *The journal of Giles Moore* (Sussex Record Society, 68, Lewes, 1971)
Boodle, J. A., ed., *The registers of Boughton-under-Blean* (Parish Register Society, 49, 1903)
Bray, G., ed., *The Anglican canons 1529–1947* (Church of England Record Society, 6, Woodbridge, 1998)
Broadway, J., Cust, R., and Roberts, S. K., eds., *A calendar of the docquets of Lord Keeper Coventry 1625–1640* (4 vols., List and Index Society, Special Series, 34–7, Kew, 2004)

Calendar of state papers colonial, America and West Indies (41 vols., 1860–1969)
Calendar of state papers domestic: Charles II (28 vols., 1860–1939)
Caley, J., Ellis, H., and Bandinel, B., eds., *Monasticon anglicanum: or, the history of the ancient abbies, and other monasteries, hospitals, cathedral and collegiate churches in England and Wales* ... , collected in Latin by Sir William Dugdale (8 vols., 1823)
Cardwell, E., *Documentary annals of the reformed Church of England: being a collection of injunctions, declarations, orders, articles of inquiry, from the year 1546 to the year 1716* (2 vols., Oxford, 1839)
Clarke, A. W. H., ed., *The parish register of Wimbledon, co. Surrey* (Surrey Record Society, 8, 1924)
Cliffe, J. T., ed., 'The Cromwellian Decimation Tax of 1655: the assessment lists' *Seventeenth-century political letters and papers. Miscellany, Vol. XXXIII* (Royal Historical Society, Camden 5th series, 7, Cambridge, 1996)
Cowper, J. M., ed., *The booke of regester of the parish of St. Peter in Canterbury: for christninges, weddinges and buryalls, 1560–1800* (Canterbury, 1888)
Cowper, J. M., ed., *The register booke of christeninges, marriages and buriails in Saint Dunstan's, Canterbury, 1559–1800* (Canterbury, 1887)
Foster, J., ed., *The register of admissions to Gray's Inn, 1521–1889* (1889)
Gregory, J., ed., *The Speculum of Archbishop Thomas Secker* (Church of England Record Society, 2, Woodbridge, 1995)
Harrington, D., ed., *Kent Hearth Tax assessment Lady Day 1664* (2000)
HMC, *The forty-sixth annual report of the deputy keeper of the public records.* 11 August 1885 Appendix I Nos. 1 and 2 Presentations to Offices, on the Patent Rolls; Charles II, vol. XXXVII, Readex Microprint Edition
HMC, *Calendar of the proceedings of the Committee for Compounding, etc., 1643–1660, preserved in the State Paper Department of Her Majesty's Public Record Office* (3 vols., 1889–92)
Journals of the House of Lords (42 vols., 1767–1830)
Larking, L. B., ed., *Proceedings principally in the county of Kent ... in 1640* (Camden Society, o.s, 80, 1862)
Le Neve, J., *Fasti ecclesiae anglicanae 1541–1857*, ed. J. M. Horn *et al.* (13 vols., 1969–2013)
Littledale, W. A., ed., *The registers of St Vedast, Foster Lane and of St Michael le Quern, London* (2 vols., 1902–3)
Lodge, E. C., ed., *The account book of a Kentish estate 1616–1704* (1927)
Lyon Turner, G., ed., *Original records of early nonconformity under persecution and indulgence* (2 vols., 1911)
Pickering, D., *The statutes at large*, XIV (Cambridge, 1765)
Robinson, C. J., ed., *A register of the scholars admitted into Merchant Taylors' School 1562–1874* (Lewes, 1882)
Rushworth, R., *Historical collections: 1625 (Charles I), historical collections of private passages of state*, I: 1618–29 (1721)
Wilkie, C. H., ed., *The parish registers of Elmstone, Kent, 1552–1812* (Kingston, 1891)
Wilkie, C. H., ed., *The parish registers of St. Giles, Kingston* (Brighton, 1893)
Wilkie, C. H., ed., *The parish registers of St. Peter's, Beaksbourne, Kent, 1558–1812* (Canterbury, 1896)
Wilkins, D., ed., *Concilia magnae Britanniae et Hiberniae* (4 vols., 1737)

(III) SECONDARY PRINTED SOURCES

Unless otherwise specified the place of publication is London.

Armytage, G. J., ed., *A visitation of the county of Kent, begun A.D. 1663 and finished A.D. 1668* (Harleian Society, 54, 1906)
Bate, F., *The Declaration of Indulgence 1672* (1908)
Beardmore, H. L., 'A list of the rectors of Ripple', *Archaeologia Cantiana*, 27 (1905)
Beaumont, G. F., *A history of Coggeshall, in Essex* (1890)
Beaven, A. B., *The aldermen of the city of London* (1908)
Beddard, R., 'The privileges of Christchurch, Canterbury: Archbishop Sheldon's enquiries of 1671', *Archaeologia Cantiana*, 87 (1972)
Bennett, N., *Lincolnshire parish clergy c. 1214–1968: a biographical register*, Part II: *The deaneries of Beltisloe and Bolingbroke* (Lincoln Record Society, 105, Lincoln, 2016)
Berry, W., *Pedigrees of the families in the county of Kent* (1830)
Besse, J., *A collection of the sufferings of the people called quakers* (2 vols., 1753)
Best, G. F. A. *Temporal pillars: Queen Anne's Bounty, the ecclesiastical commissioners, and the Church of England* (Cambridge, 1964)
Blomefield, F., *et al.*, *An essay towards a topographical history of the county of Norfolk* (11 vols., 1805–10)
Bloomfield, P., 'The Cromwellian Commission in Kent, 1655–57', in *Studies in modern Kentish history*, ed. A. Detsicas and N. Yates (Maidstone, 1983)
Bosher, R. S., *The making of the Restoration settlement, 1649–1662* (1951)
Boys, W., *Collections for an history of Sandwich* (Canterbury, 1791)
Bradfer-Lawrence, H. L., *A short history of the castle honor and borough of Castle Rising* (King's Lynn, 1932)
Bramston, W., *A history of the abbey church of Minster* (1896)
Brooks, P. N., *Reformation principle and practice* (1980)
Brydges, E., *Peerage of England* (9 vols., 1812)
Bucholz, R. O., *et al.*, eds., *Office-holders in modern Britain* (12 vols., 1972–2006)
Burke, J. and J. B., *A genealogical and heraldic history of the extinct and dormant baronetcies of England* (1841)
Burrage, C., 'The Fifth Monarchy insurrections', *English Historical Review*, 25 (1910)
Cartwright, E., *et al.*, *A history of the western division of the county of Sussex ...* (3 vols., 1815–32)
Cass, F. C., *Monken Hadley* (1880)
Cave-Browne, J., *The history of Boxley parish* (Maidstone, 1892)
Cave-Browne, J., *The story of Hollingbourne* (Maidstone, 1890)
Cave-Browne, J., *The history of the parish church of All Saints, Maidstone* (Maidstone, 1889)
Cavell, J., and Kennett, B., *A history of Sir Roger Manwood's School Sandwich 1563–1963* (1963)
Chalkin, C. W., *Seventeenth-century Kent* (1965)
Chamberlain, J. S., *Accommodating high churchmen: the clergy of Sussex, 1700–1745* (Urbana, 1997)
Chester, J. L., and Armytage, G. J., eds., *Allegations for marriage licences issued by the bishop of London, 1611 to 1828* (Harleian Society, 26, 1887)

Chester, J. L., and Armytage, G. J., eds., *Allegations for marriage licences issued from the faculty office of the archbishop of Canterbury at London, 1543 to 1869* (Harleian Society, 24, 1886)
Churchill, I. J., *Canterbury administration* ... (2 vols., 1933)
Clark, P., 'Josias Nicholls and religious radicalism, 1553–1639', *Journal of Ecclesiastical History*, 28 (1977)
Coates, W. H., Snow, V. F., and Young, A. S., eds., *The private journals of the Long Parliament* (3 vols., New Haven, 1982–92)
Cobbett, W., *Parliamentary history of England* ... (36 vols., 1806–20)
Cockburn, J. S., ed. *Calendar of assize records Kent indictments 1649–1659* (1989)
Cockburn, J. S., ed. *Calendar of assize records Kent indictments Charles II 1660–1675* (1995)
Cockburn, J. S., ed. *Calendar of assize records Kent indictments Charles II 1676–1688* (1997)
Cokayne, G. E., ed. *Complete baronetage* (5 vols., Exeter, 1900–6)
Collinson, P., Ramsay, N., and Sparks, M., eds., *A history of Canterbury cathedral* (Oxford, 1995)
Crisp, F. A., *The parish registers of Stifford, Essex* (privately printed, 1885)
Cross, C., ed., *Patronage and recruitment in the Tudor and early Stuart church* (Borthwick Studies in History, 2, York, 1996)
Dobson, M. J., 'Death and disease in the Romney Marsh area in the 17th to 19th centuries', in *Romney Marsh Environmental Change and Human Occupation in a Coastal Lowland* (University of Oxford Committee for Archaeology, Monograph No. 46, 1998)
Draper, G., 'The first hundred years of quakerism in Kent', *Archaeologia Cantiana*, 112 (1994)
Dunkin, E. H. W., 'Admissions to Sussex benefices (temp Commonwealth) by the commissioners for the approbation of public preachers', *Sussex Archaeological Collections*, 33 (1883)
Dunkin, E. H. W., 'Contributions towards the ecclesiastical history of the deanery of South Malling', *Sussex Archaeological Collections*, 26 (1875)
Dunkin, E. H. W., Jenkins, C., and Fry, E. A., *Index to the Act Books of the archbishops of Canterbury 1663–1859* (2 vols., 1929–38)
Ecton, J., *Liber valorum & decimarum: being an account of such ecclesiastical benefices* ... (2nd edn, 1723)
Elwes, D. G. C., 'The parish of South Bersted', *Sussex Archaeological Collections*, 24 (1872)
Erwood, E. F. C., 'Notes on the churches of Romney Marsh in the county of Kent, 1923' *Archaeologia Cantiana*, 37 (1925)
Everitt, A., *The community of Kent and the Great Rebellion 1640–1660* (Leicester, 1966)
Everitt, A., ed., 'An account book of the committee of Kent, 1646–7', in *A seventeenth century miscellany* (Canterbury, 1960)
Faussett, T. G., 'Family chronicle of Richard Fogge, of Danes Court, in Tilmanstone', *Archaeologia Cantiana*, 5 (1863)
Fielding, C. H., *The records of Rochester* (Dartford, 1910)
Fincham, K., *Prelate as pastor. The episcopate of James I* (Oxford, 1990)
Fincham, K., and Lake, P., ed., *Religious politics in post-Reformation England* (Woodbridge, 2006)

Fincham, K., and Taylor, S., 'Episcopalian conformity and nonconformity, 1646–1660', in *Royalists and royalism during the Interregnum*, ed. J. McElligott and D. Smith (Manchester, 2010)

Fincham, K., and Tyacke, N., *Altars restored: the changing face of English religious worship, 1547–c. 1700* (Oxford, 2010)

Fishwick, H., *The history of the parish of Rochdale in the county of Lancaster* (Rochdale, 1889)

Fletcher, A., 'The enforcement of the Conventicle Acts 1664–1679', *Studies in Church History*, 21 (1984)

Foster, J., ed., *Alumni Oxonienses* (4 vols., Oxford, 1891–2)

Fox, J., *The king's smuggler: Jane Whorwood ...* (Stroud, 2010)

Frampton, T. S., 'List of forty-five vicars of Tilmanstone', *Archaeologia Cantiana*, 20 (1893)

Frampton, T. S., 'St. Mary's church, Minster, Isle of Thanet' *Archaeologia Cantiana*, 25 (1902)

Frampton, T. S., 'The vicar, masters or provosts, and perpetual curates of the church of SS. Gregory and Martin, Wye', *Archaeologia Cantiana*, 28 (1909)

Greaves, R. L., *Deliver us from evil: the radical underground in Britain, 1660–1663* (Oxford, 1986)

Green, I. M., *The re-establishment of the Church of England, 1660–1663* (Oxford, 1978)

Gregory, J., *Restoration, reformation and reform, 1660–1828* (Oxford, 2000)

Gregory, J., ed., *The Oxford history of anglicanism*, II: *Establishment and empire, 1662–1829* (Oxford, 2017)

Gregory, J., and Chamberlain, J. S., eds., *The national church in local perspective. The Church of England and the regions 1660–1800* (Woodbridge, 2005)

Haggard, J., *Reports of cases argued and determined in the ecclesiastical courts ...* (2 vols., 1829–30)

Haines, R. M., 'Some arguments in favour of plurality in the Elizabethan church', *Studies in Church History*, 5 (1969)

Hardman Moore, S., *Pilgrims: new world settlers and the call of home* (New Haven and London, 2007)

Harris, T., *London crowds in the reign of Charles II* (Cambridge, 1990)

Hart, W. G., *The register of Tonbridge School* (1935)

Haslewood, F., *Memorials of Smarden, Kent* (Ipswich, 1886)

Haslewood, F., *The parish of Benenden Kent* (Ipswich, 1889)

Hasted, E., *The history and topographical survey of the county of Kent* (2nd edn, 12 vols., 1797–1801)

Hegarty, A., ed., *A biographical register of St. John's College, Oxford 1555–1666* (Oxford Historical Society, n.s., 43, Woodbridge, 2011)

Hennessy, G. L., *Novum repertorium ecclesiasticum parochiale londinense* (1898)

Heygate Lambert, F. A., *The registers of Banstead, Surrey* (1896)

Hill, C., *Economic problems of the church* (Oxford, 1968)

Houston, J., *Catalogue of ecclesiastical records of the Commonwealth 1643–1660 in the Lambeth Palace Library* (1968)

Hudson, T. P., ed., *A history of the county of Sussex*, Victoria County History of Sussex, VI, Part 1: *Bramber rape (southern part)* (1980)

Hussey, A., 'Visitations of the archdeacon of Canterbury', *Archaeologia Cantiana*, 25 (1902)

Hussey, A., 'Visitations of the archdeacon of Canterbury', *Archaeologia Cantiana*, 26 (1904)
Ingram Hill, D., *The Six Preachers of Canterbury cathedral 1541–1982* (Ramsgate, 1982)
Ivimey, J., *A history of the English baptists* (4 vols., 1811–30)
Jones, M. V., 'The divine Durant: a seventeenth-century independent', *Archaeologia Cantiana*, 83 (1968)
Kilburne, R. *A topographie or survey of the county of Kent* (1659)
King, T. W., 'Some remarks on a brass plate formerly in the church of Holy Trinity at Guildford', *Surrey Archaeological Collections*, 3 (1865)
Latham R., and Matthews, W., eds., *The diary of Samuel Pepys* (11 vols., 1970–83)
C. Lee, '"Fanatic magistrates": religious and political conflict in three Kent boroughs, 1680–1684', *Historical Journal*, 35 (1992)
Lightfoot, W. J., 'Notes from the parochial register of Orlestone', *Archaeologia Cantiana*, 2 (1859)
Lightfoot, W. J., 'Notes on Warehorne church and its ancient stained glass, with indices to the parochial registers of Warehorne and Newenden', *Archaeologia Cantiana*, 4 (1861)
Lipscomb, G., *The history and antiquities of the county of Buckingham* (4 vols., 1847)
Lutton, R., 'Heresy and heterodoxy in late medieval Kent', in *Later medieval Kent, 1220–1540*, ed. S. Sweetinburgh (Woodbridge, 2010)
McCartney, M. W., *Virginia immigrants and adventurers, 1607–1635: a biographical dictionary* (Baltimore, 2007)
Mackenzie, E., and Ross, M., *An historical, topographical, and descriptive view of the county palatine of Durham* (Newcastle upon Tyne, 2 vols., 1834)
Massue, M. H., *The Plantagenet Roll of the Blood Royal ... Mortimer-Percy Volume* (1911)
Mastin, J., *The history and antiquities of Naseby* (Cambridge, 1792)
Matthews, A. G., *Calamy revised* (Oxford, 1988)
Matthews, A. G., *Walker revised* (Oxford, 1948)
Newcourt, R., *Repertorium ecclesiasticum parochiale londinense* (2 vols., 1708–10)
Oechsli, W., *History of Switzerland 1499–1914* (Cambridge, 1922)
Orridge, B. B., *Some account of the citizens of London ...* (1867)
Overton, J. H., *The nonjurors* (1902)
Packer, B., 'Nonconformity in Tenterden: 1640–1750', *Transactions of the Unitarian Historical Society* 20 (1992)
Page, W., ed., *The Victoria history of the county of Buckingham* (2 vols., 1905–8)
Pearce, E. H., *Sion College and Library* (Cambridge, 1913)
Pearman, A. J., *Ashford: its church, vicars, college, and grammar school* (Ashford, 1886)
Pearman, A. J., 'Bethersden, its church, and monumental inscriptions', *Archaeologia Cantiana*, 16 (1886)
Pearman, A. J., 'The Chutes of Bethersden, Appledore, and Hinxhill', *Archaeologia Cantiana*, 18 (1889)
Pearman, A. J., 'Rainham church', *Archaeologia Cantiana*, 17 (1887)
Pearman, A. J., 'Rectors of Merstham', *Surrey Archaeological Collections*, 17 (1902)
Peile, J., *Biographical register of Christ's College 1505–1905* (2 vols., 1910–13)
Plomer, H. R., *A dictionary of the printers and booksellers who were at work in England, Scotland and Ireland from 1668 to 1725* (Oxford, 1922)

Poole, A., *A market town and its surrounding villages* (Chichester, 2005)
Pruett, J. H., *The parish clergy under the later Stuarts: the Leicestershire experience* (Urbana, 1978)
Puckle, J., 'The ancient fabric of the church of St. Mary the Virgin, Dover', *Archaeologia Cantiana*, 20 (1893)
Ray, J. E., 'The church of SS Peter and Paul, Bexhill', *Sussex Archaeological Collections*, 53 (1910)
Reeves, A., and Eve, D., 'Sheep-keeping and lookers' huts on Romney Marsh', in *Romney Marsh environmental change and human occupation in a coastal lowland*, ed. J. Eddison, M. Gardiner and A. Long (Oxford, 1998)
Richardson, D., *Magna Carta ancestry: a study in colonial and medieval families*, I (Baltimore, 2011)
Rushworth, J., *Historical collections of private passages of state ...* (8 vols., 1721)
St Croix, W. de, 'Parochial history of Glynde', *Sussex Archaeological Collections*, 20 (1868)
Sawyer, F. E., 'Proceedings of the committee of plundered ministers relating to Sussex', *Sussex Archaeological Collections*, 30 (1880)
Scott, J. R., *Memorials of the family of Scott, of Scot's-hall ...* (1883)
Scott Robertson, W. A., 'Bexley', *Archaeologia Cantiana*, 18 (1889)
Scott Robertson, W. A., 'Church of St. Botolph, Lullingstone', *Archaeologia Cantiana*, 16 (1886)
Scott Robertson, W. A., 'Patricksbourne church, and Bifrons', *Archaeologia Cantiana*, 14 (1882)
Scott Robertson, W. A., 'Rectors of Preston-by-Faversham', *Archaeologia Cantiana*, 21 (1895)
Shaw, W. A., *A history of the English church during the civil wars and under the Commonwealth, 1640–1660* (2 vols., 1900)
Shaw, W. A., *The knights of England* (2 vols., 1906)
Shaw, W. F., *Memorials of the royal ville and parish of Eastry* (1870)
Smith, G., *Royalist agents, conspirators and spies* (Oxford, 2016)
Smith, P. M., 'The advowson: the history and development of a most peculiar property', *Ecclesiastical Law Journal*, 5 (2000)
Somner, W., *The antiquities of Canterbury ...* , rev. N. Battely (2nd edn, 1703)
Spaeth, D. A., *The church in an age of danger: parsons and parishioners, 1660–1740* (Cambridge, 2000)
Spurr, J., *The Restoration Church of England, 1646–1689* (1991)
Squibb, G. D., *Doctors' Commons: a history of the College of Advocates and Doctors of Law* (Oxford, 1977)
Stieg, M., *Laud's laboratory. The diocese of Bath and Wells in the early seventeenth century* (1982)
Sterry, W., *The Eton College register 1441–1698* (Eton, 1943)
Stevens, R., *Protestant pluralism: the reception of the Toleration Act, 1689–1720* (Woodbridge, 2018)
Tapsell, G., *The personal rule of Charles II, 1681–85* (Woodbridge, 2007)
Tarbutt, W., *The annals of Cranbrook church* (Cranbrook, 1870)
Taylor, A. H., 'The chapel of St. John the Baptist, Smallhythe', *Archaeologia Cantiana*, 30 (1914)
Taylor, A. H., 'The grammar free school at Tenterden', *Archaeologia Cantiana*, 44 (1932)

Taylor, A. H., 'The rectors and vicars of St. Mildred's, Tenterden', *Archaeologia Cantiana*, 31 (1915)
Thomas, H. R., and Ryan, J., eds., *Wolverhampton Grammar School register* (Kendal, 1926)
Throsby, J., ed., *Thoroton's history of Nottinghamshire* (3 vols., 1790–7)
Tomlinson, E. M., *A history of the minories London* (1907)
Turner, E., 'The College of Benedictine Canons at South Malling', *Sussex Archaeological Collections*, 5 (1852)
Unknown author, 'Monumental inscriptions in St. Alphage church, Canterbury', *The Topographer*, 1 (1789)
Venn, J. and J. A., eds., *Alumni Cantabrigienses, Part 1: From the earliest times to 1751* (4 vols., Cambridge, 1922–7)
Weston, D. W. V., 'The origins, development and demise of perpetual curacy', *Ecclesiastical Law Journal*, 5 (1998)
Whiteman, A., 'The re-establishment of the Church of England, 1660–1663', *Transactions of the Royal Historical Society*, 5th series, 5 (1955)
Whiteman, A., ed., with M. Clapinson, *The Compton Census of 1676: a critical edition* (1986)
Willis, A. J., ed., *Canterbury licences (general) 1568–1646* (Chichester, 1972)
Willis, A. J., ed., 'Canterbury licences (general) 1660–1714' (unpublished typescript, Canterbury, 1975) (see also KHLC, DCb/L/R/17–27)
Willis, B., *Parochiale anglicanum: or the names of all the churches and chapels within the dioceses of Canterbury, Rochester, London, Winchester ...* (1733)
Wilson, H. B., *The history of Merchant-Taylors' School, from its foundation to the present time* (1814)
Woodruff, C. E., 'Letters relating to the condition of the church in Kent, during the primacy of Archbishop Sancroft', *Archaeologia Cantiana*, 21 (1895)
Woodruff, C. E., 'The records of the courts of the archdeaconry and consistory of Canterbury', *Archaeologia Cantiana*, 41 (1929)
Woodruff, C. E., and Cape, H. J., *Schola Regia Cantuariensis: a history of Canterbury School* (1908)
Wykes, D. L., 'Protestant dissent and the law: enforcement and persecution, 1662–72', *Studies in Church History*, 56 (2020)

(IV) UNPUBLISHED THESES

Barratt, D. M., 'The condition of the parish clergy between the Reformation and 1660, with special reference to the dioceses of Oxford, Worcester and Gloucester', D.Phil. thesis, University of Oxford, 1949
Daeley, J. I., 'The episcopal administration of Matthew Parker, archbishop of Canterbury, 1559–1575', Ph.D. thesis, London University, 1967
Fincham, K. C., 'Pastoral roles of the Jacobean episcopate in Canterbury province', Ph.D. thesis, London University, 1984
Freeman, J., 'The parish ministry in the diocese of Durham, c. 1570–1640', Ph.D. thesis, Durham University, 1980
Green, I. M., 'The process of re-establishment of the Church of England, 1660–1663', D.Phil. thesis, University of Oxford, 1973

Jones, S. A., 'The Church of England in the Forest of Arden, 1660–1740', Ph.D. thesis, University of Birmingham, 2009

Skea, K., 'The ecclesiastical identities of puritan and nonconformist clergy, 1640–1672', Ph.D. thesis, Leicester University, 2015

Marshall, W. M., 'The administration of the dioceses of Hereford and Oxford, 1660–1760', Ph.D. thesis, University of Bristol, 1978

Potter, J. M., 'The ecclesiastical courts in the diocese of Canterbury, 1603–1665', M.Phil. thesis, University of London, 1973

Reid, T., 'The clergy of the diocese of Canterbury in the seventeenth century', Ph.D. thesis, University of Kent, 2011

Salter, J. L., 'Warwickshire clergy, 1660–1714', Ph.D. thesis, Birmingham University, 1975

Stieg, M. F., 'The parochial clergy in the diocese of Bath and Wells, 1625–1685', Ph.D. thesis, University of California, 1970

Thomson, A. B. de L., 'The diocese of Winchester before and after the English civil wars: a study of the character and performance of its clergy', Ph.D. thesis, University of London, 2004

(V) UNPUBLISHED PAPER

Fincham, K., 'Somner and Laud', 2019.

(VI) ELECTRONIC SOURCES

Individuals

Asherst, John	www.hastingleigh.com/OPR/Warehorne-Burials
Buffkin, Captain	www.kentarchaeology.org.uk/Research/Libr/MIs/MIsLoose/01.htm
Cooper, John	Kent Family History Society transcriptions on CD-ROMs Cranbrook Burials
Couteur, Clement	www.theislandwiki.org/index.php/Clement_Le_Couteur
Crosswell, Samuel	www.familysearch.org England Deaths and Burials
Hurt, John	Kent Family History Society transcriptions on CD-ROMs Sittingbourne Burials
Mackallir or Mackallar, John	Kent Family History Society transcriptions on CD-ROMs Patrixbourne Burials
Malbon, John	Kent Family History Society transcriptions on CD-ROMs Sheperdswell Burials
Master, Robert	Kent Family History Society transcriptions on CD-ROMs Molash Burials
Morris, Richard	Kent Family History Society transcriptions on CD-ROMs Rolvenden Burials

Paynter, Allington	www.british-history.ac.uk/office-holders/vol11
Philips or Phillipps, Thomas	Kent Family History Society transcriptions on CD-ROMs Headcorn Burials
Pibus, Henry	www.hastingleigh.com/hast-rectors.html
Sclater or Slatyer, William	www.innertemplearchives.org.uk
Soutchote or Southcote, John	www.british-history.ac.uk/vch/surrey/vol3
Sowton, Stephen	Kent Family History Society transcriptions on CD-ROMs Staplehurst Burials
Taverner, Samuel	www.doverhistorian.com/2013/07/29/samuel-taverner-the-dissident-preacher-who-was-imprisoned-in-the-castle
Winsmore, Nathan	www.freepages.genealogy.rootsweb.ancestry.com/~wrag44/chaceley/chaceleyvol1pt2
Worrall, Francis	Kent Family History Society transcriptions on CD-ROMs Preston next Faversham Burials

General

British History Online	www.british-history.ac.uk
The Clergy of the Church of England database 1540–1835	www.theclergydatabase.org.uk
The History of Parliament	www.historyofparliamentonline.org
Oxford dictionary of national biography	www.oxforddnb.com

Biographical index

Numbers within square brackets [ ] refer to page numbers in the Introduction or to folio numbers in the original manuscript. Page numbers of entries from the Introduction are in Roman numerals and folio numbers of entries from the transcription are in Arabic numerals. '(2)' signifies that the person is mentioned that number of times on the folio or page, and 'n.' is added where the person is mentioned in a footnote. Only the highest recorded degree is given. Names scored out in the manuscript are listed if legible. Folios 70r to 72v and 79r to 87r have not been indexed.

Abberfeild, Mr [42] Not identified.

Abbot, Sir Morrice [8] Merchant and politician. Maurice brother of George Abbot, archbishop of Canterbury and of Robert Abbot, bishop of Salisbury. Sometime MP, governor of the East India Company and lord mayor of London. Died in 1642. *ODNB*.

Adams, Charles [lxvi, lxvi n. 182, 59a] MA. Presented to the rectory of St Michael Paternoster Royal with St Martin Vintry and instituted to the former in 1662, holding it until 1672. Chaplain to James, Viscount Saye and Sele in 1663. Instituted to the vicarage of Great Baddow, Essex, in 1663, and dispensed to hold it with Chadwell St Mary, Essex, in 1670, holding them until his possible death in 1684. CCEd Person ID: 142729; LPL, VH 2/35/4, F V/1/II fo. 50, F II/10/1a–b.

Adey, Mr [7] Not identified.

Adman, – [38] Robert Adman was assessed for the 1664 Hearth Tax on two houses in the parish of Smarden: one with five hearths and the other with one. Harrington, pp. 314–15.

Alderne, Daniel [l n. 93, li, 40 n. 95] MA. Presented to the vicarage of Aylesford in Rochester diocese in July 1662 and there is a record of his institution in the same month, but he was not inducted. He was presented to the vicarage of Chart Sutton in October of the same year and recorded as the vicar at the metropolitical visitation in May 1663, but the vicarage is shown as vacant in the Catalogue. He was presented again in June 1663 to Aylesford, inducted in July and probably remained there until his death in 1667. CCEd Person ID: 18; KHLC, DCb/J/Z/7/4.

Aldersey, Henry [45] Named as patron of Bredgar, but probably Terry Aldersley, of Bredgar, who matriculated at Magdalen Hall, Oxford, in 1637, aged eighteen. In the 1664 Hearth Tax he (Terry) was assessed for four houses in Bredgar: one with eight hearths, two with three hearths each and one with nine hearths. The three hearth and nine hearth houses were all empty. Foster, I, 12; Harrington, p. 262.

Alderson, Martin [lxvii, 61] MA. Licensed as curate of Little Dunmow, Essex, in 1640 and may have stayed until he was presented to the rectory of Latchingdon, by the lord protector in 1656. He was admitted as a preacher at Latchingdon in 1662, but his death, as rector of Latchingdon, is recorded in 1680. CCEd Person ID: 44738; LPL, COMM II/411, VB 1/4/129; Venn, I, p. 13.

Aldey, Edward [xliv n. 54, xlviii n. 82, 1] MA. Collated to the rectory of Canterbury St Andrew in 1624 and probably held it throughout the Interregnum. Appointed a canon of Canterbury cathedral in 1660 and held the prebend along with his rectory and the mastership of Eastbridge Hospital from 1664 until his death in 1673, at the age of seventy-eight. CCEd Person ID: 2023; Horn, III, 37; Hasted, XII, 133.

Aldworth, – [9, 17] Not identified.

Alexander, Henry [63] *See* **Alexander Erwin**

Allen, Richard [10] MA. One of three generations of rectors in the diocese. Curate of Canterbury St Andrew from 1634, he was given dispensation to succeed his father, Richard, as rector in 1637 and may have held it until after the Restoration. He is noted at the 1662 visitation as rector of Crundale and was buried there in 1671, being succeeded by his son, Richard. CCEd Person ID: 37692, 37693; **Broadway, Cust and Roberts, 34, p. 141;** Dunkin, I, 10; Hasted, VII, 380.

Alleyn or **Allen, Thomas** [lxvi n. 176, 46, 56a] MA. Already vicar of the parish of Grain by 1664, but left before he was instituted as rector of Kingsdown in 1668. He died in December 1668. CCEd Person ID: 139862; LPL, VH 96/2981; MA, P314/1/1.

Alleyn, Stephen [49] Not identified.

Amherst or **Amhurst, George** [43] BA. Vicar of Marden from 1662 until his death in 1707. CCEd Person ID: 141382; Venn, I, 28.

Anderson, Robert [60 n. 147] MA. Curate of Mortlake from 1662, and may have remained until he was instituted to the vicarage of Sandon, Herts., in 1675. CCEd Person ID: 85617; LPL, VG 1/2 fo. 16, 1/3 fo. 59; Venn, I, 29.

Andrewes, Mr [24] John Andrewes, a gentleman, had a nineteen hearth house in Denton. Harrington, p. 408.

Ansell, John [9] MA. Rector of Brook from 1672 until 1682, he was given dispensation to succeed his father, **Reginald Ansell**, at Stowting in 1679 and served until his death in 1725. CCEd Person ID: 139367; Dunkin, I, 15; Venn, I, 33.

Ansell, Reginald [26] MA. Instituted rector of Fordwich in 1630 but moved to the rectory of Stowting, probably after the death of Richard Allen in 1652. He remained until his own death in 1679. CCEd Person ID: 37709; TNA, PROB 11/221/153.

Archbold, Edward [46, 46 n. 109] LLB. Admitted to the rectory of Luddenham in 1658 but gone by 1662. As chaplain to **John Warner**, bishop of Rochester, he was dispensed to hold the rectory of Kingsdown with Mappiscombe and the rectory of Fawkham in 1662, but he had officiated at the latter since 1650. Both were in the diocese of Rochester. In 1666, he resigned from Fawkham and became rector of Trottiscliffe, also in the diocese of Rochester. He held Kingsdown and Trottiscliffe until 1690. CCEd Person ID: 3929; LPL, VB 1/2/17, F I/C fo. 98, F I/C fo. 203; Fielding, p. 318.

Arderne, James [xliii, xlviii n. 80, 2, 2 n. 9, 4, 5] DD. Ordained in March 1661 and recorded as rector of Canterbury St Mildred and vicar of Canterbury Holy Cross Westgate in July 1662, but in August 1662, **Richard Burney** is noted as the rector of Canterbury St Mildred. Arderne was licensed to the cure of Thanington, Kent, in 1663 and instituted as rector of Canterbury St Mildred in August 1664. He ceded Thanington, resigned from Canterbury St Mildred and Canterbury Holy Cross Westgate in 1666 and became curate of St Botolph Without Aldgate, London, in the same year. Later becoming chaplain to Charles II and pluralist rector in Lincolnshire and Cheshire, he became dean of Chester in 1682 and was subsequently involved in 'high Tory' versus 'Whig' controversies. Died in 1691. CCEd Person ID: 139369; Dunkin, I, 17; LPL, VG 1/2 fo. 6, 1/2 fo. 33, VG 1/4 fo. 3; *ODNB*.

Arinir, – [38] Not identified.

Asherst, John [33] MA. Instituted to the rectory of Warehorne in 1652 and served until his death in 1669. CCEd Person ID: 139371; Green (1973), p. 369; www.hastingleigh.com/OPR/Warehorne-Burials.

Asthare, Andrew [21] Not identified.

Atkinson, Isaac [41] Instituted to the rectory of Frinsted in 1662, resigned in 1675 without further record. CCEd Person ID: 139372; LPL, VB 1/3/241.

Aucher, Anthony [11, 25] Sir Anthony Aucher fought for the king in both civil wars. Had a twenty hearth house in Bishopsbourne and compounded for £700. MP for Canterbury in 1660, created first baronet in 1666, and held numerous other positions under the crown, until his death in 1692. Cliffe, p. 472; Harrington, p. 410; Venn, I, 56.

Aucher, Anthony [34] Eldest son of **Sir Anthony Aucher** and died in 1673. Venn, I, 56.

Aucher, John [58] DD. A younger son of **Sir Anthony Aucher**, he was a canon of Canterbury cathedral from 1660 until his death in 1701. Rector of Westbere, 1661–3, and rector of All Hallows Lombard Street, London, 1663–86. CCEd Person ID: 139374; *ODNB*.

Aucher, Robert [11] MA. Another son of **Sir Anthony Aucher**. Instituted as rector of Kingston in 1672, he soon obtained dispensation for non-residence for three years, renewed in 1675 for a further three years. He was to reside in Oxford to gain some more knowledge in the study of divinity. In 1676, he was dispensed to receive the vicarage of Eastchurch, but he was never instituted. In 1678, his father made a further, unsuccessful, application for non-residence – 'the parish being well satisfyed with the Life and Doctrine of the Curate'. He died in 1682. His curate at Kingston was **Robert Garret**. CCEd Person ID: 139864; LPL, VB 1/3/155, 169, 267, 1/4/3; Wilkie (1893), p. xii.

Austen, Robt. [55 (2), 56a] Sir Robert was created a baronet in 1660. Sheriff of Kent in 1660–1 and a JP in 1665 and 1666. He had a twenty-nine hearth house in Bexley. Died in 1666 aged seventy-nine. Cokayne, III, 78; KHLC, Q/J/C/10, 11; Harrington, p. 91.

Axon, William [36] LLB. Collated to the rectory of Halstead in Rochester diocese in 1635, he was collated to the rectory of Great Chart in 1639, but was sequestrated in 1644. He was restored in 1660, and died before June 1667. CCEd Person ID: 37837; LPL, VG 1/5, p. 16; Matthews, *Walker*, p. 210.

Ayling, John [6] MA. Appointed vicar of Monkton in 1662 and remained there until his death in 1710. CCEd Person ID: 139375; LPL, VG 1/3 fo. 9, VB 1/6/25.

Ayres, John [18] Not identified.

Ayres, Mr [7] 'Of London'. Not identified.

Bagnoll or **Bagnal, William** [50, 52] MA. Instituted to the rectory of Badlesmere in 1661, and dispensed to hold it with the rectory of Leaveland in 1662. He held both livings until his death in 1713. CCEd Person ID: 121712; LPL, F I/C fo. 75v, VB 1/6/127.

Baker, John [lv] Possibly the schoolmaster at St Peter in Thanet, 1630–4. Admitted as vicar of Boughton under Blean in 1646 and buried in 1648. CCEd Person ID: 37896; Matthews, *Walker*, p. 225; Boodle, p. x.

Baker, John [64] Recorded as the patron of Mayfield in 1662. The advowson was then owned by his family until the eighteenth century. *SAC*, 26, p. 66.

Baker, William [20] William Barker of Ratcliffe, Middx., mariner, was the lessee of the rectory of Whitfield from March 1662. He owned, or had interests in, over 2,000 acres of land in Virginia, imported tobacco from the colony and returned with goods. LPL, TA 696/4; McCartney, p. 112.

Baker, William [61 n. 153] MA. Instituted as rector of Monks Eleigh in 1660 and remained until his death in 1706. CCEd Person ID: 142730; LPL, VB 1/5/234.

Balderston, William [lxiii] MA. Instituted as the vicar of Northbourne with the chapel of Shoulden in 1678. Died in 1703. LPL, MS 1137, pp. 35–6, VG 1/5, p. 70, VB 1/5/66.

Bale, John [lii, 29] MA. MD conferred by royal mandate in 1663. Instituted as the rector of the ruined church of Hope in 1663. He is noted in visitations until 1677 and was succeeded by **John Gostling**. He died in 1682. CCEd Person ID: 139378; Hasted, VIII, 420; *AC*, 37, p. 191.

Bamster, Lady [53] Not identified.

Bancroft, Richard [xliii, 44] Archbishop of Canterbury, 1604–10. CCEd Person ID: 2098; *ODNB*.

Bankes, Henry [30 n. 69] DD. Rector of Thakeham, Sussex, 1640–80, and dispensed to hold it with the rectory of the derelict church of Midley, 1669–80. He died in 1680 and his inventory totalled £1,337, all willed to family members, except for four shillings to the poor of the parish. CCEd Person ID: 139379; LPL, F I/C fo. 259v, VB 1/2/212; Dallaway, p. 250; *SAC*, 91, p. 215; Venn, I, 79.

Bargrave, Isaac [li] DD. Rector of Eythorne, 1614–42, canon of Canterbury cathedral, 1622–5, and dean, 1625–43. Rector of St Margaret's, Westminster, 1622–42, vicar of Tenterden, 1626–7, and vicar of Lydd, 1627–8, both ceded. Rector of Chartham, 1628–43. Died in 1643. CCEd Person ID: 38049; Matthews, *Walker*, p. 210; *ODNB*.

Bargrave, John [xli, 2, 38] DD. Nephew of **Isaac Bargrave**. Rector of Harbledown from 1661 and dispensed to continue to hold it along with the rectory of Pluckley from 1662. In addition, he was one of the Six Preachers of Canterbury cathedral but resigned when he became a residentiary canon in 1662, holding the latter position for life. Ceded Harbledown in 1670 and resigned from Pluckley in 1677. Given dispensation for non-residence in 1662 and probably only paid brief visits to his parishes. He was acclaimed as the rescuer of English hostages from Algiers and for his collection of curiosities. **John Sargenson** acted as his curate at Harbledown from 1663 to 1670. CCEd Person ID: 20238; LPL, F I/C fo. 79; Horn, III, 25; *ODNB*.

Barham, John [21] BA. Collated to the rectory of Hawkinge in 1676, and dispensed to hold with the rectory of Charlton in 1679. He retained both offices until his death in 1690. CCEd Person ID: 139381; Dunkin, I, 37.

Barker, Mr [6] Not identified.

Barker, William [xl n. 24] DD. Canon of Canterbury cathedral 1660–9. Not mentioned in the Catalogue as he was not an incumbent of a living in Canterbury diocese. Rector of Hardwick, Bucks., 1661–9. CCEd Person ID: 6904, 67480; Horn, III, 39.

Barling, Clement [xlii] MA. Curate at Woodchurch in 1638 and at Appledore with Ebony, 1638–43. Rector of Denton from 1644 to his sequestration in 1662 but did not leave the parish until 1663. Died in 1670 and six ministers carried him to his grave, five of whom were nonconformists who had been ejected from their livings in 1660 or 1662. Barling's will takes up seventeen pages of the register and fourteen clergymen are named. CCEd Person ID: 38057; Matthews, *Calamy*, p. 29; Reid, pp. 149–57.

Barne or **Barnes, Miles** [xl n. 24, 21, 21 n. 42, 25] MA. Instituted to the rectory of Lyminge with the chapels of Stanford and Paddlesworth in 1632, he was sequestrated in 1644 and restored in 1660. Instituted as rector of Brook in 1640, he may have kept it until 1662. He may have been at Tenterden in 1649, and was instituted to Kingston in 1660, but did not displace **Nicholas Dingley**. Appointed as a Six Preacher of Canterbury cathedral in 1663, he became curate to **John Lee** at Barham in 1667 and curate of Folkestone in the same year, keeping his four positions until his death in 1670. CCEd Person ID: 38061; Ingram Hill, p. 65; Matthews, *Walker*, p. 210.

Barney, William [20, 20 n. 40, 22, 23, 23 n. 50] MA. Vicar of Westcliffe and curate of St Margaret at Cliffe from 1662, and noted at the former in visitations up to 1695.

He was instituted as vicar of Buckland near Dover in 1674 and probably retained all three livings until his death in 1700. CCEd Person ID: 67490; LPL, VG 1/5, p. 49; Hasted, IX, 418.

Barnham, Martin [27] Sir Martin Barnham was one of the London members of the extensive family that owned lands and mansions in Hollingbourne, Boughton Monchelsea, Linton and Bilsington. Harrington, pp. 100, 105, 177; Hasted, V, 340, VIII, 348.

Barnham, Mr [7] 'Of London'. Probably related to Sir **Martin Barnham**.

Barrow, Isaac [73r] DD. Bishop of Sodor and Man, 1663–70, and translated to the diocese of St Asaph in March 1670 but was permitted to retain Sodor and Man in commendam until 1671. *ODNB*.

Barry, Matthew [lix] *See* **Nathaniel Barry**

Barry, Nathaniel [lix, lix n. 134] Son of John Barry, rector of Cottesmore, Rutland. Intruded into Tenterden as lecturer in 1642 and later became vicar. Appointed vicar of Dover St Mary the Virgin in 1654 but was ejected in 1660. Named as a presbyterian preacher in St Mary the Virgin in 1669. Matthews quotes Archbishop Sheldon, writing that Barry 'holds his private meetings and conventicles there'. He became a licensed Presbyterian preacher in 1672 and died in 1675. He is mentioned in **Clement Barling**'s will. CCEd Person ID: 45386; Matthews, *Walker*, p. 223, *Calamy*, p. 31; Lyon Turner, I, 16; Venn, I, 99.

Barton, David [50, 50 n. 114] MA. Described as minister of Bromley in London diocese, already in office, when he subscribed in August 1662. Later that year, he was collated to the rectory of St Margaret New Fish Street, London, which was destroyed in the Great Fire of 1666. He was granted the sequestration of the vicarage of Boughton under Blean in 1666 and given dispensation to hold the rectory of Chislehurst in Rochester diocese in 1670. He left Boughton under Blean in 1671, but retained his two rectories until his death in 1683. CCEd Person ID: 435; LPL, VB 1/2/22, 217, 1/3/81; Willis (1733), p. 22.

Bate, – [35] Not identified.

Bates, Isaac [45 n. 105] MA. Vicar of Sheldwich from 1667, and rector of Bicknor from 1669, holding both until his death in 1674. CCEd Person ID: 139865; Hasted, V, 569.

Bayley, Simon [4, 30] MA. Succeeded **William Hawkins** (not recorded) at Thanington and at St Mary in the Marsh in 1674. He was also a Six Preacher of Canterbury cathedral for just over a year from 1677 and died or moved away in 1679. CCEd Person ID: 7545; LPL, VB 1/3/224, VG 1/5, p. 50; CCA, DCc-TB/1–35; Foster, I, 91.

Beane, Henry [34] Not identified.

Beck, John [19] MA. Vicar of Woodnesborough in 1670, and licensed to the cure of the vacant vicarage of Waldershare in the following year. Master of Sir Roger

Manwood's Free School, Sandwich, in 1672 and died in that year. CCEd Person ID: 86184; Willis (1975), pp. 45, 51, 91; LPL, VB 1/3/199; Matthews, *Calamy*, p. 43; Cavell and Kennett, Appendix B.

Beeching, Abel [42] Not identified.

Belke, Thomas [13] DD. Canon of Canterbury cathedral and rector of Wickhambreux from 1676 until his death in 1711. Rural dean of Bridge in 1683. CCEd Person ID: 118546; Dunkin, I, 57; Venn, I, 127.

Belke, William [xlvi, xlviii n. 82, 13, 13 n. 28] DD. Father of the above. Rector of Wooton from 1641 until sequestration in 1644. Allowed to be vicar of Chilham from 1646 until 1656. Cromwell granted him permission to continue his ministry whereby he became curate of Wye in 1657, probably remaining until 1662. He was presented to the rectory of Wickhambreux in 1658 and appointed a canon of Canterbury cathedral in 1660, retaining both offices until his death in 1676. CCEd Person ID: 67593; Dunkin, I, 57; LPL, COMM I/21, II/717; Matthews, *Walker*, p. 211; Venn, I, 127.

Benchskyn, James [9] BD. A former Fellow of Queens' College, Cambridge, he was rector of Kelsale, Suffolk, from 1641 until his sequestration in 1643. Instituted vicar of Eastry in 1660, he stayed until 1661 and was appointed perpetual curate of Ash in 1662, remaining until his death in 1679. CCEd Person ID: 67599; Matthews, *Walker*, p. 327; Venn, I, 135.

Bennet, – [36, 38] Probably John Bennet, a Quaker clothier whose home was used for meetings of Friends, 1655–80. In 1656, some of his goods were distrained for refusal to pay 'Steeple-house rates', and in 1661, he was one of many who were committed to Maidstone prison, for refusing to swear an oath of allegiance. He was a trustee or purchaser of the Cranbrook Meeting House in 1680. Besse, pp. 289, 290; *AC*, 112, p. 326.

Bernard, Edward [59b n. 146] DD. Arabist and mathematician and was briefly the rector of Cheam, Surrey, in 1673 and rector of Brightwell, Berks., from 1691 until his death in 1697. CCEd Person ID: 7672; *ODNB*.

Betton, John [xxxix n. 16, lxvii, 62, 63, 63 n. 167] MA. Curate at Boxgrove, Sussex, 1666–75. Presented and collated to the prebend of Selsey, Chichester cathedral, in 1669, but this was ineffective as the incumbent was not dead. Instituted to the rectory of West Stoke, Sussex, in 1670 and dispensed to hold it with the rectory of Tangmere in 1674. Chaplain to Richard, earl of Dorset, in 1675. Resigned from Tangmere in 1676, having been dispensed to hold West Stoke, with the rectory of East Lavant, and instituted to the latter in 1676, but he was reinstituted, to corroborate his title in 1680 and 1682. His death in 1721 ended his incumbencies in his two rectories after forty-five and fifty-one years, respectively. CCEd Person ID: 61467; LPL, VB 1/2/204, 214, 1/3/237, 1/4/11, 108, VH 2/27/2, 3, 4, 2/53/6, 7, F V/1/II fo. 103v, F I/D fo. 139; Horn, II, 50; Venn, I, 145.

Birch, Nicholas [36] Not identified.

Birchin, Thomas [35] Not identified.

Birkenhead, John [xlviii] DCL. The author mostly responsible for the editions of *Mercurius Aulicus*, the newsbook of the king's party from 1643 to 1645. He was MP for Wilton, 1661–79, and was knighted in 1662. He died in 1679. *ODNB*.

Bishop, John [43] Not identified.

Bishop, Thomas [43] Not identified.

Bisson, Michael [51] BA. Collated to the vicarage of Graveney in 1660, and may have stayed until 1666, but not found thereafter. CCEd Person ID: 139868; Venn, I, 159.

Blackmore, James [35 (2)] An Anabaptist preacher at a conventicle in Marden in 1669, and he was licensed in 1672 to teach congregations in Biddenden and Tenterden. See also under **George Hammond** below. Lyon Turner, I, 19; Bate, p. xxxii.

Blackstone or **Blaxton, Benjamin** [xxxix n. 13, lxv n. 170, 56b, 56b n. 125] MA. Appointed vicar of Orpington in 1664, and died in 1671. CCEd Person ID: 142731; LPL, VH 2/44/3.

Blandford, Walter [73r] Bishop of Oxford, 1665–71, bishop of Worcester, 1671–5. *ODNB*.

Blechinden, – [11] Thomas Blechinden DD, rector of Sowton, Devon, from 1625 to his resignation in 1635. Dispensed to hold Norton Fizwarren, Somerset, in 1627, and held it until 1638. Canon of Canterbury cathedral from 1633, vicar of Eastry with Worth from 1638 and rector of Kingston from 1640, but sequestrated from all of his offices in 1644. Probably not restored and died in 1663. CCEd Person ID: 39294; Matthews, *Walker*, p. 211.

Blemell, John [58] MA. Preacher at Dulwich College, Surrey, in 1630, and curate of St James', Bury St Edmunds, Suffolk, in 1638, and may have been there until 1657. Appointed as rector of Bradfield St Clare, Suffolk, in 1644, and still there in 1648, although under harassment. Admitted, by the Triers, to the vicarage of Tostock, Suffolk, in 1658, but resigned this and his rectory in 1661. Instituted to the rectory of All Hallows the Great, London, in 1662, and died in 1665. CCEd Person ID: 122796; Matthews, *Walker*, p. 328, Venn, I, 166.

Blomer, Thomas [58] DD. Instituted as a canon of Canterbury cathedral in 1673 and instituted to the rectory of All Hallows Bread Street with St John the Evangelist, London, in 1681. He resigned his prebend in 1706, being replaced by his son, Ralph, and died in 1723. CCEd Person ID: 139869; Horn, III, 37; LPL, F II/8/10, VH 2/28/1, 2/28/2, VG 1/3, fo. 75, VB 1/5/213, 218; Venn, I, 168.

Blood, Thomas [lviii (2)] Conspirator involved in the plot to seize Dublin castle in 1663 and the attempted robbery of the crown jewels in 1671. *ODNB*.

Bonny, Peter [21, 30 n. 65] Recorded as the minister of Alkham in 1655, he was instituted to the rectory of Hawkinge in 1667, and was licensed to the cure of Lympne in 1670. In 1676, he signed the Compton census as curate of Hawkinge, Lympne and West Hythe. He died in the same year. LPL, MS 1643, p. 27, VG 1/5, p. 15; Dunkin, I, 83; Willis (1975), p. 44.

Bonwick, John [59b] DD. Rector of Newdigate, Surrey, 1663–98. Chaplain to the earl of Chesterfield. Dispensed to hold the rectory of East Horsley in 1663 and retained it until 1669. Dispensed in 1669 to hold the rectory of Mickleham, Surrey, and held it until his death. CCEd Person ID: 92175; LPL, F I/C fo. 109, VB 1/2/181.

Boraston, George [lxvi, lxvi n. 176, 56a] MA. Instituted to the rectory of Hever in 1662, following the resignation of his uncle, **John Petter**. He served until his death in 1699. CCEd Person ID: 67826; LPL, VH 96/3335; Matthews, *Calamy*, p. 387.

Bosse, Richard [lxv n. 170, 57] MA. Curate of Otford, a chapel of Shoreham, in 1663, and appointed vicar of Sevenoaks in 1664, succeeding his father of the same name. He died in 1677. CCEd Person ID: 61938; LPL, CM 48/3; Hasted, III, 31.

Bostocke, Robert [xlix (3), 21, 22, 33] BD. Under-master at Tonbridge School, 1651–3. Inducted as vicar of New Romney in 1662, he held it until his death in 1680. Given dispensation also to hold Hougham in 1664, he resigned in 1675, and was dispensed to hold the rectory of Paglesham, Essex. He was granted sequestration of Dover St James the Apostle from 1664 until 1675. CCEd Person ID: 161180; Willis (1975), p. 70; LPL, F II/5/11b; Dunkin, I, 85; Sterry, p. 42.

Boston, Paul [4] MA. Licensed to the cure of Thannington in 1666 and ceded it in 1671. May have been the same man who was curate of St Giles in the Fields, London, from 1661, and vicar of St Bride's, London, from 1666. As Thanington was a perpetual curacy, it would not have been considered pluralism if he also held a London benefice; he would, however, have had to supply an assistant curate at Thanington, of which there is no surviving record. In 1672, Paul Boston, vicar of St Bride's and curate of St Giles, refers in his will to his mother Mrs White and his brother **Blasé White**. The latter was rector of Canterbury St George the Martyr. CCEd Person ID: 161181; Venn, I, 184; LPL, VB 1/2/28, VB 1/3/87; TNA, PROB 11/337/545.

Bothell, – [38] Reported in the Catalogue as a Quaker shoemaker, but he is probably Ephraim Bothell, living in a two hearth house in Newenden. He had been 'vicar' of Hawkhurst, 1651–62, but probably then ejected and took up his trade. Matthews does not consider him as being ejected, but notes that Calamy called him a nonconformist. At the Maidstone Assizes in July 1661, he was indicted for uttering perverse opinions in contempt of the Book of Common Prayer, and refusing to administer the sacraments according to the Book of Common Prayer. Indicted again for the latter offence in 1662. He was ordained in 1667, and became vicar of Chiddingley, Sussex. Matthews, *Calamy*, p. 65; Harrington, p. 222; Cockburn (1995), pp. 27, 44.

Bourchier, Thomas [62, 62 n. 159] Cardinal archbishop of Canterbury, 1454–86. *ODNB*.

Bourne, Robert [56b] MA, LLD. Curate of Emmington, Oxon., in 1666. Instituted as vicar of Orpington in 1671, and dispensed to hold the rectory of Hayes, Kent, in 1679. He died in 1687 in possession of both livings. CCEd Person ID: 7941; LPL, VB 1/4/64, VH 2/44/4.

Boys, – [45] Probably an error. The patronage of Bicknor had been owned by the crown since the dissolution of the monasteries. Hasted, V, 568.

Boys, Dr [40] John Boys DD was rector of Hollingbourne from 1604 until his death in 1625. CCEd Person ID: 39373.

Boys, Edward [16] Probably Sir Edward Boys of Fredville, Kent, who owned the manor of Elmington in the parish of Eythorne. The owners of this manor and of Waldershare manor, in the adjoining parish, were alternate patrons of Eythorne. Hasted, X, 68, 70; Armytage, p. 21.

Boys, John [16, 32, 32 n. 74] MP for Kent, 1645, 1654 and 1656. Lord of the eleven hearth manor of Betteshanger. Died in 1678. Venn, I, 195; Hasted, X, 45; Harrington, p. 409.

Boys, John [32] Probably the hero of the defence of Donnington castle, Berks., in 1643, who was knighted in 1644. Involved in the royalist conspiracies of the 1650s. Bloomfield, p. 17; *ODNB*.

Boys, John [34] Recorded as 'John Boice gent' with an eight hearth house in Willesborough in the 1664 Return. He may have been one of the larger family. Harrington, p. 307.

Boys, Major [26] Probably John Boys Esq. who had an eighteen hearth house in Nonington. He served as a JP in 1665, 1666 and 1670. Harrington, p. 407; KHLC, Q/J/C/10, 11, 12.

Boys, Robert [29, 40] BD. Fellow of Corpus Christi College, Cambridge, from 1641 until 1664. Ordained priest in 1642 and instituted to the rectory of Ivychurch, Kent, in 1663 and to Canterbury St Dunstan, in February 1664. He died before December 1666, when he was succeeded, at Ivychurch, by Edward Ladbroke. CCEd Person ID: 139873, 140043; Venn, I, 196; LPL, VG 1/3 fo. 22v, VB 1/1/42, 1/2/36.

Boys, Samuel [38] Of Hawkhurst. He was a JP 1665, 1666 and 1670. KHLC, Q/J/C/10, 11, 12; Plantagenet, p. 518; Hasted, VII, 147.

Boys or **Boise, Thomas** [15] The Boys family had many branches in various parishes in Kent. The advowson of Barfreston was held by John Boys of Denton in the sixteenth century. He passed it to his son, Thomas, and ownership then descended until it was sold to Ewell, of Denton, and then Sir **Basil Dixwell**. Hasted, X, 77.

Brabourne, William [62] DD. Prebendary of Hereford cathedral and of St Paul's, London, from 1660 and already in office as vicar of Northolt, Middx.; when he subscribed in 1662, he was dispensed to hold the rectory of Newington, Oxon., in the same year. He died in possession of all his preferments in 1685. CCEd Person ID: 8095.

Bradbury, Dudley [61] MA. Vicar of Freckenham, Suffolk, from 1674 until, possibly, 1696. Rector of Moulton, Suffolk, from 1678 until his death in 1734, and rector of Herringswell, Suffolk, 1700–34. CCEd Person ID: 4679.

Bradford, William [59a, 59a n. 139] An error, should read **John Bradford**. DD. Master of Camberwell Grammar School, 1661–74. Rector of St Edmund the King and Martyr, London, from 1670 until his death in 1685. Rector of Sefton, Lancs., 1675–8, and vicar of Bexhill St Peter, Sussex, 1678–85. Royal chaplain, 1670–85, and canon of Canterbury cathedral in 1685. CCEd Person ID: 62029; LPL, F I/D fo. 109, VB 1/4/47; *SAC*, 53, p. 107; Venn, I, 199.

Bradley, Alexander [11, 12] Instituted to the rectory of Ford, Sussex, in 1647, but by 1656, he was signing the church register as minister in Elmstone and was recognized as the rector in the visitation of 1662. He was vicar of Preston by Wingham by 1664 and held both livings until his death in 1691. CCEd Person ID: 80615; KHLC, DCb/V/V/56, 58; LPL, VB 1/4/473, 474; Wilkie (1891), p. 10.

Bradshaw, John [59a] BD. Vicar of Bedford St Paul, Beds., from 1638, possibly until 1652. Rector of St Michael Crooked Lane, London, 1666–71, and rector of St George Botolph Lane, London, 1664–9. Rector of Cublington, Bucks., from 1670 until his death in 1682. Chaplain to successive bishops of Lincoln, 1669–76. CCEd Person ID: 35752; Matthews, *Walker*, p. 64; Venn, I, 202.

Brames or **Braems, Arnold** [21] Arnold Braems, a Dover merchant of Flemish descent, built and resided in Bridge Place, a twenty-four hearth mansion in Bridge. He had compounded for £800, was knighted in 1660 and died in 1681. Hasted, IX, 288; Harrington, p. 417; Cliffe, p. 472.

Brett, Nicholas [21] BD. Schoolmaster at Sutton by Dover in 1622 and collated to the vicarage of Headcorn in 1639, from which he was sequestrated in 1645. He is reported as the minister of Eastry in 1647 and 1653–5, probably holding it until he was restored to Headcorn in 1660. In 1662, he resigned Headcorn and was appointed curate of Folkestone, and probably remained until 1666. CCEd Person ID: 39391; Shaw (1870), p. 161; Matthews, *Walker*, p. 212; KHLC, DCb/V/V/57, 58.

Brett, Thomas [1 n. 93, 15, 18] MA. Intruded into the desolate rectory of Little Mongeham in 1656, he was licensed to the perpetual curacy of Sutton by Dover in 1662 and instituted rector of Betteshanger in 1663. He retained the Sutton and Betteshanger until his death in 1680. CCEd Person ID: 139875; LPL, VG 1/2 fo. 32v, 1/3 fo. 73; Venn, I, 211.

Brewer, William [21, 22] MA. Instituted as vicar of Hougham in 1675 and granted the sequestration of Dover St James the Apostle. In 1690, he was dispensed to hold the vicarage of Charlton, along with Hougham, and he retained his three appointments until his probable death in 1701. CCEd Person ID: 139876; Dunkin, I, 100.

Briggs, Thomas [lxiv] LLD Dean of South Malling, Pagham and Tarring 1678–1703, vicar-general of Chichester, commissary for Lewes archdeaconry in 1680 and chancellor of Chichester in 1703. Died in 1713. CCEd Person ID: 175809; LPL, VB 1/4/36, 1/5/75, Arches A 14; Venn, I, 218.

Brockman, James [20, 23, 26] Son of Sir William, below, he had a sixteen hearth house in Newington. Berry, p. 118; Harrington, p. 354.

Brockman, William [22, 27, 28 (2)] Sir William Brockman of Newington. Berry, p. 118.

Brodnax or **Broadnax, Major** [11] Probably John Brodnax, a major in the civil war royalist army who immigrated to Virginia and died in 1657. A Mr William Brodnax had a fifteen hearth house in Godmersham and he was knighted in October 1664. Richardson, I, 329; Harrington, p. 326; Shaw (1906), II, 240.

Brokesby or **Brookesby, Obadiah** [9, 29] MA. Curate of Carlton cum Willingham, Cambs., in 1672, he was instituted rector of Ivychurch and vicar of Bekesbourne in 1677. He died in 1685. CCEd Person ID: 5009; LPL, VG 1/5, p. 63; Venn, I, 229.

Bromskell, John [33 n. 79] MA. Instituted to the rectory of Warehorne in 1670 and served until 1675, but nothing further is known. CCEd Person ID: 139880; Dunkin, I, 107.

Brook, Joyner [27] MA. Instituted as rector of Bonnington in 1643 and probably remained until his death in 1669. He was licensed to serve the cure of Newchurch in 1664 and probably assisted **George May senior**. CCEd Person ID: 80602; LPL, VB 1/2/187; Willis (1975), p. 43.

Brown, Mr [13] A descendant of patrons of Wickhambreux since the sixteenth century. Hasted, IX, 162.

Browne, James [43] MA. Vicar of Sutton Valence with East Sutton, 1666–79, but no further record. CCEd Person ID: 139881; LPL, VG 1/5, p. 79.

Browne, Joseph [59a] MA. Rector of St Matthew Friday Street, London, 1637–40, and rector of St Michael Crooked Lane from 1640, possibly surviving in office, until his death in 1666, although Thomas Carter was lecturer, 1652–7, and Thomas Mallory lecturer, 1659–61. CCEd Person ID: 80611; LPL, VB 1/1/183; Matthews, *Calamy*, pp. 102, 335; Venn, I, 235.

Browne, Peter [li, 40, 40 n. 95, 42] MA. Ordained presbyter for Hedley, Surrey, by 4th Classis of London in 1659. Instituted rector of Langley in 1662 and served until his death in 1692. Vicar of Chart Sutton from 1664 until his resignation in 1688. CCEd Person ID: 7188.

Browne, Thomas [lxv, lxvi, xlviii (2), lxvi nn. 175 & 178, 38 (2), 56a (2)] BA. Licensed to teach in the chapelry of Otford, and elsewhere in the deanery of Shoreham in 1638 and acted as curate to John Emerson. Began baptizing infants in 1646 and admitted in 1647 as vicar of Farningham. Noted in the parliamentary survey of 1650 as the vicar and the birth and death of several of his children are recorded from 1649 through 1660. Instituted as vicar of Farningham in 1660 and made the required declaration as 'vicar' of Newenden in August 1662. Did not receive dispensation to hold Newenden along with Farningham until November 1662, when noted as chaplain to Richard, earl of Dorset. He was collated as rector of Newenden in December 1662, but resigned in 1664 and as chaplain to Thomas, Lord Culpepper, was dispensed to hold Farningham along with the rectory of Halstead. Buried as vicar of Farningham in 1678. CCEd Person ID: 139884; LPL, VH 98/1/93, VG 1/2 fo. 38v, F I/C fo. 96v, F V/1/I fo. 54, VB 1/1/99, 104; KHLC, TR/2322/23, pp. 13, 49, 50, 51, 53; Hasted, II, 526; Larking, pp. 128–9; Matthews, Walker, p. 227.

Bryan, William [33].A. Instituted as vicar of Stone-in-Oxney in 1663 and served until his death in 1696. CCEd Person ID: 139877; LPL, VB 1/4/545; Venn, I, 244.

Buffkin, Captain [43] Probably Ralph Bufkin, buried in the cemetery of All Saints church, Loose, in 1710 in his eighty-fourth year. The family do not appear in the Kent Hearth Tax records for 1664. Harrington; www.kentarchaeology.org.uk/Research/Libr/MIs/MIsLoose/01.htm.

Burges or **Burgiss, Edmund** [3 n. 11, 34 n. 80] Minor canon of Rochester cathedral in 1662 and vicar of Allhallows, Rochester, in 1663. He was curate of Canterbury St Mary Bredman from 1664 and became a minor canon of Canterbury cathedral in the same year. In 1679, he became vicar of Willesborough and retained all three positions until his probable death in 1681. He was omitted from the Catalogue. CCEd Person ID: 7189; LPL, VG 1/3 fo. 71; CCA, DCc-TB/4–17.

Burley, Thomas [56b n. 123] MA. Instituted as rector of Ifield in 1662 but ceded it in 1666. May be the same man who was briefly rector of Chilton Candover, Hants., in 1665 and rector of Kingston, Hants., from 1670 until his death in 1682. CCEd Person ID: 142736, 92389; LPL, VB 1/1/196.

Burney, Richard [lvi, 1, 2, 2 n. 9, 4 n. 14 (2), 5 n. 17] MA. Active in some Kent parishes during the 1640s and 1650s. He was expelled from the vicarage of Tudeley with Capel in 1647 and although he had officiated in Old Romney from 1652, he was considered unfit in 1657, and sequestrated. Ordained priest in July 1661, was appointed a chaplain in extraordinary to the crown in the following August, and instituted to the rectory of Canterbury All Saints in September 1661. He was rector of Canterbury St Mildred, 1662–4. Reinstituted to Canterbury All Saints in August 1664, he was licensed to serve the cure of Canterbury St Peter in October 1674, but had signed the parish register transcript in 1671. He retained these two livings until his death, aged seventy-eight in 1692. CCEd Person ID: 86655; LPL, VG 1/2 fo. 33, 1/4 fo. 3; Matthews, *Walker*, p. 213; Bucholz, pp. 251–78; Foster, I, 215.

Burney, William [20] *See* **William Barney**

Burton, Richard [28, 32] MA. Teacher at Ashford in 1623 and Smeeth in 1630. Rector of Dymchurch from 1625 until his death in 1676 and dispensed to hold the vicarage of Sellindge from 1638 until 1676. CCEd Person ID: 39451; Willis (1972),

p. 17, KHLC, DCb/V/V/43; LPL, VG 1/2 fo. 9; Whiteman, pp. 28, 32; Broadway, Cust and Roberts, 34, p. 159.

Burville, James [16, 17] MA. Schoolmaster at Sutton by Dover in 1631 and curate of Betteshanger in 1634. Appointed as one of the Six Preachers of Canterbury cathedral in 1645, rector of the ruined church of Little Mongeham in 1646 and vicar of Northbourne with Shoulden in 1647; he was sequestrated from all three in 1655. Having retired to Ireland during the Commonwealth, he was restored to his parish offices in 1660, and to the cathedral in 1661. He ceded Little Mongeham and received the rectory of Ham in 1662, retaining it along with Northbourne and his cathedral office until his death in 1678. In 1668, Archdeacon Sancroft noted that he was 'a prisoner for debt'. CCEd Person ID: 39454; Matthews, *Walker*, p. 213; LPL, COMM I/17, 69, VB 1/4/41; Bodl., MS Sancroft 99, p. 87.

Burville, James junior [18, 20, 20 n. 37] BA. Curate to his father at Northbourne with the chapel of Shoulden from 1674 to 1676. Vicar of Tilmanstone and curate of Whitfield from 1675 until his death in 1697. CCEd Person ID: 161630; Venn, I, 269; LPL, VB 1/4/559.

Butler, Daniel [10, 11] BA. Vicar of Godmersham with Challock from 1664 until his death in 1675. CCEd Person ID: 139921; LPL, VG 1/4 fo. 2v.

Cadman, John [24] Curate at Folkestone in 1569, vicar of Alkham with Capel-le-Ferne, 1569–94, vicar of Brabourne and rector of the desolate church of Bircholt from 1594 until his death in 1617. CCEd Person ID: 39455.

Caldicott or **Caldecott, Randolph** [59a] DD. Instituted to the rectory of Fovant, Wilts., in 1646, he had left before 1662. In that year, he became rector of Whaddon, Wilts., but ceded in 1669 and was instituted as rector of Rodmarton, Gloucs., which he ceded in 1671, becoming rector of Bishopston, Wilts. He died in 1688. He and **Michael Selby** disputed institution to the rectory of Hayes, Middx., in the deanery of Croydon, but Selby was instituted in 1661. Caldecott was instituted in 1664, but no record has been found of his tenure and he was probably not inducted. CCEd Person ID: 21273; LPL, VH 77/1–2, 2/20/3, VG 1/2 fo. 22, 1/4 fo. 3, F II/3/219.

Caldwall, Edward [59a] BA. Vicar of Hayes, Middx., from 1673 until his cession in 1675. Instituted to the vicarage of Stottesdon, Shrops., in 1675, he served until his death in 1687. CCEd Person ID: 142739; LPL, VH 2/21/6; SA, X7381/225/1246.

Campian or **Campion, Abraham** [62] DD. Chaplain to Archbishop Sheldon. Rector of Monks Risborough, Bucks., from 1675 until his death in 1701. Prebendary of Lincoln cathedral, 1679–1701, and dean, 1700–1. CCEd Person ID: 11569; LPL, VG 1/5, p. 58; Lipscombe, II, 420; Foster, I, 233.

Campleshon, John [xxxix, xxxix n. 12, 48 (2), 49 (2)] MA. Vicar of Rainham, 1662–5. The parochial accounts reveal controversy in 1666; a shilling was paid 'for a wareant to distrayne Mr. Campleshon' and £2.5.0 was paid 'to Cleare the p'ish of Mr. Campleshon's children'. Collated to the vacant vicarage of Upchurch in 1664 and possibly stayed until 1666. The Catalogue, fo. 48, has Campleshon as the vicar of Rodmersham, but **John White** was instituted in 1662 and noted in the visitations of 1662 and 1664, whereas Campleshon is scored out in the 1664 call book. CCEd Person ID: 139924; *AC*, 17, p. 65.

Carew, Reginald [29] MA. Rector of Mablethorpe St Peter, Lincs., 1630–4, and Belleau with Claythorpe, Lincs., from 1632, but was deprived in 1634. He was instituted as rector of the derelict church of Hurst in 1662 and probably retained it until 1683. CCEd Person ID: 68145.

Carre or **Carr, William** [33] MA. Curate of Cambridge St Michael in 1628. Instituted as vicar of Mountfield, Sussex, in 1628 and was dispensed to hold it with the rectory of Hastings St Clement in 1638 but was sequestrated in 1643. He was presented to the vicarage of Bexhill, Sussex, in 1660 but the presentation was disputed by Thomas Delves, who had probably officiated since the late 1650s. Carr was collated to the rectory of Old Romney in December 1660 and held it until his death in 1670. Prebendary of Chichester cathedral, 1660–70. CCEd Person ID: 74576, 63300; Venn, I, 297; LPL, Arches A 2 fos. 2, 5–9, 12; Horn, II, 41; *SAC*, 53, p. 106; Matthews, *Walker*, p. 354.

Carter or **Cater, Thomas** [26] MA. Intruded into the rectory of Saltwood with the chapel of Hythe in 1648, and vicar of Teynham, 1660–3. He remained at Saltwood until his death in 1673. CCEd Person ID: 10263; LPL, VG 1/2 fo. 9v; Shaw (1900), II, 353; KHLC, DCb/V/V/56; Willis (1975), pp. 32, 33, 72; Foster, I, 250.

Casaubon, Meric [xlviii n. 82, 11] DD. Rector of Bleadon, Somerset, 1626–30, resigned. Canon of Canterbury cathedral, 1628–43, then sequestrated, restored, 1660–71. Rector of St Mary in the Marsh, 1630–4, and rector of Old Romney for eleven months in 1634, resigning from both; he became rector of Minster in Thanet and vicar of Monkton with Birchington. He was ordered to resign from Monkton in 1643 and left Minster in 1644. Restored to the latter in 1660, he exchanged it for the rectory of Ickham with Well in 1662. He died in 1671. CCEd Person ID: 25253; Matthews, *Walker*, p. 213; Horn, III, 33; *ODNB*.

Castilion, John [xlviii (2), lxvi, 7, 30, 58] DD. A pluralist on the grand scale, Castilion was curate of St Mary Magdalen, Oxford, in 1641 and was instituted to the rectory of Colsterworth, Lincs., in 1646, but he was unable to gain possession. Subscribed as rector in 1662 and remained until his resignation in 1681. He was made a canon of Canterbury cathedral in 1660, a chaplain to Charles II in 1662 and vicar of Minster in Thanet in 1662 then, having received dispensation in 1665, he combined the vicarage with the rectory of Mersham. Meanwhile, he is recorded as the rector of St Dionis Backchurch, London, in or after 1662, resigning in 1665. He was made dean of Rochester cathedral in 1676, and in 1683, he became rural dean of Westbere. He resigned Mersham in 1677 but retained his deanery and prebend along with the vicarage of Minster until his death in 1688. CCEd Person ID: 6540; LPL, F I/C fo. 176v, VG 1/4 fo. 4; *AC*, 25, p. 108; Hennessy, p. 81; Bennett, p. 70; Bodl., MS Tanner 124, fo. 107.

Cater or **Carter, Thomas** [51, 52] MA. Curate to David Platt at Graveney from 1630 until at least 1637. Licensed to teach at Faversham Grammar School in 1637, and at Sittingbourne in 1665. Granted the sequestration of the vicarage of Ospringe in 1643 and was admitted in 1657, serving until 1678. Rector of Goodnestone by Faversham from 1662 until his death in 1678. CCEd Person ID: 39499; Willis (1972), pp. 67, 72, 140; Willis (1975), p. 3; Matthews, *Walker*, pp. 221, 228; KHLC, DCb/V/V/56, 58, 64, 69–71.

Cave, William [58] DD. Instituted as vicar of Islington St Mary, London, in 1662, he ceded it in 1691. Rector of Ryton, Durham, from 1676, until his resignation in 1679, and rector of All Hallows the Great, London, from 1679, until his resignation in 1690. Canon of Windsor from 1684, until his death in 1713, and vicar of Isleworth, Middx., from 1690 to 1713. Chaplain to Charles II. CCEd Person ID: 86991; Mackenzie **and** Ross, pp. 186–7; Venn, I, 310; *ODNB*.

Chadwick, John [55] MA. Instituted to the vicarage of Darenth in 1669 and probably rector of Longfield in Rochester diocese, 1672–1705. In 1685, James II recommended Chadwick, now chaplain to Isabella, marchioness of Winchester, for the vicarage of Sutton at Hone in Rochester diocese. The patron was the dean and chapter of Rochester cathedral, but the prebendaries refused to agree to the presentation, alleging that Chadwick was a Roman catholic and a man of immoral character. After some months, they agreed to the appointment and Chadwick resigned from Darenth and was instituted to Sutton in December 1685, serving until his death in 1705. CCEd Person ID: 726, 727; LPL, VH 2/9/2, F V/1/III fo. 122; MA, DRc/AC3/7 fos. 108a–136a; Hasted, II, 366.

Chamberlain or **Chamberlayne, Edward** [lxv n. 169, 57 (2)] MA, LLD, FRS. Writer and diplomat. Instituted to the sinecure rectory of Sevenoaks in 1661 and remained until his death in 1703. CCEd Person ID: 142740; LPL, VB 1/5/103; Venn, I, 316; *ODNB*.

Chapman, Stephen [35] Not identified.

Chaworth, Richard [xli, liv, 63, 64] DCL. Knighted in 1663. Advocate of Doctors Commons, 1660, chancellor of the diocese of London, 1637–63, and of Chichester, 1660–3, vicar-general of the province of Canterbury, 1663–9. CCEd Person ID: 161815; LPL, MS 2216, fo. 20; Foster, I, 265.

Chewney or **Chowney, Nicholas** [6, 7] DD. Chewney had served in Deal, Kent, in 1646 and Stow Maries, Essex, in 1648, before St Nicholas at Wade in 1650, ejected 1655. He is recorded at Iver, Bucks., from 1657 to 1661 and was collated to the vicarage of St Nicholas at Wade in 1662. He was given dispensation to hold it with the vicarage of St John in Thanet, where he was instituted in 1666, and served until his death in 1685. He resigned St Nicholas at Wade in 1671, probably because of his presentment to the archdeacon's court for neglect. CCEd Person ID: 138910; Matthews, *Walker*, p. 214, LPL, F I/C fo. 194; Dunkin, I, 157; *AC*, 26, p. 43.

Child, William [56b] A descendant of Nicholas Child, lord of the manor of Ifield, who repaired the church and died in 1638. Hasted, III, 351.

Chittenden, Thomas [37] Not identified.

Christmas, James [xxxix, 11, 11 n. 24] MA. He was rector of the derelict church of Midley for a short time in 1681, and then collated to the vicarage of Godmersham with Challock in 1682. In 1688, he was noted as chaplain to the earl of Devon and allowed the vicarage of Ulcombe in plurality with Godmersham. He died in 1713. CCEd Person ID: 138305; LPL, F II/28/18; Dunkin, I, 157.

Chute, George [29 (2), 35] According to his will of 1664, Sir George Choute, of Bethersden. Died of smallpox at the age of twenty-three. He was a grandson of **Nicholas Toke** and married Elizabeth, daughter of Sir **Basil Dixwell**. *AC*, 18, p. 69; Berry, p. 173.

Clarke, Edward [lxv n. 174, lxvi n. 175, 55] DD. Held the rectory of Chevening from 1645 and was noted as the incumbent in the parliamentary survey of 1650. He had also held the rectory of Bowers Gifford, Essex, but was dispossessed in 1651 by order of the committee of plundered ministers against pluralities. He was instituted to Chevening in August 1660 and to Bowers Gifford in November 1661, receiving dispensation to hold the two together, and held them until his death in 1681, along with a prebend of Rochester cathedral from 1670. CCEd Person ID: 142741, 7191; Hasted, III, 125; Foster, I, 279; LPL, VB 1/4/158, VG 1/2 f.14, COMM XIIa/19 fo. 94; Fielding, p. 57; Horn, III, 61.

Clarke, Robert [37] Nominated rector of Frittenden by parliament in 1647 and survived the Restoration, dying in 1666. Shaw (1900), II, p. 341; LPL, VB 1/2/38.

Clarke, Thomas [xxxix n. 17, 63, 63 n. 176] BA. Instituted rector of St Thomas at Cliffe in 1666, but became rector of Lewes St John sub Castro, Sussex, in 1670. He disappears from the record by 1674. CCEd Person ID: 62978; LPL, VG 1/5, pp. 11, 39v.

Clayton, Mr [44] Sir Robert Clayton FRS was a member of the Scriveners Company from 1658 to 1679, and master, 1671–2. Master of the Drapers Company, alderman, sheriff and lord mayor of London, MP for London and Bletchingley. Said to be 'a political ally in London of the nonconformists, whom he would never prosecute'. Died 1707. *HoP*; *ODNB*.

Clerke, Francis [44] Sir Francis, of Rochester and Ulcombe, was MP for Rochester in 1661, 1681 and 1685–6. JP; receiver of the Hearth Tax for Kent and the city and county of Canterbury, 1664–7. Had an eighteen hearth house in Ulcombe. Died in 1686. *HoP*; Harrington, pp. cix, 108.

Clewer, William [59b] DD. Vicar of Croydon from 1660, but deprived in 1684, 'for the reformation of his manners and excesses, ... neglect of his Cure of Souls ... not preaching, nor reading the common prayers ... not baptizing infants; and not reading prayers for the burial of the dead; and for omitting the due celebration of the Sacrament' following a legal case lasting three years. Also tried and convicted at the Old Bailey for stealing a silver cup. CCEd Person ID: 142743; LPL, VH 77/12/1–35; Haggard, App. B, p. 2; Venn, I, 355.

Cliff, Alan [30] Patron of the desolate church of Midley, but he only presented in 1669. Hasted, VIII, 413.

Codd, John [xlviii n. 81, 44] DD. Instituted as vicar of Leybourne, Rochester diocese, in 1640. Sequestrated in 1643 but restored in 1646 and may have remained until his resignation in 1663. Canon of Rochester cathedral, 1660–72. Vicar of Rochester St Margaret from 1662 and was dispensed to hold it in plurality with the rectory of Ulcombe. He retained his three offices until his death in 1672. CCEd Person ID: 766; Matthews, *Walker*, p. 214; Horn, III, 62.

Cole, Robert [xlviii n. 80, 32, 35, 38] BD. Probably the curate of Steeple Aston, Oxon., in 1645, he was appointed by parliament to Lyminge *pro tempore* in 1651 but continued there until, in August 1660, he was instituted to the rectory of Shadoxhurst. In October of the same year, he was collated to the vicarage of Bethersden, and in 1662, he was dispensed to hold it in plurality with the rectory of Smarden. He held all three livings until his death in 1667. CCEd Person ID: 11157; LPL, F I/C fo. 90; Haslewood (1886), pp. 37–9; *AC*, 16, p. 89.

Colebrand, Richard [lxiv, 60] DD. Dean, commissary and rector of Bocking, Essex, from 1660, and as chaplain to the king, received dispensation to hold the rectory of Toppesfield, Essex, in 1664. Held both livings until his death in 1674. Canon of Westminster cathedral, 1673–4. CCEd Person ID: 138975; LPL, F I/C fo. 164; CCA, DCc-CantLet/121; Venn, I, 368.

Coleman or **Coaleman, William** [15] Curate to **John Castilion** at Minster in Thanet in 1663, he was instituted as vicar of Sandwich St Clement in 1666, resigning in 1677. He signed the Compton census in 1676, as vicar of Sandwich St Mary, Sandwich St Peter and Sandwich St Clement, but was acting as curate to **Gervase How** at the former two parishes. He is recorded as the curate of Stodmarsh and vicar of West Hythe from 1678 and held these livings until his death in 1720. CCEd Person ID: 139936; Whiteman, p. 21; KHLC, DCb/V/V/74, 79, 84, 95; Dunkin, I, 174.

Collington, Nathaniel junior [38, 38 nn. 88, 91] MA. Curate of Smallhythe Chapel in 1668 and 1670. Instituted rector of Pluckley in 1677 and remained until his death in 1735. He was the son of Nathaniel Collington, vicar of Tenterden. CCEd Person ID: 139938; LPL, VG 1/5, p. 65, VB 1/8/45; KHLC, DCb/V/V/64; Dunkin, I, 176.

Collington, Nathaniel senior [10, 10 n. 22, 11, 11 n. 23, 29, 29 n. 64, 38, 38 n. 90, 38 n. 91] MA. Chaplain to the earl of Winchelsea. Vicar of Boughton Aluph at the visitation of 1662 but was vicar of Godmersham with the chapel of Challock from August 1662 until his resignation in 1664. Vicar of Tenterden from November 1662 with dispensation to hold the rectory of Kenardington from 1664, and was pursued by **Henry Nicolls** for dilapidations at Boughton. He held Tenterden and Kenardington until his death in 1682. CCEd Person ID: 63030; LPL, VB 1/1/34, 39; KHLC, DCb/PRC/18/30/152; *AC*, 31, pp. 228–9.

Collins, Francis [57 n. 129] MA. Licensed to officiate at Sundridge in 1634. Named in the parliamentary survey of 1650, as the incumbent of Knockholt and subscribed in 1662 as curate. Buried there as minister in 1670. LPL, VH 98/1/57, VG 1/2 fo. 17; Hasted, II, p. 82.

Collins, John [39] Possibly rector of Allington, Rochester diocese, from 1656, but was instituted in 1660, serving until his death in 1677. He was presented to the vicarage of Bearsted in 1663 and again in 1667, and received dispensation to hold it, along with Allington, in 1664, but was not admitted until 1668. He held the vicarage until 1677. CCEd Person ID: 777; LPL, VB 1/1/68; Fielding, p. 18.

Collins, Walter [38] BA. Instituted rector of Newenden in December 1664, but not recorded after 1668. CCEd Person ID: 5237; LPL, VG 1/4 fo. 3v.

Colpeper [38] Probably **Thomas Culpeper** below.

Colt, Ann [45] The wife of **Henry Colt** below.

Colt, Esq [45] Probably Henry Colt, a lay rector. His family acquired the rectory of Borden in Elizabethan times. Hasted, VI, 77.

Colvill, – [36] John Colvill, a quaker clothier, lived in a seven hearth house in Cranbrook and was a trustee or purchaser of quaker property in 1658. Some of his sheep were distrained for non-payment of tithes in 1660, and he was imprisoned 1670–2. Besse, pp. 290, 295; *AC*, 112, p. 326; Harrington, p. 231.

Compton, Henry [lxii, 73r, 73r n. 191] DD. Bishop of Oxford, 1674–5, and bishop of London, 1675–1713. *ODNB*.

Conway, Thomas senior [49, 53] MA. University preacher, 1653, and Fellow of Gonville and Caius College, Cambridge, 1651–6. Admitted to the rectory of Wychling in 1656, and reinstituted in 1661. Collated to the vicarage of Stalisfield in 1665, he retained both livings until his death in 1690. His son, Thomas, was curate at Wychling from 1682 and succeeded to the rectory in 1690. CCEd Person ID: 139940, 5253; LPL, COMM III/4, p. 607, COMM III/5, p. 501; Venn, I, 381; Dunkin, I, 181.

Cooke, – [38] Not identified.

Cooke, Alexander [6] BA. Collated to Chislet in June 1662 and is recorded as the vicar in the visitations of 1662, 1664 and 1670. He died in 1672. CCEd Person ID: 139941; KHLC, DCb/V/V/56, 58, 64; Venn, I, 382.

Cooke, John [30] MA. A chaplain of Christ Church, Oxford, from 1669, he was appointed to the rectory of Cuxton, Kent, in 1674, but ceded in 1677. He was collated to the rectory of Mersham in the same year, holding it until his death in 1726. Chaplain to Thomas, earl of Thanet in 1685, he was made a Six Preacher of Canterbury cathedral in 1687, and he also became rector of Canterbury St George the Martyr with St Mary Magdalen in 1692, holding these positions until 1726. He was vicar of Hernhill, 1690–8, and was rector of the derelict church of Bircholt in 1692. CCEd Person ID: 788, 12305; LPL, F V/1/IV fo. 87v; Willis (1975), p. 52; Dunkin, I, 182; Ingram Hill, p. 70.

Cooke or **Cook, Ralph** [lxvii, 38, 59b] DD. Rector of Burythope, Yorks., 1636–7, rector of Burstow from 1637 until his death in 1685. Rector of St Gabriel's Fenchurch, London, from 1638, sequestrated in 1644 but restored by 1662. The church was destroyed in the Great Fire in 1666. Canon of Rochester cathedral, 1660–85. CCEd Person ID: 789; Matthews, *Walker*, p. 45; Horn, III, 65; Foster, I, 321.

Cooke, Thomas [60 (2)] DD. Instituted to the rectory of Great Mongeham in 1665, but ceded it in the same year. Chaplain to Archbishop Sheldon. Rector of Hadleigh, Suffolk, from 1665, and rector of Stiste from 1666, holding both until his death in 1679. Archdeacon of Middlesex, 1669–79, and prebendary of St Paul's cathedral 1670–79. CCEd Person ID: 18626; LPL, VG 1/4 fos. 4, 5, VB 1/1/154; Dunkin, I, 183; Venn, I, 387.

Cooper, John [xliv, lix, 36] BA. Curate and schoolmaster at Goudhurst in 1661. Collated to the vicarage of Cranbrook and licensed to teach in the school in 1662. He was buried in 1668. CCEd Person ID: 139942; LPL, VG 1/2 fo. 28v; KFHS, Cranbrook Burials.

Coppin, Jo. [26] Descendant of John Coppin of Bekesbourne, who became lord of the manor of Wooton in 1606. Hasted, IX, 366–7.

Corutier, Clement [18] *See* **Clement Couteur**.

Cosby, Phineas [42] MA. Instituted as vicar of Linton in 1660 and died in 1677. CCEd Person ID: 139943.

Cosin, John [xli (2), xli n. 31] Bishop of Durham, 1660–72. CCEd Person ID: 23012; *ODNB*.

Cottingham, John [lxvi n. 175, 56a] MA. Instituted as rector at Halstead in 1644, having been curate to Thomas Whitfield, who resigned. He is recorded as minister from 1651 to 1655 and subscribed in 1662. He died in 1664. CCEd Person ID: 80692; LPL, COMM I/47, V/1, VIa/2, 3, 6, 7, VB 1/1/100; Matthews, *Walker*, p. 227.

Cotton, Jo. [lxvi, 56a] Sir John Cotton, third baronet, was MP for Huntingdon, 1661–79, and for Huntungdonshire in 1685. He negotiated the transfer of the Cotton library, which had been started by his grandfather and augmented by his father, to the nation at his death and later it formed one of the foundation collections of the newly established British Museum and therefore the British Library. He had a thirteen hearth house in Farningham and died in 1702. *ODNB*; *HoP*; Harrington, p. 77.

Courtenay, William [62] Archbishop of Canterbury, 1381–96. *ODNB*.

Couteur, Clement [18] Clement Le Couteur MA. Scion of an old-established family in Jersey, he was instituted as rector of the derelict church of Little Mongeham in 1661 and to the 1st Mediety of the rectory of Sedgebrooke, Lincs., in 1662. He is noted in visitations as holding the former until 1677, and resigned from the latter in 1688. He succeeded his brother Phillippe as dean of Jersey in 1672 and held the office until his death in 1714. CCEd Person ID: 94093; *46th report*, p. 41; Foster, I, 337; www.theislandwiki.org/index.php/Clement_Le_Couteur.

Coventry, John [33] MA. Rector of Warehorne, 1675–80, and died in 1681. CCEd Person ID: 139945; LPL, VB 1/3/253; *AC*, 4, p, 102.

Cowes, James [52] MA. Instituted to the rectory of Luddenham in 1661 and remained there until his death in 1675. Curate of Oare, 1668–75, and curate of Davington, 1671–5. CCEd Person ID: 139970; Dunkin, I, 195; Willis (1975), p. 45.

Cradock, Thomas [48 (2)] MA. Vicar of Tonge, 1672–7, and licensed to read prayers in the chapel of Sheerness Fort in 1673. In 1675, his institution as rector of Frinsted was refused, as the living was not void. Curate to **William Walter** at Rainham in 1675, he signed the Compton census in 1676. Later that year he was instituted to the vicarage, and as chaplain to Elizabeth, countess dowager of Thanet, he was dispensed to hold Rainham with the rectory of Frinsted in 1682. He died in 1723. CCEd Person ID: 139971; Dunkin, I, 198; Willis (1975), p. 47; Hasted, VI, 14; Whiteman, pp. 29, 30; TNA, PROB 11/593/387.

Crawford, John [37] BA. Intruded rector of Halden in 1645 who remained until his death in 1683.

LPL, VB 1/4/317; Matthews, *Walker*, p. 226; Venn, I, 415.

Crayford, William [17] Patron of Ripple and referred to as 'Sir' William, but called William Crayford esquire by Hasted. Mr Crayford had a twelve hearth house in Great Mongeham in 1664. Hasted, IX, 569; Harrington, p. 400.

Crew, John [47] MA. Schoolmaster in the parish of St Peter le Poer, London in 1673, Usher at Rochester School in 1676 and licensed to teach at Elham in the same year. Instituted as vicar of Hartlip in 1677 and remained until his death in 1704. Minor canon of Rochester cathedral, 1684–1704. CCEd Person ID: 7193; Dunkin, I, 201; Willis (1975), p. 5.

Crew, Nathaniel [73r] Bishop of Oxford, 1671–4, and bishop of Durham, 1674–1717. *ODNB*.

Crips, – (Captain) *See* **Crispe, Thomas.**

Crips, Henry [18] The patron of the desolate church of Stonar was Henry Crispe of Quex, Birchington, a relative of **Thomas Crispe** below. Hasted, X, 420.

Crispe, Thomas [6] Referred to as Captain Crips, one of the chief men in the parish of Monkton, honest and a JP. He only attended the assizes in 1661 and 1662. He lived in Quekes or Quex manor in Birchington parish. Cockburn (1995), pp. 4, 16, 50; Hasted, X, 297–301.

Croft, Herbert [xli] Bishop of Hereford, 1660–91. CCEd Person ID: 11883; *ODNB*.

Crompe, Benjamin [xlviii n. 81, 42, 47] MA. Curate to John Viney at Westwell in 1634. Rector of High Halstow in Rochester diocese, 1639–64, and canon of Rochester cathedral, 1660–4. Presented to the vicarage of Boxley in 1663, but not instituted. Dispensed in 1662 to hold the vicarage of Hartlip in plurality with High Halstow, serving the former until his death in 1664. CCEd Person ID: 822; Willis (1972), p. 66; LPL, F I/C fo. 116.

Crosswell, Samuel [34] Instituted as rector of Wittersham in 1647 and remained until the appointment of **Francis Drayton junior** in 1667. No other records found but probably buried at Appledore in 1701. CCEd Person ID: 173692; England Marriages, 1538–1973, England Deaths and Burials, 1538–1991, www.familysearch.org.

Cuckow, Daniel [7] MA. Perpetual curate of Fairfield, 1631 to 1637, and curate of Brookland, 1632 to 1637. Instituted to the rectory of Swalecliffe in 1641, he appears to have remained, throughout the Interregnum, until his death in 1691. CCEd Person ID: 11917; KHLC, DCb/V/V/57, 58, 64, 69–71, 74, 79, 84.

Cuffen, Henry [29, 29 n. 20] MA. A peripatetic curate in the 1620s and 1630s, Cuffen served in West Langdon, Whitfield, Sevington and Old Romney and was schoolmaster at Lydd. Not found in the Commonwealth records, he is noted as curate of Fairfield and Ruckinge in 1662, and was instituted to the rectory of Brook in April 1667, but died before July of that year. CCEd Person ID: 40538; LPL, VG 1/2 fo. 32v; Venn I, 431.

Cullen, John [10] BA. John Culling or Cullen was appointed to Chillenden in 1652 and served as the rector until his death in 1709. He was Usher of King's School, Canterbury, 1663–81, and curate of the donative of Goodnestone by Wingham, 1679–81. The dean and chapter of Canterbury presented him to the sinecure rectory of Orgarswick on his resignation from the school. CCEd Person ID: 139974; BL, Add MS 36792, fo. 51; LPL, VB 1/6/4; Venn, I, 431; Woodruff and Cape, p. 150.

Cullen, Thomas [20] Not identified.

Culmer, Richard junior [7] Master of Sir Roger Manwood's Free School, Sandwich, from 1673, until his death in 1689. CCEd Person ID: 139975; Venn, I, 431; Cavell and Kennett, p. 58.

Culmer, Richard senior [7] Father of the above. The infamous presbyterian iconoclast was minister, at various times from the 1620s to 1640s, in Goodnestone by Wingham, Harbledown, Chartham and Hackington. He became a Six Preacher of Canterbury cathedral in 1644 and probably retained the position until 1660. He was also vicar of Minster in Thanet from 1645 until his ejection in 1660. He died in 1662. *ODNB*; Ingram Hill, p. 52; Matthews, *Calamy*, p. 154.

Culpeper, Cheyney [27] Sir Cheyney Culpeper, eldest son of **Sir Thomas Culpeper**, had been chairman of the Kent committee after the rebellion of 1648. He died in 1663. *ODNB*; Cliffe, p. 473.

Culpeper, Lady [41] The widow of Sir Cheyney, above, or Sir Thomas, below.

Culpeper, Thomas [41] This could be Sir Thomas Culpeper, died 1662, or his youngest son, Thomas, who was knighted soon after the Restoration. He published a number of pamphlets and died in 1697. *ODNB*.

Cumberland, Robert [l, 10] BA. Recorded as vicar of Petham in 1662, he was instituted to the vicarage of Chilham in the same year and served until his death in 1711. CCEd Person ID: 139976; Hasted, VII, 291.

Cunningham, Henry [56b] MA. Instituted to the vicarage of Northfleet in 1632, and probably remained until his death in 1665. CCEd Person ID: 40545; LPL, VB 1/1/160.

Curtis, George [53] Lived in the twenty hearth manor house in Otterden. Harrington, p. 96, Hasted, V, 537.

Dale, Thomas [63] MA. Instituted to the rectory of Kingsdown with Mappiscombe, Rochester diocese, in 1639, following the death of his father, Christopher. Possibly sequestrated at sometime in the succeeding years, but his resignation is recorded in 1662. He successfully petitioned the king in 1660, for the rectory of West Tarring and held it until his death in 1672. CCEd Person ID: 837; LPL, VG 1/2 fo. 25; *CSPD*, 1660, p. 62.

Dalton, John [lv, 58] MA. Perhaps the intruded rector of Hornsey, Middx., 1654–8. Vicar of Boughton under Blean in 1657 but resigned in 1658. Already in office when he subscribed as rector of St Swithin London Stone with St Mary Bothaw in 1662. He resigned as rector of St Mary Bothaw in 1666 and probably became vicar of Aylesbury, Bucks., where he died in 1682. CCEd Person ID: 162355; Matthews, *Walker*, p. 260; LPL, COMM II/332, VH 2/32/5; Boodle, p. x.

Danby [lxii] Thomas Osborne, first duke of Leeds, previously earl of Danby and marquess of Carmarthen. Lord treasurer, 1673–9. He was the originator of the Compton census of 1676 and died in 1712. *ODNB*.

Darell, John [36] The Darrell family owned the manor of Little Chart from the fourteenth to the eighteenth century. It had seventeen hearths. Hasted, VII, pp. 457–60; Harrington, p. 313.

Davies, Francis [73r] Bishop of Llandaff, 1667–75. *ODNB*.

Davis, John [20, 22] From around 1646 to 1660 he was the pastor of a congregational church, which held its meetings in the church of Dover St James the Apostle. Matthews quotes Anthony Wood saying that Davis was MA, Cambridge, and was chaplain to Dover castle under Major General Kelsey. In 1654, he was assistant to the Kent Commission. He was ejected from St James in 1660 and possibly died in 1663. Matthews, *Calamy*, p. 158; perhaps Venn, II, 15.

Davis, John [l n. 93, 43 (2)] Rector of Otham in 1655 and remained until his death in 1677. Curate of Maidstone from 1661 until 1677. LPL, COMM III/4, fo. 183; Dunkin, I, 223.

Davis or **Davies, William** [53] MA. Recorded as the vicar of Selling at the 1662 visitation. Chaplain to William, earl of Marlborough, in 1668, but died in 1669. KHLC, DCb/V/V/56; LPL, F V/1/II fo. 38v, VB 1/2/202.

Davyes or **Davis, John** [lxvi n. 176, 55] MA. Approved as minister of Darenth on 31 December 1658. He made the required declaration in 1662 and died in 1669. LPL, COMM II/223, VG 1/2 fo. 10v, VH 2/9/1, 96/3910.

Dawling, John [15, 17] MA. Rector of East Langdon, curate to **Isaac Lovell** at Guston and curate of the desolate church of West Langdon from 1674, holding all three offices until 1679, when he became rector of Ringwould, succeeding his father, **Richard Dawling**. He died in 1727. CCEd Person ID: 139978; LPL, VB 1/4/75, 76; Dunkin, I, 224.

Dawling, Richard [17] MA. Instituted as rector of Frinsted in 1645, he was rector of Ringwould from 1651 until his death in 1679. CCEd Person ID: 80817; Venn, II, 20.

Deering or **Dering, Edward** [28 (2)] BA. Sir Edward, second baronet. MP in 1660, 1670, 1679 and 1681. His manor house of Surrenden in Pluckley had thirty-four hearths. *ODNB*; *HoP*; Hasted, VII, 465; Harrington, p. 316.

Deering, Henry junior [44] MA. Curate to William Sutton at Detling, 1670–3. Instituted to the vicarage of Thurnham with Allington in 1674 and dispensed to hold it with the vicarage of Bearsted in 1693. He held both livings until his death in 1720. CCEd Person ID: 139979; Willis (1975), p. 62; LPL, VB 1/3/214, F II/34/24; Hasted, V, 513.

Deering, Henry senior [41, 47 (2)] MA. Vicar of Newington next Sittingbourne from 1626, but sequestrated in 1645. Restored in 1660 and died in 1666. Vicar of Lower Halstow from 1632 but also sequestrated and restored in 1660. CCEd Person ID: 40372; Matthews, *Walker*, p. 215; Venn, II, 36.

De L'angle, John Maximilian [lxiii] DD. Vicar of Ruislip, Middx., 1674–82. Canon of Canterbury cathedral, 1678–1724. Rector of Kingston, 1682–92, and dispensed to hold Sibertswold with Coldred in plurality, 1684–6. In 1686, he replaced Sibertswold with the rectory of Canterbury St George the Martyr with St Mary Magdalen, Canterbury. He resigned Kingston in 1692 for the rectory of St Michael Paternoster Royal, and St Martin Vintry London but resigned in 1695 to become the rector of Chartham. He died in 1724. CCEd Person ID: 24486, 162481; LPL, VB 1/4/413, 485, 534, VB 1/7/74; Venn, II, 29; Hasted, IX, 349.

Dicus or **Dicas, Humphrey** [l n. 93, 18, 20] MA. Vicar of Tilmanstone from 1651 until his death in 1675. Also, curate of Whitfield from at least 1663 until 1675. CCEd Person ID: 173403; BL, Add MS 36792, fo. 21; Matthews, *Walker*, p. 68; *AC*, 20, p. 113; Foster, I, 402.

Diggs or **Digges, Thomas** [10] Thomas Digges Esq. lived in the twenty-six hearth Chilham castle and presented the vicarage of Chilham to **Robert Cumberland** in 1662. He died in 1687. Harrington, p. 321; Hasted, VII, 275, 291.

Dillingham, Samuel [59a] MA. Collated to the rectory of St Pancras Soper Lane, London, in 1662, but after the Great Fire, he removed to the curacy of Monken Hadley, Middx., where he died in 1672. CCEd Person ID: 142824; Cass, pp. 90–1.

Dingley, Mr [44] Francis Dingley Esq. was once the patron of Wormshill, but it was sold to the Sedley family in Elizabethan times. Hasted, V, 563.

Dingley, Nicholas [xliv, 11] BA. Intruded into the rectory of Kingston in 1647, he survived an attempt to institute **Miles Barne** in his place and remained until 1672. At the 1662 visitation, he was also noted as the rector of Buckland by Faversham but he is not shown there in the Catalogue. He is recorded as chaplain to Francis, Lord Willoughby, in 1662 and died in 1672. CCEd Person ID: 124723, 38061; Matthews, *Walker*, p. 212; LPL, F V/1/I fo. 73v, VB 1/3/155; Wilkie (1891), pp. xi-xii.

Dixon, Robert [xlviii n. 81, 49] DD. Instituted to the rectory of Tunstall in 1647, but sequestrated in the same year. Restored in 1660, he resigned in favour of his son Robert in 1676. Vicar of Rochester St Nicholas with St Clement and canon of Rochester cathedral, 1660–88. CCEd Person ID: 878; Matthews, *Walker*, p. 215; Dunkin, I, 239; *ODNB*.

Dixwell, Basil [50] Sir Basil, who lived in a twenty hearth house in Barham. He married Dorothy, daughter of Sir **Thomas Peyton**, of Knowlton. Harrington, p. 411; Berry, p. 469.

Dodd, John [xlii] MA. Instituted to the rectory of Betteshanger in October 1661 but was not ordained until May 1662. Ejected in 1662 and no further record found. Matthews confuses him with John Codd at Ulcombe. CCEd Person ID: 139875; Matthews, *Calamy*, p. 165.

Dodson, Jeremy [13] MA. Curate of Wye, 1661–5, and probably the rector of St Katherine Coleman, London, from 1665 until his death in 1692. CCEd Person ID: 139982, 162680; *AC*, 28, pp. 321–2; Venn, II, 52.

Doe, Sir Charles [40] Alderman of London, 1664–7, and knighted as sheriff in 1665. Beaven, p. 343; Shaw (1906), II, 241.

Dolben, John [lxix] DD. Married Catherine Sheldon, niece of **Gilbert Sheldon** in 1657. Rector of Newington, an archbishop's peculiar in Oxfordshire, 1660–3. Prebendary of St Paul's cathedral, 1661–7. Archdeacon of London and vicar of St Giles Cripplegate, 1662–4. Dean of Westminster, 1662–83. Bishop of Rochester, 1666–83. Archbishop of York, 1683–8. Died in 1688. CCEd Person ID: 142825; *ODNB*.

Dorrell, James [47] Esq. Lessee of the parsonage of Halstow and possibly the Mr James Dorell said to be one of the ringleaders of the Kentish Royalist Rebellion of 1648. Rushworth, VII, 1136.

Dorset, earl of [62, 63, 64] Thomas Sackville, first Baron Buckhurst and first earl of Dorset. Patron of the rectories of East Lavant, Framfield and Buxton until his death in 1608. *SAC* 26, p. 12; *ODNB*.

Doughty or **Doughtie, John** [59b, 59b n. 146] DD. Rector of Wood Norton, Norfolk, in 1616. Probably sequestrated and subscribed in 1662. Rector of Rushock, Worcs., in 1631 but unknown tenure. Rector of Lapworth, Warwicks., from 1634 and Beaudesert, Warwicks., from 1636, he was sequestrated from both by 1646. Canon of Westminster, 1660–72. Chaplain to James, earl of Northampton, in 1666. Rector of Cheam, Surrey, from 1662, until his death in 1672. CCEd Person ID: 80130; LPL, F V/1/II fo. 17; Matthews, *Walker*, p. 363; *ODNB*.

Downes, Elkanah [lxvi, 58] DD. Curate at St Edmund the King and Martyr, London, in 1640. Minister of Holy Trinity Minories from 1643, and remained, undisturbed, until admittance as curate in 1661, still there in 1664. Having taken the Solemn League and Covenant, he was appointed to the rectory of Digswell, Herts., in 1647, by the House of Lords, tenure unknown. Curate of Chatham, Rochester diocese, in 1661. Instituted as rector of St Leonard Eastcheap in 1661 and dispensed to hold the rectory of Ashtead, Surrey, in 1662. St Leonard Eastcheap was not rebuilt after the Great Fire, and the parish was united with St Benet Gracechurch in 1670. Downes was referred to as the minister of St Leonard in 1671. He remained as rector of Ashtead until his death in 1683. CCEd Person ID: 92909; LPL, F I/C fo. 85; *LJ*, 8, p. 652; Tomlinson, p. 222; Fielding, p. 51; Venn, I, 293.

Drayton, Francis junior [27, 34, 34 n. 81, 39] MA. Vicar of Bearsted and of Appledore with Ebony from 1661, he ceded Bearsted in 1667, and was dispensed to hold the rectory of Wittersham along with Appledore. He retained them both, until his death in 1697, although he received dispensation to live at Tenterden in 1667, 1670 and 1673. CCEd Person ID: 139984; LPL, F V/1/II fo. 27, VB 1/2/106, 113, 115, 232, 1/3/185, 1/4/556, 557.

Drayton, Francis senior [36] MA. Curate to Thomas Hieron at Hernhill in 1635. He was an intruder at Great Chart, in 1646. Presented to the rectory of Little Chart in 1646 and appears to have remained there throughout the Interregnum, dying in 1669. CCEd Person ID: 40672; LPL, COMM I/68; Dunkin, I, 249.

Drury, John [56b] Not identified.

Drury, Walter [38] MA. was collated to the rectory of Sandhurst in 1632, sequestered in 1645 and restored in 1660. He remained until his death in 1680. CCEd Person ID: 40673; LPL, VB 1/4/132; Matthews, *Walker*, p. 215.

Dryden, Jonathan [20] MA. Rector of Cheriton from 1668 until his cession in 1676. Rector of Keighley, Londesborough and Scrayingham, all in Yorkshire, and a canon of York cathedral between 1676 and his death in 1702. CCEd Person ID: 15042; LPL, VB 1/3/291.

du Bray or **de Bray** or **Deffray, John** [17] MA. Instituted as rector of Sandwich St Peter in 1671, he ceded in 1673, subsequently holding seven other positions in the diocese. Curate of Minster in Thanet, 1675–8, curate of Adisham in 1683, and Westbere in 1689. He was rector of Hawkinge, 1690–5, curate of River, the chapel to Lydden, in 1692 and curate of Brookland from 1696 until his death in 1738. CCEd Person ID: 123648; LPL, VB 1/3/102; Willis (1975), pp. 47–54; CCA, U108/16.

du Moulin, Peter [xlviii n. 82, 8] DD. Holder of several livings in England and Wales before the civil wars, he suffered many sequestrations. He was instituted to the rectory of Adisham in 1658, became a royal chaplain and succeeded his father as a canon of

Canterbury cathedral in 1660. He retained both offices until his death in 1684. CCEd Person ID: 139986; *ODNB*.

Ducy, Ed. [21] Not identified.

Duke, Edward [30, 30 n. 69] MA. Collated to the derelict church of Midley in 1629. In 1662, he was described as the rector of Midley and curate of Edenbridge, Kent. Died in 1669. CCEd Person ID: 40682; LPL, VG 1/2 fo. 7v, VB 1/2/212.

Dukeson, Dr. [42] DD. Probably Richard Dukeson, the sequestrated rector of St Clement Danes, London, who was restored in 1660. CCEd Person ID: 63421; Venn, II, 73.

Dunbar, William [50, 52] MA. Admitted as vicar of Woodnesborough in 1657, ordained deacon and priest in 1660, and by 1661, he was vicar of Doddington, adding the vicarage of Newnham by 1664. He was granted a licence for non-residence at Doddington in 1669, signed the Compton census for both his livings and probably died in 1694. CCEd Person ID: 87877; LPL, COMM III/6, p. 26, VB 1/2/183; Whiteman, pp. 31–2.

Durant, John [lix, lx, 4] Held the lectureship of Sandwich St Peter from 1643 and later formed a congregation of independents in Canterbury. The intruded rector of Canterbury St George the Martyr and a Six Preacher in the cathedral in 1649, he was ejected from both positions in 1660. He preached at conventicles in Canterbury St Peter and St Paul in 1669, and received a licence as a congregationalist in 1672. He died in 1689. *AC*, 83, pp. 193–203; Matthews, *Calamy*, p. 173; Lyon Turner, I, 13.

Durell or **Durel, John** [1] Minister of the French congregation in London, which met in the chapel at the Savoy Palace, where **Gilbert Sheldon** was master. *ODNB*.

Eales, Alban [27] MA. Rector of Holton, Oxon., from at least 1646 and possibly stayed until 1664. He was collated to Aldington in 1665, and was appointed as a Six Preacher of Canterbury cathedral in the same year, probably dying in 1670. CCEd Person ID: 12413; Ingram Hill, p. 65; Mastin, p. 139; Fox, *passim*.

Edmonds, John [9] LLB. Collated to the vicarage of Bekesbourne in 1661, he served until his death in 1666. CCEd Person ID: 139996; Wilkie (1896), p. 110.

Edwards, Jo. [50] John Edwards died in 1631 and the patronage of Davington was passed to his daughter, Anne, who married into the family of Bode, of Essex. Mary Bode (daughter of Sir **Edward Boys**) owned the patronage by 1663. Hasted, VI, 376.

Edwards, John [42, 47] MA. Master of King's School, Rochester, 1663–77. Vicar of Hartlip from 1664 until his death in 1677. Presented to Ashford in 1673, but not instituted. Vicar of Halling in Rochester diocese, 1646–77. CCEd Person ID: 904; LPL, VB 1/3/306.

Edwards, Richard [15] MA. Rector of Chislehurst, Rochester diocese, in 1653 but unknown tenure. Rector of Barfreystone from 1662 until his death in 1702. In the

Compton census of 1676, it is noted that there was no return for the parish because Edwards was in hiding, possibly to avoid creditors. CCEd Person ID: 121711; LPL, VG 1/2 fo. 31, VB 1/5/39; Matthews, *Walker*, p. 213; Whiteman, p. 21.

Ellis, Robert [xlviii n. 81, 35] MA. May have held the vicarage of Burham, Rochester diocese, from 1647. As chaplain to Philip, earl of Chesterfield, he was instituted to the rectory of Boughton Malherbe in 1661, having obtained dispensation to hold it along with Burham. He held both livings until his death in 1675. CCEd Person ID: 68790; Fielding, p. 44.

Elward, William [45] BA. Teacher at Tunstall in 1666 – '*literatus*'. Curate to **John Lynch** at Harrietsham in 1669 and instituted to the vicarage of Bicknor in 1674. Curate to William Thomas at Hucking in 1683. As chaplain to John, Lord Culpeper, baron of Thoresway, he was dispensed to hold Bicknor with the vicarage of Borden in 1690. He retained the two livings until his death in 1704. CCEd Person ID: 14076; Willis (1975), pp. 3, 49; LPL, F II/30/29, VB 1/5/139, 141, 164.

Erwin, Alexander [63, 63 n. 175, 64 n. 183] Probably the 'Henry Alexander' recorded in the Catalogue as the rector of Buxted. He is noted as curate of Lindfield, 1678–82, curate at Chailey, Sussex, in 1686 and as a curate at Buxted in 1687. CCEd Person ID: 63418.

Eve, Henry [30, 50, 52, 54] DD. Intruded at Sandwich St Clement in 1643, he was nominated as vicar of Lynstead in 1647, and is noted in visitations until 1681. Rector of Buckland (by Faversham), 1663–86, and vicar of Teynham, 1663–81, he was rector of the derelict church of Midley, 1681–6. Died in 1686. CCEd Person ID: 68853; Matthews, *Walker*, p. 216; Shaw (1900), II, 341; KHLC, DCb/V/V/56–71.

Evering [xliii, 20 (2)] Robert Evering of Evering manor, later borough, was assessed for four hearths in 1664. Hasted, VIII, 137–8; Harrington, p. 352.

Ewell, Mr [15] Possibly Edward Ewell, 'gent', who had a three hearth house in Herne. According to Hasted, the advowson of the rectory of Barfreston was alienated to Ewell during the reign of Charles I, but was in the possession of **Basil Dixwell** in 1640. Harrington, p. 365; Hasted X, 77.

Fagge, – [10] Mentioned as one of the 'persons of quality' in the parish of Chilham. Rather than the son of Colonel Fagge, he is probably Mr Whittingham Fogge, a member of the extensive family in the county, who resided in a nine hearth house in Chilham. Harrington, p. 321; *AC*, 20, pp. 124–5.

Faversham, Lady [53] Catherine Sondes was the daughter and coheir of Sir **George Sondes**. She married **Louis Watson** in 1677, and died in 1695. *HoP*.

Fellow, Edward [xlii] MA. Curate at Stourmouth, 1620–2, schoolmaster at Wingham in 1629, curate at Staple, 1629–37, and at Birchington, 1644–61. Rector of the derelict church of Stonar, 1647–63, and rector of Canterbury St Alphege from 1661 until his death in 1663. CCEd Person ID: 40893; Ingram Hill, p. 61.

Felton, Nich. [56a] MA. Fellow of Pembroke College, Cambridge, 1633–44, ejected. Instituted as vicar of Teston, Rochester diocese, in 1664, but resigned before October 1667. Instituted to the vicarage of Eynsford in 1666, but resigned in 1669, when he was collated to the rectory of Hardwick, Cambs., again resigned and was instituted as rector of Rettendon, Essex, in 1670. He ceded Rettendon in 1672 on his collation to the rectory of Newton in the Isle, Cambs., where his travels were ended by his death in 1675. CCEd Person ID: 15524; LPL, VB 1/2/9, VH 2/10/2; Matthews, *Walker*, p. 38.

Fenne, James [41] MA. Instituted as vicar of Rochester St Margaret in 1673, but resigned in 1677, having been instituted to the vicarage of Goudhurst in 1676. Died in 1709. CCEd Person ID: 14821; LPL, VB 1/4/10, 1/5/332; Foster, II, 492.

Fermor, Mr [62] A member of the family who owned the advowson of the parish church of Halton at various times in the seventeenth and eighteenth centuries. Page, II, 341.

Fidge or Fige, John [lvi, 12] BA. Noted as rector of Bishopsbourne with Barham at the visitation of 1662, he was instituted vicar of Patrixbourne in 1663 and died in 1667. CCEd Person ID: 68976; KHLC, DCb/V/V/56; *AC*, 14, p. 179.

Finch, – [6] Not identified.

Finch, John, baron of Fordwich [2, 6] Bequeathed the manor and advowson of Fordwich to **Heneage Finch**, third earl of Winchelsea. His widow, Mabel (daughter of Charles Fotherby, dean of Canterbury), presented to Fordwich in 1663. Hasted, IX, 67; *ODNB*.

Finch, Thomas [46] A descendant of Thomas Finch who purchased the manor and advowson of Kingsdown in the sixteenth century. This Thomas may have died before 1664, as he is not listed in the Hearth Tax return for that year. Hasted, VI, 113–16.

Finney, Thomas [l, 32] BA. Curate at Warehorne in 1681 and at Brookland in 1683. No other record. CCEd Person ID: 88344; LPL, VB 1/4/141.

Finnis, John [22] Not identified.

Fisher, Edward [53, 53 n. 118] MA. Curate to **Henry Eve**, at Teynham in 1676, possibly remaining until 1680. Vicar of Selling, 1680–1710. Chaplain to Mary, duchess of Buckingham in 1689, and dispensed to hold the rectory of Buckland in plurality with Selling. Curate at Sheldwich, 1684–90. He resigned from Buckland in 1708 and died in 1710. CCEd Person ID: 123668; Whiteman, p. 32; LPL, F V/1/IV fo. 30, F II/29/30a–b, VB 1/5/281; Venn, II, 142.

Floate, John [23] MA. Instituted to the vicarage of Tillingham, Essex, in 1647 but in 1651, he was admitted to the living of Acrise. He served the rectory until his death in 1699. CCEd Person ID: 68100; Matthews, *Walker*, p. 223.

Fly, William [xxxix n. 14, l, 59a, 59a n. 141] MA. Curate of Idlesteye, Herts., in 1662. Curate of Norwood, Middx. (chapel of Hayes) who was suspended for conducting a clandestine marriage in 1667. Instituted as vicar of Hayes in 1670, and died in 1673. CCEd Person ID: 69022; LPL, VH 77/3/1–2, VB 1/3/41, 201.

Fogg, – [18] Richard Fogge Esq. lived in an eight hearth house in Tilmanstone and died in 1680. He was the father of Whittingham Fogge (*see under* **Fagge**). *AC*, 5, pp. 112–32; Harrington, p. 405.

Fowle, Mr [38] Not positively identified, but Mrs Elizabeth Fowle was assessed for eleven hearths in a house in Sandhurst in 1664. Harrington, p. 229.

Fowler, Edward [58] DD. Curate of Northill, Beds., 1656–63, rector of All Hallows Bread Street, London, 1673–81, canon of Gloucester cathedral, 1676–91, vicar of St Giles Cripplegate, London, 1681–1714, Bishop of Gloucester from 1691 until his death in 1714. CCEd Person ID: 35525; LPL, VG 1/3, fo. 75; *ODNB*.

Fowler, James [1, 1 n. 5] Master of Sir Roger Manwood's Free School, Sandwich, in 1672 and curate of Canterbury St Dunstan in 1674. Willis (1975), p. 46; Cavell and Kennett, Appendix B.

Francis, Jo. [9] Not identified.

Frembley, Ralph [10] Lived in a six hearth house in Boughton Aluph. Harrington, p. 332.

Frere, Mr [48] Henry Frere had an eight hearth house in Rainham. Harrington, p. 274.

Fryday, John [40] BA. Noted as curate at Ospringe during the visitation of 1662, subscribed as vicar of Detling in 1663, but disappeared before 1668 and nothing else known. Detling suffered from continuous sequestration from 1668 until 1674. CCEd Person ID: 88605; KHLC, DCb/V/V/56; LPL, VG 1/2 fo. 39; Willis (1975), pp. 61–3.

Fuller, William [73r] Bishop of Limerick, 1664–7, and bishop of Lincoln, 1667–75. *ODNB*.

Gamlyn, John [51] MA. Curate to Samuel Parker at Chartham in 1673, he signed the Compton census in 1676. Collated to the vicarage of Hernhill in the same year, he ceded in 1683, having been appointed to the vicarage of Faversham. He stayed in Faversham until his death in 1715, but was absent for some time in 1690, as John Blackstone was licensed to serve the cure in that year, 'John Gamlyn in civil custody'. He held the sequestration of Boughton under Blean from 1676 until 1684, and as chaplain to Margaret, countess dowager of Marlborough, was dispensed to hold the vicarage of Preston by Faversham, along with Facersham from 1684 until 1715. CCEd Person ID: 140002; Whiteman, p. 23; LPL, VB 1/3/295, F II/25/24; Willis (1975), pp. 51, 62, 65; *AC*, 21, p. 149.

Garbrand, Nicholas [63 n. 170] BD. Instituted as vicar of Washington, Sussex, in 1638, and may have been undisturbed until 1671. Prebendary of Chichester cathedral,

1660–71. Rector of Patching from 1660 until his death in 1671. CCEd Person ID: 7629; Horn, II, 52; Foster, II, 546.

Garnons, Luke [64 n. 182] MA. Vicar of Pagham from 1678 until his resignation in 1680. Vicar of Ringmer from 1680 until his death in 1681. CCEd Person ID: 15935; *SAC*, 26, p. 75; Venn, II, 197.

Garret, Robert [4, 26, 26 n. 57] MA. Curate at Bishopsbourne, Kent, from 1667 to 1677, and curate at Kingston, Kent, from 1673 to 1682. He signed the Compton census as such in 1676. He was licensed to the cure of Thanington in 1679, and became rector of Wooton, Kent, in 1680, probably retaining both livings until his death in 1712. CCEd Person ID: 63537; LPL, VB 1/4/189; Whiteman, p. 23; Dunkin, I, 319; Venn, II, 197.

Gatford, Lionel [58] DD, LLD. Presented to the vicarage of Martham, Norfolk, in 1668, but not instituted. Chaplain to Charles, earl of Norwich in 1669, and chaplain to Prince Rupert in 1679. Instituted to the rectory of Laceby, Lincs., in 1670 and ceded in 1678. Curate at St Giles in the Fields, London, in 1672. Rector of Clewer, Berks., 1677–80, rector of St Dionis Backchurch, London, 1680–1715, archdeacon of St Albans, 1713–15, treasurer and precentor of St Paul's cathedral, London, from 1714, until his death in 1715. CCEd Person ID: 88733; LPL, F V/1/III fo. 17v, F V/1/II fo. 47; Venn, II, 200.

Gell, Robert [58] DD. Curate at Bottisham, Cambs., in 1635, and Fellow of Christ's College, Cambridge, for many years. Rector of St Mary Aldermary from 1641, and survived an attempt to remove him in 1645. Sometime chaplain to Archbishop Sheldon, he died in office in 1665. CCEd Person ID: 24341; *ODNB*.

Gerrard, Henry [16, 30, 30 n. 66] MA. Vicar of Lenham from 1670 until 1677, and dispensed to also hold the vicarage of Lydd in 1672. Appointed a Six Preacher of Canterbury cathedral in 1676. In the following year, he was dispensed to hold the rectory of Deal with Lydd and he was noted as a chaplain to Ralph Brideoake, bishop of Chichester. He died in 1711. CCEd Person ID: 140007; LPL, F V/1/III fo. 4; Dunkin, I, 324; *AC*, 21, p. 181; Ingram Hill, p. 68.

Gibbons, Mr [22] Probably Thomas Gibbon of West Cliffe who had compounded for £200. Cliffe, p. 472.

Gibbs, William [11] Sold the patronage of Elmstone in the 1640s to Robert Jaques who was sheriff of Kent in 1669. Hasted, IX, p. 133; Berry, p. xi.

Gibson, William [lxv n. 174, lxvi n. 175, 56b] MA. Instituted to the vicarage of West Malling, Rochester diocese, in 1637, but tenure uncertain. In 1661, he stated in a petition that he had 'lost his living' but no date given. 'Minister' of Meopham in 1646 and received a payment from the Trustees for the Maintenance of Preaching Ministers in 1651. Instituted as vicar in 1662 serving until his death in 1670. He was instituted to the rectory of Lullingstone in Rochester diocese in 1663 and remained until 1670. CCEd Person ID: 977; LPL, MS 1104, fos. 103, 107; CCA, DCc-PET/211; *AC*, 16, p. 113; Matthews, *Walker*, p. 223; Venn, II, 212.

Gifford, George [56a] The lay lessee of the parsonage of Eynsford. Possibly the father of **George Gifford** below, but certainly a relative. Hasted, II, 537–8.

Gifford, George [58 (2)] DD. Rector of St Dunstan in the East, London, from 1656, but collated in 1661, and served until his death in 1686. Reader at Gresham College, London, in 1662 and president of Sion College in 1677 and 1678. CEd Person ID: 142828; LPL, VG 1/2 fo. 14v; Hennessy, p. 136; Pearce, pp. 126, 364; Foster, II, 563.

Gipps, George [28] MA. Licensed to the cure of Lympne in 1676 and to that of Fairfield in 1678. He left Lympne in 1679 and became curate of Wye, where he stayed until his death in 1707. He had been instituted to the vicarage of Brenzett in 1677 and retained it until his death. CCEd Person ID: 140013; Willis (1975), pp. 47–8; Dunkin, I, 329.

Glemham, Henry [73r] DD. Rector of Symondsbury, Dorset, 1631–45 and 1660–70. Dean of Bristol, 1660–7. Bishop of St Asaph, 1667–70. Died in 1670. CCEd Person ID: 7789; Venn, II, 222.

Goddard, – [11] Not identified.

Godden, – [30] Not identified.

Godden, Robert [7] MA. Vicar of Ryarsh in Rochester diocese in 1661 and instituted as vicar of Reculver in the same year. He died in 1672. CCEd Person ID: 985; Willis (1975), p. 62.

Goddin or **Godden, John** [44] Purchased the patronage of Thurnham in the middle of the seventeenth century, but nothing else known. Hasted, V, p. 523.

Godfry or **Godfrey, Thomas** [10] Husband of **Lady Moyle**, patron of Boughton Aluph. Lived in the fourteen hearth Nuckwell Manor in Boughton Aluph, and paid Hearth Tax for a four hearth empty house in the parish. Harrington, p. 332.

Goldsmith, Thomas [37] Not identified.

Goodrich or **Goodridge, William** [36] MA. Vicar of Steeple, Essex, in 1650. Vicar of Cranbrook from 1654 until his resignation in 1662. LPL, COMM III/3/1, fo. 262; Matthews, *Calamy*, p. 226; Tarbutt, p. 38.

Goodwin, Henry [56a] This clerk is shown in the Catalogue succeeding Thomas Allen in Grain, but James Nairne succeeded in 1669 following the death of Allen. In 1664, Henry Goodwin is recorded as living in a one hearth house, not chargeable for Hearth Tax in Kingsdown. He may have been curate to Allen at Grain and Kingsdown. Harrington, p. 78.

Gostling, John [12] BA. From 1689 until his death in 1733, the renowned bass singer simultaneously held the positions of canon of Lincoln cathedral, minor canon of St Paul's cathedral, minor canon of Canterbury cathedral, vicar of Littlebourne and rector of the ruined church of Hope. The two benefices in the diocese of Canterbury were allowed by dispensation but the distances involved and his attendance on the royal family make it difficult to imagine that he often attended to them. He was also the absentee vicar of Lenham, before the institution of **John Lord**. The Catalogue records it as vacant but 'John Goslyng' was assessed for seven hearths 'in the vicarage house' in the Hearth Tax return for 1664. Gostling 'served' at Canterbury cathedral and Littlebourne for the fifty-nine years 1675–1733. CCEd Person ID: 16479; *ODNB*; Horn, IX, 82; Dunkin, I, 339; *AC*, 37, p. 191; Harrington, p. 94.

Gould, Mr [55] Thomas Gould, who lived in a six hearth house in Crayford. Harrington, p. 36.

Greene, – [38] Peter Greene was assessed for three hearths in the parish of Smarden in 1664. Harrington, p. 315.

Greene, Francis [lxvi n. 176, 55] Vicar of East Farleigh from 1661 and died in 1685. In 1683, **James Wilson**, rural dean of Sutton, said that Greene 'was never qualified for the office of a priest, haveing been a common trooper in the late Rebellion, so his moralls have been no credit to the church since he crept into holy orders'. LPL, VG 1/3 fo. 3v, VH 96/4423; Hasted, IV, 383; Fielding, p. 414; *AC*, 21, p. 182.

Green, Thomas [xxxviii n. 9] Vicar of Minster, 1695–1708, canon of Canterbury cathedral, 1701–21, rector of Adisham, 1708–17, archdeacon of Canterbury, 1708–21, bishop of Norwich, 1721–3, bishop of Ely, 1723–38. Died in 1738. Venn, II, p. 258; ODNB.

Gregory, Thomas [39] Chaplain of HMS *Rainbow* in 1672. Instituted as vicar of Bearsted in 1677, he ceded it in 1685. Curate to the sinecure rector, **Ralph Staunton**, at Hollingbourne in 1680. Collated to the vicarage in 1684, he served until his death in 1696. CCEd Person ID: 142002; Dunkin, I, 349–50.

Griffin, Thomas junior [22, 22 n. 44] BA. Son of **Thomas Griffen senior**, below. Licensed as the schoolmaster in Borden in 1669, his father noted as giving his consent. Curate to **William Russell** at Ewell from 1675 to 1677, vicar of Lydden and curate of River from 1675 and schoolmaster in Dover St Mary the Virgin in the same year. Curate to John Warley at Charlton from 1676 to 1677 (Warley not mentioned in the Catalogue, although he was the rector there 1666–78), and curate of Canterbury St Dunstan in 1680. By 1685, he was curate to **John Castilion** at Minster in Thanet and was licensed as the schoolmaster there in 1686. He signed the Compton census as curate in Charlton, Ewell, River and Lydden. He died in 1704. CCEd Person ID: 123691; Dunkin, I, 351; Willis (1975), pp. 4, 5, 47, 48, 50; *AC*, 25, p. 35.

Griffin, Thomas senior [45, 45 n. 107] MA. Instituted as vicar of Borden in 1660 and licensed to the cure of Iwade in 1664, serving both until his death in 1670. CCEd Person ID: 44461; Willis (1975), p. 43; Hasted, VI, 79.

Griffith, Paul [lv] MA. Subscribed as vicar of Boughton under Blean in October 1662 but by February 1663 he was curate at Ashford Chapel, Staines, Middx., and became vicar of Feltham, Middx., in the following year. He remained until his death in 1676. CCEd Person ID: 163602; LPL, VG 1/2 fo. 37v.

Grindal, Edmund [xxxviii n. 5, 70r] Archbishop of York, 1570–6, archbishop of Canterbury, 1576–83. CCEd Person ID: 42650; *ODNB*.

Gumble, Thomas [62 n. 163] DD. Sometime 'vicar' of Chipping Wycombe between 1650 and 1657, he was not ordained deacon and priest until December 1660. Chaplain to General Monck, he accompanied the parliamentary army on its journey south in 1659 and was sent ahead to canvas support from parliament and the City of London. Canon of Winchester cathedral, 1661–76, and absentee rector of East Lavant from 1663 until his death in 1676. CCEd Person ID: 63621; LPL, F V/1/I fo. 1, VG 1/3 fo. 22v; Matthews, *Calamy*, p. 210; *ODNB*.

Gunning, Peter [xl n. 24, 73r] DD. Canon of Canterbury cathedral, 1660–9. Not an incumbent of a living in Canterbury diocese. Bishop of Chichester, 1670–5, and bishop of Ely, 1675–84. *ODNB*.

Haddes or **Hadde,** – [12, 41] One of the family who had owned the manor of Frinsted from the fourteenth to the sixteenth century. Henry Hadde presented to the rectory in 1580. A family member owned the patronage of the vicarage of Petham at some time in the seventeenth century. Hasted, V, 559, IX, 318.

Hadley, – [35] Not identified.

Hales, Edward [30, 38, 42, 48, 49, 56a] Sir Edward Hales, second baronet. His main residence was Tunstall Place, which had thirty-one hearths, but he had three other houses in Kent and one in London. A staunch royalist, he was the nominal leader of the Kent rising in 1648. He compounded for £2,000. Returned as MP for Maidstone in 1660, and sat for Queenborough from 1661 until 1680. He died in 1683. Harrington, 245, 261, 263, 264; *HoP*.

Hales, Edward [51] Edward Hales Esq. Eldest son of **Sir Edward**, later the third baronet and Jacobite first earl of Tenterden, who converted to Roman catholicism. He lived in an eleven hearth house in Charing. Harrington, p. 311; *ODNB*.

Hales, Elizabeth [3] Only daughter and heir of Sir James Hales, who had an eighteen hearth house in Canterbury. She compounded for £350. Hasted, XI, 238; Harrington, p. 444; Cliffe, p. 477.

Hales, Sir Robert [9] Created a baronet in 1660 and resided in the manor of Howlets in the parish of Bekesbourne. Hasted, IX, 271.

Hall, George [xli (5)] DD. Bishop of Chester, 1662–8. In October 1662, he was dispensed to hold in commendam the archdeaconry of Canterbury and rectory of Wigan, Lancs. CCEd Person ID: 97700; LPL, F I/C fo. 95; *ODNB*.

Halyfax [30] George Savile, first marquess of Halifax. *ODNB*.

Hammond, George [lx, 35 (3), 36, 37 (2), 38, 42] An anabaptist preacher, who lived in a four hearth house in Bethersden, but influenced surrounding parishes. He was joint pastor, with **James Blackmore**, of the baptist church at Biddenden, with congregations also at Cranbrook and Rolvenden. They were both imprisoned at Maidstone, 1660–1, along with other baptists, but said to be freed by the jailer. Packer, pp. 86–7; Lyon Turner, I, 17; Harrington, p. 318.

Hammond, Mr [38] Not identified.

Hammond, Thomas [64 n. 178] Thomas Hamon or Hammond was refused institution to the vicarage of Framfield in 1663 but in 1666, he is referred to as the minister in the parish register. He is recorded, as vicar, several times between 1673 and 1682 and his cession is noted in 1686. CCEd Person ID: 63650; LPL, VH 2/12/1; Matthews, *Calamy*, p. 92; *SAC*, 26, p. 45.

Hannington, Henry [24] Admitted to Gonville and Caius College, Cambridge, in 1637, but no record of degree. Curate of Buckland near Dover in 1639 and curate to Edward Ward, at Dover St James the Apostle in the same year. Vicar of Elham from at least 1662 until his death in 1691 and vicar of Lyminge with Paddlesworth and Stanford from 1672 until his resignation in 1685. He married the widow of **William Somner**, the antiquary, and her son, William, became curate to Hannington at Elham in 1683 and vicar of Lyminge in 1685. CCEd Person ID: 140021; LPL, VB 1/4/405, VG 1/6 fo. 43; Venn, II, 299.

Harding, Richard [lv] Appointed to the vicarage of Boughton under Blean on the sequestration of **Samuel Smith** in 1641. He 'returned to the West' in 1646. Boodle, p. x; Matthews, *Walker*, p. 225.

Hardres, Edward [11, 13] Members of the Hardres family would have, undoubtedly, been patrons of the church of Greater Hardres and the chapel of Stelling, but Edward has not been found, and there is no record of a knighthood. Shaw (1906), II, Index, p. 106; Hasted, IX, 306–9; Armytage, p. 73.

Hardres, Peter [xlviii n. 82, 11, 13] DD. Had been rector of Upper Hardres with the chapel of Stelling since 1632 and likely held it without interruption until his death in 1678, the advowson being owned by his family. He was a canon of Canterbury cathedral, 1660–78. CCEd Person ID: 41339; Hasted, IX, 309; Horn, III, 35.

Harfleete, Charles [22] MA Curate to **Peter Hardres** at the chapel of Stelling from 1634 and may have remained there until the Restoration. Vicar of Newington by Hythe from at least 1662, until his death in 1671. CCEd Person ID: 41337; KHLC, DCb/V/V/56, 58, 64; Dunkin, I, 374.

Harman, John [20, 22] See **Romswinckell**.

Harris, Christopher [24] MA. Curate to **Thomas Risden** at Ashford in 1670 and to **William Wickens** at Eastwell in 1673. Appointed curate of Wingham in 1672, he retained it until his probable death in 1719. Instituted to the ruined church of Bircholt in 1673, he was instituted to the rectory of Stourmouth in 1690. CCEd Person ID: 1074; LPL, VB 1/3/103, VB 1/6/324; Dunkin, I, 376.

Harris, John [59b] BD. Instituted to the rectory of Passenham, Northants., in 1632 and again in 1640, tenure unknown, but he may have remained until 1660. Dispensed to hold the rectory of Overstone in 1633, he resigned in 1642. Prebendary of Hereford cathedral, and vicar of Merstham, from 1660 until his death in 1678. CCEd Person ID: 118652; *Surrey AC*, 17, p. 21; Venn, II, 312.

Harris, Richard [61] BA. Curate of Southchurch from 1662 and rector from 1668, until his death in 1680. CCEd Person ID: 163763; LPL, VB 1/2/120, VG 1/5, p. 21; Venn, II, 312.

Harrison, Benjamin [15] Admitted to the rectory of Sandwich St Clement, but sequestrated sometime between 1650 and 1653. He was vicar of South Tawton, Devon, from 1654, possibly until 1660, when he was restored to St Clement's. He ceded the latter in 1666, and was said to have moved to another living in the West Country. CCEd Person ID: 140023; Matthews, *Walker*, p. 218; LPL, VB 1/2/32; Boys, p. 293.

Harrison, John [63] LLD, DD. Prebendary of Chichester cathedral from 1677 until his death in 1698. Rector of Pulborough, Sussex, 1677–98. Vicar of Crondall, Hants., from 1679 until his resignation in 1684. Instituted to the vicarage of West Tarring in 1676 but ceded it in 1677, whereupon **Richard Pawley** became vicar, probably until 1684, when he replaced Harrison at Crondall. Harrison returned to the vicarage of West Tarring and is recorded there in 1693 and 1697. CCEd Person ID: 63768, 64802; LPL, VG 1/5, p. 59.

Harward, William [62 n. 157] MA. Rector of Monks Risborough from 1624 until his sequestration in 1647. Restored in 1660 and served until his death in 1671. CCEd Person ID: 175041; Matthews, *Walker*, p. 74.

Hawe, George [38] Admitted to the vicarage of Tenterden by the Commissioners for Approbation of Public Preachers ('Triers') in 1655. Served until his ejection in 1662 when he became the founder and first minister of the Tenterden Presbyterian congregation. Imprisoned for preaching in 1665 and died in 1683. Matthews, *Calamy*, p. 253; *AC*, 31, p. 227.

Hawke, Mr [24] William Halke or Hawke was a descendant of the family who had owned the manor of Bircholt and two-thirds of the advowson of the church, since the fifteenth century. He died during the reign of Elizabeth I and left a daughter. Hasted, VIII, 11.

Hawkins, William [2, 30, 30 n. 68] MA. Licensed to teach at Biddenden School in 1638 and collated to St Mary in the Marsh in 1639. There in 1642 and probably remained throughout the Interregnum, as there is no record of his sequestration. Noted in the visitation of 1662 and subsequent visitations until his death in 1674. Minor canon of Canterbury cathedral from 1660 until 1670, curate of Canterbury St Margaret from 1662 and became the perpetual curate of Thanington, Kent, in 1671. He held St Margaret's, St Mary's and Thanington until 1674. CCEd Person ID: 41691; Willis (1975), p. 21; CCA, DCc-TB/1–35; KHLC, DCb/V/V/56, 58, 61, 64, 67; Dunkin, I, 389.

Hawtry, – [35] John Hawtry had a four hearth house in Ashford. Harrington, p. 296.

Haynes or **Haymes, Thomas junior** [40, 45 n. 107, 56b] MA. Fellow of King's College, Cambridge, 1661–9. Probably the son of **Haynes senior** below. Curate of Bredhurst from at least 1663 until 1675, and curate to **Robert Dixon**, at Tunstall, 1670–73. Vicar of Borden, 1670–3, and vicar of Northfleet from 1673 until his death in 1704. CCEd Person ID: 35725; Venn, II, 340; Whiteman, p. 35.

Haynes or **Haymes, Thomas senior** [40] Intruded vicar of Boxley from 1644 until his death in 1679. CCEd Person ID: 7199; LPL, VB 1/4/69; Cave-Browne (1892), p. 94.

Head, Merick [44] DD. Instituted to the rectory of Ulcombe in 1672 and to the rectory of Leybourne, Rochester diocese, in 1675. He retained both livings until his death in 1687. CCEd Person ID: 1150.

Henchman, Humphrey [lxix, 73r, 73r n. 191] Bishop of Salisbury, 1660–3, and bishop of London, 1663–75. *ODNB*.

Henden, John [35 (2), 37, 38 (2)] Nephew and heir of Edward Henden, one of the barons of the exchequer in the reign of Charles I, who died in 1662. John Henden was knighted in 1641 and served as high sheriff of Kent in 1646. He had a twenty-five hearth house in Benenden, another with six hearths in Biddenden and another with four hearths in Stone-in-Oxney. Harrington, pp. 240, 242, 350; Kilburne, p. 412; Shaw (1906), II, 210.

Hensly, Mr [47] Not identified.

Hering or **Herring, James** [lxvii, 63, 63 n. 166] MA. Rector of Hitcham, Bucks., from 1660 until his resignation in 1666. Prebendary of Chichester cathedral from 1664 until his death in 1673. Chaplain to Henry King, bishop of Chichester in 1666 and, with dispensation, held the rectory of Slinfold and the vicarage of Cuckfield, Sussex, from 1666 until 1673. CCEd Person ID: 97206; LPL, F V/1/II fo. 19v, VB 1/2/13; Horn, II, 59; Venn, II, 358.

Heskith or **Hesketh, Henry** [lxvii, 59b] MA. Curate of Nutfield, Surrey, in 1662 and rector of Ashton upon Mersey, Cheshire, 1662–3. Rector of Long Ditton, Surrey, 1663–5, and rector of Charlwood, Surrey, 1663–1710. Collated to the vicarage of St Helen Bishopgate, London, in 1678, he resigned in 1695 and died in 1710. Sometime chaplain to Anthony, earl of Shaftesbury, and to Charles II. CCEd Person ID: 74834; LPL, VG 1/2 fo. 9, F I/C fo. 129, F V/1/II fo. 91, III fo. 17; *ODNB*.

Heyman or **Hayman, Peter** [32] Sir Peter Heyman, second baronet. His Somerfield manor in Sellinge, had sixteen hearths. Cockayne, II, 136; Harrington, p. 347.

Hickford, – [48] Henry Higford 'gent' had a thirteen hearth house in Rainham. Harrington, p. 273.

Hickford, James [lxvi n. 175, 56b] MA. Instituted as rector of Ightham in 1644, and probably retained his living until his death in 1693. CCEd Person ID: 80931.

Hieron, Thomas [27 n. 59] MA. Vicar of Hernhill, 1630–53, curate at Otham, 1647–58, Six Preacher of Canterbury cathedral, 1655–9, rector of Boughton Malherbe, 1656–9, vicar of Bekesbourne, 1656–9, and vicar of Appledore, 1656–9. Probably died in 1659. CCEd Person ID: 42470; LPL, MS 1643, p. 46; Cave-Browne (1889), p. 125; Ingram Hill, p. 58; Matthews, *Walker*, p. 211.

Hieron, William [38] MA. Instituted to the rectory of Newenden in September 1661 but is not recorded again. The Catalogue reports his imprisonment for debt. CCEd Person ID: 140026.

Hill, Hercules [lv] Minister of Boughton under Blean in 1649 and probably remained until 1653. Boodle, p. x; LPL, MS 1104, fos. 114r–118v.

Hind, Samuel [22, 22 n. 45] DD. Presented to the rectory of Standish, Lancs., in December 1639 but John Chadwicke was instituted in August 1640. Reported as vicar of Richmond, Surrey, 1653–5. Vicar of Banstead, Surrey, from 1658 to 1660. Curate of Dover St Mary the Virgin, possibly in 1660 but resigned in 1663. Reappointed in 1664, and may have served until 1675. CCEd Person ID: 171251; Venn, II, 377; LPL, VB 1/1/12; Heygate Lambert, p. 127; Willis (1975), p. 32.

Hinton, Giles [lii, 8, 51, 51 n. 115] DD. Ordained presbyter by 4th Classis of London in 1659, Hinton was instituted rector of Westbere in 1663 and vicar of Faversham in 1666, holding both benefices until 1681. Collated to the rectory of Biddenden in 1682, he became rector of Wormshill in 1683, having received dispensation. He died in 1702. CCEd Person ID: 140028; Dunkin, I, 412; LPL, VB 1/5/22, 23; *AC*, 21, pp. 185–6.

Hirst, – [38] Possibly Ed. Hirst, named as an 'abetter' of independents in 1669. Lyon Turner, I, 13.

Hirst, Martin [xliv (2)] BCL. Son of Edward, the vicar of Lynstead and of Teynham who had died in 1618. Expelled from the University of Oxford for his refusal to submit to the parliamentary visitors in 1648, he became a public notary, clerk and registrar in assorted courts and was involved in the visitation of the University of Oxford in 1660. Admitted as registrar of the archdeacon's court during its first session in Canterbury St Margaret in September 1661. He had an eight hearth house in Canterbury. CCEd Person ID: 41712; CCA, DCc-BB/W/13; Wilkins, IV, 583–4; Hegarty, p. 326; Potter, p. 184; Harrington, p. 445.

Holder, John [xxxix n. 16, lxvii, 62, 62 n. 162] LLB. Rector of Chichester All Saints, 1676–81, and vicar of Chidham, Sussex, 1677–81. Vicar of Aldingbourne, Sussex, from 1681 until his death in 1709. CCEd Person ID: 63902; LPL, VH 2/6/1, VB 1/5/326.

Holland, Philip [lv, 56b, n. 125] MA. Rector of Willey, Warwicks., vicar of Boughton under Blean, 1660–2, and of Caversfield, Bucks., 1661–2. Vicar of Orpington, 1663 and ceded in 1664. CCEd Person ID: 97367, LPL, VH 2/44/1, 2.

Holman, Richard [25] Not identified.

Honeywood, Sir Robert [9 (2), 35, 36] Tenant to the parsonage of Bekesbourne and had a twenty hearth house in the parish of Charing. His son, Robert 'was attainted for treason in 1667, having refused to answer a proclamation recalling him from service with the Dutch forces against the English in the Second Anglo-Dutch War'. *ODNB*; Harrington, p. 312.

Honywood, – [30] Not identified.

Honywood, Lady [26] Frances Vane, married to Sir **Robert Honywood** above. *ODNB*.

Honywood, Robert [46] Not identified.

Hood, Dr [52] DD. Paul Hood, incumbent at various times in four counties and prebendary of Southwell minster and Lincoln cathedral. Rector of Lincoln College, Oxford, 1621–68. CCEd Person ID: 13379.

Hopper, Simon [41] Should be Simon Hooker who presented **Isaac Atkinson** to Frinsted in 1662. CCEd Person ID: 139372.

Horsmonden, John [38] Said to be of the Middle Temple. JP in 1665, 1666 and 1670. Lived in a nine hearth house in Goudhurst. Berry, p. 363; Harrington, p. 251; KHLC, Q/J/C/10, 11, 12.

Hosman, William [37] Not identified.

How, Gervase [17] MA. Rector of Sandwich St Peter Sandwich and of St Mary from 1673, holding both until 1679. He, or a namesake, is recorded as being instituted to the vicarage of Battersea in the diocese of Winchester in 1676. CCEd Person ID: 16760; KHLC, DCb/V/V/69–71.

How or **Howe, Simon** [24 n. 54, 32] MA. Rector of Sevington from 1656. Licensed to teach in the 'Common School' at Ashford in 1662. He ceded Sevington in 1668 and was instituted to the rectory of Waldingfield, Suffolk, but this was disputed by Samuel Newson, who was instituted in 1669 and held the rectory until his death in 1695. How was instituted to the rectory of Bircholt (a derelict church) in 1664, following the death of **John Rosse**, retaining it until his death in 1673. CCEd Person ID: 125677, 117534; LPL, COMM III/5, fo. 135, Arches A 5, VB 1/2/158, VB 1/3/203.

Howard, Luke [22] A quaker preacher at Dover St James the Apostle, named in the Episcopal Returns of Conventicles in 1669. He had been converted in 1655. He was imprisoned with others at Dover in 1660, held for twelve weeks and was imprisoned again in 1661. In 1675, some of his goods were distrained for refusing to bear arms and he was again imprisoned in 1682 and 1683, with goods again distrained in 1690, for non-attendance at church. Besse, pp. 288–9, 291–2, 297–9; *AC*, 112, p. 322; Lyon Turner, I, 16.

Howard, Richard [6] BA. Collated to the vicarage of Chislet in 1672 and remained until his death in 1682. CCEd Person ID: 63940; LPL, VB 1/3/149; Venn, II, 416.

Hugeson, William [52] Sir William Hugessen compounded for his estate with the Kent committee for £600. He had a twenty hearth house in Lynsted. Cliffe, p. 471; Harrington, p. 276.

Hughes, Henry [1 n. 5 (2), 7] MA. Curate of Aldington in 1671, minor canon of Canterbury cathedral, 1672–8, vicar of Reculver from 1672 until his resignation in 1679, curate of Canterbury St Dunstan in 1675 and vicar there 1676 to 1677. Willis (1975), pp. 47, 103; CCA, DCc-TB/1–35; LPL, VG 1/5, p. 43; Whiteman, p. 35.

Hulks or **Hulse, Mr** [52] John Hulse, who owned a moiety of the advowson of the vicarage of Newnham. Hasted, VI, 420.

Hulse, Richard [35 (2), 38 (2)] Gentleman of Bethersden, who lived in the eleven hearth manor of Lovelace. Harrington, p. 303; Berry, p. 326; Hasted, VII, 489.

Huntington or **Huntingdon, Benjamin** [40, 55] BA. Instituted as vicar of Bexley in 1666 and served until his death in 1707. He paid for church improvements and left £50 to the poor in his will. He was a brother of Dr Robert Huntington, the orientalist and bishop of Raphoe. CCEd Person ID: 142839, 36198; Foster, II, 773; Hasted, II, 183; *ODNB*.

Hurst, Robert [35] Not identified.

Hurt, Henry [l, 30 (2), 30 n. 68] BA. Licensed as curate to **John Hurt** at Burmarsh in 1666 and retained the curacy under **George Jones** until 1699. Licensed curate to **William Hawkins** at St Mary in the Marsh in 1668, he was instituted as rector in 1679 and served until his probable death in 1699. In the Compton census of 1676, he signed as rector of the derelict churches of Blackmanstone and Eastbridge. CCEd Person ID: 63970; LPL, VG 1/5, p. 74; Whiteman, pp. 27–8; Dunkin, I, 448; Willis (1975), p. 44.

Hurt, John [28 n. 61, 46] MA. Instituted as vicar of Milton Regis in 1661 and, as chaplain to the earl of Peterborough, he was dispensed to hold it in plurality with Burmarsh in 1662. He had probably officiated at Milton or Sittingbourne during the Interregnum, as John Hurt, vicar, performed baptisms at Sittingbourne in 1652, 1655, 1657 and 1659. He was licensed to the cure of Bobbing in 1671 and collated to the ruined church of Eastbridge in the same year. He probably died in 1673. CCEd Person ID: 140031; LPL, F I/C fo. 84; KFHS, Sittingbourne Burials; Dunkin, I, 448; Willis (1975), p. 45.

Huxley, William [61] MA. Vicar of Dullingham, Cambs., from 1674 until his death in 1707. Vicar of Moulton, Sussex, for one month in 1677. CCEd Person ID: 16768; LPL, VG 1/5, p. 61, VH 2/40/3.

Ibbott, Edmund [16] MA. Rector of Deal from 1662 until his death in 1677. CCEd Person ID: 140032; LPL, VG 1/2 fo. 36; Willis (1975), p. 72.

Ireland, Rich [xxxix n. 17, 64, 64 n. 182] MA. Instituted as vicar of Wilmington, Sussex, in 1664, and may have held it until his death in 1680. Vicar of Ringmer, 1667–80. CCEd Person ID: 63993; Venn, II, 450; *SAC*, 26, p. 75.

Jackson, Joseph [19] MA. Intruded into the vicarage of Headcorn in 1645, he was replaced by the incumbent Nicholas Brett in 1660. Curate of Bromley in the diocese of Rochester from 1647 until 1653 and vicar of Aylesford from 1654 until his deprivation in 1663. Instituted to the vicarage of Woodnesborough in 1661, he held it until his death in 1667. CCEd Person ID: 1284; Matthews, *Walker*, p. 212; Venn, II, 456.

Jemmat, Samuel [51] MA. An intruder at Pluckley in 1642, at Eastry in 1652 and at Eastling in the same year. He remained as rector of Eastling, was chaplain to Robert, Lord Brooke in 1671 and signed the Compton census, the year before his death. LPL, F V/1/II fo. 71v; Matthews, *Walker*, pp. 212, 214; Whiteman, p. 31.

Jemmet, John [29] MA. Instituted rector of Hinxhill in 1666 and served until his death in 1689. He may be the John Jemmatt who was licensed to the cure of Brook in 1683. CCEd Person ID: 140034; Willis (1975), p. 50.

Jenkins, Lionel [49] DCL. Advocate of Doctors Commons, 1661, principal of Jesus College, Oxford, 1661–73. Judge of high court of admiralty, 1668–73, and of the prerogative court of Canterbury, 1668–85. Knighted in 1669. Secretary of state, 1680–4, and an MP. LPL, MS 2216, fo. 20; *ODNB*.

Jeriard, Henry *see* **Henry Gerrard**.

Johnson, Peter [6] MA. Ordained in 1654 as a presbyterian and officiated at Maresfield, Sussex, but moved to St Laurence in Thanet in the same year. According to Hasted, he resigned in 1662 'refusing to own the invalidity of his former ordination by taking episcopal orders'. Matthews, *Calamy*, p. 299; Hasted, X, 406; Venn, II, 480.

Johnson, William [lxiii (2), 9, 9 n. 20, 9 n. 21, 24, 24 n. 53] BA. Noted as curate at Stourmouth in April 1663, he was collated to Brabourne in 1664 and instituted to Brook in 1667. He retained Brabourne until his death in 1676 but resigned Brook in 1669 for the rectory of Monks Horton, which he kept until 1676. CCEd Person ID: 140035; KHLC, DCb/J/Z/7/4; Dunkin, I, 473.

Jones, George [27, 28, 30, 30 n. 67, 45, 48] BA. Chaplain to Charles, Lord Gerard, Baron Brandon in 1662, he was collated to Sittingbourne. Vicar of Bapchild from 1663 until 1690. His son, George, was licensed to the cure in 1679. Instituted to the derelict rectory of Blackmanstone in 1667 he was recorded in visitations until 1680. He was dispensed to hold the rectory of Burmarsh along with Sittingbourne in 1673 and held them both until his death in 1705. CCEd Person ID: 140036; LPL, F V/1/II fo. 85v, VG 1/2 fo. 37, 1/5 p. 16, VB 1/3/190, 1/5/180, 200.

Jones, Philip [xxxix n. 13, lxv n. 172, 57] BA. Curate of Southwark St Saviour, Surrey, in 1672 and curate of Downe, 1672–80, but in 1681 it is recorded that he was 'incapacitated to reside, Mr. Wardroper to officiate'. Vicar of Addington, Surrey, from 1680 and probably died before 1695. CCEd Person ID: 16969; LPL, VG 1/3 fo. 76v, VB 1/4/533, VH 5/1.

Jones, Thomas [4] MA. Collated to the vicarage of Sturry in 1661 and died in 1680. This 'good old poore man' may have been the teacher in the parish of Canterbury

All Saints noted at the 1630 visitation. CCEd Person ID: 180554; LPL, VB 1/4/99; KHLC, DCb/V/V/43.

Jordan, Lieutenant [37] Not identified.

Jorden or **Jordan, William** [xliv n. 54, 4, 31] MA. Instituted to Canterbury St Paul in 1627 and became a minor canon of Canterbury cathedral in 1634, but was forced out of both positions by 1644. Reinstated in 1660 he was also instituted to the sinecure of the derelict church of Orgarswick and held all three appointments until his death in 1680. CCEd Person ID: 42415; Matthews, *Walker*, p. 220; CCA, DCc-TB/1–35.

Juxon, Elias [xl n. 24, 27] MA. A distant relative of **William Juxon**, he was a Fellow of King's College, Cambridge, 1653–60. Rector of Aldington from 1661 and a Six Preacher of Canterbury cathedral from 1663 until his death in 1665. CCEd Person ID: 140037; LPL, VB 1/1/140; Venn, II, 492.

Juxon, William [i, xli (3), li n. 98, liv] Archbishop of Canterbury, 1660–3. CCEd Person ID: 8468; *ODNB*.

Kay, Arthur [1, 24 n. 56] MA from St Andrews University, Scotland. Curate to **David Nairne** at Brook in 1664. Collated to the vicarage of Elmsted in 1665 but resigned in 1673 in favour of **Charles Kay**. Appointed a Six Preacher of Canterbury cathedral in 1670, he was collated to Canterbury St Andrew in 1673 and probably held it with St Mary Bredman, the parishes being united in 1682. He served the cathedral and the latter two parishes until his death in 1701 aged eighty. He is omitted from the Catalogue entry for Elmstead. CCEd Person ID: 140038; Willis (1975), p. 42; Ingram Hill, p. 67.

Kay, Charles [24, 24 n. 56] MA from Edinburgh University, Scotland. Perhaps the son of **Arthur Kay**, to whom he was curate at Elmsted, 1672–5. Curate to John Crocker at Preston by Faversham in 1672. Vicar of Elmsted from 1673 until his cession in 1676. CCEd Person ID: 14157; Dunkin, I, 483.

Kay, James [25, 38 n. 87, 53 n. 118] MA. Possibly another son of **Arthur Kay**, as he was also licensed as a curate at Brook in 1664. Vicar of Postling from 1662 until his cession in 1668, when he became rector of Newenden. In 1671, he was dispensed to hold the vicarage of Selling. He retained Newenden and Selling until his death in 1677. CCEd Person ID: 140039; Dunkin, I, 483; KHLC, DCb/V/V/56, 58; CCA, DCc-SVSB/2/167/2; Willis (1975), p. 43.

Kelley, Geo. [56b] MA. Rector of Ifield from 1667 until his death in 1692. As chaplain to the earl of Winchelsea, he was dispensed to hold the rectory of Nursted, Rochester diocese, in 1673 and held it until 1692. CCEd Person ID: 1318; LPL, F I/D fo. 62v, VH 2/25/3–4.

Kemp, – [63, 63 n. 172, 64, 64 n. 185] William Kempe, owner of the rectory and advowson of the vicarage of South Malling. *SAC*, 26, p. 82; Gregory, p. 227.

Kempe, Reynold [10] Not identified.

Kempe, Sir Thomas [10, 26] Lord of the manor of Chilham, who died in Elizabethan times. His descendant,

Thomas Digges Esq. presented the vicarage of Chilham to **Robert Cumberland** in 1662. Hasted, VII, 275, 291.

Kennet, Basil [25, 28] Teacher in Bekesbourne in 1661 and curate to **John Reading** at Cheriton in 1664. He was collated to the vicarage of Postling in 1668 and dispensed to hold it with the rectory of Dymchurch (where he had been curate to **Richard Burton** since 1673) in 1676. He held both livings until his probable death in 1686. He was the father of the future bishop of Peterborough, White Kennett. CCEd Person ID: 140040, 36223; Dunkin, I, 487; Willis (1975), pp. 1, 42.

Kenrick, or **Kenwrick, William** [lviii (2)] The son of Colonel William Kenwricke of Boughton under Blean. Admitted at Trinity College, Cambridge, in 1657 and at Gray's Inn in 1658, but no degree found. A member of the Kent committee from 1643 to 1652, deputy lieutenant of the county and a member of the Convention Parliament of 1653, representing Kent. Imprisoned in the Tower of London for some time in late 1662 for suspicious activity. He had a twelve hearth house in Boughton under Blean. Everitt (1960), pp. 130, 152; Cobbett, III, 1407; Greaves, p. 124; Harrington, p. 295.

King, William [4, 37] MA. Chaplain to John, earl of Thanet, he became rector of Hothfield, Kent, in 1661 and was given dispensation to hold Hackington. He became a Six Preacher of Canterbury cathedral in 1671 and held all of his appointments until his death in 1682. CCEd Person ID: 140041; CCA, DCc-MAND/SP/1671/1, DCc-TB/1–35.

King, William [27] MA. Collated to the rectory of the derelict church of Blackmanstone in 1637, he was instituted to the vicarage of Warlingham, Surrey, in 1660 and probably remained in possession of both until his death in 1667. CCEd Person ID: 45940.

Knatchbull, Norton [23, 25, 26, 30, 35] BA. Sir Norton, first baronet. MP for Kent, 1640; for New Romney, 1640–8, 1660–79. Owned the mansion of Mersham Hatch, with its twenty-five hearths. Died in 1685. Venn, III, 27; *HoP*; Harrington, p. 305.

Knatchbull, Norton [27] MA. One of the many of that name. He was curate to Thomas Allen, at Kingsnorth, 1633–6, and may have been the vicar of Waltham noted in the visitation of 1662. Curate of Bilsington from 1663 until at least 1670. CCEd Person ID: 39946, KHLC, DCb/V/V/56; Venn, III, 28.

Knell, Paul [31 (2)] DD. Curate of Whitstable from 1638 until at least 1642. Royalist military chaplain during the first civil war and joined the king at Oxford. Minister at Canterbury St Dunstan in 1647, but preached and published sermons in London, where he became minister of St Benet and St Peter Paul's Wharf in the 1650s. Instituted as vicar of Newchurch in 1660 and became the sinecure rector in 1662, retaining both until his death in 1664. He was buried at St Dunstan in 1664, but was not the vicar. CCEd Person ID: 39942; Cowper (1887), p. 128; *ODNB* (which has errors).

Knight, John [59a (3)] Sir John Knight, of Bristol, who was a relentless persecutor of radical sectarians under the old recusancy laws and the Conventicles Act of 1664. Died in 1683. LPL, VH 2/20/2; *ODNB*.

Knollis, Lady [29] Cecilia, widow of Robert Edolph Esq., married Sir Frances Knolles, of Reading. Hasted, VII, 561–6.

Ladbroke, Edward [9, 29] MA. In 1666, he was instituted to the vicarage of Bekesbourne and dispensed to hold the rectory of Ivychurch. Appointed as a Six Preacher of Canterbury cathedral in 1671, he held the three offices until his death in 1676. CCEd Person ID: 140043; LPL, VB 1/2/34, 1/2/32, VG 1/5, p. 14; Ingram Hill, p. 66.

Laney or **Lany, Benjamin** [73r] Bishop of Peterborough, 1660–3, bishop of Lincoln, 1663–7, and bishop of Ely, 1667–75. *ODNB*.

Langham, Richard [12] MA. Minor canon of Canterbury cathedral and vicar of Littlebourne, 1660–74. He graduated BA in 1641 but has not been traced during the Interregnum although, in a petition to the dean and chapter after 1660, he says that he is 'in debt, with … a troublesome estate to run in Northamptonshire'. He died in 1674. CCEd Person ID: 8569; CCA, DCc-PET/45, DCc-TB/1–35; LPL, VB 1/3/274; Venn, III, 43.

Latham, – [lxvi, lxx, 56b] George Latham MA. Rector of Wavendon, Bucks., in 1647 and vicar of Ealing, 1647–8. Admitted as rector of Hunton in Shoreham deanery in 1656 and there until his ejection in August 1662. His successor was instituted in the following month. Matthews, *Calamy*, p. 315.

Latimer, John [62 n. 158] MA. Instituted as rector of Halton in 1629, sequestrated in 1645, restored in 1660 and served until his death in 1678. CCEd Person ID: 52270; Matthews, *Walker*, p. 75.

Lawder, William [33] MA. Appointed rector of Snargate in 1656, noted as rector in 1662 and died in 1667. At the Maidstone Assizes in 1665 he was indicted as a common drunkard and disturber of the peace, and for refusing to administer the sacraments according to the Book of Common Prayer. LPL, COMM III/5, fo. 521, VG 1/2 fo. 6v, VB 1/2/88; Cockburn (1995), p. 156.

Lawrence, Paul [63 n. 167] MA. Instituted to the rectory of Tangmere in 1660 and to the vicarage of Poling, Sussex, in 1661. Probably died in 1674. CCEd Person ID: 142849; LPL, VG 1/3 fo. 11v; Venn, III, 53.

Layfeild or **Layfield, Edward** [lxv, 57, 59b] DD. Son of Archbishop Laud's half-sister. Rector of Ibstock, Leics., 1633–5; prebendary of St Paul's Cathedral, 1633; archdeacon of Essex, 1634; vicar of All Hallows Barking, London, 1635; rector of East Horsley, Surrey, 1637; sinecure rector of Wrotham, 1638; rector of Chiddingfold, Surrey, 1640. Sequestrated from Barking in 1643 and probably lost all other preferments around the same time. He was restored in 1660 to his prebend, archdeaconry, sinecure rectory of Wrotham, and vicarage of Barking, and he held them all until his death in 1680, with the exception of Wrotham, which he resigned in 1677 in favour of his son, Charles. Instituted to the rectory of Barnes, Surrey, in 1663, he retained it until his death. CCEd Person ID: 8599; Matthews, *Walker*, p. 53; LPL, VG 1/2 fo. 3, VB 1/3/307.

Layfield, Charles [57] DD. Succeeded his father, **Edward Layfield**, as rector of Wrotham in 1677, and held it until his death in 1715. Rector of Croston, Lancs., 1683–9, of Chilbolton, Hants., 1689–1715, and of Buriton, Hants., 1688–99. CCEd Person ID: 94089; LPL, VB 1/3/307, 1/6/183; Foster, III, 890.

Lee, John [xlvi (3), xlviii n. 81] DD. Instituted to the rectory of Milton-next-Gravesend in Rochester diocese in 1642, he was sequestrated before 1650 and formally resigned the living in 1663. Inducted to the rectory of Southfleet, also in Rochester, in 1652, he was collated to it in 1660 and held the living until his death in 1679. Appointed archdeacon of Rochester and as a canon of Rochester cathedral in 1660, he was collated to the rectory of Bishopsbourne with the chapel of Barham in 1662 and held all of these offices until his death. In 1666, he changed his surname to Warner in accordance with the provisions of the will of his uncle, **John Warner**, late bishop of Rochester. CCEd Person ID: 1366; Horn, III, 52, 58, 70.

Lee, Moses [35] MA. Instituted rector of Biddenden in 1660 and remained until his death in 1682. CCEd Person ID: 142146; Foster, III, 894; LPL, VB 1/4/171.

Lee, Thomas [lxvi n. 176, 56b] Vicar of Leigh, Rochester diocese, from 1653, but ceded it in 1661. Vicar of Penshurst from 1660 until his death in 1709. CCEd Person ID: 1368; LPL, VH 2/47/1; Fielding, p. 168.

Leicester, earl of [56b] Robert Sidney, second earl of Leicester. Owner of Penshurst Palace (twenty-one hearths) and Ford Palace (six hearths) in Hoath parish. *ODNB*; Harrington, p. 55.

Leversidge, John [64] Rector of Stanmer by 1656 and probably remained until 1670. Rector of Hamsey, Sussex, from 1670 until his death in 1674. CCEd Person ID: 78120; LPL, VB 1/2/215, VB 1/3/5; *Sussex RS*, 68, p. viii.

Lewknor, Mr [23] Robert Lewknor owned the manor of Acrise, with its twelve hearths, until he sold it in 1666. Hasted, VIII, 113; Harrington, p. 340.

Liddell, Andrew [35] Andrew Lidall had an eleven hearth house in Bethersden. Harrington, p. 302.

Lightfoot, Richard [29, 29 n. 63] MA. Instituted to the rectory of Kenardington in 1632, he may have served throughout the Interregnum until his cession in 1664. He became rector of Chadwell, Essex, in 1663 and remained until his death in 1670. CCEd Person ID: 46162.

Lillie, John [64] MA. Collated to the vicarage of Ringmer in 1681 and remained until his cession in 1690. In the same year, he was instituted to the rectory of Lamarsh, Essex, and died in 1717. CCEd Person ID: 17399; LPL, VB 1/4/147; Venn, III, 85.

Linch or **Lynch, John** [41] Prebendary of Salisbury cathedral from 1619 and vicar of Aldbourne, Wilts., from 1620. He resigned both offices in 1630 and was instituted to the rectory of Harrietsham. Sequestrated in 1644, he was restored in 1660 and remained until his death in 1680. CCEd Person ID: 27914; Matthews, *Walker*, p. 221.

Lloyd, Humphrey [73r] DD. Bishop of Bangor, 1674–89. *ODNB*.

Lloyd, Nicholas [59b] MA. Rector of Oxford St Martin, 1665–70. Chaplain to Walter Blandford, bishop of Oxford. Rector of Newington, Surrey, from 1673, until his death in 1680. CCEd Person ID: 142856; *ODNB*.

Lodwick or **Lodowick, John** [17 n. 33] Instituted to the vicarage of Sandwich St Mary in 1661 and probably stayed until 1672. He was also the rector of Sandwich St Peter in 1666 when he approved the appointment of the parish clerk, but he is not noted in the Catalogue, as by 1668 he had been sequestrated. Archdeacon Sancroft notes that Lodwick 'pretends a presentation, but hath no Institution nor Induction'. In 1672, he commended Daniel Joyce as a teacher in Dover St James the Apostle and by 1675 he was curate of Dover St Mary the Virgin, resigning in 1698. The Catalogue does not note his presence in Dover. CCEd Person ID: 99291; Bodl., MS Sancroft 99, p. 162.

Lord, John [xxxix, 42] MA. Instituted as vicar of Stone in Oxney in 1661, and as chaplain to John, earl of Bath, was dispensed to also hold the vicarage of Salehurst, Sussex. He ceded Stone in 1663 and was collated to the vicarage of Lenham in 1664 holding it until his cession in 1670 and subsequent appointment (succeeding his father) as rector of Cooling, which he ceded in 1673. CCEd Person ID: 1390; LPL, VB 1/2/229, 3/22.

Lorkin or **Larkin, Thomas** [48] MA. Instituted as vicar of Stockbury in 1638 and may have remained, undisturbed, until his death in 1670. Canon of Rochester cathedral, 1667–70. CCEd Person ID: 46080; LPL, VB 1/3/24; Horn, III, 60.

Lorrington, William [9] Not identified.

Louth, Simon [2, 5, 5 n. 17] MA. Instituted to the rectory of Canterbury St Mildred with St Mary de Castro in 1666 and collated to the vicarage of Canterbury Holy Cross Westgate in the same year, having received dispensation for the pluralism. He was chaplain to Frances Grey, dowager baroness of Ruthin. Instituted rector of Harbledown, Kent, in 1670 and probably resigned from St Mildred's around the same time. In 1676, he signed the Compton census as rector of Harbledown and vicar of Holy Cross Westgate and became chaplain to William, earl of Derby in 1679. In the same year, he resigned Holy Cross Westgate and took up the vicarage of Blean. He was instituted to the deanery of Rochester in 1688, but not installed. In 1689, his refusal to take the oaths of allegiance caused his suspension from his Kentish parishes and he was deprived in 1690. Reported as having held the vicarage of Canterbury St Dunstan, but there is no direct evidence of this. CCEd Person ID: 7204; Venn, III, 111; Hasted, IX, 41; LPL, VG 1/4 fo. 5v, 1/3 fo. 70, F I/C fo. 203, F V/1/II fo. 17, V/1/III fo. 21v, VG 1/5, p. 35; Dunkin, II, 43; Whiteman, pp. 19, 20; *ODNB*.

Lovel or **Lovell, Isaac** [19] BA. Rector of Sandwich St Peter in 1671, curate of Guston from 1672 until 1711 and vicar of Woodnesborough from 1673 until his death in 1729. CCEd Person ID: 142149; Dunkin, II, 42; Whiteman, p. 33; Hasted, IX, 409.

Lovelace, William [xliv n. 54, 3 (2)] MA. Licensed to the cure of Ash, Kent, in 1638 and may have remained there until 1655, when Ephraim Crocker was appointed. Matthews has not recorded a sequestration. May have been vicar of Canterbury St Paul in 1659, but was instituted to St Mary Magdalen in 1660 and was vicar of St Mary Bredin (both Canterbury) from at least 1662. He became rector of Canterbury St Margaret in 1674 and served all three churches until his death in 1683. CCEd Person ID: 46219; Venn, III, 107; CCA, U108/2/25, KHLC, DCb/V/V/ 56, 69; Hasted, X1, 233.

Lovell, Robert [17 n. 32] MA. Instituted to Sandwich St Peter in 1639 and there in 1642, but not recorded thereafter. CCEd Person ID: 46220.

Lunne [49 n. 113] Not identified.

Lunne, William [xlvi (2), 24] MA. Curate to **John Lee** at Bishopsbourne in 1663, he was instituted to the rectory of Denton in the same year. He was appointed to the curacy of Swingfield in 1675 and held it until 1695 when he became curate of Nonington with Womenswold. He retained Denton and Nonington until his death in 1704. CCEd Person ID: 140256; KHLC, DCb/J/Z/3/44; Whiteman, p. 25; LPL, VG 1/7 fo. 3, VB 1/5/172, 174.

Lynde, Humphrey [40, 43, 43 n. 103] MA. Curate at Maidstone from 1677 and vicar of Boxley from 1679, holding both until his death in 1690. CCEd Person ID: 64354.

Maccorne, David [38] MA. Curate to **James Kay** at Newenden in 1673 and instituted as rector in 1677. He died in 1687. CCEd Person ID: 140257; LPL, VG 1/5, p. 66; KHLC, DCb/V/V/67.

Mackallir or **Mackallar, John** [12, 12 n. 27, 53] MA. Curate to **James Cowes** at Luddenham, 1662–3, he was curate of Oare from 1662 until his cession in 1668. Instituted to the vicarage of Patrixbourne with Bridge in 1667, he signed the Compton census in 1676 as vicar there and as the curate of Stodmarsh. He was finally recorded at Stodmarsh in 1677 but retained Patrixbourne until his death in 1698. CCEd Person ID: 140258; LPL, VG 1/2 fo. 4, 1/3 fo. 33, VB 1/2/132; Whiteman, p. 24; KHLC, DCb/V/V/71; KFHS, Patrixbourne Burials; Dunkin, II, 51.

Malbon, John [li, 30 n. 65] The vicarage of Lympne is recorded in the Catalogue as being vacant, but John Malbon is noted in the visitation of 1662 as the vicar, and he was buried at Sibertswold in 1666 as 'Curate of this Parish & Vicar of Lym'. KHLC, DCb/V/V/56; KFHS, Sheperdswell Burials.

Man or **Mann, William** [27] A descendant of Sir Christopher Mann, who gained the advowson of Bonnington by an exchange with Sir James Hales. Hasted, VIII, 333.

Marsh, John [11] Had a seven hearth house in Kingston. Harrington, p. 412.

Marsh, Richard [xxxix n. 13, vii (2), xviii, lxv n. 170, 31, 56a] MA. Curate of Leeds with Broomfield, 1635–41, and a Six Preacher of Canterbury cathedral, 1636–40. Rector of Ruckinge from 1641 until his sequestration in 1645. Restored in 1660, he held the rectory until his death in 1687. Prebendary of Totenhall, St Paul's, London, 1660–87. Possibly curate of Bromley, Kent, 1663–6. Vicar of East Peckham, Kent, 1664–87. CCEd Person ID: 46269; Ingram Hill, p. 47; Matthews, *Walker*, p. 222; Fielding, p. 40; Horn, I, 58.

Marshall, Mr [46] Not identified.

Martin, Mr [42] Possibly Francis Martin 'of Langley, gent.' a member of the grand jury at the Maidstone Assizes in 1685. Hasted, IV, 370; Cockburn (1997), p. 225.

Master, James [xli] DCL. Son of Edward Master of Ospringe. Admitted to Doctors' Commons in 1640; advocate in 1648 and treasurer 1655–61. Conducted the archidiaconal visitation of Canterbury diocese in 1662. Will proved in February 1664. KHLC, DCb/V/V/56; Squibb, p. 177; Venn, III, 159.

Master, Richard [15] A descendant of John Master, who had been granted the manor and patronage of East Langdon, by Henry VIII. Hasted, IX, 551.

Master, Robert [l, 12] Minister of Molash, the chapel to Chilham, in 1656. Noted as the curate in 1662 and served until his death in 1668. CCA, U108/2/25; KHLC, DCb/V/V/56; KFHS, Molash Burials.

Master or **Masters, William** [59a, 61] BD. Rector of Woodford, Essex, from 1661 until his death in 1684. Rector of Southchurch, Essex, 1666–7. Prebendary of St Paul's cathedral, 1663–84. Dispensed to hold the rectory of St Vedast Foster Lane London in 1671, holding it until his death. CCEd Person ID: 144627; LPL, VB 1/3/74, VG 1/5, p. 9; Foster, III, 987.

Masters, Mr [20] Richard Masters served as a JP in 1665 and 1666. KHLC, Q/J/C/10, 11.

Masters, Mr [34] Probably Edward Masters, who had a nine hearth house in the parish of Willesborough. Hasted, VII, 575; Harrington, p. 307.

Mauduit, John [lxvi] MA. Ordained deacon in 1645. Curate of Hammersmith, Middx., in 1647 and rector of St Nicholas, Abingdon in 1648. Rector of Penshurst in 1650 but ejected in 1660. CCEd Person ID: 8811; Matthews, *Calamy*, p. 345; Foster, III, 990.

May, George junior [30, 58] DD. Held the sequestration of Great Chart 1655–8 and probably moved to Mersham in 1658, although not collated until 1661. He was a Six Preacher of Canterbury cathedral from 1660 until his death in 1703. He resigned from Mersham in 1664 and became rector of St Dionis Backchurch, London, in the following year with a dispensation to hold the rectory of Warnford, Hants. He resigned St Dionis in 1680 and was dispensed to hold the rectory of Bishopstoke, Hants. He was appointed to the prebend of Middleton in Chichester cathedral in 1678 and then to the prebend of Heathfield in 1681. At his death in 1703, he held his two Hampshire rectories and the Six Preachership along with his two prebends. CCEd Person ID: 94403; Dunkin, II, 73; Matthews, *Walker*, pp. 210, 222; Ingram Hill, p. 62.

May, George senior [31 (2), 31 n. 70, 34] MA. Probably vicar of Willesborough from 1613 until his death in 1671. Schoolmaster at Marden in 1622 and a Six Preacher of Canterbury cathedral, 1660–71. Instituted as vicar of Newchurch in 1664, he resigned in 1665, becoming the sinecure rector. CCEd Person ID: 42263; LPL, VG 1/4 fo. 3, VB 1/1/123; Willis (1975), p. 71; Ingram Hill, p. 62; Matthews, *Walker*, p. 222.

Maynard, John [lxviii, 64] MA. Instituted to the vicarage of Mayfield in 1624, he was also appointed as vicar of Camberwell, Surrey, in 1646 having installed a curate at Mayfield. He was selected as a representative of Sussex to the Westminster assembly of divines in 1643. Subscribed as a preacher and schoolteacher in 1662 but was ejected from Mayfield in that year. CCEd Person ID: 46369; *ODNB*; Matthews, *Calamy*, p. 346.

Megges, James [lxvii, 59b] DD. Instituted as rector of St Margaret Pattens, London, in 1637, sequestrated by 1645 but restored in 1660 and resigned in 1661. Collated to the rectory of Newington, Surrey, in 1641, sequestrated in 1643, but was restored by 1661 and retained it until 1673. As chaplain to Bishop Warner of Rochester, he was dispensed in 1661 to hold the rectory of Theydon Garnon, Essex, which he kept until his death in 1673. CCEd Person ID: 70314; LPL, VG 1/2 fo. 3v; Matthews, *Walker*, p. 54; Venn, III, 173.

Mell, Thomas [lxviii, 64] MA. Rector of Isfield, 1663–6. As chaplain to the earl of Lincoln, was dispensed to hold the vicarage of Leatherhead, Surrey, in 1663 and held it until his death in 1671. CCEd Person ID: 72326.

Mellis, John [63 n. 166] MA. Admitted to Slindon in 1654 and conformed at the Restoration. Died in 1683.

CCEd Person ID: 64533; *SAC*, 33, p. 222.

Mereton or **Meriton, John** [58] MA. Rector of St Nicholas Cole Abbey, London, 1661–2. Rector of Little Fakenham, Suffolk, 1662–3, and rector of St Michael Cornhill, London, 1664–1704. Instituted as rector of St Mary Bothaw, London, in 1666 but the church was destroyed by the Great Fire and the parish united with that of St Swithin London Stone, whose church was also destroyed in 1666 but rebuilt in the 1670s. CCEd Person ID: 72349; LPL, VH 2/32/5, VG 1/2 fo. 24v; *ODNB*.

Mews, Peter [73r] DCL. Bishop of Bath and Wells, 1673–84, and bishop of Winchester, 1684–1706. *ODNB*.

Meynell, Alderman [49, 49 n. 113] Francis Meynell was a member of the Goldsmith Company, an alderman, 1660–6, and sheriff of London in 1661. He was one of a group of bankers who advanced large sums to Charles II. Pepys called him 'the great money man' and estimated his income as £10,000 per annum. Orridge, pp. 237, 343; Pepys, III, 200, IV, 17.

Michenbourn, – [64] Edward Michelborne Esq. of Stanmer was the patron of Stanmer in 1670. LPL, VB 1/2/215; *Sussex RS*, 68, p. viii.

Middleton, Robert [lxviii, 63] MA. Rector of Buxted from 1661 until his death in 1674. CCEd Person ID: 81261; LPL, VG 1/2 fo. 21v; Matthews, *Calamy*, p. 466; *SAC*, 26, p. 20, 91, pp. 41–2.

Millington, Thomas [xxxix n. 14, 60] BA. Vicar of Cheswardine, Shrops., 1655–62. Curate of Newport, Shrops., 1662–5, also schoolmaster in the parish. Vicar of Market Drayton and rector of Adderley, Shrops., from 1667 until his probable death in 1679. Chaplain to John, Viscount Mordaunt of Aviland, in 1671. Probably absentee perpetual curate of Wimbledon, 1665–7, as Humphrey Williams is named in the parish register as the curate from 1665 until 1668. CCEd Person ID: 54649; LPL, VG 1/4 fo. 4v, F V/1/II fo. 66, F I/D fo. 72v; *SRS*, 8, pp. 21–3.

Mills, Richard [lix] Not identified. Named as an anabaptist preacher who lived in Shatterling, a hamlet situated between Ash and Wingham. BL, SP 29/93.

Milway, Thomas [45] MA. Vicar of Borden, 1673–94, and 'during the absence of Titus Oates', curate at Bobbing from 1679 (see **Titus Oates** below). Dispensed in 1694 to hold the vicarage of Upchurch and the rectory of Newington, he died in the same year. CCEd Person ID: 72581; Dunkin, II, 88; Willis (1975), p. 48.

Mockett, John [lix] Named as an anabaptist preacher in Ash, where he had a two hearth house. Nothing further known. BL, SP 29/93; Harrington, p. 391.

Monings, Captain [9] Hasted refers to a Captain Monins as 'the treasurer and manager' of the revenues of the dean and chapter of Canterbury cathedral from 1648 to 1660, appointed by parliament. Possibly Sir Thomas Monins, third baronet, who inherited in 1663. Captain Thomas Monnings or Monins was one of the commissioners appointed to secure the 'Peace of this Commonwealth' in 1655 and was named as an 'abetter' of independents in 1669. Cockayne, I, 77; Lyon Turner, I, 13; Bloomfield, pp. 11, 22; Hasted, XI, viii.

Monings or **Monins, Edward** [16, 20, 26] Second baronet, who inherited the nineteen hearth family seat in Waldershare and died in 1663. Cockayne, I, 77; Hasted, X, 70; Harrington, p. 414.

Monings or **Monins, Thomas** [20] A descendant of John Monins, who owned the advowson of Charlton in the sixteenth century. A relative of **William** and **Edward**. Hasted, IX, 473.

Monings or **Monins, William** [16] First baronet of Waldershare. He died in 1643 and **Edward** became the patron of Eyethorne. Cockayne, I, 77; Hasted, X, 53.

Montague of Cowdrey, Lord [42] The Catalogue has a query about the patron of Lenham being Lord Montague of Cowdray. According to Hasted, Henry Browne, Fifth Viscount Montague, sold the manor and the advowson with the agreement of his son Anthony born in 1686. Hasted, V, 422.

Monyman, Rich. [35, 35 n. 83] MA. Nicholas Monyman was schoolmaster at Cranbrook, 1658–62, and was instituted vicar of Benenden in September 1662, remaining until his death in 1700. CCEd Person ID: 72593; Haslewood (1889), p. 149; Venn, III, 203.

Moore, John [40, 42] MA. Curate of Leeds with the chapel of Broomfield from 1662 until 1664, when he disappears from the records. LPL, VG 1/2 fo. 37, 1/4 fo. 3v.

Moore, Thomas [35] Not identified.

Moore, Thomas Sir [16 n. 31] Not identified.

More or **Moore, George** [45] Created in 1665 first baronet of Maids Moreton, Bucks., married Frances Sandford and became patron of Bobbing. *HoP*.

Morgan, Robert [73r] Bishop of Bangor, 1666–73. *ODNB*.

Morley, Coll [64] Herbert Morley patron of Glynde. MP for Lewes in 1640, Sussex in the 1650s and Rye in 1660–7. He died in 1667. Parliamentary colonel of horse, 1643–5 and 1659–60. *HoP*; *SAC*, 20, p. 61.

Morley, William [63] Knighted in 1661, he was MP for Sussex in 1667–78 and MP for Midhurst in six parliaments to 1698. He died in 1701. His father was Sir William, the MP for Chichester in the Long Parliament until disabled as a royalist and fined £1,000. Foster, III, 1034; *HoP*.

Morreland, Thomas [lix] Possibly Thomas Moreland, who had a four hearth house in Sevenoaks. He was probably a quaker who travelled to Cranbrook and disturbed a church service in April 1663. Harrington, p. 44.

Morris, Abdias [32, 32 n. 77] BA. Curate to **Peter Hardres** at Upper Hardres, 1671–3, then curate to **John Castilion** at Mersham, 1674–6. In 1676, he was instituted to the vicarage of Sellindge and he was licensed to the cure of Lympne in 1679 holding both offices until his probable death in 1680. CCEd Person ID: 17970; LPL, VB 1/3/288; Willis (1975), pp. 46, 48.

Morris, Richard [li, 38, 40 n. 95] Instituted to the vicarage of Rolvenden in January 1663 but may not have been inducted. Presented to Chart next Sutton in June 1663 but Chart is noted as vacant in October 1663. At Rolvenden, John Viner, 'vicar of this parish', was buried on 18 July 1668. CCEd Person ID: 64597; KFHS, Rolvenden Burials.

Morton, Timothy [59a, 59a n. 141] MA. Vicar of Hayes, Middx., from 1662 until his resignation in 1670. Rector of Salisbury St Martin, Wilts., from 1670 until his cession in 1687. Possibly the curate of Stratford sub Castle, Wilts., in 1670. Prebendary of Salisbury cathedral from 1679 until his resignation in 1687. Probably rector of Peakirk, Northants., from 1687 but tenure unknown. CCEd Person ID: 53200; LPL, VB 1/3/41; Foster, III, 1039.

Mountague, Henry [64, 64 nn. 179, 184] BA. Instituted as vicar of Glynde in 1662 but may not have been inducted. Possibly curate of South Malling, 1662–8. Instituted as vicar of Laughton, Sussex, in 1663 and ceded in 1685. Rector of Westmeston, Sussex, from 1686 until his death in 1708. CCEd Person ID: 64609, 72849; Foster, III, 1021.

Moyle, Lady [10] Mary Moyle, the widow of Sir Robert Moyle, presented **Henry Nicholls** to the vicarage of Boughton Aluph. One of the numerous Moyles in Kent. Married to **Thomas Godfrey**. LPL, VB 1/1/35; Armytage, p. 67.

Mund or **Mun, Stephen** [34] MA. Intruded rector of Woodchurch in 1654 serving until his death in 1684. CCEd Person ID: 72858; LPL, COMM III/3, 2, fo. 429, VB 1/4/418.

Munn, Richard [10, 11] MA. Vicar of Godmersham with Challock from 1675 until his death in 1682. CCEd Person ID: 54792; LPL, VG 1/5, p. 54, VB 1/4/205; Venn, III, 226.

Myles, Henry [59a] MA. Instituted rector of St Michael Crooked Lane, London, in 1671 but died in 1673. CCEd Person ID: 17998; Venn, III, 188.

Nairne, David [l n. 93, lxii, lxiii, 9, 23] MA. Probably served as the perpetual curate of Swingfield from 1627 until 1667. He became rector of Brook after 1662 and resigned in 1666. CCEd Person ID: 37908; LPL, VB 1/2/48.

Napleton, John [48] MA. Vicar of Tonge from 1677 until his death in 1712. Dispensed to hold the vicarage of Bobbing in 1703, retaining it until 1712. CCEd Person ID: 72881; LPL, VB 1/5/104, 1/6/93, 102.

Naylor, John [35] BA. Born in 1604, of Sturry, Kent, was admitted to Gray's Inn in 1628, called to the Bar in 1636 and to the Bench in 1659. He attended the Maidstone Assizes as a JP in seven of the Interregnum years and in March 1661. He died in 1669 leaving property in Sturry and Ashford and had 'moneyes outstanding in Ireland'. After bequests to sisters and nieces, the residue of his estate was left to his executrix, Katherine, Viscountess Ranelagh, a daughter of the first earl of Cork. Sister of Robert Boyle, the scientist, and a noted intellectual, she was a patron to the Hartlib circle and although she was closely associated with independents and presbyterians, during the Interregnum, she flourished following the Restoration. Venn, III, 234; Foster (1889), p. 186; Cockburn (1989) *passim*, (1995), p. 5; *ODNB*; TNA, PROB 11/360/410.

Neale, William [18] Not identified.

Neame, Silvester [10] Paid Hearth Tax in 1664 on a three hearth house in Chillenden. Harrington, p. 406.

Negus, Thomas [lxvii, 63] MA. Instituted to the rectory of Albourne, Sussex, in 1635 and may have served until his death in 1676. In 1662, as chaplain to Mildmay, earl of Westmorland, he was dispensed to also hold the vicarage of West Tarring, where he was buried. CCEd Person ID: 64658; LPL, F V/1/I fo. 54, F I/C fo. 97, VB 1/3/294; Venn, III, 239.

Newman, – (Captain) [6] Not identified.

Newman, Stephen [45, 45 n. 105] MA. Rector of Bicknor in 1653, instituted in 1662 and died in 1669. CCEd Person ID: 72908; Venn, III, 250; Green (1973), p. 387.

Nichols, Charles [lix (4)] BA. Grandson of Josias Nicholls who married the widow of the puritan, Dudley Fenner, and was deprived from the rectory of Eastwell in 1603. Never ordained in the Church of England but became pastor of the congregational church formed at Adisham in 1649. Remained in east Kent after the Restoration. Imprisoned twice but escaped, excommunicated and named as an itinerant preacher in Sandwich, Ash and Dover. Licensed to preach in 1672 and died in 1679. Mentioned in **Clement Barling**'s will. KHLC, DCb/V/V/43; *JEH*, 28 (1977), 133–50; Fincham and Lake, pp. 113–27; Matthews, *Calamy* p. 365; Lyon Turner, pp. 14–16; *ODNB*.

Nicolls, Daniel [lxvii, 60 (2)] DD. Already in office as rector of Hadleigh, when he subscribed in September 1662. Collated to the rectory of Chislet in 1663, but not instituted. As chaplain to Archbishop Juxon, he was dispensed to hold Hadleigh with the rectory of Stisted in 1663. He died in 1665. CCEd Person ID: 143689; LPL, F I/C fo. 114, VB 1/1/177; Peile, I, 276; Venn, III, 254.

Nicolls or **Nicholls, Henry** [10] Served as a minor canon of Canterbury cathedral from 1661 to 1663, but not continuously. He was instituted vicar of Boughton Aluph in 1662 and in spite of the condemnation of his abilities in the Catalogue, remained until his death in 1708. He was also the perpetual curate of Harty from 1680 until 1695 and subscribed as a curate at Crundale in 1696. The Boughton Aluph vicarage house had six hearths. CCEd Person ID: 124183; CCA, DCc-TB/2–4, V/V/ 74, 89; LPL, VB 1/5/305; Harrington, p. 332.

Nightingale, Thomas [lvi, 44] MA. Admitted to the rectory of Wormshill in 1655 and remained until his death in 1673. CCEd Person ID: 72952; LPL, COMM III/4, p. 78, VB 1/3/200.

Nitingale, Sibil [41] Possibly the wife of **Thomas Nightingale** above.

North, Francis [61] An error. Should be Sir Henry North of Mildenhall, created baronet in 1660. LPL, VH 2/40/2; Burke, p. 390.

Northumberland, Earl [55] Algernon Percy, tenth earl of Northumberland. *ODNB*.

Norton, – [12] Not identified.

Nurse, Rich. [55] MA. Fellow of Trinity College, Cambridge, was collated to Chiddingstone in 1667. He died in 1705. CCEd Person ID: 158769; LPL, VB 1/5/188.

Oates, Titus [45] The notorious fabricator of the Popish Plot. Curate of Theydon Bois, Essex, in 1669. Instituted as vicar of Bobbing in 1673 and given dispensation for non-residence in 1674 'by reason of the unwholsomnesse of the ayre'. **Thomas Milway** and **Thomas Turner** appear to have acted as curates at Bobbing during the whole of Oates's tenure ending in 1689. CCEd Person ID: 18169; Willis (1975), pp. 48–9; *ODNB*.

Oliver, – [22] One 'William Olliver' had a house in the parish of St Margaret at Cliffe, which was not chargeable for the Hearth Tax in 1664. Harrington, p. 414.

Oliver, Edward [l, lxvi n. 176, 57, 57 n. 127] MA. Curate of Shoreham in 1661 but described as vicar, when his death was recorded in 1674. LPL, VG 1/2 fo. 17v, VB 1/3/238, Venn, III, 279.

Oliver, John [17, 17 n. 32 (2)] DD. Instituted as rector of Chenies, Bucks., in 1631 but resigned in 1632. Rector of Broughton Poggs, Oxon., 1632–8, instituted as rector of Little Laver, Essex in 1637 and was still there in 1640, rector of Monks Eleigh, Suffolk, 1638–9, and rector of Adisham, 1639–55, sequestrated but restored in 1660. Possibly vicar of St Margaret at Cliffe, 1655–8. Many other appointments. CCEd Person ID: 14385; *ODNB*; Matthews, *Walker*, p. 223; Foster, III, 1089.

Osborne, Thomas [59b] LLB. Rector of Cheam, Surrey, from 1673 until his death in 1686. LPL, VH 2/5/2, 3; Foster, IV, 1532.

Osborne, William junior [2, 2 n. 6, 3, 3 n. 13, 15 n. 29, 19 n. 36] MA. The son of **William Osborne** below. Collated to the rectory of Canterbury St Martin in 1661 and instituted to Fordwich in August 1663. Died in 1693, still holding Fordwich along with the combined rectories of St Paul and St Martin. Another William Osborne, probably his son, was inducted to the rectory of Canterbury St Martin on 28 June 1693. CCEd Person ID: 73139, 61261; Willis (1975), pp. 42, 74; Venn, III, 286.

Osborne, William senior [l n. 93, 15, 19, 19 n. 34, 21] MA. The son of William Osborne, rector of East Langdon, 1616–41. Curate to Alexander Chapman at Deal in 1627, curate to Walter Richards at Buckland and Dover St James the Apostle, 1632–6, and curate of Eastry and Worth, under Samuel Nicolls, 1636–7. Rector of East Langdon from 1641 and the desolate church of West Langdon from 1661, he was licensed to the cure of Guston in 1663. In the Catalogue, fo. 15, he is labelled 'A Presbyterian', probably indicating that he stayed in East Langdon throughout the Interregnum. He retained the three livings until his death in 1674. CCEd Person ID: 39096; Willis (1972), pp. 64, 65, 67; Willis (1975), pp. 59, 92; Venn, III, 286.

Overing, John [6] Collated to the vicarage of St John in Thanet in August 1662, but in 1665 he had to request the release of his living from sequestration. The judge of the archdeacon's court admonished him that 'he do reside upon his vicarage of St John's and duly discharge the Cure according to the Canons'. He is not recorded in the parish thereafter and may be the Johannes Overing collated to the rectory of Wickham St Paul, London, in 1670. CCEd Person ID: 140264, 165554; *AC*, 26, pp. 29–30.

Owen, Jonas [15, 17, 26] LLB. Probably the rector of Ruskington, Lincs., from 1630 until 1662 when he resigned and moved to Kent. He was collated to the vicarage of Sibertswold with the chapel of Coldred in 1662 and instituted as the rector of Wootton in 1663. Reputed to have been a Fellow of St John's College, Oxford, for seventeen years, he was said to be seventy-five years old in 1665, but he retained both of his livings until his death in 1680. CCEd Person ID: 100014; LPL, VB 1/4/108; Hegarty, p. 109; Robinson, p. 61; *AC*, 25, p. 260; Foster, III, 1100.

Palmer, Samuel [lxvi n. 176, 56a] BA. Appointed to the vicarage of Eynsford in 1662 but ceded in 1666. Not identified thereafter. CCEd Person ID: 73190; LPL, VB 1/2/9.

Palmer, Thomas [lviii] MA. Rector of St Lawrence Pountney, London, 1644–6. Rector of Aston-upon-Trent, Derbs., from 1646 until his ejection in 1660. Imprisoned several times for preaching and for involvement with the Farnley Wood plot. Went to Ireland with **Thomas Blood** and not further recorded. Matthews, *Calamy*, p. 380; Venn, III, 301; *ODNB*.

Palmer, Thomas [14, 23] Sir Thomas Palmer of Wingham, a baronet, who died in 1656. Compounded with a fine of £1,000. Cliffe, p. 472.

Parker, Mark [15] BA. Instituted as vicar of Sandwich St Clement in 1677 and died in 1680. CCEd Person ID: 18251; Dunkin, II, 151.

Parker, Matthew [xliii, 29, 53, 60, 62 (2), 66 n. 190] Archbishop of Canterbury, 1559–75. *ODNB*.

Parker, Robert [40] Not identified.

Parker, Samuel [10, 11] MA (DD). Instituted to the rectory of Chartham in 1667 and received dispensation to hold the rectory of Ickham in plurality in 1671. He held both livings until his death, but was probably rarely seen in them, as he was appointed a chaplain to Archbishop Sheldon in 1667, archdeacon of Canterbury in 1670 and canon of Canterbury cathedral in 1671. Died in 1688 as bishop of Oxford, having been appointed in 1686. A fierce opponent of religious toleration. CCEd Person ID: 100686; LPL, VG 1/5, pp. 18, 34, VG 1/6 fo. 59v; *ODNB*.

Parkhurst, Henry [13, 52] DD. Fellow of Magdalen College, Oxford, 1631–48. Rector of Compton Abbas, Dorset, in 1637 but then disappears from the record until the 1662 visitation when he was recorded as the rector of Norton. He was made a canon of Southwell in the same year and dispensed to hold the rectory of Stourmouth along with Norton in 1663. He died in 1669. CCEd Person ID: 73226, 14461; LPL, F I/C fo. 110; Venn, III, 310.

Partherich, Edward [12, 51] Sir Edward had lived in the parish of Bridge and was the patron of Patrixbourne, but the family sold all their Kentish estates in 1638 and moved to Cambridgeshire. He married Catherine Throckmorton, of Northamptonshire. By the time of the Catalogue, **Arnold Braems** was the patron of Patrixbourne. *HoP*; Hasted, 9, p. 279.

Paul, Obadiah [49 n. 112] MA. Curate of Bapchild in 1667 and curate of Leysdown, with a licence for the sequestration of the rectory of Warden in 1669. In 1672, as chaplain to Benjamin, Viscount Fitzwalter, he was dispensed to hold the rectories of Aythorpe Roding and Little Birch, both in Essex. He died in 1703. CCEd Person ID: 165632; LPL, VB 1/2/47, 71, 1/3/156, F V/1/II fo. 75v; Venn, III, 320.

Paul, Onesiphorus [53 n. 118] MA. Curate of Little Somborne Chapel, Hants., in 1663 and of Chilton Foliat, Berks., in 1664. Instituted as vicar of Leysdown in 1668, and in 1669 he was appointed to the vicarage of Selling, remaining until 1671. Also recorded as a curate at Mersham in 1673. Instituted to the rectory of Lawshall, Suffolk, in 1675, he resigned in the following year, and was instituted to the vicarage of Wanborough, Wilts., where he may have remained until 1692. CCEd Person ID: 22684; LPL, VG 1/5, p. 24, VB 1/2/202; KHLC, DCb/V/V/67.

Pauley or **Pawley, Richard** [63] MA. Vicar of West Tarring from 1677 until 1684 when he replaced **John Harrison** as vicar of Crondall, Hants. He is recorded until 1708 and probably died in 1713. CCEd Person ID: 64802; LPL, VG 1/5, p. 65; Foster, III, 1128.

Pawley, William [xxxix n. 13, l (2), lxv n. 172, 57, 57 n. 129] MA. Ordained in 1663, but not traced until he is licensed to the cure of Knockholt in 1670. He died in 1674. CCEd Person ID: 65032; TNA, PROB 11/346/372; LPL, VB 1/3/37; Hasted, II, 83.

Payne or **Paine, George** [62 n. 164] BA. Curate of Earnley and Almodington in 1662. Collated to the vicarage of Pagham in 1662 and remained until 1678. CCEd Person ID: 64806.

Payn or **Payne, William** [41] DD, FRS. Instituted to the rectory of Wormshill in 1673 and dispensed to hold it with Frinsted in 1675. Moved to London to become rector of St Mary, Whitechapel, in 1681, and in 1689, lecturer at St Mildred Poultry, London, and chaplain-in-ordinary to William and Mary. CCEd Person ID: 18280; *ODNB*; LPL, VB 1/3/241.

Payne, John [37] Not identified.

Paynter, Allington [56a] A Gentleman Pensioner in Extraordinary in 1660 and promoted to be a Gentleman Pensioner in 1662, serving until 1671. The fifty Gentlemen Pensioners were part of the royal guard and were in waiting by quarter, in the presence chamber with their axes, and on ceremonial occasions. www.british-history.ac.uk/office-holders/vol11.

Payton or **Peyton, Thomas** [lii, 16 (2), 18, 26] Sir Thomas Peyton second baronet of Knowlton. MP for Sandwich, 1640–5, and for Kent in 1661, and in 1663 he was added to the committee for the bill to provide remedies against meetings of dissenters. One of the leading royalist conspirators in Kent during the 1650s. JP in 1665, 1666 and 1670. He had a twenty-one hearth house in Knowlton. *HoP*; KHLC, Q/J/C/10, 11, 12; Cliffe, p. 477.

Pead, Deuel or **Duel** [4, 4 nn. 14 (2), 15] M. Instituted rector of Canterbury St Peter in 1672 but is not recorded again until he signs a testimonial as minister of St Botolph Without Aldgate, in 1679. Subsequently, he held several other livings in London, before his death in 1727. CCEd Person ID: 73436; LPL, VB 1/3/163, VX IA/10/142/1–2; Venn, III, 326.

Peake, – [17] Not identified.

Pearne or Perne, Andrew [1 n. 93, 22] BA. Curate of Swingfield from 1667 and instituted as vicar of Lydden in 1673, he died holding both in 1675. CCEd Person ID: 18299; KHLC, DCb/V/V/61, 64, 69.

Pearson, Richard [59a] MA. Instituted rector of St Michael Crooked Lane, London, in 1675 but deprived in 1690. LPL, VG 1/5, p. 56; Venn, III, 331.

Peck, Francis [26, 28, 28 n. 61] BA. Licensed to serve as curate of Nonington with Womenswold in 1672 and as a deacon, curate of Folkestone in the same year. He was instituted as the rector of the derelict church of Eastbridge in 1673 and rector of Saltwood with Hythe in 1673, retaining both until his death in 1706. CCEd Person ID: 73447; LPL, VB 1/3/139, 1/5/221, VG 1/5 pp. 48, 49; Willis (1975), p. 45.

Peck, Robert [xxxix n. 17, 64, 64 n. 180] MA. Vicar and schoolmaster of Codicote, Herts., from 1661 but ceded the vicarage in 1665. Instituted to the vicarage of Mayfield in 1664 and served until his death in 1696. CCEd Person ID: 64753; LPL, VH 2/38/3.

Pell, – [38] Robert and Thomas Pell were assessed for the 1664 Hearth Tax on three houses in the parish of Smarden. Harrington, pp. 314–15.

Pell, William [48] MA. Vicar of Tonge from 1661, until his death in 1672. In 1667, he was required to perform penance, in his own church and at Sittingbourne, for 'a constant and habitual course and practice of marrying all sorts of people, both of my own and other parishes, that would hire me to do it, without either banns or licence'. CCEd Person ID: 140266; LPL, VB 1/3/155; *AC*, 41, p. 102.

Pengry, Moses [56a] BD. Appointed as vicar of Gillingham in 1676, he was dispensed to hold the living with the rectory of Nevendon, Essex, in 1678 but died in that year. CCEd Person ID: 66244; LPL, VB 1/4/44.

Penny, James [xlvi, 1] MA. Collated to the vicarage of Canterbury St Dunstan in 1615 but sequestrated in 1646. He was restored before Michaelmas, 1662, when he signed the return to the archdeacon as vicar. Remained as vicar until his death in January 1664. CCEd Person ID: 39038; Matthews, *Walker*, p. 223; Cowper (1887), pp. 126, 128.

Percivall, Mr [21] Not identified.

Perkins, James [33] MA. Instituted as rector of Warehorne in April 1680 but ceded in December 1680. Rector of Braughing, Herts., from 1680 until his death in 1714. CCEd Person ID: 126707; LPL, VB 1/4/133.

Perne, Thomas [20 (2)] MA. Instituted rector of Charlton in 1660, and held it until his death before 1666. Instituted as vicar of Buckland near Dover in 1660, but no further record. CCEd Person ID: 73829.

Perry, – [10] Richard Perry lived in a two hearth house in Chartham. Harrington, p. 324.

Petit, Henry [6] Captain Henry is mentioned as a chief man and a friend of the church in the parish of St John in Thanet. He owned the ancient estate of Dandelion in the parish but died in 1661 and was buried in the parish church. Hasted, XII, p. 337.

Petter, John [lxvi] MA. Instituted as rector of Hever in 1632, noted there in 1650 and remained until 1662. During his tenure, he appointed curates in 1632, 1634 and 1636. He is listed as ejected in 1662 but the presentation of **George Boraston**, his nephew, is 'on the resignation of John Petter, former incumbent'. CCEd Person ID: 46892; LPL, VH 98/1/38v, 60, 73v, 2/22/1, VG ½ fo. 7v; Matthews, *Calamy*, p. 387; Hasted, III, p. 202.

Peyto, Joshua [62 n. 162] BA. Rector of Chichester All Saints from 1619 until his death in 1662. Rector of Rumboldswke, Sussex, 1661–2. CCEd Person ID: 78607.

Philips or **Phillipps, Thomas** [37] MA. Curate to **Robert Cole** at Smarden in 1662, then collated to the vicarage of Headcorn in 1663. In 1668, archdeacon **William Sancroft** records in his Parochial Notebook that Philips had been 'presented for scandal, & suspended & yet in prison'. He died in 1673. CCEd Person ID: 173741; LPL, VG ½ fo. 39v; Bodl., MS Sancroft 99, p. 97; KFHS, Headcorn Burials.

Phinnies or **Phineas, Benjamin** [49] Vicar of Upchurch from 1667 until his death in 1684. CCEd Person ID: 74078.

Pibus, Henry [25] MA. Appointed rector of Hastingleigh in 1647 and remained until his death in 1686. CCEd Person ID: 81130; Shaw (1900), II, 347; www.hastingleigh.com/hast-rectors.html.

Peirce, Edmund [15] LLD. Knighted in 1645. Master in Chancery, 1660–7, and MP for Maidstone, 1661–7. Appointed commissary-general for Canterbury by the dean and chapter *sede vacante* in 1660. Died in 1667. *HoP*; Potter, pp. 183, 204; Venn, III, 328.

Pierce, Thomas [xxxix n. 24] DD. Canon of Canterbury cathedral, 1660–91. Not mentioned in the Catalogue as he was not an incumbent of a living in Canterbury diocese. Rector of Brington, Northants., 1656–76, prebendary of Lincoln cathedral, 1660–91, and dean of Salisbury cathedral, 1675–91. CCEd Person ID: 59205; *ODNB*.

Pindar, William [lxv n. 174, lxvi n. 176, 55] DD. Sequestered from Langdon Hills and Stock Harvard in Essex but officiated at the former in the 1650s at the request of sequestrators. He was restored to Langdon before November 1660, when he was collated to Brasted, but resigned Langdon in March 1662. Instituted to Springfield Boswell, also in Essex, in December 1661 and held it and Brasted until his death in 1692. CCEd Person ID: 56334; Venn, III, 367; Matthews, *Walker*, p. 161.

Plaine, William [60 n. 151] MA. Instituted as rector of Borley in 1661 but was instituted again in 1663. As chaplain to the earl of St Albans, he was dispensed to hold in plurality Borley with Langenhoe, Essex, in 1662. He held both rectories until his death in 1681. CCEd Person ID: 142895; LPL, F II/3/212.

Pleydall or **Pleydell, Jonathan** [37] BA. Ordained as a deacon in September 1662 and was appointed curate of the donative of Hawkhurst in December of that year, but he was not ordained priest until June 1663. Licensed to teach at Hawkhurst in 1666, he moved to Ewhurst, Surrey in 1691 and held the rectory until 1725. CCEd Person ID: 64884; Willis (1975), p. 3; Foster, III, 1172.

Plymley, John [16] MA. Rector of Ham from 1678 until his death in 1734. Second undermaster of Merchant-Taylors' School in 1679 and first undermaster in 1680–5. He was thought to have died in 1729, and the rectory was sequestrated, but it was discovered that he had been resident at Wolverhampton. He was headmaster of Wolverhampton School from 1685 until 1710, and a prebend of Wolverhampton Collegiate Church. He died in 1734. CCEd Person ID: 19265, 432; Hasted, X, 43; Venn, III, 374; Thomas **and** Ryan, p. xii; Wilson, p. 1180.

Pollard, William [35] Not identified.

Pollington, Thomas [43] MA. Instituted in 1661 as vicar of Sutton Valence with East Sutton but resigned in 1666. Not further recorded, but the same name appears in Gloucestershire as a curate and a preacher in 1665 and 1670. CCEd Person ID: 74162, 161297; LPL, VB 1/1/188; Venn, III, 376.

Pordage, Mr [48] Thomas Pordage junior; his father died in 1637. Two-thirds of the Pordage estates had been sequestered for recusancy by the late 1640s, but may have been restored later. Thomas Pordage Esq. was assessed for thirteen hearths in his house in Rodmersham in 1664. TNA, PROB 11/172/178; Compounding, III, 1908; Everitt (1966), p. 247; Hasted, VI, 117; Harrington, p. 261.

Porter, – [lxvi, 56a] Francis Porter MA was ordained deacon and priest in 1644 and noted as chaplain to Henry, marquess of Dorchester, in 1649. He compounded for first fruits as rector, without cure, of Eynsford in 1653 but was instituted in 1660. In 1662, he was instituted to the vicarage of North Wheatley, Notts., and received dispensation to hold Saundby, Notts., with North Wheatley in 1667. Probably died in 1687. CCEd Person ID: 14619; LPL, F V/1/I fo. 27v, VB ½/9, ½/61; BL, Add MS 39506, p. 51; Foster, III, 1182.

Pory, Robert [41, 41 n. 96] DD. Collated to the sinecure rectory of Hollingbourne in 1661 and retained it until his death in 1669, although he may never have visited. Related, by marriage, to Archbishop Juxon, he had many other offices. CCEd Person ID: 74181; *ODNB*; Matthews, *Walker*, p. 55.

Potter, Thomas [lxv n. 174, lxvi n. 176, 55] DD. Possibly sequestrated from the rectories of Nympsfield, Gloucs., and Sundridge in Shoreham Deanery in the 1640s. Installed in the prebend of Louth in Lincoln cathedral in October 1660. Noted in the Episcopal Register of 1662 as rector of Broadwater, Sussex, and was given dispensation on 30 September 1662 to hold Chiddingstone, to which rectory he was collated on 4 October. A chaplain to Archbishop Juxon, he held Broadwater, Chiddingstone and his prebend until his death in 1667. CCEd Person ID: 142896, 64923, 101099; LPL, F I/C fo. 90; Horn, IX, 88; Matthews, *Walker*, pp. 224, 402.

Powel or **Powell, Roger** [31, 31 n. 72] BA. Curate of Aldermaston, Berks., in 1680 and rector of Orlestone in 1682. Suspected of simony and replaced in 1684 by Jerman Dunn. CCEd Person ID: 119514, 87882 (Dunn institution to Orlestone).

Powell, Nathaniel [30] Purchased the manor of Kingsnorth in the 1640s and was created a baronet in 1661. He died in 1675. Burke, p. 423.

Pownall, Samuel [20] BA. Vicar of Alkham with the chapel of Capel-le-Ferne from 1627. Sequestrated by 1646, when John Richards is said to have been the vicar. Not mentioned in Matthews, *Walker*. Pownall recorded as vicar in 1662 and remained until his death in 1676. CCEd Person ID: 14662; Venn, III, 450; Foster, III, 1196; KHLC, DCb/V/V/56; LPL, VB 1/3/279.

Prestwich, John [46] Fellow of All Souls College, Oxford. Instituted to the derelict church of Elmley in 1661 and retained it until his death in 1679. CCEd Person ID: 74356; KHLC, DCb/V/V/56, 58, 64, 70, 71.

Price, Denzill [60, 60 n. 150] Dispensed to receive orders of deacon and priest in May 1667, when it was noted that he was of the universities of Leyden and Utrecht. Instituted to the vicarage of Roydon, Essex, in 1667 but resigned in 1668. Signed a Dutch and English translation of a Dutch deposition in 1668. Instituted to the rectory of Harston, Leics., in 1669 but ceded in 1672. The Catalogue locates him, in error, at Stisted, Essex. He was rector of Stifford, Essex. from 1674 until his death and burial there in 1678. CCEd Person ID: 64966; LPL, VB ½/62; *CSPC*, 1746, IV; Newcourt, II, 561; Stifford, p. 87.

Primrose, Dr [11] Probably Gilbert Primrose DD, a Scottish born minister of the French Reformed church who was exiled from his church in Bordeaux in 1623 and returned to London, where he was chosen as one of the ministers of the French and Walloon refugee church. He died in 1642. The Catalogue mentions Sir Anthony Aucher and Primrose as patrons of Kingston but Aucher sold the advowson to Thomas Gibbon in 1647 and it descended to his granddaughters Dorothy and Anne. When **Robert Aucher** was instituted as rector of Kingston, the joint patrons were Dorothy and Anne Gibbon and Frederick Primrose. LPL, VB 1/3/155; Hasted, IX, 342; *ODNB*.

Pritchett or **Prichett, John** [73r] DD. Rector of Bratoft, Lincs., 1634–41, rector of St Andrew Undershaft, London, 1641–64, prebendary of St Paul's Cathedral, London, 1662–80, rector of Harlington, London, 1661–81, vicar of St Giles Cripplegate, London, 1664–81, and bishop of Gloucester from 1672 until his death in 1681. CCEd Person ID: 14721, 74264; Foster, III, 1211; Horn, VIII, 42.

Proctor, Luke [7] MA. Curate of Chartham from 1628 to 1630 and curate of Eyethorne in 1634. Rector of St Mary Bothaw, London, in 1639 and rector of St Michael Paternoster Royal, London, from 1637 until his sequestration in 1643. He was again sequestered from the vicarage of Forest Hill, Oxon., in 1652. Instituted vicar of St Peter in Thanet in 1666, he resigned in the same year and became rector of Snodland in Rochester diocese in 1667, dying in 1673. CCEd Person ID: 38981, 1738; LPL, VG 1/5, p. 3; Dunkin, II, 206; Matthews, *Walker*, p. 56.

Prolling, John [56a] Not identified.

Provost, John [63] MA. Collated to the sinecure rectory of West Tarring in 1672 and held it until his death in 1711. Nothing else known. CCEd Person ID: 65026; LPL, VB 1/3/154, 1/6/46.

Pulford, Gregory [xlviii n. 80, 1 n. 93, 2, 3, 4] MA. Incumbent of the curacy of Nackington, Kent, in 1659 and instituted to Lower Hardres in September 1660. Appointed chaplain to Henry, earl of Monmouth, in 1661 and given dispensation to hold two livings. In the same year, he became rector of Milton. Resigned from Milton in 1669 and not recorded thereafter in Nackington or Lower Hardres, next being noted as the preacher in St Stephen's, St Albans, in 1678, although he was probably the vicar. Died in 1693, aged seventy. CCEd Person ID: 74295; LPL, F I/C fo. 34v, VB ½/191; Venn, III, 405.

Pury, Peter senior [li, 11 n. 25, 16] MA. Curate at Stourmouth, 1633–4, curate of the donative of Goodnestone by Wingham from 1636, probably remaining until 1682. Vicar of Knowlton from 1639 until his death in 1684. See fo. 11 n. 25. CCEd Person ID: 38920; Venn, III, 409.

Quinton, Francis [17 n. 32] Possibly admitted to Trinity College, Cambridge, in 1645 but no degree recorded. Intruded into the rectory of Adisham 1655 and died in 1658. LPL, COMM II/8; Matthews, *Walker*, p. 223; Venn, III, 413.

Radcliffe, Percival [lv, 50] MA. Curate of Wetherell and Warwick in 1662. Instituted as vicar of Boughton under Blean in 1663 and to the vicarage of Sheldwich, possibly in the same year. He died in 1666. CCEd Person ID: 173912; Foster, III, 1228; LPL, VG ¼ fo. 2, VB ½/103; *AC*, 18, p. 299.

Rands, Richard [35, 38] MA. As chaplain to Henry, earl of Peterborough, he was dispensed to be instituted as vicar of Bethersden and rector of Smarden in 1668. In 1669, he was instituted as rector of Turvey, Beds., remaining until his death in 1700. CCEd Person ID: 75008; LPL, F V/1/II fo. 30; Dunkin, II, 215.

Reading, John [xlvi, 10, 20, 20 n. 41] MA. Licensed to the perpetual curacy of Dover St Mary the Virgin in 1618, he was sequestrated in 1643 but instituted rector of Cheriton in 1644, where he survived the Interregnum. In 1660, he became chaplain to **Heneage Finch**, third earl of Winchelsea, appointed a canon of Canterbury cathedral and instituted rector of Chartham. He died in 1667. CCEd Person ID: 14929; Matthews, *Walker*, p. 224; *AC*, 5, p. 120; Foster, III, 1242.

Remmington, – [36] Alexander 'Rimington', a quaker, who was imprisoned in 1661, along with others, at Maidstone, for refusing the oath of allegiance. Besse, p. 290.

Reny, Andrew [40, 42] MA. Instituted as vicar of Detling in 1674 and as chaplain to the earl of Middlesex, was dispensed to hold it with Linton in 1677. He ceded Detling and became vicar of Hadlow, Rochester diocese, in 1680, retaining both vicarages until his death in 1701. CCEd Person ID: 2477; LPL, VG 1/5, p. 49, F I/D fo. 145, VB ¼/102.

Reve, Adam [47] BA. Vicar of Newington next Sittingbourne, 1666–84. Suspended for scandal in 1668, Curate to Theophilus Becke at Reculver in 1688 and vicar of Reculver with Hoath from 1689 until his death in 1692. CCEd Person ID: 74490; Willis (1975), pp. 66, 74; Bodl., MS Sancroft 99, p. 149.

Rich, Jo. [35] Not identified.

Richards, John [24] MA. Licensed to teach at Biddenden in 1662. Collated to the vicarage of Brabourne and the rectory of Monks Horton in 1676 and served both until his death in 1727. CCEd Person ID: 75012; Dunkin, II, 227; Willis (1975), p. 2.

Richards, John [27 n. 59] MA. Vicar of Godmersham, 1645–6, vicar of Alkham in 1646 and vicar of Appledore from 1646 until his death in 1651. LPL, MS 1104, fo. 38; Hasted, VII, 261; BL, Add MS 36792; Venn, III, 450.

Richards, Robert [31, 31 n. 72] MA. Curate to **Richard Marsh** at Ruckinge and rector of Orlestone, 1666–9. Given dispensation to hold the rectories of Snargate and Snave, instituted to both in 1669 and held them until his death in 1683. CCEd Person ID: 65217; LPL, VB ½/166, VG 1/5 pp. 27–8; Dunkin, II, 227.

Richards, Samuel [24] MA. Instituted as vicar of Elmsted in 1676 and served until his death in 1686. Also, curate to **John Ansell** at Brook in 1680. CCEd Person ID: 75014; Willis (1975), p. 48.

Ridgeway, Henry [36] MA. Instituted as vicar of Charing in 1663 and possibly remained until **John Shephard** was instituted in 1674. No further records found. CCEd Person ID: 74531.

Riggs, Edward [lviii (2)] Rector of Sevington in 1654 and vicar of St John in Thanet from 1657 until his ejection in 1660. Involved in the Tong Plot of 1662, imprisoned in the Tower of London and confessed. Gave a bond for good behaviour and became a government informer in Rotterdam. Greaves, pp. 122–3, 171–2; Matthews, *Calamy*, p. 412.

Risden, Thomas [35, 58] BD. Curate of Holy Trinity Minories, London, 1640–2. Admitted as vicar of Rainham, Essex, in 1644, subscribed as vicar in 1662 but ceded in 1663. Collated to the rectory of All Hallows Bread Street, London, in 1662, but when the church burnt down in the Great Fire of London in 1666 he was, as chaplain to the bishop of St David's, given dispensation to hold the vicarage of Ashford. He died holding both offices in 1673. CCEd Person ID: 74546; Venn, III, 461; LPL, F I/C fo. 208, VB 1/3/10, 121.

Roberts, Mr [25 (2)] A descendant of Sir John Roberts of Canterbury who died in 1658. Hasted, VIII, 84.

Robertson, George [54] MA. Instituted to the vicarage of Leysdown in 1661 and there in 1662, but instituted to Throwley in that year and kept the vicarage until his possible death in 1688. CCEd Person ID: 140271.

Robins, Stephen [63] MA. Rector of Tangmere from 1677 until his cession in 1680. Instituted to the rectory of Little Ilford, London, in 1680 and held it until his death in 1713. As chaplain to George Howard, earl of Suffolk, he was dispensed in 1690 to hold Little Ilford with the vicarage of East Ham, London, resigning the latter in 1710. CCEd Person ID: 142897; LPL, F V/1/IV fo. 48.

Robinson, Elisha [2, 4 n. 14] MA. Received dispensation to be ordained deacon although under twenty-three years of age, in order to take up the office of minor canon of Canterbury cathedral in March 1666. He gave a presentation bond of £100 to the dean and chapter in June 1666, received letters dimissory for priest's orders on 21 September and was instituted rector of Canterbury St George three days later. He received his last payment as a minor canon on 25 December 1670 and died in 1671. At the 1670 visitation, he is recorded as the minister of Canterbury St Peter. CCEd Person ID: 140272; Venn, III, 469; CCA, DCc-TB/6, DCc-ChAnt/C/825E; KHLC, DCb/V/V/64; LPL, F I/C fo. 195, VB ½/22, 23.

Roborough, Stephen [lxiv, 63, 63 n. 173, 64] BA. Rector of Ardingly, Sussex, from 1667 until his death in 1723. Also named, in the Catalogue, as incumbent of South Malling and surrogate to **Richard Chaworth**. He was the dean of South Malling deanery and sinecure rector of the parish, which was a curacy. See **Henry Mountague**. CCEd Person ID: 65249; *SAC*, 5, pp. 132–9, 26, p. 83; Venn, III, 476.

Romswinckell, John Herman [20, 20 n. 39, 22, 22 n. 43, 22 n. 47, 55, 55 n. 120] BD. Subscribed as a schoolmaster in Market Bosworth, Leics., and licensed to preach throughout the diocese of Lincoln in 1662. Probably the 'Mr. Romwinkle' noted as living in Crayford. On 5 April 1666, he received ordination as deacon and priest, on the same day, and was presented to Buckland near Dover. Instituted to the vicarage two days later; he was also granted the sequestration of the vicarage of Lydden with River in July of the same year. He was noted acting as curate at Charlton in 1673 and died in that year. CCEd Person ID: 75368; LPL, F I/C fo. 200, VG 1/5, p. 8, VB ½/14; Dunkin, I, 401, II, 242.

Rooke, William [6, 24] Probably William Rooke Esq. who had a seven hearth house in Monkton. Named as captain of the county troop, an 'honest gent.' and one of the chief men in the parish of Monkton. He attended the assizes five times from 1661 to 1665. Harrington, p. 395; Cockburn (1995), pp. 5, 16, 50, 83, 130.

Roper, Lord [52] Sir Christopher Roper, Fourth Baron Teynham. A Roman catholic recusant. Resided in a forty-three hearth house in Lynstead. Hasted, VI, 300; Harrington, p. 275; Brydges, p. 84.

Rose, Gervase [6] Mr Gervase Rose had a ten hearth house in Chislet, near to that of **Alexander Cooke's** three hearth house. Harrington, p. 369.

Rosse, John [24 (2), 24 n. 54 (2)] MA. Vicar of Brabourne from 1625 probably remaining throughout the Interregnum until his death in 1663. Also rector of the derelict church of Bircholt, 1662–3. CCEd Person ID: 38130; LPL, VB 1/1/78.

Roundtree, Ralph [lv, 46, 49 n. 112] Curate at Boughton under Blean in 1662 and curate during the sequestration of the rectory of Warden from 1664 until 1667. Instituted to the vicarage of Leysdown in 1663 holding it until his possible death in 1667. CCEd Person ID: 140273; Willis (1975), p. 42.

Rudge, John [58 n. 136] MA. Curate at Camberwell, Surrey, in 1667. Instituted rector of St Mary Aldermary, London (not rebuilt after the Great Fire until 1682), in 1669, and retained it until his death in 1679. Possibly also rector of St Thomas Apostle, London (united to St Mary Aldermary after the Great Fire), from 1672 until 1679. CCEd Person ID: 95290; LPL, VG 1/5, p. 31; Venn, III, 496.

Russell, Thomas [xlviii n. 80, 13, 28 (2)] MA. Curate of Saltwood with Hythe in 1637 but no further record found until he is noted at the 1662 visitation as vicar of Brookland and of Brenzett, and curate of Stodmarsh. He was replaced at the latter in 1675 but retained his other two livings until his probable death in 1677. CCEd Person ID: 15198, 38126; LPL, VG ½ fo. 29; KHLC, DCb/V/V/56.

Russell, William [li, 21, 22 n. 46] A minister with this name was intruded into Folkestone in 1654, and recorded as relinquishing Woodnesborough in 1657, having been approved as the minister of Old Romney. Instituted as vicar of Ewell in 1661 he is also noted in visitations as the vicar of Lydden until 1667, and probably also held River, as they were frequently held together. Instituted vicar of Alkham in 1676, he retained it, possibly along with Ewell, until his death in 1694. CCEd Person ID: 140275; Dunkin, II, 250; Matthews, *Walker*, p. 224; LPL, COMM III/2, p. 39, VG 1/5, p. 58; Willis (1975), pp. 47, 49; KHLC, DCb/V/V/56, 58, 61; Hasted, VIII, 132, 141.

Rutton, Matthew junior [43, 43 n. 104] MA. Instituted as rector of Otham in 1677 and served until his death in 1701. CCEd Person ID: 140276; Venn, III, 503.

Rutton, Matthew senior [39, 39 n. 92] MA. Instituted to the vicarage of Cobham, Rochester diocese, in 1637 but unknown tenure. Master of King's School, Rochester, 1647–60, and intruded vicar of Boughton Monchelsea in 1649. He may have remained at Boughton until his death in 1686. CCEd Person ID: 3075; Matthews, *Walker*, p. 213; Foster, III, 1293; Venn, III, 503.

Sabin, John [9, 36] John Sabine MD, who resided in Bekesbourne and whose father, Avery Sabin, had been an alderman in Canterbury in the 1640s. Venn, IV, 1; Hasted, XII, 127.

Sackett, John [16] BD. Curate, at various times in 1623 and 1624 in Dover St James the Apostle, Hawkinge and Herne. Rector of Betteshanger from 1626 until ceding in 1628 for the rectory of Great Mongeham, which he retained until his death in 1664. He had also been rector of the ruined church of Eastbridge and master of Eastbridge Hospital. CCEd Person ID: 38334; Willis (1972), p. 62; Venn, IV, 2.

Sackett, Stephen [1, 33] MA. Instituted to Blean in 1632 and to West Hythe in 1633, following dispensation as chaplain to Cecilia, baroness de la Warr. After his appointment as chaplain to Edmund, bishop of Bangor, he was again given dispensation and reinstituted as vicar of Blean. He probably retained both livings until his death in

1679. He was not the master of Eastbridge Hospital. His brother, **John Sackett**, was master from 1628 to 1664 and was succeeded by **Edward Aldey**. CCEd Person ID: 37877; Hasted, XII, 133; Dunkin, I, 7; Venn, IV, 2.

St George, Thomas [55] Sir Thomas St George. At the Restoration, he was appointed Somerset herald, knighted in 1669, and garter king of arms in 1686. Died in 1703. *ODNB*.

St John, Tho. [55] An error for the above.

Salter, Nathaniel [59a] MA. Vicar of Culham, Oxon., 1670–2. Rector of St Michael Royal with St Martin Vintry London 1672–83. Chaplain to the king in 1683 and was dispensed to hold the rectory of Paglesham, Essex, to which he was collated in May 1683 and died in September of that year. CCEd Person ID: 82048; LPL, F V/1/III fo. 80, F II/24/61, VH 2/35/6.

Sancroft, William [xxxviii n. 9, iii (2), iv (2), v, x, xvi (4), xix] Archbishop of Canterbury, 1678–90. CCEd Person ID: 137820, *ODNB*.

Sanders or **Saunders, Anthony** [41 n. 96, 63, 73r, 73r n. 191] DD. Rector of Hollingbourne from 1669 until he resigned in 1677. Rector of Buxted, Sussex, 1674, and dispensed to hold it with the rectory of Acton, Middx., in 1677. He held these two benefices until his death in 1720. Chancellor of St Paul's cathedral, 1672–1720. CCEd Person ID: 65335; LPL, VG 1/5, pp. 30, 34, 48, VB 1/3/172, 321; Cave-Browne (1890), pp. 53–4; Venn, IV, 13.

Sandford, Mr [45] Henry Sandford Esq. of the twenty-two hearth Bobbing Court manor. His daughter, Frances, married Sir **George Moore**, baronet, who then became the next patron of Bobbing. Hasted, VI, 198; Harrington, p. 267.

Sands, Richard [16] Not identified.

Sandys, Richard [16, 17] Son of Edwin MP and grandson of Edwin, archbishop of York. He was a colonel in the parliamentary army, knighted in 1660 and JP in 1665 and 1666. Owned the twenty-eight hearth Northbourne Court and died in 1669. *HoP*; Burke, p. 468; Shaw (1906), II, 230; Hasted, IX, 590.

Sargenson, John [1 n. 5, 2] MA. Licensed to preach at St Edward's, Cambridge, in 1662 and appointed a minor canon of Canterbury cathedral in 1663, holding the position until his death in 1684. Served as curate in Canterbury St Dunstan in 1671 and instituted rector of Canterbury St George in the same year, retaining the living until 1680. Received dispensation to hold Canterbury St Mildred in 1672 and served until his death. He preached a sermon in Canterbury cathedral, on Charles II's birthday, 29 May 1683, on the text 'By me kings reign, and princes decree justice.' CCEd Person ID: 18995; CCA, DCc-TB/1–35; Willis (1975), p. 45; LPL, VG 1/3 fo. 52v, VB 1/3/155, 1/3/133, MS 1753 fos. 1–17; Venn, IV, 20.

Savery, Daniel [10] Not identified.

Say, Robert [lxvi, 56a, 56b (2)] DD. Provost of Oriel College, Oxford, 1653–91, and vice-chancellor, 1664–6. Sinecure rector of Orpington from 1660 until his death in 1691, and rector of Marsh Gibbon, Bucks., 1661–91. CCEd Person ID: 102354; Foster, IV, 1321; Lipscomb, III, 54.

Saye, Lady [55] Frances, the daughter of Sir Edward Cecil, First Viscount Wimbledon and widow of James Fiennes, Second Viscount Saye and Sele. After the death of her husband, she married **Joshua Sprigg** in 1675. She died in 1684. *HoP*; *ODNB*.

Scarlett, William [l n. 93, 45, 46] MA. Chaplain of Trinity College, Cambridge, 1639–45 and 1661–2. Curate of Iwade and vicar of Bobbing, 1662–8. Rector of High Halstow from 1664 until his death in 1668. Minor Canon of Rochester cathedral. CCEd Person ID: 2959; KHLC, DCb/V/V/56, 58; Bodl., MS Sancroft 99, p. 23.

Sclater or **Slatyer, William** [53] BA. Student of the Inner Temple in 1642. Succeeded his father as rector of Otterden from 1647 until his death in 1668. Matthews, *Walker*, p. 225; LPL, VB ½/160; www.innertemplearchives.org.uk.

Scott, Ed [25] Probably Sir Edward Scott DCL, the husband of Catherine Goring. Lady Catherine Goring lived apart from her husband for twelve years, and it was rumoured that **Thomas Scott**, below, was her illegitimate son, by Prince Rupert. Edward Scott died in 1663 having acknowledged Thomas as his son and heir. Scott, pp. 229–32; Pepys, IV, 254.

Scott, Lady [56a] Probably Hester, widow of Sir Humphrey Style and wife of John Scott Esq., who was not of the Scot's Hall family. Hasted, II, 24.

Scott, Mr [25] A nephew of **Edward Scott**, above. Possibly the Tho. Scot named as 'a Ringleader of the Petition for the King's tryall' in the Episcopal Returns of Conventicles in 1669. Lyon Turner, I, 13.

Scott or **Scot, Thomas** [30, 31 (2)] The acknowledged heir of **Edward Scott**, above. He was knighted in 1663 and owned the thirty-six hearth Scot's Hall in Smeeth. He was the lord of the manor of Orlestone, but not of Kingsnorth. Scott, p. 236; Hasted, VII, 585, VIII, 6–7; Harrington, p. 335.

Scott, William [56b] MA. Chaplain in HMS '*The St George*' in an expedition against the Dutch, and instituted as vicar of Northfleet in 1665. Resigned in 1672. LPL, VB 1/1/160, 1/3/179, 182.

Screven or **Scriven, George** [30 n. 66] MA. Instituted as vicar of Hemel Hempstead in 1661 and remained until his cession in 1670. Curate of Flaunden and of Bovingdon, Herts., but tenure unknown. Collated to Lydd and as chaplain to Anthony, earl of Kent, was dispensed to hold it with Aldington, then received a licence for non-residence at Lydd. He died in 1672. CCEd Person ID: 102387; LPL, F I/D fo. 8, VG 1/5, p. 35, VB 1/3/13; Willis (1975), p. 72.

Sedley, Charles [17] Sir Charles, fifth baronet. MP for New Romney. Said to have been a libertine. *HoP*.

Selby, Michael [59a] MA. Vicar of Pampisford, Cambs., 1638–45, then instituted as vicar of Riseley, Beds., being succeeded by his son, Francis, in 1672. In that year, he became rector of Ingoldsby, Lincs., and died in 1685. He and **Randolph Caldecott** disputed institution to the rectory of Hayes, Middx., in the deanery of Croydon in 1661, but Selby was instituted. In 1680, he granted a lease of the rectory to Roger Jenyns, which provided for augmentation of the vicarage, and William Bishop was presented to the rectory on the death of Selby in 1685. CCEd Person ID: 75543; LPL, VB 1/3/175, VH 77/1–2, 2/20/4; Bodl., MS Tanner 125, fos. 101, 108.

Selyard or **Seyliard, Francis** [lxvii, 61, 61 n. 154, 64 n. 180] MA. Vicar of Mayfield from 1663 until his cession in 1664. Curate of Moulton in 1662 but may have been there since 1657. Instituted as rector in 1663 and served until his death in 1676. CCEd Person ID: 143693; LPL, VG ½ fo. 30v, VB 1/1/27, 1/3/305, 311; Venn, IV, 46.

Seyliard, Mr [56b] Robert Seyliard, gentleman, had an eleven hearth house in Penshurst. Harrington, p. 57.

Seyliard, Thomas [lv] MA. Vicar of Boughton under Blean in 1653, remaining until made rector of Deal in 1657 from where he was ejected in 1662. He died in 1671. Boodle, p. x; Matthews, *Calamy*, p. 434.

Seyliard, Thomas [lxvi] MA. Intruded rector of Chiddingstone from at least 1647 he was ejected in 1662 but was perhaps the rector of Runwell, Essex, 1660–7. CCEd Person ID: 166723; Matthews, *Walker*, p. 224, *Calamy*, p. 433; Venn, IV, 46.

Seymour, Lucius [43] MA. Curate of Loose in 1663 and curate at Stalisfield in 1664, he is last recorded at Loose in 1666. CCEd Person ID: 65372; LPL, VG 1/2 fo. 40, Willis (1975), p. 42.

Sharpe, Samuel [lxvi n. 175, 57] MA. Instituted as rector of Sundridge in 1645 and reinstituted in 1661, he remained until his death in 1680. CCEd Person ID: 80443; LPL, VG 1/2 fo. 15v, VB 1/4/120.

Sheldon, Gilbert [xxxvii (2), xxxviii (5), xli (3), xlviii, li, lxi (4), lxii (2), lxiii (2), lxiv, lxix (2), lxx, lxxi (2), 49 n. 113] Archbishop of Canterbury 1663–78. CCEd Person ID: 15373; *ODNB*.

Shephard, John [36] MA. Appointed vicar of Charing in 1674 and signed the Compton census as vicar in 1676, but ceded in 1678. No further record. CCEd Person ID: 140281; Dunkin, II, 280, Whiteman, p. 33.

Shepheard, Nicholas [63] MA. Admitted to the rectory of Edburton in 1656, subscribed to the Act of Uniformity in 1662 and served until his death in 1681. CCEd Person ID: 65751; *SAC*, 33, p. 213.

Sherman, Mark [xlviii n. 81, 31] BD. Probably the rector instituted to Claydon, Suffolk, in 1632 who was sequestrated in 1644 and restored, 1660–5. Rector of Orlestone from 1656 until his death in 1665. CCEd Person ID: 90876; Matthews, *Walker*, p. 344; LPL, VG 1/2 fo. 16; *AC*, 2, p. 93.

Sherman, William [20] Not identified.

Sherwin, John [52] MA. Curate to Edward Lake, at Norton, in 1672. Curate of Davington, curate of Oare and rector of Luddenham from 1675 until his death in 1714. CCEd Person ID: 82819; Willis (1975), p. 46; KHLC, DCb/V/V/69–84; LPL, VB 1/6/137.

Shipton, James [7] MA. Curate at Kingston in 1634 and at Adisham in 1637, he was vicar of Patrixbourne from 1659 to 1662 and was then collated to St Peter in Thanet in 1663, remaining until his death in 1665. CCEd Person ID: 38489; *AC*, 14, p. 179; Hasted, X, 377.

Shore, John [60, 63 n. 176] BA. Entered in the Catalogue as an incumbent at Putney, but no trace of him in the records. He was probably the curate at Tangley, a chapel of Faccombe, Hants., in 1672 and went on to be rector of Lewes St John sub Castro, Sussex, 1674–1722, and rector of Hamsey, Sussex, 1674–1722. He had been collated to the rectory of Lewes St Thomas at Cliffe, Sussex, in 1674 but ceded it in 1675. CCEd Person ID: 95473; LPL, VB 1/3/216, 248; *SAC*, 26, p. 27.

Shrawley, John [41, 42] MA. Vicar of Bearsted, 1652–7. Collated to the vicarage of Hollingbourne with the chapel of Hucking in 1661 and died in 1668. CCEd Person ID: 140283; LPL, VB 1/2/147, CCA, U108/2/25; Matthews, *Walker*, p. 225.

Shute, Christopher [lxvi, lxvi n. 182, 59a] DD. Rector of Navenby, Lincs., from 1642 possibly until 1656 and then rector of Watton, Herts., until his death in 1671. Given dispensation to hold St Vedast Foster Lane London in 1661 but had been there since at least 1658. Prebend of St Paul's, 1660–3, and prebend of Rochester cathedral, 1664–71. Archdeacon of St Albans, 1664–71. CCEd Person ID: 741; Venn, IV, 71; Littledale, I, 69.

Simpson, George [9] Not identified.

Skeane, Robert [51] MA. Admitted to the rectory of Monks Horton in 1656, he left in 1660. Admitted to Hernhill in 1659 he was collated to the vicarage in 1660 and remained until his death in 1676. Curate to **David Barton** at Boughton under Blean from 1666, he was granted the sequestration in 1671 and served until 1676. CCEd Person ID: 140284; LPL, COMM III/5, fo. 547, COMM III/7, fo. 579, VB 1/3/81; Dunkin, II, 293.

Skinner, Augustine [37] MP for Kent, 1642–53 and 1654–5. Subscriber to the parliamentary oath and covenant and the Solemn League and Covenant. Named as a commissioner for the trial of the king, but refused to act or sign the death warrant. He and his brother William, below, were members of the Cromwellian Commission, 1655–7, and regularly attended as JPs at the assizes between 1649 and 1659. Died in 1672. Snow and Young, p. 476; Cockburn (1989), *passim*; Bloomfield, p. 22.

Skinner, Robert [73r, 73r 191 (2)] Bishop of Bristol, 1637–41, bishop of Oxford, 1641–3, bishop of Worcester, 1663–70. *ODNB*.

Skinner, William [37] Brother of Augustine, above.

Slaughter, – [lix (3), lx, 17] Isaac Slaughter or Slatter was listed as an anabaptist teacher in 1664 and had a four hearth house in Northbourne. BL, SP 29/93, fo. 124; Harrington, p. 400.

Slaughter or **Sclater, Edward** [60, 60 n. 148] MA. Entered as William in error. Vicar of Fyfield, Berks., 1647–58. Vicar of Esher, Surrey, 1658–89, and curate of Putney, 1664–89. Became a catholic in 1686 and was dispensed by James II, to continue in his livings. He recanted in 1689, retired from teaching and died *c*. 1699. LPL, VG 1/4 fo. 2v; *ODNB*.

Sleighton, Edward [31, 31 n. 71, 32, 32 n. 76] MA. Instituted as vicar of Newchurch in 1665 and as chaplain to the earl of Peterborough, was dispensed to hold it with the rectory of Sevington in 1668. He was licensed to the cure of Monks Horton in 1666. He became the sinecure rector of Newchurch in 1671 and held his two rectories along with his vicarage until his death in 1686. CCEd Person ID: 140287; LPL, F I/C fo. 242v; Dunkin, II, 296; Willis (1975), p. 43; Bodl., MS Sancroft 99, p. 102.

Smallwood, George [59a] MA. Rector of St Mildred Poultry and of St Margaret New Fish Street, London, 1660–2. Collated to the rectory of St Mary le Bow in 1662 and served until his death in 1679. CCEd Person ID: 143696; Venn, IV, 91; LPL, VG 1/2 fo. 3v, VB 1/4/86.

Smith, – [43] Not identified.

Smith, Edward [lxvi n. 176, 56b] MA. Instituted as rector of Keston in 1660, subscribed in 1662 and remained until his death in 1678. CCEd Person ID: 175803; LPL, VG 1/2 fo. 3, VH 97/1/379v.

Smith, John [lxviii, 64] BA. Fellow of King's College, Cambridge, 1650–62. Vicar of Wadhurst from 1662 until his death in 1714. CCEd Person ID: 142900; *SAC*, 26, p. 94; Venn, IV, 102.

Smith or **Smythe, Matthew** [l n. 93, 7, 8] MA. Perpetual curate of Whitstable from 1661 to 1667 and vicar of Seasalter from 1661 until his resignation in 1669. KHLC, DCb/V/V/57, 58, 61; LPL, VB 1/2/170.

Smith, Mr [48] An Anthony Smyth was assessed for two hearths in 1664. Harrington, p. 274.

Smith, Mr [63, 64] Henry Smith (nicknamed Dog Smith). Alderman of London, moneylender, landholder and benefactor, always followed by his dog. Died in 1628 having founded, by his will, a charitable trust which remains in existence in 2020. *SAC*, 26, p. 64; Gregory, p. 228 n. 5; *ODNB*.

Smith, Samuel [lv (2), 24, 28] MA. Vicar of Boughton under Blean from 1637 until his sequestration in 1641. Restored in 1660, he ceded the living in the same year and became rector of Monks Horton and of the derelict church of Eastbridge. In 1666, he was appointed a Six Preacher of Canterbury cathedral and he was licensed to the cure of Wye in 1667. He resigned from Monks Horton in 1669 but retained his other preferments until his death in 1671. CCEd Person ID: 47108; Matthews, *Walker*, p. 225; Willis (1975), p. 44; Ingram Hill, p. 66.

Smoult, Thomas [lxvi n. 176, 55] DD. Appointed as minister of Bexley in 1659 and subscribed in July 1662 but he resigned and was instituted to Barkway, Herts., in May 1666 serving until 1693, when he was instituted as rector of Great Berkhampstead, Herts. First Professor of Moral Theology at Cambridge and chaplain to the king. He died in 1707. CCEd Person ID: 104911; Venn, IV, 116; LPL, VH 2/2/1, VG 1/2 fo. 8v, VB 1/2/24; *AC*, 18, p. 380; Hasted, II, p. 183.

Smyth, Miles [xxxviii (2), xxxix, xli (2), xlii (2), xliii (2), lxi (2), lxii, lxvi, lxx, lxxi, 49 n. 113 (2)] BCL. Secretary to Archbishop Sheldon from 1663. In addition to his secretarial duties, he managed the compilation of the Catalogue. His authorship of the Act Book, commenced in August 1663, and his obviously extensive research into the registers of previous archbishops, gave him a unique insight into the affairs of the diocese and allowed him to make many annotations in the Catalogue. Contrary to the statements in the ODNB article, we know that his wife's Christian name was Jane and that he died in 1672 not in 1671. LPL VB 1/1/57; *AC*, 87, p. 87; *ODNB*.

Snatt, William [63] BA. Rector of Denton, Sussex, 1671–5. Prebendary of Chichester cathedral, 1675–90. Rector of Lewes St Thomas at Cliffe from 1674 until his cession in 1682. Curate of Lewes St Michael and of Lewes All Saints, Sussex, 1675–8. Vicar of Seaford, 1679–81, and vicar of Cuckfield, Sussex, 1681–90. Deprived by 1690 as a nonjuror, lost his remaining preferments and was briefly imprisoned in 1696 for his part 'in publicly absolving, with the imposition of hands, Sir John Friend and Sir William Parkyns on the scaffold when they were executed for their share in the Assassination Plot against William III'. He died in 1721. CCEd Person ID: 66785; LPL, VG 1/5, p. 52, VB 1/4/173; *ODNB*; Overton, pp. 216–18.

Snelling, Thomas [32, 33] BD. Possibly the Thomas Snelling ejected from St John's College, Oxford, in 1648 'as having been in arms against Parliament'. Rector of Snave in 1662 and curate to **Samuel Crosswell**, at Wittersham in 1663. Received dispensation to hold Snargate with Snave in 1667 and held both rectories until **Robert Richards**, was collated in 1669. CCEd Person ID: 103214; Matthews, *Walker*, p. 33; LPL, VG 1/2 fo. 20, VB 1/2/69, 168.

Somner, William [xxvi, xliii, xliv (3), li, lxiii] Antiquary, Anglo-Saxon scholar and important official of the diocese of Canterbury. Proctor of the consistory court at Canterbury from 1638 and acted as deputy registrar from 1639 to 1643 (his father was the registrar). In 1660, he was appointed registrar of the commissary and consistory court for the city and diocese of Canterbury, and auditor and deputy receiver general of the cathedral. In 1662, he was the effective deputy to the principal registrar to the archbishop. CCA, DCc-ChAnt/S/406, BB/W/12, VP/6, 9, DCc/LitMS/C/5; LPL, CM 28/4; Fincham, 'Somner and Laud', unpublished paper, 2019; *ODNB*.

Sonds or **Sondes, George** [16, 50, 52] First earl of Feversham. MP for Higham Ferrers in 1628 and sheriff of Kent in 1637. Imprisoned in 1645 and only released in 1650 by compounding for his estate by paying £3,350. In 1655, Major General Kelsey called him 'a great enemy of the state', but his worst tragedy was the murder of his son, George, by his younger brother, Freeman, who was hanged at Maidstone in August 1655. He was MP for Ashburton, Devon, 1661–76 and died in 1677. He had a thirty-two hearth house in Sheldwich and other houses in Eastry and Throwley. *ODNB*; Cliffe, p. 476.

Sonds, Mart. [53] This should be Sir Michael Sondes, of Throwley, who died in 1617. He had been sheriff of Kent in 1684 and was MP for Maidstone in 1584 and for Queenborough between 1586 and 1604. *HoP*; Hasted, VII, 42.

Soutchote or **Southcote, John** [59b] John Southcote was knighted in 1646 and made his will in 1685, having purchased the manor of Albury, Merstham, in 1678. Nothing else known. TNA, PROB 11/380/282; Shaw (1906), II, 220; www.british-history.ac.uk/vch/surrey/vol3.

Southland, Mrs [11] Probably the widow of Thomas Southland of Ickham, who compounded for £500. She lived in an eight hearth house in Ickham. Cliffe, p. 474; Harrington, p. 384.

Sowton, Stephen [44] MA. Instituted to the rectory of Staplehurst in 1662 and was buried there, as rector in 1684. Archdeacon Sancroft feared that Sowton was 'somewhat vain in his conversation'. CCEd Person ID: 140288; Bodl., MS Sancroft 99, p. 192; KFHS, Staplehurst Burials.

Sparrow, Anthony [73r] DD. Bishop of Exeter, 1667–76, and bishop of Norwich, 1676–85. *ODNB*.

Speed, Matthew [62 n. 165] BA. Vicar of South Bersted from 1650 until his death in 1678. In 1671, it was reported that 'The Vicar is one Mr. Speede his tattered thatched howse hard by the Church. By his more than beggarly habit and his sottish look, and as I heard his wicked life are all great scandalls to the Church.' CCEd Person ID: 68756; LPL, COMM II/73; Venn, IV, 129; *SAC*, 24, pp. 172, 174, 178, 53, p. 196.

Spencer, John [24, 24 nn. 55, 56] MA. Vicar of Newchurch in 1657 but replaced by **Paul Knell** in 1660. Vicar of Elmsted in 1661 noted in the visitations of 1662 and 1664, and remained until his death in 1665. LPL, COMM III/6, p. 91; KHLC, DCb/V/V/56, 58; Matthews, *Calamy*, p. 455.

Spier, James [43] Not identified.

Spinedge, Anthony [58] BD. Vicar of Impington, Cambs., 1677–9, and vicar of Guilden Morden, Cambs., in 1677. Fellow of Jesus College, Cambridge, 1671–80 and rector of St Mary Aldermary united to St Thomas the Apostle from 1679 until his death in 1694. Lawrence Newton, John Burdett and William Polhill were appointed in 1685, 1691 and 1692, respectively, to be coadjutors 'to be responsible for cure of souls there on account of the rector's infirmity'. CCEd Person ID: 19618; Venn, IV, 135.

Spraling, – [10] Probably Robert Sprackling, who lived in an eight hearth house in Chilham. Harrington, p. 323.

Sprigg, Joshua [55] Independent minister and chaplain to the New Model Army who opposed the execution of Charles I. Retired to his estate in Crayford after the Restoration, and married Frances **Lady Saye**, the widow of James Fiennes, Second Viscount Saye and Sele. Local hostility to them keeping conventicles in their house caused them to move to Highgate, London. He died in 1684. *ODNB*.

Stacey, John [xxxix n. 13, lxv n. 171, 56b] MA. Instituted as rector of Ridley, Rochester diocese, in 1660 and remained until his death in 1680. As chaplain to the duke of Lennox and Richmond he was dispensed to hold the rectory of Ifield in 1666, but resigned to become rector of Hartley in Rochester diocese in 1667, holding it until 1680. CCEd Person ID: 3375; LPL, VH 2/25/1, 2/25/2, F I/C fo. 197; Venn, IV, 141.

Stanhope, Michael [35] BA. As chaplain to the marquess of Winchester, was instituted to the rectory of Boughton Malherbe in 1675 and held it in plurality with the rectory of Langton, Yorks., having obtained a royal warrant, as the two livings were beyond canonical distance from each other. He remained rector of Boughton Malherbe until his death in 1724. CCEd Person ID: 55950; LPL, VB 1/3/268, 1/7/70, F I/D fo. 112v.

Stanley, William [17, 19, 19 n. 36] MA. Curate of Hawkinge in 1633 and curate of Folkestone from 1633 until 1637. In the following year, he became vicar of West Tarring and its chapels, which were peculiars of the archbishop in Sussex. He was ejected in 1645 'because of his service in the royalist army in the Sussex campaign of 1643', restored in 1646 but left the parish in 1648. He was appointed rector of Ripple and curate of Walmer in 1648 and served them both until his death in 1680. In the Catalogue, the entries for Stanley and Osborne have been transposed on fo. 19. CCEd Person ID: 38615; *AC*, 27, p. 241; Shaw (1900), II, 261; West Tarring, pp. 270–80; *SAC*, 30, pp. 132–3.

Stanton or **Staunton, Ralph** [41, 41 n. 97] MA. Said to be curate of Bredhurst in 1677. Sinecure rector of Hollingbourne, 1677–94, and vicar of Ickleton, Cambs., 1678–84. Briefly rector of Avington, Hants., in 1684, he was instituted as rector of Wilford, Notts., in 1685, serving until his death in 1694. CCEd Person ID: 20415; LPL, MS 1137, p. 82, VG 1/5, p. 67.

Starre, – [35, 38] Comfort Starre MA (Harvard). Emigrated from Ashford with his father to New England in 1635. Fellow of Harvard in 1650. Returned to England in that year and settled in Cumberland, becoming curate of St Cuthbert's, Carlisle, in 1656. Attended the Savoy Conference in 1658. Ejected from Carlisle in 1660 and returned to Kent. Congregational minister at Lewes around the turn of the century and died there in 1708. Hardman Moore, p. 180; Matthews, *Calamy*, p. 460.

Stede, William [xliv (2)] DCL. Son of Sir William below. Advocate of Doctors' Commons in 1623 and official principal of the archdeacon of Canterbury, 1628–72. Ordered to appear before the Cromwellian Commission in 1655 regarding his presence in Maidstone during the rebellion of 1648 and accused of 'supplying arms, money, horses and men to the Royalist party'. Potter, p. 188; Bloomfield, p. 14; Foster, IV, 1415.

Stede, William [49] Sir William was a member of the Stede family, who had their seat in Harrietsham. He married one of the Culpepers and presented William Culpeper to

Wychling in 1628. His son, William, presented **Thomas Conway** in 1661. Hasted, V, 449 *et seq.*, VI, 143, 553.

Steed, Mr [48] Edwin Stede Esq. Another member of the Stede family. Hasted, V, 449 *et seq.*, VI, 143.

Stephens, Samuel [14] BA. Curate at Adisham with Staple in 1617 and curate of Wingham from 1619 until his death sometime before 1676. He was registered as an approved minister in 1656. CCEd Person ID: 38626; LPL, COMM III/1, p. 56; Whiteman, p. 35.

Sterry, Nathaniel [60] BD. Described as an 'ardent Cromwellian' but conformed after the Restoration. Rector of Bocking, Suffolk, from 1674 until his death in 1698. In 1676, he was commissioned, jointly with **Thomas Cooke**, 'to exercise jurisdiction within deanery of Bocking' and this was renewed in 1678 and in later years until his death in 1698. He is alleged to have been rector of Stuston, Suffolk, in 1662 but he was only dispensed to receive orders of deacon and priest together in 1666. Venn also gives details of Nathaniel Sterne, rector of Stuston from 1662 until his death in 1673. CCEd Person ID: 142901; LPL, F II/7/111, VB 1/3/233; Venn, IV, 160; Foster, IV, 1422; *ODNB*.

Stockar, John [1, 3] MA. Possibly related to Johannes Jakob Stockar, who, at the instigation of the Swiss protestant canons, met Cromwell in 1653 and mediated between England and the Netherlands. John Stockar was instituted rector of Canterbury St Alphege and vicar of Canterbury St Mary Northgate in September 1663, serving them both until his death in 1708, aged eighty-four. CCEd Person ID: 140291; Dunkin, II, 332; Oechsli, p. 421; *Topographer*, 218.

Stokes, John [lxiii, 9] MA. Licensed as a teacher in Elham in 1661, he was instituted to Brook in 1669 and died in 1672. CCEd Person ID: 70474; Willis (1975), p. 1; LPL, VB 1/2/196; Venn, IV, 166.

Stoyning, or **Stoning, John** [58] MA. Instituted as rector of St John the Evangelist Friday Street, London, in 1663 but the church was destroyed in the Great Fire of 1666. Rector of St Andrew by the Wardrobe, London, from 1673 until his death in 1694, and probably also rector of St Ann, Blackfriars, London, during the same period. CCEd Person ID: 166694; Foster, IV, 1430; LMA, P69/JNE, P/69/ALH2, P/69/ANN.

Stradling, George [lxv n. 174, lxvi, 176, 49 n. 113, 55] DD. Son of a baronet, Fellow of All Souls, Oxford, he was ordained in November 1660 and became chaplain to **Gilbert Sheldon**, while the latter was bishop of London. Prebendary of St Paul's Cathedral and of Westminster Abbey, vicar of Cliffe at Hoo in 1663 until his death in 1688, whilst holding the rectory of Fulham, Middx. Later the dean of Chichester Cathedral. CCEd Person ID: 3443; *ODNB*; LPL, VB 1/1/23.

Strangford, Lord [4, 23, 31] Philip Smythe, second viscount. MP for Hythe in 1660. He had houses in Stanford (sixty hearths), Sturry (twenty hearths) and Herne (nine hearths). *HoP*; Harrington, pp. 346, 364, 370.

Stringer, – [35] Not identified.

Stringer, William [31 n. 72] BA. Instituted as rector of Orlestone in 1669 and possibly remained until 1682 but no further record. CCEd Person ID: 140292; LPL VB 1/2/184.

Sutton, William [44] MA. Vicar of Detling and curate of Sutton by Dover in 1639 then disappears from view until 1661 when he was instituted to the rectory of Thurnham with Allington. Died in 1673. CCEd Person ID: 38662; LPL, VB 1/3/214; Venn, IV, 188; Hasted, IV, 359.

Swadlin or **Swadling, Thomas** [21, 22 (2), 22 n. 45] DD. Curate of Tredington, Worcs., from 1622 to 1628 then curate of St Botolph Without Aldgate, London, from 1628, but imprisoned several times from 1642, and formally sequestrated in 1655. Restored in 1661 but resigned in 1662. Appointed vicar of Hougham in 1662 and curate of Dover St Mary the Virgin in 1663, he also held Dover St James the Apostle from 1662 until 1664, when he resigned all of his Kent livings and became rector and vicar of All Saints with St Peter, Stamford, Lincs. He died in 1670. CCEd Person ID: 17118; Matthews, *Walker*, p. 59; LPL, VG 1/2 fo. 5v, VG 1/4 fo. 2, VB 1/1/100; Hegarty, p. 445.

Swan, William [56a] Sir William of Hook Place, Southfleet, with fifteen hearths. JP in 1665, 1666, 1670. Hasted, II, 435; KHLC, Q/J/C/10, 11, 12; Harrington, p. 71.

Sweit, Giles [lxiv, lxix] LLD. Knighted in 1664, he was variously: president of Doctors Commons, dean of the Arches, official principal of the court of Canterbury and dean of Shoreham, Croydon and Risborough and a prebendary of Salisbury cathedral. He died in 1672. CCEd Person ID: 75656; Squibb, pp. 46, 117; LPL, VH 98/3/84; Foster, IV, 1446.

Swift, Thomas [59a, 59a n. 139] MA. Possibly rector of Thorpe Mandeville, Northants., in 1660 and rector of St Edmund the King and Martyr London from 1666 until perhaps 1670. CCEd Person ID: 166736; Foster, IV, 1447.

Sydway or **Sidway, John** [53, 53 n. 118] MA. Vicar of Selling from 1677 until his deprivation in 1680. CCEd Person ID: 65929; CCA, DCc-SVSB/2/167/2; LPL, VB 1/4/111.

Symonds, Samuel [47 (2)] BA. Curate of Minster-in-Sheppey from 1661 until 1664 and admitted as rector of Murston during the latter year. He was licensed to the cure of Rodmersham in 1675, signed the Compton census as curate in 1676 and served Murston and Rodmersham, until his probable death in 1694. CCEd Person ID: 140294; Bramston, p. 85; Willis (1975), p. 47; Whiteman, p. 29; Foster, IV, 1451.

Sympson, – [37 n. 86] A man with the surname of Sympson is noted as the vicar of Kennington in 1662 but he cannot otherwise be identified and may have been ejected. KHLC, DCb/V/V/57.

Tanner, Thomas [xlii, xliii, xliv] DD. Bishop of St Asaph, 1732–5. CCEd Person ID: 20461; *ODNB*.

Taverner, Captain [lix, lx, 16] Samuel Taverner, captain of a troop of horse in the parliamentary army, was commissioned as governor of Deal castle in 1653. He resigned in 1660 and was baptized in 1663, becoming an elder and pastor of the baptist church in Dover. He died in 1692. Ivimey, IV, 511; Lyon Turner, I, 16; https://doverhistorian. com/2013/07/29/samuel-taverner-the-dissident-preacher-who-was-imprisoned-in-the-castle.

Taylor, Francis [3 n. 11] MA. Although blind, he was admitted as rector of Canterbury St Mary Bredman in 1648 and remained until his ejection in 1660, but was still noted as rector in the visitation of 1662. Matthews, *Calamy*, p. 477; KHLC, DCb/V/V/56.

Templeman, – [46] Not identified.

Terry, David [12 n. 26, 14] MA. Curate of Eastry with Worth in 1662 and curate of Ickham in April 1663. He was instituted to the vicarage of Waltham in September 1663 and given dispensation to hold it along with the vicarage of Petham in 1669. He probably died in 1691. CCEd Person ID: 140296; KHLC, DCb/L/R/17, p. 2; LPL, VG 1/3 fo. 8v, 1/4 fo. 1v, 1/2/186.

Thanet, earl of [27, 37 (2), 64, 64 n. 177] John Tufton, second earl of Thanet. His support for the royalist cause forced him to compound and he was fined £9,000, but he sided with parliament during the Kent rising of 1648. He was patron of the rectory of Hothfield Place, but he also had a twenty-four hearth house in Maidstone and another, with twelve hearths, in Bobbing. Harrington, pp. 190, 267, 301; Cliffe, p. 475.

Thatcher, – [41 (2)] Thomas Thatcher had a ten hearth house in Frinsted and owned the advowson of the rectory. He paid Decimation Tax of £5 in 1656. Harrington, p. 97; Cliffe, p. 443.

Theaker, Thomas [xlix] MA. Curate at New Romney to the non-resident vicar **Robert Bostocke** in 1672 and appointed as curate at Old Romney and Brensett in 1689. Unknown tenures and no other records found. CCEd Person ID: 124516; Willis (1975), pp. 45, 51.

Thomas, Thomas [60] Dr. Not identified.

Thomas, William [41 n. 97] BA. Curate at Tenterden in 1668 and in the same year, he was collated to the vicarage of Hollingbourne. In 1678, several clergymen entered into an engagement to supply the cure during Thomas's illness. He probably died in 1684. LPL, VG 1/5/26; Bodl., MS Tanner 124, fo. 51; Willis (1975), p. 44.

Thompson, Mr [xxxix n. 14, 60, 60 n. 147] Joseph Thompson MA. Vicar of St Dunstan in the West, London, 1662–78, and curate of Mortlake from 1672 until his death in 1678. CCEd Person ID: 166904; LPL, VB 1/3/59, VH 5/1; Venn, IV, 225.

Throckmorton, W. [59b] Sir William Throckmorton first baronet. Died 1628. *ODNB*.

Thornhill, [51] A descendant of Richard Thornhill, who purchased the advowson of Harty in Elizabethan times. Hasted, VI, 283.

Thurman, Edward [41] MA. Father of Henry below. Schoolmaster at Staines in 1619. Curate of St Mary le Strand, London, in 1627 and rector of Great Hallingbury, Essex, from 1629 until his ejection in 1643. Minister at St Michael Royal, London, in 1658 and vicar of Goudhurst from 1662. Signed the Compton census at Goudhurst in 1676 and died the same year. CCEd Person ID: 7212; Matthews, *Walker*, p. 165; Whiteman, p. 30; Venn, IV, 239; Foster, IV, 1484.

Thurman, Henry [63, 64] Probably Henry Thurman MA. Rector of Lewes St Anne, Sussex, from 1662, and as chaplain to Joseph Henshaw, bishop of Peterborough, was dispensed to hold in plurality Lewes St John sub Castro, Sussex, from 1666. Prebendary of Chichester cathedral from 1667 until his death in 1669. CCEd Person ID: 70667; LPL, F V/1/II fo. 13v; Horn, II, 64.

Tilden, Richard [46, 47] BA. Subscribed as rector of Kingsdown in 1661 but was not instituted until 1662. He is recorded in the visitation book for that year, and again in 1664, but not thereafter. He is also recorded for these years, as the rector of Milstead, thus explaining the Catalogue entry, but he was not instituted until 1668. He died as rector in 1688. CCEd Person ID: 140297; LPL, VB 1/2/144; Dunkin, I, 9; KHLC, DCb/V/V/57, 58; Venn, IV, 283.

Tilson, Edward [56a] MA. Appointed as vicar of Eynsford in 1670, was dispensed to hold the rectory of Lullingston, Rochester diocese, in plurality in 1672. He died in 1726 and was succeeded in both livings by his son Edward. CCEd Person ID: 3567; LPL, F I/D fo. 40, F I/G fo. 55; Venn, IV, 243.

Toke *see* **Toke**, **Tooke** and **Tuck**, below.

Toke, Nicholas [36, 37 n. 86] MA. Instituted as rector of Eastwell in 1644 and remained until his death in 1670. He was also vicar of Kennington, 1664–70. He had a four hearth house in Westwell. CCEd Person ID: 81180; LPL, VB 1/3/29; KHLC, DCb/V/V/58, 64; Harrington, p. 333.

Tomkins, Tomkyns or **Thomkins, Thomas** [21, 36, 58 n. 136, 62, 73r] DD. A chaplain to Archbishop Sheldon and a 'zealous royalist' and polemicist, he was instituted to Great Chart in 1667 and held it along with St Mary Aldermary, London, which had been destroyed by the Great Fire. He resigned them both in 1669 and became rector of Lambeth and prebend of Exeter cathedral, followed by the rectory of Monks Risborough, Bucks., in 1672, retaining these three preferments until his death in 1675. The Catalogue mentions him as the curate of Folkestone, but no other evidence has been found to substantiate this. CCEd Person ID: 96305; *ODNB*.

Tooke, – [47] The patron of Milstead, this would have been another of the **Toke** family.

Tray, Richard [47] MA. Vicar of Milton Regis, 1654–5. Rector of Murston from 1659 until his death in 1664. CCEd Person ID: 151524; Matthews, *Walker*, p. 226; LPL, VB 1/1/95.

Trott, Robert [53] Very little known about this man, who was collated to Stalisfield in 1641 and may have remained throughout the Interregnum. He subscribed as vicar in 1662 and died in 1664. CCEd Person ID: 81185; LPL, VG 1/2 fo. 8, VB 1/1/111.

Tuck, Captain [27, 36] Nicholas Toke of Godinton, known as the Captain. One of a large family; he was the uncle of **Nicholas Toke**, rector of Eastwell, and of **Richard Hulse** of Bethersden. Also a brother-in-law of **Richard Tilden**, rector of Kingsdown and Milstead. Owner and tenant of extensive landholdings in Kent and sheriff of Kent in 1663. His estate was centred on the fifteen hearth Godinton House in Great Chart. Married five times, his second wife was the sister of Sir **Norton Knatchbull** and his fifth, the daughter of **Thomas Finch**, earl of Winchelsea. He died in 1680, aged ninety-two. Lodge, *passim*; Harrington, p. 301.

Tuck, Mr [22] Probably a member of the **Toke** family, but no identification made.

Tudor, John [li, 49] LLB. Curate at Lydd in 1668 and vicar of Leysdown from 1670 until his death in 1689. Dispensed to hold Warden and rector there, 1675–89. CCEd Person ID: 140298; Dunkin, II, 395; Willis (1975), p. 44.

Tufton, William [34] He had a four hearth house in Wittersham and was named as an anabaptist by the Catalogue. Bate lists Richard Tufton as a presbyterian, whose house was used for conventicles after the 1672 Declaration of Indulgence, but he is not included in the 1664 Hearth Tax schedules. Bate, p. lxix; Harrington, p. 349.

Turner, Thomas [xl n. 24] DD. Dean of Canterbury cathedral, 1644–72. Not mentioned in the Catalogue as he was not an incumbent of a living in Canterbury diocese. CCEd Person ID: 3219; Hegarty, pp. 151–2; *ODNB*.

Turner, Thomas [43] A quaker; one of several who were arrested at a meeting at Staplehurst in 1661. Besse, p. 290.

Turner, Thomas [46] Vicar of Milton Regis from 1673 until his death in 1695. Curate of Bobbing from 1676 until at least 1688 (**Titus Oates** was the absentee vicar). Confused with the president of Corpus Christi College, Oxford, by Venn, Foster and *ODNB*. CCEd Person ID: 173932; TNA, PROB 11/539/376; CCA, DCc-Bond/525; KHLC, DCb/V/V/69–84; Willis (1975), p. 48; LPL, VG 1/6 fo. 140r–v; Whiteman, p. 29.

Turner, William [59b] MA. Instituted as rector of East Horsley, Surrey, in 1670. Probably remained until 1682 but nothing further known. CCEd Person ID: 128261; LPL, VB 1/4/301; Venn, IV, 278.

Twiss or **Twisse, Ralph** [l, lxvi n. 175, 56a, 57] MA. Admitted to the vicarage of Gillingham in 1654 and instituted in 1660. He was also curate of Lidsing, a chapel of Gillingham. He died in 1676. CCEd Person ID: 143027; MA, P153/1/2.

Udney, Alexander [21] BD. He held an MA from Aberdeen University and was collated to the rectory of Hawkinge in 1612 holding it until at least 1637 and was again noted in the visitations of 1662 and 1664. As no other incumbents have been found during the Interregnum, it is conceivable that he may have been present throughout. Licensed to the cure of Folkestone in 1631, he was still there in 1634. CCEd Person ID: 8852; KHLC, DCb/V/V/56, 58.

Ullock, Henry [16] DD. Chaplain to **Heneage Finch**, third earl of Winchelsea. Instituted rector of Great Mongeham in 1665, he was appointed as one of the Six Preachers of Canterbury cathedral in 1673 and made a canon of Rochester cathedral in 1675. In 1683, he became rural dean of Sandwich, probably resigning in 1689 when he became dean of Rochester cathedral. He ceded Great Mongeham and resigned as a Six Preacher in 1690, when he was instituted to the rectory of Leybourne in Rochester diocese. He died in 1706. CCEd Person ID: 3587; LPL, VG 1/4 fo. 4v; Bodl., MS Tanner 124, fo. 84; Ingram Hill, p. 67; Horn, III, 56, 62.

Vaughan, John [27 n. 59] BA. Curate at Hernhill in 1638. Vicar of Appledore, 1651–5. CCEd Person ID: 45082; BL, Add MS 36792, fo. 32.

Venner, Thomas [lviii] Fifth Monarchist rebel and leader of a failed uprising in London in 1661. He was hanged, drawn and quartered and thirteen of his followers were hanged. *ODNB*; *EHR*, 25 (1910), 722–47.

Verier, – [17] Not identified.

Waldron, Joseph [59a] MA. Vicar of Hayes, Middx., 1675–95, and rector of Mells, Somerset, from 1695 until his death in 1719. CCEd Person ID: 143028.

Walker, Henry [34, 37] Instituted to the vicarage of Kennington in 1677 but ceded in 1682 (in favour of John Walker). Vicar of Willesborough from 1681 until 1695 and may have been curate to William Cade at Brook in 1691. Probably died in 1695. CCEd Person ID: 140300; LPL, VG 1/3 fo. 77; Dunkin, II, 421; Willis (1975), p. 52.

Wall, William [57, 57 n. 127] DD. Vicar of Shoreham, 1674–1727. As chaplain to Thomas, bishop of Rochester, he was dispensed to hold the rectory of Milton-next-Gravesend in 1708 retaining it until his death in 1727. CCEd Person ID: 3593; LPL, VH 2/51/1, F II/49/58; Venn, IV, 320; *ODNB*.

Walsall, Samuel [39] MA. Already vicar of Westwell when he subscribed in 1662. He was replaced by William Viney in 1669. CCEd Person ID: 173742; LPL, VG 1/2 fo. 3, VG 1/5 p. 30.

Walter, Henry [43, 43 n. 102] MA. Curate of Loose from 1667 until his death in 1713. CCEd Person ID: 142209; Dunkin, II, 426.

Walter, William [48] MA. Instituted to the vicarage of Rainham in 1665 but resigned in 1676. Nothing further known. LPL, VG 1/4 fo. 4; Dunkin, II, 427.

Walton, Thomas [lxiii, 16] MA. Collated to the vicarage of Waldershare in 1639, he was still there in 1642 and possibly retained it until 1685, but the living is recorded as vacant in the Catalogue fo. 18. He was probably the man intruded into the vicarage of Hougham in 1648. He approved the appointment of the parish clerk at Folkestone in

1661 and was instituted rector of Eythorne in the same year. He held Eythorne until his death in 1698. CCEd Person ID: 48379; Matthews, *Walker*, p. 218; Willis (1975), p. 31; Venn, IV, 328.

Ward, Seth [73r] Bishop of Exeter, 1662–7, and bishop of Salisbury, 1667–89. *ODNB*.

Warham, William [xliii, 38 n. 90] Archbishop of Canterbury, 1504–32. *ODNB*.

Warley, John [34] MA. Curate to Simon Potter at Fowlmere, Cambs., 1664–5. Rector of Charlton, 1666–79, curate of Wye, 1670–5, and vicar of Willesborough from 1672 until his death in 1679. At the Maidstone Assizes in 1677 he was indicted for neglecting to instruct his youthful parishioners in the catechism and neglecting to hold services in the parish church at Wye on 18 February 1677, so that the parishioners consorted instead in common tippling houses. CCEd Person ID: 15711; Willis (1975), p. 44; KHLC, DCb/V/V/69–71; Cockburn (1995), pp. 56, 57.

Warner, John [6] Bishop of Rochester, 1638–66. CCEd Person ID: 3243; *ODNB*.

Warren, Samuel [35] BA. Instituted as rector of Ashford in 1673 and served until his death in 1721, aged eighty-three. He held the sinecure rectory of Blackmanstone from at least 1695, until his death. CCEd Person ID: 4614; KHLC, DCb/V/V/74; Dunkin, II, 434; Foster, IV, 1576; Pearman, pp. 61–2.

Warwick, Earl [60] Probably Charles Rich, fourth earl of Warwick, who died in 1673. Brydges, IX, 400.

Watkins, Thomas [43] A quaker; one of several who were arrested at a meeting at Staplehurst in 1661. Besse, p. 290.

Watson, Louis [53] The Hon. Lewis Watson married Catherine, daughter and coheir of Sir **George Sondes** in 1677. He was MP for Canterbury in 1681 and for Higham Ferrers in 1689. He became third earl of Feversham in 1709 and was created earl of Rockingham in 1714. He died in 1724. *HoP*; Hasted, VII, 42.

Watts, Mr [35] A descendant of William Watts, who purchased the manor of Benenden in 1554. Hasted, VII, 176.

Web, Mr [37 (2)] Probably Richard Webb, a descendant of the Webb family, who had owned the advowson of Frittenden since the sixteenth century. He had a nine hearth house in the parish in 1664. Hasted, VII, 118; Harrington, p. 232.

Webb, John [6] 'Son of John Hog, Turk, sometime a captive', who matriculated from Pembroke College, Cambridge, in 1648. Became the vicar of Herne at some time during the Interregnum and served until his death in 1689. Hasted, IX, 95; Willis (1975), p. 65; Venn, IV, 355.

Webber, Robert [17 n. 32] MA. Appointed as rector of Sandwich St Peter in 1654 but ejected in 1662 or 1663. Master of Sir Roger Manwood's Free School, Sandwich, from 1665 until his death in 1671. Matthews, *Calamy*, p. 516; Cavell and Kennett, p. 221.

Webster, Edward [59b] BD. Rector of Little Sampford from 1660 until his death in 1689 and dispensed to hold the vicarage of Canewdon, Essex, in 1670. Chaplain to James Fleetwood, bishop of Worcester, in 1676 and presented by him to the rectory of Newington, Surrey, holding it from 1681 until 1689. Prebendary of Lichfield cathedral, 1666–89, and chancellor of the diocese of Worcester from 1680. CCEd Person ID: 60493; LPL, F V/1/III fo. 3, F II/22/89, VB 1/3/27, VH 2/42/2, 3.

Wells, Samuel [12] MA. Curate of Nonington with Womenswold, 1662–81, and curate of Folkestone, 1672–89. LPL, VG 1/2 fo. 38, 1/5 p. 41; Matthews, *Walker*, pp. 224, 227.

Wheeler, Major [36] Not identified.

Whiston, John [16] MA. Intruded minister of Brigstock, Northants., from 1655 until the restoration of the previous incumbent in 1660. Presented to the prebend of Kilsby in Lincoln cathedral and installed by proxy in 1660 but ineffective, as the precentor gained possession. Instituted to the rectory of Sudborough in 1660 but no further record. Instituted vicar of Eastry with Worth in 1661 and probably died there in 1694. CCEd Person ID: 140304; Matthews, *Walker*, p. 282; Horn, IX, 75; Venn, IV, 384.

Whiston, Samuel [37] BA. Instituted to the vicarage of Headcorn in 1673, his death was reported in 1716. He signed the Compton census in 1676 as curate of Smarden and vicar of Headcorn. CCEd Person ID: 71671; LPL, VG 1/5, p. 45, VB 1/6/227; Whiteman, pp. 26–7.

White, Blasé [2, 18] MA. Appointed minor canon of Canterbury cathedral in December 1660 and instituted to the rectory of Canterbury St George the Martyr in 1661. In 1663, he was instituted as rector of the ruined church of Stonar. He held the three positions until 1666 but probably then moved from Kent, retaining Stonar, and in 1677 becoming a vicar choral of Lichfield cathedral. CCEd Person ID: 60530; CCA, DCc-TB/1–4; LPL VG 1/3 fo. 22v, VB 1/2/23.

White, John [23 n. 49, 47, 48] BA. Curate of Bapchild in 1662 and curate to **Robert Pory** at Hucking in 1663, he was noted as the vicar of Rodmersham in 1662, probably staying until 1670. In 1666, he was instituted as vicar of Halstow and in 1671 he became curate of Iwade, serving these two parishes until his death in 1706. On fo. 23, the Catalogue lists him as the vicar of Sheperheath (Shepreth in Cambridgeshire). A John White was instituted to this parish, on 5 September 1672 but was not inducted, as Benjamin Layer was instituted eight days later and served until 1681. CCEd Person ID: 140305, 17340; LPL, VB 1/2/26, VG 1/5, p. 43; Willis (1975), pp. 42, 45; KHLC, DCb/V/V/95.

White, Thomas [lxiii, 17, 17 n. 33, 46] MA. Instituted to the rectory of St Mary on the Hill, London, in 1661 and given dispensation to hold it along with Eastchurch in 1667 as the former church had been 'consumed by the Late Lamentable Fire'. Probably the sequestrator at Sandwich St Peter 1668–71. He died in 1682. CCEd Person ID: 140308; LPL, VB 1/2/45, 46.

White, Thomas [58] DD. Vicar of Newark on Trent, Notts., 1660–6, rector of All Hallows the Great, London, 1666–79, and rector of Bottesford, Leics., 1679–85.

Archdeacon of Nottingham, 1683–5, and bishop of Peterborough from 1685 until 1690. One of the nonjuring bishops, he died in 1698. CCEd Person ID: 104963; Venn, IV, 389; *ODNB*.

Whitgift, John [xlvi, 56b, 58] Archbishop of Canterbury, 1583–1604. *ODNB*.

Whitlock, Richard [li, 35, 40 n. 95] LLB. Perhaps vicar of Elvetham, Hants., in 1656. Instituted as vicar of Stowe, Bucks., in April 1661 but did not remain. He was presented to Chart next Sutton in June 1662, then to Ashford in August before his institution there as vicar in September 1662. He died in 1666. CCEd Person ID: 7215; Foster, IV, 1620; Matthews, *Walker*, p. 227.

Whitmore, Lady [43] Identification uncertain. Possibly Mary, the widow of Sir George Whitmore, lord mayor of London in 1631–2, or could be Elizabeth, daughter and heir of Sir William Acton and wife of Sir Thomas Whitmore. *ODNB*; *HoP* (entries relating to a possible husband).

Whittaker, – [48] Not identified.

Whittle, Robert [lxvi, 56a] MA. Instituted to the vicarage of East Malling in 1628 and appears to have survived the Interregnum, serving until his death, aged eighty-one, in 1679. CCEd Person ID: 45162; Hasted, IV, 517; Venn, IV, 397.

Wickens or **Wickins, William** [51, 52] MA. Rector of Kennington, 1670–7, and rector of Eastling from 1678 until his death in 1718. Rector of Eastwell from 1670 until his resignation in 1684 and vicar of Lynstead, 1681–1718. Also noted as curate at Hothfield in 1670 and was made rural dean of Ospringe in 1683. CCEd Person ID: 104988; Willis (1975), p. 44; KHLC, DCb/V/V/64; Hasted, VI, 307, 437, VII, 411; *AC*, 21, p. 174.

Wickings, Henry [43] The quaker brother of **James**, below. He refused to pay tithes and died in prison in January 1664. Besse, p. 294.

Wickings, James [43] A quaker and a refuser to pay tithes. He had cattle taken from him in 1661 and was imprisoned in 1663. The following year, he was committed to Canterbury jail by a writ *De Excommunicato Capiendo* for not paying tithes, then removed to Maidstone jail where he is said to have remained for nine years. Besse, pp. 293–4.

Wilcox, Joseph [59a] MA. Instituted to the vicarage of Harrow on the Hill with the chapel of Pinner, Middx., in 1662 although a second institution is recorded in 1664. Also curate of Kingsbury, Middx., from 1683, he served both offices until his death in 1702. CCEd Person ID: 22949; Venn, IV, 405.

Wildbore, – [17] Not identified.

Wilde, William [58 n. 131] Sir William Wilde, judge and politician, *c.* 1611–79. *ODNB*.

Wilford or **Wilsford, Edward** [l, li (3), 22, 30, 30 n. 66] DD. Son of Sir **Thomas Wilsford** below. Captain of a troop of horse, he was wounded at the battle of Worcester. Instituted as the vicar of Lydd in 1660 but given dispensation for non-residence in 1661 and, again, by Archbishop Sheldon in 1664. He died before the collation of **George Screven** to Lydd in 1670. CCEd Person ID: 140313; LPL, F II/1/205a, 205b, VB 1/1/64; Venn, IV, 408; Hasted, IX, 343.

Wilford, Sir James [11] Knighted in 1661, he was the great grandson of the esteemed soldier and army commander in the wars against the Scots in the sixteenth century. He had a ten hearth house in Kingston. *HoP*; Shaw (1906), II, 234; Harrington, p. 412.

Wilford or **Wilsford, Sir Thomas** [l, 42] Father of **Edward** above. MP for Canterbury in 1625 and died in 1646. *HoP*; Hasted, IX, 343.

Wilkinson, James [29] MA. Instituted rector of Hinxhill in 1642. No other incumbents have been found, so he may have stayed in until his death in 1666. CCEd Person ID: 81215; Venn, IV, 410.

Wilkinson, Mr [42] Richard Wilkinson JP attended the assizes in 1657 and 1658 and 1662–5. He had two houses in Lenham; one with ten hearths, the other with six. Harrington, pp. 94, 96; KHLC, Q/J/C/8, 9; Cockburn (1995), *passim*.

Wilkinson, Robert [xl n. 24, lxiii, 17, 17 n. 32, 46] DD. Noted as vicar of Worth, chapel to Eastry in 1652 and appointed to Staple, chapel to Adisham in 1656. In 1660, he became a Six Preacher of Canterbury cathedral and curate of Ash in the same year, probably remaining in the latter until 1663, when he was appointed rector of Sandwich St Peter. He resigned his rectory in 1665 in favour of **John Lodowick**. Instituted as rector of Eastchurch in 1661, he retained it, along with his cathedral office, until his death in 1666. CCEd Person ID: 140312; LPL, COMM III, 5, fo. 656, VB 1/2/27; BL, Add MS 36792, fo. 44; Ingram Hill, p. 61.

Williams, John [lxv n. 174, lxvi n. 176, 57] Collated to the rectory of St Peter Paul's Wharf, London, in 1660, he served until the church was destroyed in the Great Fire. As chaplain to Henry, marquess of Dorchester, he was dispensed to hold the vicarage of Wrotham in 1662, keeping it until his death in 1680. CCEd Person ID: 143031; LPL, VB 1/4/108.

Willis, – [38] Not identified.

Willoughby, Sir William [8] Of Selston in Nottinghamshire, was created baronet in August 1660, and said to be very rich. The Catalogue comments that he was married to 'Sir Morrice Abbot's daughter' but he married Margaret Abbot in 1657. She was the daughter and heir of George Abbott, who was the son and heir of Sir Maurice Abbot and nephew of George Abbot, archbishop of Canterbury, 1611–33. Willoughby died in 1670. Thoroton, II, 265; *Surrey AC*, 3, pp. 254–66.

Willsted, – [38] Not identified.

Wilmot, Thomas [60] MA. Curate of Wimbledon, 1667–9, and curate of Kings Norton from 1669 until his death in 1699. CCEd Person ID: 83118, 143032; Venn, IV, 426.

Wilson, Captain [17] Captain Thomas Wilson. Said to be the incompetent lieutenant-governor of Dover castle in the 1650s. Smith, pp. 191–2.

Wilson, James [42] MA. Curate of Leeds with the chapel of Broomfield from 1664 probably until his death in 1687. Six Preacher of Canterbury cathedral, 1679–87, and rector of Hunton, a peculiar of the archbishop in the deanery of Shoreham, Kent, from 1685 until 1687. He was made rural dean of Sutton in 1683. CCEd Person ID: 143033; LPL, VG 1/4 fo. 3v; Ingram Hill, p. 70; *AC*, 21, p. 174.

Wilson, Nathaniel [30] MA. Instituted as rector of Kingsnorth in 1663 and licensed to teach there in 1664, he remained until his death. He was licensed to the cure of Shadoxhurst in 1667, signed the Compton census, as curate in 1676, and died in the same year. CCEd Person ID: 140318; Willis (1975), pp. 3, 44; LPL, VB 1/4/5.

Wilson, Timothy [30, 32] MA. The son of Thomas Wilson, who had been a member of the Westminster Assembly. Timothy was licensed to teach at Biddenden in 1665 and noted as the teacher there in 1680. He was master of the Sutton Valence Free Grammar School from 1690 until his death in 1705. Curate to **Nathaniel Wilson**, at Shadoxhurst in 1670, he was licensed to the cure of Otham in 1671 and served until 1676. In that year, he was dispensed to hold the rectories of Kingsnorth and Shadoxhurst, holding the latter until 1690, when he was instituted to Great Mongeham and appointed a Six Preacher of Canterbury cathedral. CCEd Person ID: 140319; Willis (1975), pp. 3, 45; Ingram Hill, p. 70; *AC*, 41, p. 101; Venn, IV, 432.

Winchelsea, earl of [10, 36, 51] **Heneage Finch**, the third earl. Royalist and leader of the abortive rising of 1655. After the Restoration, he was appointed governor of Dover and lord lieutenant of Kent. Appointed to the embassy in Constantinople in 1660, remaining until 1669. He owned a forty-seven hearth house in Eastwell. *ODNB*; Harrington, p. 332.

Winsmore, Nathan [45] Recorded as the vicar of Bredgar in the visitations from 1662 until his death in 1671. The birth of Elizabeth, daughter of Nathaniel Winsmore, is recorded in 1651 in Chaceley, Worcs. KHLC, DCb/V/V/56–64; http://freepages.genealogy.rootsweb.ancestry.com/~wrag44/chaceley/chaceleyvol1pt2.htm.

Wolfe, Miles [59a (2)] Described in the deeds presenting **Michael Selby** to the rectory of Hayes, Middx., as of Langford, Somerset, but nothing else found. LPL, VH 2/20/2.

Wood, Thomas [lxvi n. 175, 56a] Incumbent at Hayes, Kent, in 1652, recognized as rector after 1660 and remained until his death in 1679. CCEd Person ID: 143034; Hasted II, 28.

Wood, Thomas [73r] Bishop of Lichfield and Coventry from 1671 but suspended from 1684 until 1687. Died in 1692. *ODNB*.

Wooley, John [xxxix n. 15, xix, 59a, 62] MA. Instituted rector of St Michael Crooked Lane, London, in 1673, instituted rector of Monks Risborough, with the chapel of Owlswick, Bucks., in 1675, and died in that year. CCEd Person ID: 14205; LPL, VG 1/5 pp. 46, 55, VH 95/2188; Lipscombe, II, 420.

Worgar, Stephen [37] MA. Vicar of Ferring, Sussex, 1657–66. Instituted as rector of Frittenden in 1666 but may not have been inducted, as Robert Newton was appointed in January 1667. CCEd Person ID: 72016, 72923; LPL, COMM II/279, VG 1/2 fo. 22v, VB 1/2/38.

Worrall, Francis [51, 51 n. 115, 53] MA. Instituted to the vicarage of Kingsnorth in 1637 and possibly remained in the living until 1662. As chaplain to John, earl of Thanet, he was dispensed to hold the vicarages of Faversham and Preston by Faversham in 1662. He resigned from Faversham in 1665, becoming curate of Davington. In 1667, he was dispensed to hold Preston with the vicarage of Graveney and retained his two vicarages, along with his curacy until his death in 1671. CCEd Person ID: 77160; Dunkin, II, 503; KFHS, Preston next Faversham Burials.

Worth, Mr [73r] Not identified.

Wotton, Lady [35] Katherine Stanhope, countess of Chesterfield and Lady Stanhope. She owned a thirty-seven hearth house in Boughton Malherbe. *ODNB*; Harrington, p. 103.

Wren, George [45, 45 n. 106] MA. Minor canon of Rochester cathedral, 1667–1718. Vicar of Bobbing, 1668–72, and vicar of Chalk, Rochester diocese, from 1669 until his cession in 1680. Vicar of Hoo St Werburgh, Rochester diocese, from 1679 until his death in 1718. CCEd Person ID: 3917; Dunkin, II, 505.

Wroth, John [55] Owner of the thirteen hearth Blendon Hall, Bexley, who was created a baronet in 1660. Hasted, II, 163.

Yardley, Thomas [lxvi n. 176, 56b] MA. Ejected Fellow of Trinity College, Cambridge, became vicar of Hollingbourne in 1652. Subscribed in 1660 but not recorded thereafter. Instituted as vicar of Halling, Rochester diocese, in 1662 but successor appointed in 1663. Collated to the rectory of Hunton in 1662 and remained until his death in 1683. Master of King's School, Rochester, 1660–3. CCEd Person ID: 3927; LPL, VG 1/2 fo. 36; Venn, IV, 487.

Yate or **Yates, William** [lxvi n. 176, 56a] MA. Vicar of Gillingham from March 1679 until his death in November of that year. CCEd Person ID: 175805; Foster, IV, 1700.

Yates, – [31] Robert Yate BD. Rector of Sible Hedingham, Essex, from 1618 but resigned in 1619. Sinecure rector of Newchurch from 1621 but tenure unknown. Curate of St James, Clerkenwell, London, from 1625 until 1631. Dispensed to succeed his father, Richard, as rector of Badlesmere in 1631 but tenure again unknown. Probably died before 1661. CCEd Person ID: 41740.

Yates, John [55] MA. Instituted to the rectory of Crayford in July 1660, and may have remained until his probable death in 1702. As chaplain to Charles, earl of Westmorland, he also held the rectory of Mereworth in Rochester diocese from 1673 until 1702. CCEd Person ID: 143035; LPL, VB 1/3/183, 1/5/46, F V/1/II fo. 81v; Dunkin, II, 242.

Young, John [6] MA. Collated to the vicarage of St Laurence in Thanet in November 1662, but reinstituted in December 1663. He only served this parish and died in 1699. CCEd Person ID: 121710; LPL, VG 1/2 fo. 38, 1/4 fo. 2v; Venn, IV, 493.

General index

Personal names are only listed in the Biographical index. Page numbers of entries from the Introduction are in Roman numerals and folio numbers of entries from the transcription are in Arabic numerals. '(2)' signifies that the term is mentioned that number of times on the folio or page. Parish and chapel names are taken from The Clergy of the Church of England database. Where names from the manuscript are not easily recognized they are entered and cross-referenced to the modern spelling. Where 'Canterbury' refers to the jurisdiction over the peculiars, it has been indexed under 'archbishop'. References in the Catalogue to 'Ch.' or 'Chu. of Cant.', 'Dec. Cap. Cant.', 'D et Cap. Wigorn', 'D. & Chapter of Westminster', churches of Rochester, St Paul's London, Chichester and Windsor have all been indexed under the heading of dean and chapter of the appropriate place. Folios 70r to 72v and 79r to 87r and the entries in 'Number of Parishes' and 'Exempt Parishes' have not been indexed.

Abbreviations

bp: bishop
bpric: bishopric

Acrise   23
Act Book   xliii, 49 n. 113
Acts of Parliament
   Act for Confirming and Restoring of Ministers   liv, 64
   Act of Uniformity   liv (2), lviii
   Conventicle Act 1664   lviii
   Corporation Act 1661   lviii
   Quaker Act 1662   lviii
   Toleration Act 1689   lxxi
Adisham   lx, 8, 13 (2), 17, 17 n. 32 (2)
Albourne   lxvii
Aldington   27, 32 (2)
Alkham   xliii, 20, 21 (2)
Allington   44
anabaptists *see* nonconformity
apothecaries *see* occupations
apparitors   xliv (2),
Appledore   27, 27 n. 59, 28 (2), 34, 39
archbishop of Canterbury
   as impropriator   1, 4, 5, 9, 11, 12, 13, 14, 15, 17 (2), 37, 40
   as impropriator and patron   6 (5), 8, 15 (2), 17, 18 (2), 19 (2), 20 (2), 21 (3), 22 (2), 24 (2), 25, 27, 35, 43 (3), 47, 48, 51 (2)
   as patron   1 (2), 2, 3 (2), 4 (2), 6, 7 (4), 8, 9 (2), 10, 11 (2), 16 (3), 18 (2), 20, 21, 22 (2), 23, 24, 25 (2), 26, 27 (2), 28 (2), 29, 30 (3), 31 (2), 32 (2), 33 (2), 34 (2), 35, 36 (2), 37 (2), 38 (4), 39, 40, 41 (2), 42, 45, 48 (2), 49 (2), 50, 53 (3), 54, 55 (4), 56a (3), 56b (5), 57 (2), 58 (4), 59a (6), 59b (6), 60 (3), 61 (4), 62 (6), 63 (7), 64 (6), 66
   peculiars   xxxvii, xxxix (3), xlv, xlviii, l (2), lxi, lxii, lxiv-lxix, lxx
      administrative structure   lxiv
      definition of   lxiv
      jurisdiction over   55, 59a, 59b, 60, 62 (2), 63 (2), 65 (2)
   archdeacon of Canterbury   xl (3), xli (4), xliii, xliv, lxiii (2)
      as impropriator   13
      as patron   2, 4, 15, 17, 30, 33, 46, 50, 52, 54
   archdeaconry   xl, xli

Archdeaconry Notes ii–v
archdeacon's court xliv (2), lviii
Ash lix (2), lx, 9 (2)
Ash by Campsey *see* Campsea Ash
Ashford xl, 35, 47
Ashstead lxvii
assizes lviii; *see also* Canterbury and Maidstone
augmentation iv, 4 (2), 4 n., 6 (2), 7 (3), 8, 9 (3), 10 (2), 11, 12 (3), 14, 15, 16 (2), 17 (2), 18 (2), 19 (3), 20 (3), 21 (3), 22 (2), 23, 24 (2), 28, 29, 33, 35, 36, 37, 38 (2), 39, 40 (2), 41 (2), 42, 43 (3), 45, 46, 47 (3), 48 (2), 53 (2), 56a (3), 56b, 63

Badlesmere 50, 52
Bangor bpric 73r (2)
Bapchild 45, 48
Barfreystone 15
Barham xlvi (2), 9 (2)
barn *see* parsonage and vicaridge
Barnes lxvi, lxvii, 59b
Barston *see* Barfreystone
Bartholomew ejections *see* ejections
Bath and Wells
  bpric of 73r
  treasurer 73r
Beachborough 20
Bearstead 39
Beauxfeild *see* Whitfield
Beckley 63
Bekesbourne 9, 29
Belgium 1 n. 3
Benenden 35
Berghstead *see* South Bersted
Bersted *see* Bearsted
Bethersden 32 (2), 35, 38
Betteshanger 15, 16, 18 (2)
Bexhill 33 n. 78, 73r
Bexley 40 n. 93, 55
bible *see* church furnishings
Bichborough *see* Beachborough
Bicknor 45
Biddenden lii (2), 35
Bilsington 27
Birchington 5, 6 (2)
Bircholt lii (2), 24, 24 n. 54, 32 n. 75
Bishopridge (Horsham) 63
Bishopsbourne xlvi (4), 9 (3)
Blackmanstone 27, 28, 45

Blean 1
Bobbing 45 (2), 46
Bocking
  deanery of lxiv n. 158, lxiv, lxvii, lxix, 60, 61, 61 n. 156, 87v
  parish of lxvii, 60
Bocton *see* Boughton
Bonnington 27
Book of Common Prayer *see* church furnishings
Borden 45
Borley 60
Boughton Aluph lii n. 110, 10
Boughton Malherbe 35
Boughton Monchelsea 39
Boughton under Blean lv (2), 50
Boxley 40 (2), 40 n. 94
Brabourne 24 (3), 24 n. 52
Brasted 55
Bredgar 45
Bredhurst 1 n. 92, 40, 40 n. 94
Brenzett 13, 27 n. 60, 28 (2)
Bridge
  deanery of xlii n. 38, liii, lix n. 136, 8, 87v
  parish of 9, 12
Brightwell 62
Bristol
  city of 59a
  diocese of lxi n. 141, lxi n. 144, lxii n. 147
Bromley 50
Brook lxii, 9, 23, 24
Brookland 6, 27 n. 60, 28
Broomfield 40, 42 (2)
Broomhill 32
Brownists *see* nonconformity
Buckinghamshire lxiv n. 160, 13, 62 (3)
Buckland near Dover 20 (2), 20 n. 38
Buckland by Faversham 50, 54
Burmarsh 27, 28, 30, 30 n. 67, 46, 48
Burstow lxvii (2), 59b
Buxted lxvii, lxviii, 63

Callow Green, Essex 61
Cambridge, King's College 40 (2)
Cambridgeshire 23 n. 49
Campsea Ash lxvii, 61
canon (law), canonical xlv, xlvii (3), xlviii, xlix, lxiii, liii

Canterbury
　assizes　lix
　cathedral　xl, 1 n. 3, 2 (2), 4 (2)
　　dean and chapter of: as
　　　impropriator　6, 7, 11, 12 (2), 16,
　　　　36, 53, 56b; as impropriator and
　　　　patron　7, 28, 38, 47; as lord of
　　　　the manor　36; as patron　2, 3, 3
　　　　n. 11, 4 (2), 9, 23, 29, 31, 33, 34,
　　　　41, 46, 51, 53, 54, 56a, 56b, 58 (5)
　　　petty canon of　2 (2), 4, 10, 12, 30
　　　prebendary (canon) of　xl (2), xli (2),
　　　　xl n. 24, xlvi (2), xlviii, 1, 2, 7, 8,
　　　　10, 11 (2), 13, 30, 56a
　　　Six Preacher of　xl (2), xl n. 24, xlvi,
　　　　16, 30, 34
　　city of　xl, xlii, xliii, xliii n. 43, xliv,
　　　xlvi, xlvi n. 60, li (2), li n. 104 (2),
　　　lii, liii, lv, lviii, lxii, 1, 1 n. 4, 49 n.
　　　113
　　commissary of　xliv, lxi
　　deanery of　liii, 1, 87v
　　diocese of　xxxix–xli, 23 n. 49, 56a
　　　administrative structure　xl
　　　exempt parishes　xl, xl n. 21, xlii (3),
　　　　xl n. 33, xliii (2), xliv, lxiii, lxv
　　jail　lviii, 9
　　King's School　10
　　parishes of
　　　All Saints　1
　　　Holy Cross Westgate　5, 4 n. 14
　　　St Alphege　lxii, lxiii, 1, 3
　　　St Andrew　1, 3, 3 n.
　　　St Dunstan　xlvi, 1
　　　St George the Martyr　xliii n. 43, 2,
　　　　18
　　　St Margaret　2, 2 n. 10, 30
　　　St Martin　3, 19, 19 n. 36
　　　St Mary Bredin　3
　　　St Mary Bredman　li n. 104, 3
　　　St Mary de Castro　lii (2), 5, 5 n. 17
　　　St Mary Magdalen　3
　　　St Mary Northgate　1 n. 2, 3
　　　St Mildred　xliii, xliii n. 43, lii, 2, 4,
　　　　5, 5 n. 17 (2)
　　　St Paul　3 n. 12, 4, 31
　　　St Peter　li n. 104, 4
　　priory of St Gregory　4 (2), 4 n. 16, 9
　　　(2), 14, 24, 35, 53
　　province of　xli, lxi
Capel-le-Ferne　20, 21

Carlisle　38
carpenters *see* occupations
Catalogue
　format　lxii–lxiii
　provenance and sources of
　　information　xli–xlv
catechizing　36 (2)
catholic recusants　*see* Roman catholics
Castle Rising　lxviii (4), 65
Chadwell St Mary, Essex　29 n. 63
Challock　10, 11
chancel *see* church fabric
changes in ministers　xlii (3), liv–lvii,
　lxvi–lxvii
chaplains　1, 38 n. 90
Charing
　deanery of　lii, liii, lx (3), lxii, 35, 87v
　parish of　li, liii, 36 (2)
Charlton by Dover　20
Charles I　xlvii
Charles II　xxxvii, xli, li
Charlwood　lxvii, 59b
Chart magna *see* Great Chart
Chart parva *see* Little Chart
Chart Sutton　li, 40
Chartham　xlvi, lxiii, 10, 20
Cheam　lxvii, 59b
Chelmsford, deanery of　61 (2)
Cheriton　xlvi, 10, 20
Chevening　55
Chichester
　bp of　63
　bpric of　73r
　city of　63
　dean and chapter of　45
　diocese of　lxi n. 141, lxiv n. 159
　parishes of
　　All Saints　62
　　St Pancras　63
Chiddingstone　lxvi, 55
Chilham　l, 10, 12
Chillenden　10
chirurgeons *see* occupations
Chislet　6
church building condition　9, 10 (3), 11,
　(3), 12, 15, 16 (5), 17 (3), 18, 20
　(3), 22 (2), 23 (2), 24 (2), 25 (2), 26
　(2), 28, 31 (2), 32, 33, 34, 36 (2),
　38, 41, 42 (3), 47 (2), 48, 49, 51, 55
　(3), 56a (2)
church dues　4

church fabric, chancel   9, 10 (4), 11, 16, 18, 20 (2), 22, 24, 25 (2), 41, 42 (2), 55 (2), 56a
church furnishings   xxxviii, liii
　bible   xlv
　Book of Common Prayer   xlv, 10 (2), 24, 27, 34, 42 (2), 47, 55 (3)
　communion table   26 (2), 56a
　communion table rails   lxvi, 56a
　font   xlv, 9, 10, 11, 16, 17, 26 (2), 42, 55 (2), 56a
　surplice   xlv, 4, 9, 10 (4), 11, 12, 15, 16 (2), 17 (2), 18, 20 (3), 22 (2), 23, 24, 25, 26 (2), 27, 28, 31, 32, 33, 34, 38, 42 (2), 43, 47 (2), 48, 55 (2), 56a
churchwardens   4 n. 14, 20, 38
churchyard   38
civil disturbances   lviii
Clare, deanery of   61
classical presbyteries   lvi
Cliffe *see* Lewes St Thomas at Cliffe
Cliffe at Hoo   lxiv, 55
Clive *see* Cliffe at Hoo
cobblers *see* occupations
Coggeshall   60 n. 152
Coggeshall parva *see* Little Coggeshall
Coldred   15, 17 (2)
collation   xxxix, xxxix n. 12, lii, lv (2)
Colsterworth, Lincs.   xlviii
Commonwealth   liv n. 113, lvi (2)
communicants   2, 4, 6 (2), 7, 9, 10 (2), 16 (2), 20 (2), 22, 23, 24, 25, 26, 34, 35, 36 (2), 37 (2), 38 (2), 43, 46, 47, 48, 56b
communion   13, 18
communion table *see* church furnishings
Compton census   xxxviii n. 11, lxix, 73 n. 191
conformity   1, 33, 39
　conformable   1, 2, 6, 16 n. 31, 26, 28, 30, 35, 37, 55 (3), 56a (3), 56b, 57, 63, 64
　conforming   6, 34
　conforming intruders   lvi, lvi
　conformist   lvi (2), 51, 52
　see also orthodox
consistory court   xliv (3), lviii, lxx
conventicles *see* nonconformity
conventiclity [*sic*] *see* nonconformity
convert   lvi (3), 16, 26, 51
converted   34
corn   16, 27, 30 (2), 31, 47

corrupted   38
Cornwall   xli
Cosmus Bleane *see* Blean
Cottenham   73r
Coventry and Lichfield, diocese of   lxi n. 141
Coxhall *see* Coggeshall
Cranbrook   xliv, lii n. 110, liii (2), lix, lx, 36
Cray *see* St Mary Cray
Crayford   lxviii, 55
Cropredy, Oxon.   lxviii
Croydon
　deanery of   xxxix, lxiv, lxiv n. 158, lxvi, lxvii, lxix, 59a, 59b, 59b n. 144, 60 n. 149, 87
　parish of   lxvii, lxix, 59b
Crundale   10
Cuddesdon, deanery of   62
curacy   xlix–li, 4, 11 n. 25, 13 (2), 14 (2), 18, 19 (2), 20, 20 n. 38, 21 (2), 22, 23 (2), 27, 29, 36, 36 n. 84, 37 (2), 38, 38 n. 90, 40 (2), 43 (3), 43 n. 101, 46, 47, 50, 51, 53, 59
curates   xlvi, xlviii, xlix, xlix(2), lv, lxvi (2), 1 n. 5, 3 n. 11, 8, 12, 12 n. 26, 27, 30, 30 nn. 65, 68, 33, 38 n. 91, 40 n. 94, 43 n. 103, 50, 57 (5), 57 n. 129, 61 n. 154, 63 n. 175, 64 n. 184
　unlicensed   l, li, ix

Dallington, Sussex   64
Danbury, Essex   61
Darenth   55
Dartford   xl
Davington   l n. 92, li n. 104, 50
Deal   xl, 16
debt   1
Denge Marsh   i; *see also* marsh
Denton   xlvi (2), 24 (2)
deprivation   53
Derbyshire   lviii
Derwentdale   lviii
Detling   40
dilapidated
　churches   xxxvii, xlv, li, lii, liii, liv, lxiv
　houses   xxxvii, xlv, li, lii, liii (2), liv, lxiv
dilapidations   lii
discreet, discretion   2, 4, 6, 16, 30 (2), 31, 56b

disorderly   38
dispensation   xl, xlvii, xlix (3), l, li, lii
disputers   11
dissent, dissenters, dissenting   xxxvii, xxxviii, xlii, xlv, lviii–lxii, lxiii (2), lxiv, lxvii (3), lxviii (2), lxix (3), lxx (2), lxxi (5)
doctors *see* occupations
Doctors Commons   lxiv
Doddington   50, 52
donative   l n. 92, xlix (2), l (3)
Dover
  castle of   17
  as a Cinque Port   7, 7 n. 19, 17, 38
  deanery of   xlii n. 38, lvii, lix n. 136, lx, 20, 87v
  parishes of
    St James the Apostle   xlix, 22
    St Mary the Virgin   xlvi, 22
    St Peter   23
  town of   lx n. 139, xl, li, lix, 20, 38
Downe   lxix, 57
Dublin castle   lviii
Durrington   63
Dutch   17
Dymchurch   25, 28, 32

Earde *see* Crayford
East Farleigh   55
East Grinstead   64
East Horsley   lxvii (2), 59b
East Langdon   2, 2, n. 6, 15, 19 (2)
East Lavant   lxix n. 193, 62
East Malling   lxvi, 56a
East Peckham   xlviii, lxv (2), 56a, 56b n. 126
East Rising *see* Castle Rising
East Sutton   40, 43 (2)
Eastbridge, parish of   24, 26, 27 n. 60, 28
Eastchurch   17, 27 n. 60, 46
Easter   2, 6 (2), 10 (2), 16 (2), 20, 22, 23, 25, 36, 37, 38, 48, 51
Easter book   6 (2), 35, 58
Eastling   51
Eastry   lii n. 110, 16 (2), 19 (3),
Eastwell   36
Ebony   27, 28
Edburton   lxviii, 63
Egerton   li, li n. 104, lviii (3), 36 (2), 36 n. 84

ejections   xlii, liv (7), lvi (2), lvii, lxvi (2), lxvii, lxx
  Batholomew   lvii
  unrecorded   liv, lxvi
Elham
  deanery of   lix n. 136, lx, 23, 87v
  parish of   24
Elmley   46
Elmsted   24
Elmstone   11, 12
Ely
  bpric of   73r (2)
  diocese of   lxi n. 141, 23 n. 49
Ely Monachorum *see* Monks Eleigh
England   xxxvii (2), xl, lxx, 56b
entry fines   xlvi (2)
Essex   lxiv n. 160, lxvi n. 182, lxvii, 29 n. 63, 33, 55, 60, 60 n. 150, 61
Ewell *see* Temple Ewell
excommunicate   lix, lx, 48
exempt parishes   xl, xlii (3), xliii, xliv, 1, 3, 6 (2), 7, 8, 9, 10, 11 (2), 12, 13, 14 (2), 16, 20, 21, 22 (3), 25 (3), 27, 29 (2), 30, 31 (2), 32, 33, 36, 39, 40 (2), 41, 43 (2), 50, 51; *see also* 'Exempt parishes', pp. xxvi–xxvii
Exeter
  bpric of   73r
  cathedral chancellor   73r
  diocese of   lvi, lxi n. 144
Eynsford
  rectory   lxv n. 169, 56a
  vicarage   56a
Eythorne   16

factions *see* nonconformity
factious *see* nonconformity
Fairfield   29
Falconhurst *see* Hurst
fanatics, fanaticks *see* nonconformity
farmers *see* occupations
Farningham   xlviii, lxv, lxvi (2), 56a
Farnley Wood plot   lviii
fashion   11; *see also* quality
Faversham   lii, lv, 8, 51, 53.
Fifth Monarchists   lviii (3)
fishermen *see* occupations
Fladbury   73r (2)
Fleming   17 (2)
Folkestone   21
font *see* church furnishings

Fordwich   xlii n. 36, 2, 3, 3 n. 13, 15, 15 n. 29
Framfield   lxviii (2), 64
French   1 n. 3
Frenchman   1, 18
Frinsted   41
Frittenden   37

gentlemen   2, 7, 10, 34, 38 (3), 48 (2), 51, 59b; *see also* fashion and quality
Gillingham   l, lxviii, 56a (2)
glebe   2, 6 (2), 10, 11, 16 n. 31, 24, 27, 30 (2), 31, 35 (2), 36, 38, 42, 55, 58, 59b, 64
Glemsford   73r
Glorious Revolution   lxxi
Gloucester
  bpric of   73r
  diocese of   lxii n. 147
Glynde   lxviii (2), lxix, 64
Godmersham   10 (3), 11, 11 n. 24
Goodnestone by Dover   1 n. 92, ix (2), 11
Goodnestone by Faversham   51, 52
Goudhurst   41
Grain   46, 56a, 56a n. 121
Graveney   51
Great Baddow, Essex   lxvi n. 182
Great Chart   xliv, 36
Great Fire of London   lxvii
Great Mongeham   16
Grinstead *see* East Grinstead
Guldeford Marsh   i; *see also* marsh
Guston   3, 3 n. 13, 19, 21

Hackington   4, 37 n. 85
Hadleigh   lxvii, 60
Halden *see* High Halden
Halstead   56a
Halstow *see* Lower Halstow
Halton   62 (3)
Ham   16, 17
Harbledown   lix, 2, 38
Hardres magna *see* Upper Hardres
Hardres parva *see* Lower Hardres
Harrietsham   41
Harrow on the Hill
  rectory   lxvii, 59a
  vicarage   lxvii (2), 59a, 59a n. 142, 59b n. 143
Hartlip   42, 47
Harty   li n. 104, 51

Hastingleigh   25
Hawkhurst   l n. 92, lix, lxii, 37
Hawkinge   21
Hayes, Kent   56a
Hayes, Middlesex
  rectory   l, lxvii, 59a
  vicarage   lxvii, 59a, 60 n. 149
Headacre, Sussex   63
Headcorn   37
Hearth Tax   lix
Hedingham, deanery of   60
Heene   63
Hereford, diocese of   lxi n. 141, lxii n. 147
Herne   6, 15
Hernhill   51
Herst *see* Hurst
Hever   xviii, 56a
High Halden   37
Hinxhill   29
Hithe *see* Hythe
Hoath   6, 7
Hollingbourne
  rectory   40 (2), 41
  vicarage   41, 41 n. 97, 42 (2)
Hope   lii (2), x, 29
Horsham   62, 63
Horton monachorum *see* Monks Horton
Hospital
  Eastbridge   1 (2)
  St Thomas, Southampton (2)
Hothfield   4, 37
Hougham   xlix, 21, 22
Hucking   41 (2), 42
Hunton   lxvi, lxviii, lxxx, 56b
Hurst   29
husbandmen *see* occupations
Hythe
  parish of   25, 26
  town   xl

Ickham   lii n. 110, 11
Ifield   56b
Ightham   56b
impropriators (lay)   l, 3 4, 10, 34, 35, 36
incomes   xxxvii, xxxix, xlv (3), xlvi (6), lxvi (2), lxx
independency *see* nonconformity
independents *see* nonconformity
informants   xxxviii (2), xliv, lvi, lviii, lx, lxv, lxx
insufficiency   64 (2)

Interregnum   xlvi, lvii, lix, lxvi (2)
intruders   lvi (2), lvii (2), lxx, 6, 26, 34, 36, 56b
Ireland   lviii
Isfield   lxviii, lxix n. 193, 64
Ivychurch   li, 9, 29
Iwade   45, 46

justices of the peace   6, 16, 17, 20, 23, 25 26, 35 (2), 36, 38 (2), 42 (2), 46, 56a

Kenardington   29
Kennington   li, 37, 37 n. 86
Kent   xxxix (2), li, liii (2), lviii (2), lix (3), lix n. 135, lx n. 139, lxiv n. 160, lxv, lxx
Kentish Weald   xl, lxx
Keston   56b
king as patron   1, 2 (2), 8, 10, 15, 16, 17, 22, 23, 28 (2), 29 (2), 32 (2), 33, 45, 46, 49, 50, 52, 56b, 59b (2), 64, 65 (2)
Kings Arms   9
King's Lynn St Margaret   65
Kingsdown   46 (2), 47, 56a
Kingsdown with Mappiscombe   46 n. 109
Kingsnorth   30
Kingston   xliv, 11
Kirdford, Sussex   63
Knockholt   l, lxix, 57
Knowlton   16

labourers *see* occupations
Lamberhurst, Sussex   64
Lambeth   xl, xli, xliii (2), xliv (2)
Lancashire   66
Langley   42
Latchingdon   lxvii, 61
lathe of St Augustine   lix, lix n. 135, lix n. 136
Leatherhead   64
Leaveland   52
Leeds   40 (2), 42
Leesdown *see* Leysdown
Lenham   xxxix, li, 42, 43
Lewes St Thomas at Cliffe   lxviii, 60, 63
Lexden, deanery of   60
Leysdown   xlii n. 36, 46
Lichfield and Coventry
 bpric of   73r
 treasurer of   73r

Liddon *see* Lydden
Lidsing   l, lxv, lxix, 57
Liminge *see* Lyminge
Limpne *see* Lympne
Lincoln
 bpric of   73r
 cathedral of   lxviii, 65, 87v
 prebend of   73r
Lincolnshire   lxiv n. 160
Lindfield   lxviii, lxix, 64
Linsted *see* Lynstead
Linton   42
Little Chart   36
Little Coggeshall   lxvii, 60, 60 n. 152
Little Mongeham   18
Littlebourne   12
Llanarmon   73r
Llandaffe
 archdeaconry of   73r
 bpric of   73r
Llandinam with Banhaglog   73r, 73r n. 192
Llansanfrayd   73r (2)
Llanyrys   73r
London
 bp of   46; *see also* 'Compton, Henry', 'Henchman, Humphrey' in the Biographical index
 bpric of   73r
 city of   xl, xliii, lv, lviii (2), lxiv, lxvii, lxx, 7, 44, 46, 49, 49 n. 13, 50, 58
 deanery of the Arches   lxiv n. 158, lxiv, lxvi, lxix (3), 58, 58 n. 131, 59a n. 140, 87v
 diocese of   lxiv n. 159, 59a
 parishes of
  All Hallows ad Fenne *see* All Hallows the Great
  All Hallows Bread Street   lxvii, 58 (2)
  All Hallows the Great   58, 58 n. 132
  All Hallows Honey Lane   lxvii
  All Hallows Lombard Street   58
  Holy Trinity Minories   lxvi
  St Benet Gracechurch   lxvii
  St Dionis Backchurch   xlviii, 58
  St Dunstan in the East   xlviii, 58, 58 nn. 133, 134
  St Edmonds Lombard Street *see* St Edmund the King and Martyr
  St Edmund the King and Martyr   lxix, lxvi, 59a, 59a n. 138

178   GENERAL INDEX

London (*continued*)
    St Edmund Lumbarde Street *see* St Edmund the King and Martyr
    St John the Evangelist Friday Street   lxvii, 58, 58 n. 135
    St John the Evangelist Watling Street *see* St John the Evangelist Friday Street
    St Leonard Eastcheap   lxvi, lxvii, 58
    St Mary Aldermary   58
    St Mary Bothaw   lxvii, 58
    St Mary le Bow   lxvii, 59a
    St Michael Crooked Lane   lxix, 59a
    St Michael Paternoster Royal   59a, 59a n. 137
    St Pancras Soper Lane   lxvii, 59a
    St Swithin London Stone   lxvii
    St Vedast Foster Lane   lxvii, 59a
    St Paul's cathedral   31
        chancellor of   73r
        dean and chapter of   36, 54, 59b
    tower of   lviii
Looes, deanery of   61
lookers *see* occupations
Loose   43, 43 n. 101
lord of the manor   18, 25, 28, 29, 30, 31, 32, 35, 36, 37 (2)
Lower Halstow   41, 47 (2)
Lower Hardres   2, 3, 4
loyalty   1
Luddenham   52
Lydd   l, li (6), 30
Lydden   li, 22, 22 n. 43
Lyminge
    rectory   25
    vicarage   lii, 25 (3), 26 (2)
Lympne
    deanery of   xlii n. 38, lx, lxii, 1, 27, 87v
    parish of   li, 30
Lynn
    Benedictine priory of   lxvii
    deanery of   lxvii, 65
Lynn Regis *see* King's Lynn St Margaret
Lynstead   50, 52

Maidstone
    assizes   lix, lxx
    jail   liii
    parish of   l n. 93, 40, 43 (3), 43 n. 103

    town of   liii, lx, 38, 43
malarial mosquitoes   xl
Mappiscombe   46 n. 109
Marden   43
Margate St John the Baptist *see* St John in Thanet
marsh, marshes, marshland and marsh land   xl (2), xxix, lxx, 9, 16, 27 (4), 27 n. 60, 28, 30, 31; *see also* Denge Marsh, Guldeford Marsh, Romney Marsh, St Mary in the Marsh, Walland Marsh
masons *see* occupations
Mayfield   lxviii (3), 64
Meopham   56b
merchants *see* occupations
Mersham   30
Merstham   lxvii, 59b
Middlesex   lxiv n. 160, 59a, 59a n. 144
Midley   30
Milstead   47
Milton, Bucks. *see* Milton Keynes
Milton by Canterbury   3
Milton by Sittingbourne *see* Milton Regis
Milton Keynes   lxvii, 62, 62 n. 160
Milton Regis   28, 46
Milton Shore, Essex   61
ministers *see* nonconformity
Minster   xlvii, 7
Minster-in-Sheppey   l n. 92, 47, 48 (2)
Mintlyn   lxviii (2), 65
Molash   l, 10, 12
Mongeham magna *see* Great Mongeham
Mongeham parva *see* Little Mongeham
Monks Eleigh   61
Monks Horton   24, 28
Monks Risborough
    deanery of   xxxix, lxvii, lxiv n. 158, xviii, xix, xx
    parish of   lxvii, 62
Monkton   lix, 5 (2), 6 (2)
Montgomeryshire   73r
Mortlake   lxvii, 60
Moulton
    rectory   lxvii, 61
    vicarage   61
Murston   47

Nackington   4
New England   38
New Romney   xlix (4), li, 33

Newchurch
  rectory 31
  vicarage 31, 32
Newdigate 59b
Newenden xlviii, 27 n., 38, 56a
Newington, Oxon. lxvii, 62
Newington, Surrey lxvii (2), lxix, 59b
Newington next Hythe 22
Newington next Sittingbourne 47 (2)
Newnham xlii n. 36, 52
Nockholt *see* Knockholt
non-residency xxxvii, xl, xlvii, xlviii–xlix, lxiv
nonconformity xxxix, lvi, 6, 30, 36 xxxix, lvi,
  anabaptists 1 (2), 2, 7, 10 (2), 11 (3), 12, 17, 18, 20, 22, 34, 36, 46, 48
  Brownists 42
  conventicles lix, lxi, lxix, 4, 37
  conventiclity [*sic*] 22
  factions 17
  factious 6, 9, 41, 43
  fanatics, fanaticks 2, 21, 26, 35 (3), 38 (2), 40, 43
  independency 16
  independents 7, 9, 10, 20
  ministers (nonconformist and ejected) lx, lxi, lxx (4)
  preachers 7, 38, 46, 55
  presbyterians xii (4), 1 (4), 2, 2 n. 9, 6, 9, 10, 11 (3), 15, 16 (3) n. 31, 17 (2), 24, 26, 34, 35 (2), 36, 37, 38, 40 (2), 41, 43, 44, 51 (2), 52, 54, 57, 64
  protestant dissenters lxii
  quakers 7, 10 (2), 11, 17, 20, 22, 25, 38, 43, 46, 56a, 57
  refractory 15
  refusers 25, 26
  ringleaders 35, 36, 38, 46
  schismatics, schismaticall, schismatiques 1, 2 n. 9, 25, 30, 35, 37, 38, 51 (2)
  sectarians lviii, lxix (2)
  sectaries xlv, lvi, lx (4), lxii, 1, 15, 16 (4), 17 (2), 22 (2), 23, 25, 26, 30, 31, 32, 34, 35, 36 (2), 37 (3), 38 (3), 41, 43 (2), 46 (2), 47 (4), 51 (2), 55, 56b, 59b
  teachers 35
Nonington 12, 14 (2), 26

Norfolk liv n. 113, lxiv n. 160, lxviii (3), 65, 65 n. 188, 87v
North Wheatley 56a n. 122
North Wootton lxviii, 65
Northbourne lix (2), lxiii, 17, 18 (2)
Northfleet 56b
Northolt, Middlesex lxvii
Norton 52
Norwich, diocese of lxi n. 144, lxiv n. 159, 65
Norwood l, 59b, 60 n. 149
Nottinghamshire 56a

Oare 52, 53
occupations
  apothecaries 10, 49 n. 113
  carpenters 9, 11, 15, 18, 22
  chirurgeons 49 n. 113
  cobblers 15
  doctors lxi, 29
  farmers 8, 9, 10, 13, 25, 31, 35, 38, 46, 47, 48 (2), 49, 50, 51, 52 (2), 53 (2), 56b
  fishermen 47, 49, 51, 56a
  husbandmen 10, 32, 49, 51, 52 (2), 53 (2)
  labourers 9, 31
  lookers 27, 28 (3), 30, 31 (2), 38, 46, 48
  masons 11
  merchants 38
  scriveners 44
  seamen 7
  schoolmasters lxi, 22, 38 n. 90; *see also* school
  shepherds 27, 27 n. 60; *see also* lookers above
  shoemakers 22, 38
  showmen 35
  soldiers 36
  taylors 18, 35
  thatchers 35
  ushers 10, 66 (2)
official principal lxvi
Old Romney 33
orderly 45, 46 (2), 47, 48, 49, 51, 52 (3), 55, 56b (2)
Orgarswick 27 n. 60, 31
Orlestone 31
Orpington
  rectory lxv n. 169, 56a, 56b (2)
  vicarage 56b

orthodox   36 (2), 49
Ospringe
  deanery of   lxii, 50, 87v
  parish of   51, 52
Ostenhanger *see* Westenhanger
Otford   57 (2)
Otham   l n. 93, 43
Otterden   53
Oxford
  archdeaconry of   73r (3)
  bpric of   73r (3)
    colleges of
      All Souls   33, 41, 46, 49
      Brasenose   56a
      Christ Church   37
      Jesus 49 n.   113
      Magdalen   45
      Merton   24
      Oriol   56a
      St John's   59b
    dean and chapter of   37 (2)
    diocese of   lvi, lxi n. 141, lxii n. 147, lxiv n. 159
Oxfordshire   lxiv n. 160, 62 (3), 65
Oxney, Isle of   xxxix

Paddlesworth   25 (2)
Pagham
  deanery of   xxxix, lxiv (2), lxiv n. 158, lxvii (2), lxix (2), 62, 63 n. 168,
    87v
  parish of   62
papists *see* Roman catholics
parish clerk   9, 17 n. 33
parsonage
  barn   47 (2)
  house   11, 16 (2), 27, 58
  as rectory   6 (2), 9, 10, 21, 25 (2), 27, 28, 36, 37 (2). 40, 41, 43, 45, 47, 48, 49, 55, 58, 64 (2)
Patching   lxvii, lxix n. 193, 63
Patrixbourne   9 (2), 12
patronage   xl, xliii, l (2), liv, lxv, lxviii,
Peckham   lxv, 56b
peevish   6
Penshurst   lxvi, 56b
perpetual curacies   xlvi, xlvii, xlix (2), l (9), 11 n. 25, 20 n. 38, 36 n. 84
Peterborough, diocese of   lxii n. 147
Petham   li n. 104, 12, 14

Pinner   lxvii, 59a, 59a n. 142
Plaistow, Sussex   63
Pluckley   38
pluralism   xxxvii, xxxix, xlv (3), xlvi, xlvi–xlviii, xlvii n. 69 (2), xlviii (4), xlix, lv, lvii, lxiv, lxx
popish recusants *see* Roman catholics
Postling   25, 28
preachers *see* nonconformity
presbyterians *see* nonconformity
Preston by Wingham   12
Preston next Faversham   53
Prittlewell, Essex   61
Promehill *see* Broomhill
protestant dissenters *see* nonconformity
Purleigh, Essex   61
Putney   lxvii, 60

quakers *see* nonconformity
quality   9, 10, 15, 28, 30, 31, 32, 33, 34, 35 (2), 42, 47, 52, 55, 56a, 56b; *see also* gentlemen
Queen Anne   lxxi
Queen Anne's Bounty   l, lxi
Queenborough   l n. 92, 47, 48

radicalism   lviii
Rainham   48, 49
re-establishment   xxxviii, lv, lvi (2), lvii, lviii (2)
rebellion   xxxvii, lix
receiver general   xli, xliv
Reculver   lviii (2), 6, 7
refractory *see* nonconformity
registrar   xliv (4)
resignation   liv, lxvi, lxvii
Restoration   xxxvii, lv (2), lvi (3), lvii (2), lviii (2), lix, lxiii, lxvi (3), lxviii, 56b (2)
restored   xxxvi, xlv, xlvi, xlviii, lv, lvi (2), lxvii, 24, 36
ringleaders *see* nonconformity
Ringmer   lxviii, lxix n. 193, 64
Ringwould   17
Ripple   17, 19 (2)
Risborough, deanery of   62, 62 n. 161, 87v
Risborough Monachorum *see* Monk's Risborough
River   li, 22
Rochdale   66

Rochester
  archdeacon of   9
  bp of   6, 13, 50, 52; *see also* 'Dolben, John', 'Warner, John' in the Biographical index
  cathedral
    archdeaconry of   xlvi
    canon of   xlvi
    dean and chapter of   xl, 19, 35, 38, 39 (2), 40 (3), 41, 42, 43, 44, 47, 48, 55 (2)
    petty canon of   45
    prebendary of   44, 47, 49
  city of   xl, 38
  diocese of   xxxix, xlvi, xlviii, lxi, lxii n. 147, lxiv n. 159, lxv, 46 n. 109, 55
Rochford, deanery of   60
Rodmersham   48
Rolvenden   lxii, 38 (2)
Roman catholics   lxxi
  catholic recusants   lxii
  papists   23, 25, 26, 48
  popish recusants   48
Romney Marsh   xxxix (2), liv, lxii; *see also* marsh
Romney nova *see* New Romney
Romney ventris *see* Old Romney
Rotterdam   lviii
Roydon   lxviii, 65
Royton   43
Ruckinge   xlviii, 27 n. 60, 31, 56a
Runsell, Essex   61
rural dean   lii

St Asaph
  bpric of   73r (2)
  diocese of   lxi n. 144
St David's, diocese of   lxi n. 144, lxii n. 147
St John in Thanet   lviii, 6, 7
St Laurence in Thanet   6
St Margaret at Cliffe   lii n. 110, 22, 23
St Mary Cray   56b, 56b n. 124
St Mary in the Marsh   1, 4, 27 n. 60, 30; *see also* marsh
St Nicholas at Wade   6, 7
St Peter in Thanet   7
Salisbury
  bpric of   73r
  diocese of   lvi, lxi n. 141
  treasurer of   73r

Saltwood   liii, lxvi, 25 (2), 26, 28
Sandhurst   lxii, 38
Sandwich
  as a Cinque Port   16, 51
  deanery of   xlii n. 38, lix n. 136, lx (2), 15
  parishes of
    St Clement   lx, 15 (2)
    St Mary   lx, 17
    St Peter   xlii n. 36, liii, lxiii, 17, 17 n. 33 (2)
  town of   lx, lx n. 139, 17
schismatics, schismaticall, schismatiques *see* nonconformity
school   1 n. 4, 38, 38 n. 90 (4), 66
schoolmasters *see* occupations
Scot, Scottish   9, 12, 21, 24, 26 n. 56, 37, 50, 51, 54, 56b
scriveners *see* occupations
seamen *see* occupations
Seasalter   7, 8
sectarians *see* nonconformity
sectaries *see* nonconformity
Sellindge   32
Selling   53
sequestration   xlvi (2), xlvii, xlix (3), li, 11, 17, 17 nn. 32, 33 (2), 20, 22, 22 n. 43, 24, 25, 28, 36, 49 n. 112, 64
Sevenoaks
  rectory   lxv n. 169 (2), 57
  vicarage   57
Sevington   32
Shadoxhurst   32
Sheldwich   li n. 104, 53
Shepheardswell *see* Sibertswold
shepherds *see* occupations
Sheperheath   23, 23 n; *see also* Shepreth
Sheppey, Isle of   xxxix, 17, 46 (2), 47, 49
Shepreth   23 n; *see also* Sheperheath
shoemakers *see* occupations
Shoreham
  deanery of   xxxix, xlviii (2), lxi, lxiv, lxiv n. 158, lxv (6), lxvi (3), lxix (2), 55, 57 n. 130, 87v
  rectory   l, lxv, 57
  vicarage   57
Shoulden   17, 18
showmen *see* occupations
Sibertswold   15, 17, 26

sinecure   xlv, xlvii, xlix, lxv (3), lxvi, lxvii (3), lxix, 27, 28, 29, 31, 56a (2), 56a n. 121, 57 n. 126, 60 n. 149, 73r
Sittingbourne
  deanery of   lx, 41, 45, 87v
  parish of   27, 28, 30, 45, 48
Slindon   lxvii, 63
Slinfold   lxvii, 63 n. 166
Smallhythe   38, 38 n. 90 (4)
Smarden   liii (2), lx, lxii, 38
Smeeth   27, 32
Snargate   33
Snave   32
Sodor and Man, diocese of   lxi n. 141, lxii n. 147
soldiers *see* occupations
Solemn League and Covenant   liv
South Bersted   62 (2), 62 n. 165
South Malling
  deanery of   xxxix, lxiv, (2), lxiv n. 158, lxvii, lxix, (2), 64 nn. 184, 186, 87v
  parish of   lxvii, lxviii, lxix, xix (4), 64
South Wootton   lxviii, 65
Southchurch   lxvii, 61
Southfleet, Kent   xlvi
stable *see* vicarage
Stalisfield   53
Standish   73r
Stanford   25, 26
Stanmer   lxviii, 64
Stansted   57
Staple   8, 13, 17 n. 32
Staplehurst   44
state of the church   xlv–lxii
steeple   9
Stelling   11, 13
Stifford   60 n. 150
stipend   4, 6 (2), 8, 9, 12, 13, 18, 19 (2), 21 (2), 22, 23 (2), 29, 37, 42, 43, 53, 60
Stisted   lxvii (2), 60
Stockbury   48
Stodmarsh   1 n. 92, 13
Stonar   2, 18
Stone near Faversham   54, 54 n. 119
Stone-in-Oxney   xlii n. 36, 33
Stourmouth   13, 52
Stowting   lxvi, 26

Sturmouth *see* Stourmouth
Sturry   4
Suffolk   lxiv n. 160, lxvii, 60, 61 (3)
Sundridge   lxviii, 57
surplice *see* church furnishings
Surrey   lxiv n. 160, lxvii, 27, 59b (2), 60 n. 149, 62, 64
surrogate   xliv (2), 63, 64
Sussex   lxiv n. 160, lxvii (4), 10, 33 n. 78, 62 (2), 63 (2), 63 n. 166
Sutton by Dover   18
Sutton, deanery of   lx, 39, 87v
Sutton Valence   40 (2), 43
Swalecliffe   7
Swingfield   23, 23 n. 48
symony   41

Tangmere   lxix n. 193, 63
Tarring, deanery of   lxiv (2), lxiv n. 158, lxvii, lxix, 63, 63 n. 171, 87v
taylors *see* occupations
teachers *see* nonconformity
Temple Ewell   21, 22
Tenterden
  free school   38, 38 n. 90 (2)
  parish of   lxii, 11, 38, 38 n. 90 (2)
Terring *see* Tarring and West Tarring
Teynham   xlii n. 36, 54, 54 n. 119
Thame peculiar   lxviii
Thanet, Isle of   xxxix
Thanington   4, 30
thatchers *see* occupations
Throckington   lxvii, 59b, 59b n.
Throwley   54
Thurnham   44
Thursford   lxviii (2), 65
Tilmanstone   18, 20
tithes   1, 2, 4, 6 (2), 11 (2), 12, 15, 16 (3), 22 (3), 24, 27, 28 (2), 30 (3), 31 (2), 35, 36, 40, 41, 43 (3), 44, 46, 56b, 57, 58, 63, 64 (2)
Tong Plot   lviii (2)
Tonge   27 n. 60, 48
Totenhall, prebend of   31 n. 73
Trinitarian   lxxi
Tunstall   49
turmoil   xlv, liv–lviii

Uckfield   lxviii, 63
Ulcombe   44
Upbury   56a

GENERAL INDEX

183

Upchurch   xxxix, lii, 48, 49
Upper Hardres   11, 13 (2)
ushers *see* occupations

vacant livings   xxxvii, xxxix, xlv, li (2),
      liv, lvi, lxviii (2), lxx (2)
vicarage   6, 21 (2), 37, 45, 64 (2)
   barn   6, 41
   house   lii (2), 10, 16, 22, 25, 36, 41,
      49
   stable   41
visitations   lii, lviii
   archidiaconal   xli
   metropolitan   xlii (2), liv, (2),

Wadhurst   lxviii, 64
Waldershare   li n. 104, 18
Wales   xlviii, lxi
Walland Marsh   xl; *see also* marsh
Walloons 1 (2)
Walmer   3, 4 n. 13, 19, 19 n. 34
Walsingham   lxviii
Waltham   xlii n. 36, lviii (2), 14
Warden   li, 49, 49 n. 113
Warehorne   l, 33
Watling Street   xl
Watton, Herts.   lxvi n. 182
weaving   1 n. 3
Wells   11
West Cliffe   23
West Country   xlviii, lxi
West Hythe   1, 33
West Langdon   lii (2), 19
West Tarring
   rectory   lxvii, 63
   vicarage   lxvii, 63
Westbere
   deanery of,   xiv, xlii n. 38, liii (2), lix n.
      136, lx, 5, 87v
   parish of,   xlii n. 36, lii, 8, 51
Westenhanger   31
Westhith *see* West Hythe
Westminster Abbey
   dean and chapter of   57 (3)
   prebendary of   59b
Westwell   39

Whitfield   18, 20
Whitstable   8
Wicheling *see* Wychling
Wickhambreaux   xlvi, 13
Wigan   xli (2)
Willesborough   34
William and Mary   lxxi
Wimbledon
   chapel   lxvii, 60, 60 n. 149
   rectory   lxvii, 60
Winchester, diocese of   xlvii, lxi n. 141,
      lxiv n. 159, lxvii, 59b, 64
Windsor
   castle   lviii
   dean and chapter of   64 (2)
Wingham   14
Wittersham   34, 64
Wivelsfield, Sussex   64
Wodeton *see* Wooton
Woodchurch   34
Woodland   lxv, 57
Woodnesborough   19
Wootton   26
Worcester
   battle of   li
   bp of   59a; *see also* 'Blandford,
      Walter', 'Skinner, Robert' in the
      Biographical index
   bpric of,   73r (2)
   dean and chapter of,   60
   diocese of,   xl, xlvii
   prebendary of,   60
Wormshill   lii, 44
Worth, Kent   16 (2), 19
Worth, Sussex   64
Wotton, Sussex   64
Wrotham
   rectory   lxv, lxv n. 169, 57 (2)
   vicarage   57, 57 n. 128
Wychling   49
Wye   13
Wymynswold   12, 14

yeomen   55
York, province of   lxi
Yorkshire   lviii

Church of England Record Society
COUNCIL AND OFFICERS FOR THE YEAR 2021–2022

Patron
Professor D. N. J. MacCulloch, Kt., M.A., Ph.D., D.D., F.B.A., F.S.A., F.R.Hist.S.

President
Professor Arthur Burns, M.A., D.Phil., F.R.Hist.S. (2017–2021)
Professor Alec Ryrie, M.A., M.Litt., D.Phil., F.B.A., F.R.Hist.S. (2021–)

Acting President
Felicity Heal, M.A., Ph.D., F.B.A., F.R.Hist.S (December 2020–July 2021)

Honorary Vice Presidents
Felicity Heal, M.A., Ph.D., F.B.A., F.R.Hist.S
Professor Alexandra Walsham, C.B.E., M.A., Ph.D., F.B.A., F.R.Hist.S., F.A.H.A.

Honorary Secretary
Mary Clare Martin, B.A., Ph.D., School of Education, University of Greenwich, Maritime Greenwich Campus, London, SE10 9LS (2017–2022)

Honorary Treasurer
Sarah Flew, B.A., Ph.D., Imperial College, London, SW7 2AZ (2016–2021)
Gareth Atkins, B.A., M.Phil., Ph.D., F.R.Hist.S., Queens' College, Cambridge, CB3 9ET (2021–)

Honorary General Editor
Grant Tapsell, M.A., M.Phil., Ph.D., F.R.Hist.S., Lady Margaret Hall, Norham Gardens, Oxford, OX2 6QA

Membership Secretary
Nicholas Dixon, B.A., M.Phil., Ph.D.

Other Members of Council
Mark Byford, M.A., M.B.A., D.Phil. (2021–)
Professor Hilary Carey, B.A., D.Phil., F.R.Hist.S., F.A.H.A. (2021–)
Rt. Rev and Rt. Hon. Richard Chartres, Baron Chartres K.C.V.O., Ch.St.J., P.C., F.S.A. (2017–2021)
Alexandra Gajda, M.A., D.Phil., F.R.Hist.S. (2017–2022)
Matthew Grimley, M.A., D.Phil., F.R.Hist.S. (2018–)
The Very Reverend David Hoyle, B.A., Ph.D. (2021–)
David Ceri Jones, B.A., Ph.D., F.R.Hist.S. (2016–2021)
Professor Stephen Parker, B.Ed., M.A., Ph.D., F.R.Hist.S. (2016–2021)
Sara Slinn, B.A., Ph.D. (2018–)
Anne Stott, B.A., Ph.D. (2019–)
D. L. Wykes, B.Sc., Ph.D., F.R.Hist.S. (2000–2021)

'The object of the Society shall be to advance knowledge of the history of the Church in England, and in particular of the Church of England, from the sixteenth century onwards, by the publication of editions or calendars of primary sources of information.'

PUBLICATIONS

1. VISITATION ARTICLES AND INJUNCTIONS OF THE EARLY STUART CHURCH. VOLUME I. Ed. Kenneth Fincham (1994)

2. THE SPECULUM OF ARCHBISHOP THOMAS SECKER: THE DIOCESE OF CANTERBURY 1758–1768. Ed. Jeremy Gregory (1995)

3. THE EARLY LETTERS OF BISHOP RICHARD HURD, 1739–1762. Ed. Sarah Brewer (1995)

4. BRETHREN IN ADVERSITY: BISHOP GEORGE BELL, THE CHURCH OF ENGLAND AND THE CRISIS OF GERMAN PROTESTANTISM, 1933–1939. Ed. Andrew Chandler (1997)

5. VISITATION ARTICLES AND INJUNCTIONS OF THE EARLY STUART CHURCH. VOLUME II. Ed. Kenneth Fincham (1998)

6. THE ANGLICAN CANONS, 1529–1947. Ed. Gerald Bray (1998)

7. FROM CRANMER TO DAVIDSON. A CHURCH OF ENGLAND MISCELLANY. Ed. Stephen Taylor (1999)

8. TUDOR CHURCH REFORM. THE HENRICIAN CANONS OF 1534 AND THE *REFORMATIO LEGUM ECCLESIASTICARUM*. Ed. Gerald Bray (2000)

9. ALL SAINTS SISTERS OF THE POOR. AN ANGLICAN SISTERHOOD IN THE NINETEENTH CENTURY. Ed. Susan Mumm (2001)

10. CONFERENCES AND COMBINATION LECTURES IN THE ELIZABETHAN CHURCH: DEDHAM AND BURY ST EDMUNDS, 1582–1590. Ed. Patrick Collinson, John Craig and Brett Usher (2003)

11. THE DIARY OF SAMUEL ROGERS, 1634–1638. Ed. Tom Webster and Kenneth Shipps (2004)

12. EVANGELICALISM IN THE CHURCH OF ENGLAND C.1790–C.1890. Ed. Mark Smith and Stephen Taylor (2004)

13. THE BRITISH DELEGATION AND THE SYNOD OF DORT (1618–1619). Ed. Anthony Milton (2005)

14. THE BEGINNINGS OF WOMEN'S MINISTRY. THE REVIVAL OF THE DEACONESS IN THE NINETEENTH-CENTURY CHURCH OF ENGLAND. Ed. Henrietta Blackmore (2007)

15. THE LETTERS OF THEOPHILUS LINDSEY. VOLUME I. Ed. G. M. Ditchfield (2007)

16. THE BACK PARTS OF WAR: THE YMCA MEMOIRS AND LETTERS OF BARCLAY BARON, 1915–1919. Ed. Michael Snape (2009)

17. THE DIARY OF THOMAS LARKHAM, 1647–1669. Ed. Susan Hardman Moore (2011)

18. FROM THE REFORMATION TO THE PERMISSIVE SOCIETY. A MISCELLANY IN CELEBRATION OF THE 400TH ANNIVERSARY OF LAMBETH PALACE LIBRARY. Ed. Melanie Barber and Stephen Taylor with Gabriel Sewell (2010)

19. THE LETTERS OF THEOPHILUS LINDSEY. VOLUME II. Ed. G. M. Ditchfield (2012)

20. NATIONAL PRAYERS: SPECIAL WORSHIP SINCE THE REFORMATION. VOLUME I: SPECIAL PRAYERS, FASTS AND THANKSGIVINGS IN THE BRITISH ISLES, 1533–1688. Ed. Natalie Mears, Alasdair Raffe, Stephen Taylor, Philip Williamson and Lucy Bates (2013)

21. THE JOURNAL OF BISHOP DANIEL WILSON OF CALCUTTA, 1845–1857. Ed. Andrew Atherstone (2015)

22. NATIONAL PRAYERS: SPECIAL WORSHIP SINCE THE REFORMATION. VOLUME II: GENERAL FASTS, THANKSGIVINGS AND SPECIAL PRAYERS IN THE BRITISH ISLES, 1689–1870. Ed. Philip Williamson, Alasdair Raffe, Stephen Taylor and Natalie Mears (2017)

23. THE FURTHER CORRESPONDENCE OF ARCHBISHOP LAUD. Ed. Kenneth Fincham (2017)

24. THE HOUSEHOLD ACCOUNTS OF WILLIAM LAUD, ARCHBISHOP OF CANTERBURY, 1635–1642. Ed. Leonie James (2019)

25. THE FIRST WORLD WAR DIARIES OF THE RT. REV. LLEWE LLYN GWYNNE, JULY 1915–JULY 1916. Ed. Peter Howson (2019)

26. NATIONAL PRAYERS: SPECIAL WORSHIP SINCE THE REFORMATION. VOLUME III: WORSHIP FOR NATIONAL AND ROYAL OCCASIONS IN THE UNITED KINGDOM, 1871–2016. Ed. Philip Williamson, Stephen Taylor, Alasdair Raffe and Natalie Mears (2020)

27. THE RESTORATION OF THE CHURCH OF ENGLAND: CANTERBURY DIOCESE AND THE ARCHBISHOP'S PECULIARS. Ed. Tom Reid (2022)

Forthcoming Publications

THE PAPERS OF THE ELLAND SOCIETY 1769–1818. Ed. John Walsh and Stephen Taylor

THE CORRESPONDENCE OF WILLIAM SANCROFT. Ed. Grant Tapsell

THE SERMONS OF JOHN SHARP. Ed. Françoise Deconinck-Brossard

THE CORRESPONDENCE AND PAPERS OF ARCHBISHOP RICHARD NEILE, 1598–1640. Ed. Andrew Foster

BIRKENHEAD, ALL SOULS, AND THE MAKING OF HERBERT HENSLEY HENSON: THE EARLY JOURNALS, 1885–1887. Ed. Frank Field and Julia Stapleton

PROCEEDINGS AGAINST THE 'SCANDALOUS MINISTERS' OF ESSEX, 1644–5. Ed. Graham Hart

SHAPING THE JACOBEAN RELIGIOUS SETTLEMENT: THE HAMPTON COURT CONFERENCE, 1604. Ed. Mark Byford and Kenneth Fincham

THE 1669 RETURN OF NONCONFORMIST CONVENTICLES. Ed. David Wykes

THE CORRESPONDENCE OF FRANCIS BLACKBURNE (1705–1787). Ed. G. M. Ditchfield

THE LETTERS AND PAPERS OF WILLIAM PALEY. Ed. Neil Hichin

THE CORRESPONDENCE, DIARIES AND PERSONAL MEMORANDA OF CHARLES SIMEON. Ed. Andrew Atherstone

THE DIARY OF AN OXFORD PARSON: THE REVEREND JOHN HILL, VICE-PRINCIPAL OF ST EDMUND HALL, OXFORD, 1805–1808, 1820–1855. Ed. Andrew Atherstone and Grayson Carter

Suggestions for publications should be addressed to Dr Grant Tapsell, General Editor, Church of England Record Society, Lady Margaret Hall, Norham Gardens, Oxford OX2 6QA, or at grant.tapsell@lmh.ox.ac.uk.

Membership of the Church of England Record Society is open to all who are interested in the history of the Church of England. Enquiries should be addressed to the Membership Secretary, Dr Nicholas Dixon, coersmembers@gmail.com.